WHEN THE BONES SPEAK

WHEN the BONES SPEAK

the LIVING, the DEAD, and the
SACRIFICE of CONTEMPORARY OKINAWA

CHRISTOPHER T. NELSON

DUKE UNIVERSITY PRESS
Durham and London
2025

Project Editor: Ihsan Taylor
Designed by A. Mattson Gallagher

Typeset in Minion Pro and
Quadraat Sans Pro by Westchester
Publishing Services

Cover art: Kinoshita Tomio
(1923–2014), *Red Mask* (detail), ca.
1950. Color woodcut,
21⁵⁄₁₆ × 34½ in. (54.1 × 87.6 cm).
Cincinnati Art Museum, Ohio.
Photo © Cincinnati Art Museum /
The Howard and Caroline Porter
Collection / Bridgeman Images.
Artist's estate permission courtesy
of Tamura Atsuko.

The University Libraries and the
Institute for Arts and Humanities
at the University of North Carolina
at Chapel Hill provided funds
to publish this book with an open
license.

Library of Congress
Cataloging-in-Publication Data

Names: Nelson, Christopher T., [date] author
Title: When the bones speak : the living,
the dead, and the sacrifice of contemporary
Okinawa / Christopher T. Nelson.
Other titles: Living, the dead, and the sacrifice
of contemporary Okinawa
Description: Durham : Duke University Press,
2025. | Includes bibliographical references and
index.
Identifiers: LCCN 2024050940 (print)
LCCN 2024050941 (ebook)
ISBN 9781478031963 paperback
ISBN 9781478028727 hardcover
ISBN 9781478060970 ebook
ISBN 9781478094388 ebook other
Subjects: LCSH: Nelson, Christopher T., 1961-
| Collective memory—Japan—Okinawa-ken
| Death—Social aspects—Japan—Okinawa-
ken | Psychic trauma—Japan—Okinawa-ken |
World War, 1939–1945—Campaigns—Japan—
Okinawa-ken | Okinawa-ken (Japan)—Social
life and customs—21st century | Okinawa-ken
(Japan)—History—21st century
Classification: LCC DS894.99.O374 N457 2025
(print) | LCC DS894.99.O374 (ebook) | DDC
940.53/5229—dc23/eng/20250326
LC record available at https://lccn.loc.
gov/2024050940
LC ebook record available at https://lccn.loc.
gov/2024050941

For Fiona and Siobhan

CONTENTS

ACKNOWLEDGMENTS

Beyond ink, paper, and glue, beyond figures of darkness and light on a screen, this book is made up of gifts. They are woven into every page, every line, and my work would be nothing without them. I am proud to have this opportunity to tell you about them and to express my gratitude. I thank Gushiken Takamatsu and his fellow volunteers in Gamafuyā, Higa Toyomitsu, and Yamauchi Masayoshi and the members of the Promise Keepers for their time and their trust. This project begins and ends with them. Katsukata=Inafuku Keiko welcomed me into the Institute for Ryukyuan and Okinawan Studies at Waseda University and helped me to find my way when all I had were questions. For nearly thirty years, Maetakenishi Kazuma has shared his passion for Okinawa with me, and I will never forget his family's kindness and consideration. Hiyane Teruo took an interest in my work as a graduate student and has continued to offer his guidance and advice. I am incredibly fortunate to have had Umemori Naoyuki and Umemori Junko, and Ochi Toshio and Shikimura Yoshiko, as friends and colleagues since our days in Chicago. As I worked on this project, they have made me feel at home at times when I easily could have lost my way.

I am also grateful to my friends and colleagues who discussed my project and read my manuscript at so many different stages. Margaret Wiener has seen this book through as she did the last, and her critical readings and encouragement have been indispensable. Bill Marotti has been a constant interlocutor and supportive critic for more than three decades, and many of the ideas here have grown out of our conversations. Andrea Arai gave me the chance to present my first thoughts on this project, and I appreciate her careful and perceptive comments along the way. Greg Beckett helped me to push through the middle chapters of the book and develop my ideas when I was most unsure of them. Brad Weiss not only offered generous critiques of my work but helped me to remain committed to the project of ethnography. Matt Hull's readings made me attentive to dimensions of my argument that were not yet fully clear to me and pushed me to develop them. Emiko Ohnuki-Tierney has read my work with care and encouragement, contextualizing it against the complex history of the anthropology of Japan. Anne Allison's incisive comments and deep enthusiasm have helped me to bring my project together as a sustained argument about sacrifice and death. As always, Harry Harootunian has read everything with rigor and generosity, and reminded me that the work we do is important.

My thanks as well to David Ambaras, Chris Ames, Linda Angst, Sophie Baby, Osman Balkan, the late Barney Bate, Jeff Bennett, Michael Berman, Davinder Bhowmik, Roddy Bogawa, Leo Ching, Tae Cimarosti, Heekyoung Cho, Alan Christy, Anne Claus, Mark Driscoll, Judy Farquhar, Carol Gluck, Jean-Pierre Gorin, Yukiko Hanawa, Michael Hardt, Sharon Hayashi, Heather Hindman, Jenny Huberman, Masamichi Inoue, Marilyn Ivy, Ishihara Masaie, Tony Jenkins, Jeremy Jones, Jeffrey Kahn, Ken Kawashima, John Kelly, the late Bill Kelly, Yumi Kim, Kina Ikue, Kyoung-Lae Kang, Laura Kina, Yukiko Koga, Sabu Kohso, Tze Loo, Tom Lamarre, Jean Langford, John Leisure, Tom Looser, Gabriella Lukacs, Wendy Matsumura, Daryl Maude, Simon May, John McGowan, Levi McLaughlin, Bill Mihalopoulos, Ryo Morimoto, the late Diane Nelson, François-Xavier Nérard, Takushi Odagiri, Rob Oppenheim, Simon Partner, Janet Poole, Franz Prichard, James Robertson, Joel Rozen, Annmaria Shimabuku, Clark Sorensen, Tanaka Masakazu, Mateo Taussig-Rubbo, Tomiyama Ichirō, Ruth Toulson, John Treat, Jose Vasquez, Hylton White, Tomiko Yoda, and Vicky Young for their readings, their comments, and their kindness at different stages of my project. I am deeply grateful to Kris Troost and Matthew Hayes at Duke University, Kristin Luck at George Washington University, Lynette K. Teruya at the University of Hawai'i, and the research staff at the National Humanities Center. What would my life be without libraries and librarians?

The students, staff, and faculty in the Department of Anthropology at the University of North Carolina have given me an intellectually stimulating and amazingly pleasant environment in which to teach and to write. My thanks to Anna Agbe-Davis, Lorraine Aragon, Ben Arbuckle, Florence Babb, Brian Billman, Rachel Briggs, Jocelyn Chua, Rudi Colloredo-Mansfeld, Carole Crumley, Emily Curtin, Bob Daniels, Arturo Escobar, the late Terry Evens, Mary Elizabeth Fitts, Charles Hilton, Glenn Hinson, Morgan Hoke, Dale Hutchinson, Martha King, Valerie Lambert, Heather Lapham, Paul Leslie, Jon Marcoux, Patricia McAnany, Towns Middleton, Don Nonini, Caela O'Connell, Irina Olenicheva, Jim Peacock, Katie Poor, Charles Price, Peter Redfield, Michele Rivkin-Fish, Aalyia Sadruddin, Margie and John Scarry, Karla Slocum, Douglas Smit, Mark Sorensen, Vin Steponaitis, Angela Stuesse, Amanda Thompson, Silvia Tomášková, and Colin West for the community that they have created and sustained. I particularly want to thank Aaron Delgaty, Enomoto Sora, Chris Flaherty, Hsieh Chu-wen, Ali Maxxa, and Paul Schissel for the time that we've spent thinking and discussing our work together. I am so proud of you and everything that you have done.

It has been my good fortune to work with Duke University Press over the course of my career. My thanks to Ken Wissoker for seeing something of value in the first proposal that I offered for this book, and for his patience, guidance, and support as I worked to bring it into being. Kate Mullen, Ihsan Taylor, and the production staff at the press have been superb. I would also like to thank the two anonymous readers who took the time to understand my project and whose insight and rigor shaped it into the book that it has become.

I carried out the initial fieldwork for this project in 2010 and 2011, supported by a research grant from the Fulbright Foundation. The Frederick Burkhardt Residential Fellowship for Recently Tenured Scholars, awarded by the American Council of Learned Societies, offered me a year to think and write at the National Humanities Center, as well as a semester at the Institute for Arts and Humanities at University of North Carolina at Chapel Hill. Additional funding from the University of North Carolina's Jim and Judy Cox Asia Initiative Faculty Research Award, the C. H. Jack and Joyce E. Keller Fund for Faculty Support, and the Japan Foundation let me carry out needed fieldwork to finish my research. A semester as the Paul I. Terasaki Chair in US-Japan Relations and Japanese Studies at the Terasaki Center for Japanese Studies at the University of California, Los Angeles, gave me the opportunity to rethink the structure of this project and envision the book that it would become. I would also like to thank the School for Advanced Research in Santa Fe, and the William Y. and Nettie K. Adams Fellowship for Research in the History of Anthropology; the Institute for Ryukyuan and Okinawan Studies at Waseda University; and the Japanese Arts and Globalizations Workshop on Performing Politics in Japan and Modern East Asia at UCLA. I am also grateful for invitations to speak at Aix-Marseille Université; the University of California, Santa Cruz; Columbia University; Duke University; Harvard University; Hunter College; Johns Hopkins University; Kyoto University; New York University; the University of Toronto; Waseda University; the University of Washington; and Yale University. I owe a debt of gratitude to the students and faculty at these institutions who offered their generous and insightful critiques of my work.

A special thanks to Nerea Llamas and Anne Gilliland at the University Libraries of the University of North Carolina, and to the Institute for Arts and Humanities for creating the grants that have enabled the open access publication of this book.

Finally, my thanks to my daughters Siobhan and Fiona, and my wife Atsuko. Without their interest, love, and support, none of this would have been possible.

For more than a decade, I have been deeply conscious of each of the gifts that I have received. At long last, I can return this book to you. I hope that you can find something of your kindness and generosity reworked here in these pages.

Introduction

Images flash by on the screen, blurred and indistinct. I feel that they must be important, but they slip away before I can grasp them, no more than a faint impression before another appears. I lose them as my eyes continually shift to the dull aluminum frames, the smudged glass, the passenger safety decal posted on the windows that stand in the foreground, moving but seemingly immobile. The camera is fixed where a passenger might sit, capturing images of a dreary Tokyo landscape as the train crosses the city. It is the train that is moving and I am not, seated in a darkened theater far away in Brooklyn, decades after the train reached its destination.

I am watching Chris Marker's film essay, *Level Five*.[1] Two intertwined narratives spin out: a woman's melancholy efforts to understand the death of her lover, and an account of the Battle of Okinawa, the subject of her lover's work. Jacques Rancière has described the film as a "fiction of memory [constructed] around the battle of Okinawa and around the bone-chilling collective suicide the conquering Japanese officers imposed on the colonized of Okinawa, forcing them to 'ape' Japanese standards of honor."[2] I struggle with these same concerns—they have inspired this book. What does it mean to sacrifice everything for another: your friends, your family, yourself? How could anyone accept, request, demand this sacrifice? And I wonder why Rancière neglects an important dimension of Marker's critique, tersely explaining an event that Marker represents with intentional ambiguity. To write that Okinawans simply ape (*singer*) Japanese standards of honor is to dismiss the very voices of the people that Rancière has devoted his career to freeing from appropriation. If the meaning of the Battle of Okinawa could be summarized with such confidence, is Marker's film necessary? These questions are what has brought me to this theater at the Brooklyn Academy of Music. The hope that I will see something, rediscover something, renew my confidence in the direction that I have been following through the notes and files, audio and video recordings, photographs, books and magazines, dreams and memories that I have gathered in decades of fieldwork.

Chris Marker's voice, calm and authoritative, takes over the narration of the film. He promises to make sense of the fragments left behind by the original filmmaker, and to impose order on the traces of the past that they represent. "That's where I came in," he says. "At that point in my life, I was readier for other people's images than my own. Laura's challenge fired me up. I began with their trip to Tokyo. Like them, I loved the city. And the game offered me a new way into World War II."[3] And yet, even if the disjuncture between image and voice hasn't forewarned me, certainty is elusive in this film.[4] Instead, I find myself again and again in the space between experience and understanding. The space of the dead. A space haunted by revenants, their voices indistinct, awaiting recall. Caught up in the speed of presentation and enchanted by this fiction, I am led to assemble the narrative from fragments ready to hand, conjuring into being a memory that I do not yet possess.

There is a form to this space, crafted by Marker from elements appropriated from Otto Preminger's noir mystery, *Laura*.[5] Transforming a detective's determination to solve a crime, he has assembled a labyrinth, not a palace, of memory. A fictional film to provide the loci that might contain a history. In a violent world, he asks, what can we truly know? In an uncertain world, what is the price of not knowing? Marker challenges us to use the familiarity of fiction to construct a possible record of the real.[6] It is a project fraught with hazards and uncertainty. What is the past that we recover when its traces must be reassembled in Marker's edits, when its fragments appear only to disappear, pieced together in the final print of the film, the recorded disc, made whole in the memory of the viewer who sits, like me, before the screen? How should we understand the confidence of the narrator whose voice accompanies these dizzying images?

Why does any of this matter? It is important because, like the Chris that speaks to us from the film, I also feel compelled to find a "new way into World War II." A way that is attentive to moments in the past that remain open, to paths along which we can go back, to voices calling out to be heard. To the desire for return that is at the center of Marker's film, a practice charged with longing that struggles to escape the constraints of everyday life and draw what is remembered as a distant past into the moment. And yet, the possibility of finding hope among the dead seems so remote when I hear the voice of the seminal Japanese director and critic Ōshima Nagisa summon viewers to an accounting in the present: "to tell the truth, Okinawa was sacrificed."

Marker approaches the problem of Okinawa's sacrifice elliptically, first framing it in the narrative of his friend Laura, who has asked him to help her make sense of her partner's work and death. She tells us that late one night, as she labors to understand the experiential game about the Battle of Okinawa that her lover died designing, she receives an anonymous message from another whose path she crosses in her online research. Her interlocutor tells her that he is about to commit suicide. A famous person beyond his anonymous interface, his death will be in the news. He offers to share his death, to offer it as a sacrifice, a gift to her. As his final addressee, she will take part in the moment of fame and notoriety that his act creates.

However, she scorns his offer. She is unwilling to be defined by his acknowledgment, claiming that her own experience of death and loss is such that there is nothing that she can learn from him. Hasn't she already received the gift of a death, a burden of desire, uncertainty, and loss that organizes her work in the film? And yet, after her refusal, she feels the pangs of remorse. In the morning, she finds no notices in the press, but she is unable to escape a sense of unease as she recalls their conversation: "But what if the death part wasn't fooling, only the famous part? What if he'd only lied when he said, 'I am well-known,' to make me believe before he died, he was someone else, and I deprived him of that pleasure, one last joy before dying?"

What does it mean for Laura to be offered the gift of death? We know so little about the circumstances surrounding it. There is no reason to believe that his death is a formal sacrifice—that he died in her place, that he died to bring some sacred moment into being. Nor is there any intimation that he died because of her, out of love, out of anger, out of any emotion grounded in a relationship between the two of them. And yet, in his moment of dying, he offers to extend his care, his concern to her. He will let her, she says, benefit from the publicity, the prestige of being the final person to speak with him before his death.

Knowing nothing of the intention that guides his act, there is little we can know about the consequences of her refusal. Perhaps she has interrupted his effort to invest the moment of his action with meaning, a meaning to which she could bear witness. And yet, in the film's representation of her refusal, his act takes form with depth and meaning.

As if speaking to this ambiguous offer of sacrifice, a confident voice and a resolute image is cut into the film: Kinjō Shigeaki, carefully dressed in a conservative suit and tie, speaking in formal Japanese, a man who we will learn is a Christian minister and a survivor of genocide in Okinawa.[7] With the authority and conviction of a witness, he echoes Oshima's words about sacrifice: "The battle was lost in advance, a battle the Japanese army had no chance of winning. It was inscribed in the context of defeat. And because that was the context, the purpose was to fix the aftermath, and reinforce the Tennosei, the imperial system which had to survive the military defeat. Another direct consequence inscribed in this context of defeat, was that no effort was made to protect the civilian population, so civilian casualties far outnumbered military casualties."

While I cannot see Kinjō remember, there is something unnerving in his calm narration of the terrible past. In Okinawa, he is well known for his tireless efforts to heal the wounds of war: his public ministry, his work to establish a Christian university there, his endless availability to scholars and the press. He often said that he would like to rest, to be silent, but he feared for the present more than he longed for oblivion.[8] And so, in the film he speaks again and again, determined to do more than narrate a litany of atrocities or to fill the silence that the trauma of the past engenders. To be sure, he enumerates the experiences that led to the act: horror at the monstrous acts that Americans were said to commit, patriotism and loyalty to the emperor. He speaks of a shared sense of mission with the Japanese soldiers who entrenched themselves in Kinjō's village.[9]

> We were taught that Westerners were demons. We were told if US troops captured us, they'd cut off our noses and ears, cut off our fingers. They would drive tanks over our bodies and rape our women. We would suffer horribly, then die. We were so imbued with all this that it seemed better to suppress our loved ones than leave them to the enemy. For them, it would be a consolation to die by the hands of a loved one.
>
> . . . We were imbued with army orders stating that, if necessary, meaning when encountering the enemy, the first grenade was for the enemy and the second one we had to use for suicide.

Kinjō tries to conjure the experience of sacrifice, the sensation of killing. He wants to explain to us—insofar as any act of remembrance can—the way he felt as he and his brothers beat their mother to death because they loved her more than anything in the world.

> A village elder, a leader, was snapping off a tree branch. I watched him, intrigued. Then, in his very hand, the stick became a weapon. As if having a seizure, he began to beat the life out of his wife and children, whom he loved, using just this piece of wood. It was terribly shocking, but telepathically all of us thought this was the thing to do and others began to kill the people they loved most. They began with children, with the weak and the old, with those who lacked the strength to take their own lives. So husbands killed wives, parents killed children, brothers killed sisters. They killed them because they loved them. Such was the tragedy of those mass suicides. It was a real butchery, and the waters of the river where they threw the bodies indiscriminately became rivers of blood.
>
> As for my own family, my brother who was two years my senior and I raised our hand for the first time against the mother who had borne us. At nineteen, my brother could not help moaning. He suffered so much. My father went off to die. We also killed our younger brother and sister.

Hearing Kinjō speak of Kerama, I am torn from the flow of the film by a dreadful feeling of recognition. The cluster of islands he describes—Zamami, Tokashiki, Aka—lies twenty miles off the coast of Naha. A short ferry trip from the capital of Okinawa Prefecture, their coral reefs and sandy beaches attract tourists who fish and dive in their clear waters, perhaps watching for whales to breach against the winter sky. When I was a Marine, I was only dimly aware of their existence, occasionally seeing them floating like a mirage in the ocean haze as I jogged along the beach on the main island. I knew that they had been of brief strategic importance during the Allied invasion of Okinawa, a position captured to protect the southern flank of the massive amphibious assault directed against the main island. That distance collapsed in the 1990s when I studied with the storyteller Fujiki Hayato (later Tatekawa Shīsā, and now simply Shīsā).[10] I have written of his performance, "Memories of White Sand," which centered on a survivor of the massacres on Kerama and his painful efforts to recount the memories of his experiences to his grandson, trying to capture both the hope and despair that suffused the moment before they destroyed one another in battle. Of course, I had also read Norma Field's *In the Realm of the Dying Emperor* when I started graduate school. In her memoir of Japan during the time of imperial succession, Field wrote of the moment of horror in which villagers on the islands killed their families and took their own lives, survivors murdered by the Japanese soldiers from the local garrison. She insists upon restoring the ideological dimension of the *shūdan jiketsu* that Kinjō described. It is inadequate, she argues, to allow a neutral translation of this utterance as "collective suicide." The terror of two massive modern armies about to clash, and the suffocating weight of decades of subjection to the remorseless discipline of the imperial ideology demands its translation as compulsory group suicide. What's more, the violence done in the fields and villages of Kerama is repeated, again and again. In the days that followed, it flashed out from Kerama across Okinawa, kindled into flame by the friction between American and Japanese armies as Okinawans caught along the seam of battle beat, choked, slashed, and poisoned their friends and relatives. It is awakened in memory and reencountered in graphic traces as imperial apologists mobilize state educational apparatuses to efface the traces of murder, denying the dead the dignity of representation in textbooks and classroom discussion. She contrasts this with the courageous work of the historian Ienaga Saburō, who challenged, in the media and in the courts, every effort to obscure the military murder of Okinawan civilians. Her book captures both the brutality of the Okinawan genocide and the furious struggle over its remembrance, "the dark inmixing of coercion and consent, of aggression and victimization."[11]

What is it that I find so compelling in Kinjō's quiet narration? What is it that I hear in the measured tones of his voice, that I see in the dignified and composed features of his face? What is it in his remembrance that goes beyond Fujiki's representations of hope? It is more than a survivor's narration of wartime abjection—but what? An intimation in the montage of images that follow in Marker's film: Newsreel footage of an Okinawan woman, her simple kimono gathered at her waist, staring into the camera's lens with an enigmatic expression before throwing herself off a cliff. A shipboard memorial service for 780 Okinawan children slaughtered when the *Tsushima Maru*, carrying them to the mainland, was torpedoed by the American submarine USS *Bowfin*.[12] A time-ravaged hand tracing a name inscribed on the memorial at Itoman, several meters and half a century away from the woman who jumped to her death moments earlier. Elderly women laughing as they sort produce in the stalls at the Naha market. It is a temporality that resists signification offered by battlefield monuments and the memorials to the dead that bristle from the Okinawan landscape, refusing the comforting trauma that fixes these horrors at a moment in the past and allows a future, however painful, to emerge. It is a presence that is not simply embodied by those who survived wartime genocide or by those wounded by the struggle to bear witness. It is more than the burden borne by the uneasy dead whose presence haunts the spaces of the living. It is the immanence of war—changing, changing, changing, yet always the same. The American military did not simply remain in the islands to maintain the peace after the Japanese surrender in 1945; rather, as Allied strategic planners envisioned before the invasion, the island and its bases became a site from which war continued. Now, in our time, they do so with the Japanese state as an ally, an ever-changing array of enemies and threats stretching out beyond the sea to the west and the south, in the skies above. The photographer Higa Toyomitsu has written of *rokujūgonenme no Okinawasen*—the sixty-fifth year of the Battle of Okinawa; the novelist and critic Medoruma Shun says that he lives in *sengo zeronen*—year zero of the postwar. An unending duration of war, a peace yet to begin.[13]

You need only look past the representations of idyllic island life, or the distracted routines of everyday life, to see the shape of this war. Look for the sand-colored US military trucks and armored vehicles returned from Afghanistan and Iraq, or bound for some destination yet to be decided, moving in columns along the coastal highway. Watch them set out from Marine Corps bases that stand atop demolished Okinawan villages and rehabilitated battlefields. Follow them to the military port that dominates the harbor at Naha, occupying the ruins of the costal fortifications where centuries ago Ryūkyūan soldiers and court priestesses repelled the incursion of pirates or landing forces from Satsuma, and where wooden houses were burned to the ground by American bombing in 1944. Look above for the ungainly V-22 Osprey aircraft slowly wheeling before they bank and turn north— perhaps to land in a dioxin-scarred clearing in the forest at the Northern Training Area, or perhaps to circle Camp Schwab, where construction crews, Japanese police, and American sentries ignore the voices of Japanese citizens and Okinawan officials to set to work on a massive complex that will be the new home to these aircraft and the Marines who fly them.

There is more to see if you look closely. The white cutter of the Kaijō Hoanchō, the Japanese Coast Guard, steaming out of Naha harbor, keeping the grey silhouette of the Kerama islands to starboard as it sets a course to intercept Chinese fishing vessels in the contested waters around islands whose very names are disputed. The fit-looking young Japanese men and women at the bus stop in Chatan, carrying bags from the boutiques in the American Village shopping center, waiting for a shuttle to return them to the Jieitai (Japanese Ground Self-Defense Force) base in Onna village. Trucks, burdened with concrete and steel; buses carrying laborers, demonstrators, and security forces; ships towing drilling rigs to erect yet another base. And we must look for the intimations of the unseen. The ceaseless flows of finance capital, transmitted from mainland banks to the offices of local construction companies and contractors, circulating through networks of the Bank of Japan to local development projects, from Chinese banks to realtors and developers and businesses. Transmissions along American military and bureaucratic networks to local commanders. Mobile phones pulsing from Kasumigaseki to local counterparts in Naha and Nago. A constantly shifting war of position and maneuver. As we become attentive to this, we must rethink the seemingly unexceptional, the everyday lives of the Okinawan people.

Kinjō's narration is an effort to close this open interval, to settle accounts with the past. The repetition of actions—by Japanese and American soldiers, by men and women like Kinjō himself—that began the duration are imputable. Responsibility must be assigned; the burden of blame must be shouldered. If that happens, what was done can be forgiven and forgotten. A new path into the future can be opened.[14]

> If you look in the Bible, you'll see confessing your sins and expressing remembrance cleanses people of their past. But Japanese mentality, the way of thought, considers that errors committed in the past remain errors forever. They cannot be erased. I decided that my mission must be to proclaim the value of human life to counter the nation, the idea of the past, that held life in such contempt, for that was the lie they taught. That was the motivation for my becoming a missionary, a Christian minister.

However, a countervailing force exists, one that struggles to sustain this duration and the narratives that reference it. It is not about Japanese efforts to efface the violence of the past—there seems to be little taste for silencing discussions of the brutality that marked the battle of Okinawa.[15] Rather, it is about reinvesting these moments with patriotic significance.[16] These ideological interventions are constantly repeated: the work of the conservative novelist Sono Ayako has been a bellwether for these interventions for decades.[17] They are given shape by the Reversion era claims of survivors like Akamatsu Yoshitsugu, the wartime commander of Japanese forces on Tokashiki, to solidarity with the loyal, patriotic villagers who lived and died on the island and his frustrated efforts to join survivors at a ceremony commemorating the installation of a memorial to the dead there.[18] The recent failed lawsuit launched by his comrades and family against Nobel laureate Ōe Kenzaburō and Iwanami Publishing Company mark precisely the same flashpoints.[19] Whether it is in the immediate aftermath of war, at the moment of reversion, or in the politically charged present, it is necessary to reenlist Okinawans and to reestablish the absolute, manifestly communal but murderously hierarchical, imperial edifice. Like the images of unhappy souls, conscripted even in death to imperial service at Yasukuni shrine, the sacrifices of Okinawans like Kinjō and his family are constantly recalled, remembered, and reworked. And in this moment—if in few others—Okinawans are unequivocally granted identity with mainland Japanese. Any question that they acted under the influence of orders by the Japanese army is dismissed.[20] Without compulsion, without constraint, they are hailed as both sacrificer and sacrifice, celebrated and mourned for the massive offering of their lives that preserved the imperial institution and the Japanese state.

This is the temporality that I struggle to understand. It is not one that I recognized or understood for much of my life. As a boy growing up in a mill town in Western Pennsylvania, World War II seemed like something that had ended long ago. It was my uncles' war, a war of black and white photographs, of action films and comic books, of histories in school libraries that described combat with pride and enthusiasm at a job well done. Sacrifice was acknowledged, but in a way that was both quotidian and heroic. The actuality of the war had faded like the bluing tattoos on the forearms of the steelworkers that sat at the bar at the Knights of Columbus or the VFW. The new war in Indochina that dominated our televisions, the specter of McCarthyism that seeped into our factories and churches, the newfound prosperity lit by the fires that blazed over the refineries and mill furnaces, thick with its choking chemical stench—all of that stood between the everyday life that I experienced and the consequences of an older war. I could have known more, understood more. I could have seen the ties between the aftermath of that war and the long slide into poverty and ruin that was already at work, even during the best times. I could have questioned the sour edge of racism and xenophobia that shaded workers' anxiety as their jobs in my hometown factories were swept away.

Even when I became a Marine, the war that we spoke of so often had been reduced to commemoration: battle streamers on my battalion's colors;

a training area named after a horrific battle or a street after a heroic Marine; an example in a class on tactics or logistics. The past was useful to us if we could abstract it and learn from it in planning to fight on NATO's northern flank, in Korea, in Central America, in Iran.

Which is not to say that I was not conscious of the weight of the past. As a young officer, I was continually reminded of it. As a platoon commander, I often thought of the countless lieutenants who had commanded the platoon before me, who had set an example that I did not fully understand and could never completely meet. For too long I used it to motivate myself, to challenge my Marines. The gaze of the dead is not only appropriated by right-wing Japanese ideologues.[21]

And yet, I gradually became aware of another set of relations to the past. In Okinawa, in South Korea, in the Philippines, I saw what had been done, and what we were still doing. I became aware of an immediacy that could not be overcome by a day filled with training for a war to come along the Korean DMZ, or on a beach or highway in one of the Gulf States. The names on our battle streamers and the towns and villages clustered around our bases began to move into alignment. This tension of intersecting temporalities became painfully clear to me as I read Marine Corps combat veteran E. B. Sledge's memoir, *With the Old Breed*. It haunted me from the first time I read it in my bunk on an aircraft carrier steaming toward the Persian Gulf until I read it again in my apartment in Okinawa during the fieldwork for this book. It demanded that I acknowledge the responsibility that I bear. Not simply as an American anthropologist who could come and go from the field as he pleased, but as a Marine who had labored in these islands, who had inherited the debt for what my predecessors had done on these battlefields. Sledge's vision from Okinawan battlefields comes back to me:

> I imagined Marine dead had risen up and were moving silently about the area. I suppose these were nightmares, and I must have been more asleep than awake, or just dumbfounded by fatigue. Possibly they were hallucinations, but they were strange and horrible. The pattern was always the same. The dead got up slowly out of their waterlogged craters or off the mud and, with stooped shoulders and dragging feet, wandered around aimlessly, their lips moving as though trying to tell me something. I struggled to hear what they were saying. They seemed agonized by pain and despair. I felt they were asking me for help. The most horrible thing was that I felt unable to aid them.[22]

I.1.   The Naha cityscape seen from empty tombs in Shintoshin.

Like Sledge, like the protagonists of Marker's film, my attempt to come to grips with a ghostly past has unearthed a revenant that has never been absent, a material duration that persists into the present. And sacrifice is the key to its understanding. Bataille once wrote that sacrifice will illuminate the conclusion of history just as it clarified its dawn.[23] His hope that the force of sacrifice could act against the pressure of conquest gave way to the realization that it was the desire to sacrifice, the anticipation of destruction in the name of love, that gave birth to the catastrophe.

My concerns with sacrifice are different. I have my own obligations to the past, and I bring my own tools as an anthropologist. With those, I have tried to understand the ways in which ordinary Okinawans, haunted by memories of their own sacrifice and exploitation, have struggled to live with the unbearable. The past is not simply theirs to work through, to move beyond. They are caught up in a web of people and practices—living and dead, visible and immaterial—that exert powerful forces often beyond their control. I have listened for the voices of Okinawan *yuta* or shamans, fortune tellers, artists, dead soldiers trapped in battlefield graves, ethnographers, members of war survivor associations, anti-base and antiwar activists, unhomed and unemployed laborers, evangelical Christian missionaries, and ordinary citizens who find their vocation in service to others. I have seen how their actions, individual and collective, unconscious and reflexive, produce and reproduce the complexity and unevenness of their social world. I have tried to make sense of the experiences that frame sacrifice and violence: the production, loss, and remembrance of the self and the social world; the creation of value, and the production of space and time; and the possibilities of creative action grounded in the everyday. I have paid attention to those who offer themselves up in the act of sacrifice, with reluctance, with terror, and with hope. I have also considered those who are critical of its demands, yet who open themselves to its practices, struggling to reach those who have been drawn into its logic, into its clockwork execution. This is where my project is written: at the intersection of temporalities and possibilities, where the hard finality of the past may be broken open to reveal a "not yet" that has always remained just beyond reach.

Opening a Rift in the Everyday 1

"It was possible to live here," he says to himself, "because it is possible to live here and will in the future be possible to live here, for we are tough and cannot be broken overnight."

Nietzsche, *Unfashionable Observations* (1874)

The dead had a longer memory than the living.

Pierre Clastres, *Chronicle of the Guayaki Indians* (1972)

City Assemblyman's Office, Okinawa City, July 2006

The video seemed to be on an endless loop. An overhead shot of the missile showed the white flash of ignition. The frame trembled as it began to move, then the video cut to a wide tracking shot as it gained altitude. For several moments, it continued to climb before, in another hasty cut, it was returned to the launch pad to begin all over again.

I sipped a cold bottle of jasmine tea while I watched. The air conditioning was running hard and I felt a chill as I leaned back against the metal folding chair. The same clip had been playing on the news for days, while reporters and politicians delivered urgent statements about the danger of North Korea. Everyone seemed all too aware that Okinawa was within missile range. They worried that North Korea might already be targeting the surrounding bases. My friends had probably seen the launch a hundred times, but they continued to stare intently at the screen. Outside, Route 330 was empty. Apart from the air conditioner, the office was quiet and everyone seemed enthralled by the video.

The assemblyman sat down with a sigh and ran his fingers through his hair. After a decade in office, he had assumed leadership of the committee managing the city's relationship with the US military. Bases continue to occupy much of Okinawa City, spaces that had been farms and villages before their appropriation. It was difficult and largely thankless to represent the interests of local landowners, merchants, and ordinary citizens. As a community leader and a city assemblyman, he had worked to mitigate the effects of the bases. He was particularly concerned with the precarious lives of young people. For years, he organized anti-delinquency and youth employment programs. "Just when it feels like we're making some headway, North Korea starts launching missiles. What's next?" He shook his head.

I asked my friends—working-class men in their thirties and forties—what they thought about the tests. They deferred to the assemblyman for a moment, but he nodded for them to have their say.

"How much longer will this go on? My grandmother had a good income from base leases when she was old. Now, my brothers and I are working—we don't need it. Besides, by the time the money gets divided up between everyone, it doesn't amount to much. Still, it doesn't seem like anything will ever change."[1]

"North Korea. China. If the US closes its bases, where does that leave us? Will *naichi* protect us?"[2]

"And do we want Jieitai [Japanese Self-Defense Forces] bases? I feel like we're stuck."[3]

On the screen, the missile was struggling to take off again, a persistent, anxious figure grinding against the rhythms of everyday life.

A Yuta Story, May 2011

I slowly drove down the deeply rutted road, worried that I would bounce into one of the drainage ditches along either side of the track. Thick vegetation arched overhead, as if we were somewhere deep in the rainforest. Actually, we were driving through a dense patchwork of fields in suburban Nishihara, not far north of the capital. Nansei Sekiyu's oil storage site along the coast was close.[4] If I stood on the roof of the car, I could probably see it. We were on our way to help the Promise Keepers clear a field they were borrowing from one of Reverend Yamauchi's parishioners so that they could begin growing traditional Okinawan vegetables for local markets.[5]

With his light-blue *sagyōfuku* (work clothes) and a thin towel knotted around his head, Hiroshi looked more like he was on his way to a construction site than the fields. "Work is work," he laughed. "Besides, every Okinawan is at least a little bit a farmer." We had been talking about summers he spent working in his grandfather's fields and winter weekends cutting cane. After a pause, his tone became serious: "My brother was doing *dekasegi* (transient labor) in Saitama. We were working at the Honda factory there, but I moved home when I got a job with a construction company here. He stayed and got married to an Okinawan girl who was working there too."[6]

When their first daughter was born, she was very sick. Hiroshi wasn't certain, but he told me that something hadn't developed right. As soon as she could, his brother's wife came back, and she and her mother went to see a *yuta* (shaman). The *yuta* scolded her for ignoring her departed family while she was away. A branch of her family had died out a generation ago and no one had been carrying out memorial rites for them. They needed offerings. That's why the illness was inflicted on her daughter. The ancestral spirits wanted to get her attention so that she would take care of them. On top of the child's medical treatments, she was told to come back to Okinawa throughout the year to conduct the necessary rituals.

In the end, her daughter died anyway. She complained to the *yuta* that she did everything that she was told but it didn't help. The *yuta* coldly reminded her that there was never any guarantee that the baby would recover. Her ancestors needed to get her attention and they did. That's what mattered.

The *yuta* did not offer any prophetic claim to the future; her reference to the past merely set the stage for her intervention. She disclosed something in the now, the relationship between the living and the dead that had been allowed to pass unseen, the voices of the dead that went unheard, the responsibility to those invisible forces that had gone unnoticed. Now it was up to the living and the dead to work together.[7]

The Insistence of the Past, December 2023

All morning I'd been trying to read Jon Mitchell's scathing revelations about the US military's careless use of toxic herbicides in Okinawa and the relentless denial of responsibility that followed.[8] My attention constantly shifted to the lines of winter light that moved along the rough bark of the pines that stood outside my office window. Like a rhythm frozen in space, the alternating bands of light and darkness fascinated me. With an effort, I returned to Mitchell's book.

His words pulled me into a chain of memories. I recalled standing along a highway in northern Okinawa in the winter of 2011, just above the village of Takae. I had spent the morning sitting in a tent drinking tea and talking with local activists. The walls of the tent were decorated with images highlighting the Takae struggle, a citizens' movement protesting the Marine Corps' plans to expand landing zones in the nearby jungle, and the effect that their V-22 Osprey aircraft would have on their lives.

Looking at the jungle beyond the encampment reminded me of my own experiences as a Marine training there in 1985, leading helicopter assaults and infantry patrols, little consideration given to these neighbors. I had been too preoccupied with dreams of an abandoned war in Indochina and wars that might one day begin in places like the Philippines and the Persian Gulf. The Northern Training Area was a practice field where we gave shape and presence to those fantasies in the paths we beat through the jungles. Of course, we knew that the surrounding communities were real; perhaps just not as real as the exercises that filled our days.[9] The people of Takae always knew the US military as a demanding neighbor. Residents who own the forests encircled by military fences have no choice in how the land is used or conserved. Aircraft noise and weapons firing is a constant reminder to survivors and their families of the battles that were fought in Okinawa during the Pacific War, and of the wars that are still prosecuted by those who plan and train here. Posters and pamphlets scattered across the community remind them of the hope and the failure of democracy. And now, anxiety over the possibility that Agent Orange, the toxic dioxin-based defoliant used in the Vietnam War, had been used to keep the base's landing zones clear.

As much as we are divided, there is a reserve of memory that I share with the people of Takae. Memories of moments inflicted and endured. And now, perhaps something more than memory. I wonder if, beneath the skin, we share something else brought by the US military in the name of democracy and sacrifice, something working silently in the interior of our bodies. Something more powerful and relentless than what I feel at these other reminders of the past.

I look again at the lines of light and shadow in the trees. Although they are just beyond my window, they seem so formal and distant.

Designers kept the feeling of a schoolhouse. The walls were freshly painted light and dark olive green. The floor was a highly polished pattern of tan and brown linoleum. Opaque glass-globed lights cast a warm glow. We found the exhibit of Okinawan and South Korean photography in one of the classrooms.[10] There was no furniture inside, few explanations on the walls.

Along one wall, a series of large, stark, black-and-white photographic portraits by Higa Toyomitsu represented elderly Okinawans exposing the scars of war injuries. A frightful, glossy seam along a thigh; a missing arm healed to a smooth, rounded stump; a toothless mouth in an age-dappled face.

Next, a vertical column of color photos by the South Korean photographer Lee Yong Nam depicted the intrusion of the US Army into everyday life in South Korea. Armored vehicles lined up; grain drying on the road, crushed and ruined by treads; "Yan kee go home" painted on the highway's surface. A scene from the American military exercises that occupy the rural South Korean landscape after the rice harvest is over and the paddies are dry.

To the right, a stunning series began. A column of armored personnel carriers halted, drivers and commanders in battle gear, conversing. A young woman in a plastic raincoat wailing in the rain. Then, shockingly, a color close-up of two young women along the side of the road. The first, curled up, arm extended beneath her head as if she has fallen asleep. On the sodden highway, a pool of blood, her entrails clumped alongside her. The two young girls were crushed by the US armored vehicles as they walked to a friend's birthday party. A caption noted that the driver was never convicted and was released. My head spun—next to me, several well-dressed visitors gasped in horror. One woman cried quietly, sadness, anger, and shame washing over her face.

After this, we saw two parallel sets of panels in glossy color. Noh Suntag's meditation on affect and occupation. To the left, overhead and close-up views of anti-base demonstrations. Huge South Korean and American flags held aloft, torn to pieces. Two girls, impassive expressions—"fucking America" written on a sign. To the right, demonstrators declare their support for US bases. Two aging women, one holding a sign "We Want America." Their own American and South Korean flags held aloft, together.[11]

Entering a smaller space, we found Ishikawa Mao's images from Okinawa. Photos of the helicopter crash on the grounds of Okinawa Kokusai Daigaku

(Okinawa International University), Marines blocking her lens with their hands.[12] More photos showed the Inochi o Mamoru Kai (Society for the Preservation of Life), their long-standing sit-in at the beach in Henoko, protestors marching in the streets at Nago.[13] The exhibit wrapped around to the back wall, Marines training and relaxing in Okinawa. One, a Japanese former Marine showing his tattoo, a skull pierced with a dagger—"Kill them all and let God sort them out." Next to him, a portrait of a shirtless, shaven-headed Marine. His name and blood type tattooed on the left side of his chest. The right side of the space shows photos of married couples—GIs and Okinawan women. Poverty, hopefulness. On the back wall, stark black-and-white photos of Okinawan women in Kin. Several young women in a rumpled bed with equally young GIs. A thin, haggard-looking soldier with two wildly laughing women. A half-dozen girls on the beach.

The Streets of Koza, June 2011

After breakfast, I decided to walk to the Ichibangai, a *shōtengai* (covered arcade), and visit Hisutorīto, the new museum created by the Okinawa City government. My head thick with fatigue, I felt almost overwhelmed by the disjointed sensations of anticipation and sadness that greeted me on my return to Okinawa. It was as if all of the selves that I have been here were sluggishly rearranging themselves to make a place for the new arrival. I had slept fitfully. A succession of middle-aged presenters murmured on the television that I left on all night in my room. Patterned wallpaper, a thin comforter, the functional furniture gray and anonymous. I could have been in an institutional cell anywhere. As I left the hotel, the grand lime-stone stairs flanked by vermillion pillars that led down from the lobby to the street were a weird contrast to the dull, reinforced concrete buildings that made up the rest of neighborhood.

The sky above promised nothing but rain, a mottled gray like the US Air Force interceptors that traced indistinct lines across it. I turned south, the narrow asphalt street wet and oily. I could already feel my shirt clinging to me in the warm, humid air. At the back doors of bars, bags of garbage were stacked neatly next to orange plastic crates filled with empty amber bottles of Orion beer. Turning again to my right, I saw the Terurinkan, a *sanshin* (a three-stringed musical instrument, similar to a Japanese shamisen) store and performance space. It had been the home of the great storyteller, musician, and ethnographer Teruya Rinsuke. I found it somehow reassuring to see that his widow had kept it open after his death.[14]

I paused for a moment and looked up Ipē Dōri (Ipē Street).[15] As listless as I felt, I experienced the rush of memories of other times lived in this place. The luminous yellow of the blossoms of the *ipē* tree in the early spring, vivid against the dirty, streaked, gray-and-beige walls of the buildings that lined the street. A line from the author Medoruma Shun: "their color reminded me of the Brazilian Team's World Cup uniform."[16] A question that often troubled me here: Who had planted these beautiful Brazilian trees in this back alley? Were they a memorial to generations of laborers who had left Okinawa to work in the farms and the factories of Brazil? A gift to remind those who remained of their success or their sacrifice? An aesthetic exchange to counterbalance the loss of value that these men and women could have created here?

I remembered that the narrator of one of Medoruma's Koza stories once stood at perhaps the same spot, attentive to this city as a place of intersection and troubling encounters:

> I went to buy a canned coffee from a vending machine. As I was heading back to my apartment, the dog appeared, walking toward me, with something clamped between his jaws that looked like a yellow plastic bag. The semi-transparent, jellied mass swayed with the dog's gait. The moment our eyes met, he stopped and let out a low growl. Surprised at his change of character, I held up the coffee can as if to throw it at him, at which he shrank back, spun around, and tore off at a clip that didn't seem possible for a crippled dog.[17]

The streets around me were empty, but it would not be unusual to see a stray dog scavenging in the garbage. The gelatinous blob that it carried? From Medoruma's description, it seems that the dog is clutching a *mabui*, a human spirit. I've never met anyone who told me that they've seen a *mabui* just as Medoruma described it, but it's often represented in the Okinawan media as a luminous, golden mass.[18]

The dog's burden evokes Okinawan concern and anxiety about life, spoken of as *inochi* in Japanese, *nuchi* in Uchināguchi, the Okinawan language. While there may be a historical basis for their interest, it is clear that the memory of the experience of colonial oppression, military occupation, and wartime genocide is the ground against which this history should be understood today. *Nuchi dū takara*—life is a treasure, life is to be treasured. This simple affirmation, taken from a postwar folksong celebrating survival in the ruins of war, stands in stark contrast to the Japanese wartime valorization of *gyokusai*, the representation of life as a jewel to be smashed in service and in sacrifice to the state.[19] *Nuchi dū takara.* I have seen it painted on banners and printed on the clothing of activists at anti-base demonstrations. It appears in advertising campaigns that try to capture the essence of Okinawa for curious tourists. The citizen's collective that sat before Ishikawa Mao's lens, protesting the proposed construction of a Marine Corps heliport in Henoko felt that the Inochi o Mamoru Kai best expressed its objectives.[20]

The value of life is continually affirmed because it has been so threatened in the past. And yet, *inochi* or *nuchi* indicates a state, the condition of being alive. In contrast, the *mabui* or *mabuya*—the mass carried by Medoruma's dog—is an entity. It resides throughout the body, everywhere and nowhere at once.[21] Usually thought to be beyond the direct sensory experience of human beings, it is known in its effects. It is the *mabui* that allows a person to act with intention, and to be creatively engaged with the social world. An *uranaishi* (fortune teller) once told me that a *mabui* is what opens people up to the spiritual, connecting them with the spirits of the living and the dead. Without it, a person is no more than an insensate organism, unable to meaningfully participate in the world around them. People live their lives, conscious of their *mabui* perilously attached to their all-too-vulnerable material bodies.

There are rituals to separate a *mabui* from the remains of the deceased, but people say that *mabui* can also be dislocated or lost by shock or misfortune. It can be dislodged by the unpleasant or insensitive actions of its owner, whether intentional or inadvertent. Because of this, there are a wide range of situations in everyday life ranging from the misbehavior of a child to neglect of responsibilities toward the ancestral spirits in which a person might be warned that their *mabui* will fall out.[22]

Since the *mabui* is thought to be composed of seven interdependent segments, it can also be lost, piece by piece. A person will become diminished, unable to act in a meaningful manner. They may even die without it to sustain them. Cut loose, their *mabui* might wander endlessly through the streets it knew in life. I've heard that a lost *mabui* will eventually try to make its way to the family tomb. If it reaches the tomb, not even the most powerful *yuta* (shaman) can recall it to its owner.[23]

It is also possible that an evil spirit can occupy the space left by the absent *mabui*, or a more powerful entity can force the *mabui* aside and crowd itself into the body. I've read that, long ago, malicious rivals could call upon powerful shamans to send their own spirit or spirits under their control out to occupy the bodies of their enemies. For example, Ifa Fuyū writes of the efforts of seventeenth-century Ryūkyūan officials to criminalize these practices and punish any *yuta* who engaged in them.[24] It may be that these incidents of spiritual violence continue to happen, but it is much more common to hear about possession by lost, disembodied *mabui*.

While the stories that my friends tell often have contemporary settings, they also have suggestive relationships to the memory and indeed the ongoing effects of events in the past. Several years ago, I heard a story about a young couple who, after a visit to a new children's park near the battlefields in Itoman, discovered that their infant son had been possessed by the spirit of a dead Japanese soldier. His remains never recovered or repatriated, the soldier had no comrades or family to care for him. Another friend told me that the spirit of an elderly man who had died in their house before they bought it had possessed his brother. The dead man had been left behind when his family moved to the mainland. There was no one to care for him, to see that he was properly buried, or to carry out his memorial rites. In both cases, the dead did not actively control the bodies they chose; they could only inhibit their movement, leaving its owner in a trance. Neither demonstrated any malice toward their hosts. They were simply reaching out for help. Through the intercession of *yuta*, the dead were given voice and allowed to express their needs. After that, the living were able to help them to complete their passage to the community of ancestral spirits.[25]

Mabui can also be profoundly damaged, and speakers use this trope to express the consequences of the terrible experiences they have endured. War survivors say that their *mabui* was soiled or polluted; others that it was left in tatters.[26]

My friends are concerned about the possibility of losing their *mabui* and they know what to do if it is damaged or threatened. During my dissertation research, my friends rushed past me to catch my three-year-old daughter when she tripped and fell while she was playing. As one of my friends held her in his arms, another immediately intoned the incantation familiar to most Okinawans: *Mabuya, mabuya, utikuyo!* Spirit, spirit, come back to me! On another occasion, after a minor auto accident on a stormy day, the driver of the other car insisted on doing the same for my wife before they went off together to call the police. Later, she told us that she had returned to the scene of the accident to perform a sacrifice to ensure that both she and my wife had their *mabui* firmly in place.

While historians and native ethnologists can trace the origins of these concepts and practices to the Ryūkyūan past, their articulation with contemporary experience is very different. The life of hardship in rural villages, the rituals developed at the Shuri court or in quiet village *uganju* or *ugwanju* (sacred groves) may have given them form; their meaning was transformed and intensified by life in the modern world.

In a world in which a quarter of the island's population was killed in the Battle of Okinawa, where prewar famines and postwar epidemics claimed so many, the question of life is never simple. The production of material forms of subsistence—agriculture, fishing, trade—have been brutally exploited, appropriated, and interrupted. The rural villages and urban neighborhoods that anchored life in familiar and supportive communities have been shattered again and again.

The colonial state and its successors have also intervened against local forms intended for the cultivation of life. Rituals and practices related to the generation or preservation of creative energies—from *buta benjo* and *senkotsu* to music and dance—have been prohibited or stigmatized.[27] Priestesses and shamans were ridiculed, regulated, or proscribed, although they still continue their work. Okinawans have been encouraged to reject superstition and embrace modernization as a part of Japanese assimilation and social mobility.[28]

And yet, it is in these moments of exploitation and appropriation that the value of life and its productive capacity becomes clear. The Ryūkyūan monarchy that once ruled Okinawa was aware of the importance of productive power—both human and nonhuman. As *seji*, a power that could give the King virtue and authority to protect his subjects, it could be brought into this world and used in imperial practices. Wielded by high priestesses against Satsuma invaders, it caused confusion in battle.[29]

It was the Meiji state with its related forms of appropriation that formally capitalized on the productive abilities of the Okinawan people. Here it was not *seji* but sheer *rōdō ryoku* (labor power). In late nineteenth-century discourses, Okinawans were ridiculed as backward and lazy; however, the intense efforts of state and industry to extract their labor power belie these narratives. Policies were created to outlaw communal property, separate Okinawans from their land, industrialize and consolidate Okinawan agriculture, and displace workers to jobs in mainland factories or colonial plantations. Space was cleared to construct the military bases that link Japanese and American interests and projects.[30] The legacy for Okinawan laborers has been decades of exploitation. It has brought an ongoing state of impoverishment and underemployment that has denied the Okinawan people a share in the prosperity and security experienced by their fellow Japanese citizens in the main islands. The precarity that anthropologists have explored in the cosmopolitan centers of postrecessionary Japan has deep, historical antecedents in the experiences of generations of laboring Okinawans.[31]

Against this history of expropriation, Okinawans labor to care for their valuable and fragile *mabui*. They have discovered that it can be productively transformed as well as diminished or lost, and they have created complex communal practices to shape and protect it.

However, it is not necessary to organize a formal ritual or an innovative performance to productively transform the conditions of the everyday. Ordinary life is marked with countless opportunities to create or receive *nuchigusui* (medicine for life). It may be a delicious meal prepared for the recipient with special care or an offering of seasonal fruit at an ancestral altar. It may also be the kind words of a friend or the warmth of a doting grandmother's love.

At the same time, individuals must constantly strive to develop their creative capacities. The more skillful and adept they become, the more productive their act. There is a sense that the value of the gift to the recipient is enhanced by the reputation, proficiency, character, and even the beauty of the giver.[32] Here, beauty represents more than physical attractiveness. A kind and caring person is said to be *chimujurasan*, to have a beautiful heart.[33] A self that has been reciprocally produced by intentional acts over time. For many, this requires the perfection of traditional forms of ritual and performance. The leader of my daughter's neighborhood youth group once told me, "Every Okinawan should study karate, write with a beautiful hand, and play the *sanshin*." At the same time, this commitment to self-development has been shaped by the Meiji ideology of *shusse*, the self-made man, a concept that remains influential in today's precarious world. Deep conflicts arise as the impulses to become more Japanese, to put aside rustic ways, to be conventionally successful, to be a loyal subject, run up against the valorization of the same traditional practices that one is urged to renounce. How can one be both Japanese and Okinawan?

The labor of care can take place between small groups of friends or relatives, or in rituals such as *eisā*, where hundreds of performers entertain countless spirits of the dead and tens of thousands of the living, mediating the distribution of good fortune across a community. It can extend through space and time, engaging widely dispersed participants in ongoing projects of mutual assistance. Okinawans most often speak of this as *yuimāru* (sometimes *yīmārū*), the act of binding together.[34] Creating extended networks of reciprocity is crucial to the self-definition of many Okinawans and valorized in popular and academic discourses. Historically, *yuimāru* references agrarian cooperativism, assistance given and received in labor-intensive practices such as planting and harvesting rice or building a new roof for a farmhouse. While most Okinawans spend little time in romanticized farming communities, the concept of *yuimāru* continues to encourage practices of mutual assistance in contemporary urban settings. Perhaps it has become even more important, pitted against business failure, underemployment, indebtedness, collapsing infrastructure, neoliberal reduction in services, mainland prejudice, and foreign military occupation.[35]

Given this history, how could I be surprised to think that a dog might find a lost *mabui* on the streets of Koza? Here, where there have been so many opportunities for loss? Where the Japanese army surrendered, ending the Battle of Okinawa. Where Okinawans struggled to rebuild their lives after the war. Where they undertook all kinds of labor, from dangerous salvage to sex work, to survive. Where they tried to reconcile their memories of the past and their expectations for the future with the uncertainty and commodification of the everyday. Where they were exploited, extracted, and exhausted. Where Okinawans demonstrated and rebelled against American occupation and Japanese disrespect. I cannot imagine the number of *mabui* that have been lost in these streets. And yet, I also know something of the efforts that Okinawans have made to protect and care for these fragile, creative, and necessary spirits.

In the Arcade

I crossed Pāku Abenyū Dōri (Park Avenue) and followed a narrow alley to the entrance to the arcade. A wan green light trickled down from the skylights, fading as it met the darkness that filled the passage. The faint illumination seemed overwhelmed by the water that leaked around the seals on the high windows, covering the tiled floor below with deep, brackish puddles. Most of the shops were dark, the passageway only lit by the weak, blue glow from the fluorescent lights of a couple of stores. Even in the ghost light, I could see that many of the storefronts were vacant.

The arcade was a strange place, changing and unchanging. It remained at the center of a once-vibrant business and entertainment district located just to the east of Kadena Air Base. It was made up of about a dozen blocks of small shops connected when the streets were paved with decorative tiles and a roof constructed overhead, joining the ferroconcrete buildings that had been built and rebuilt, again and again, since the end of the war. For the last thirty years, there seems to have been gradual decline, more stores

1.1.　A passageway in the arcade.

closed each time I returned. The tiled floors of several of the northernmost passages in the Ichibangai seem to have been recently restored and new, illuminated signs representing local *seinenkai* (youth groups) famous for their *eisā* had been hung above. But other writing was already on the walls. Business couldn't compete with places like the Aeon Mall at Rycom, two miles to the south, where upscale shops, restaurants, and cinemas offered tourists and locals an up-to-date experience of cosmopolitan, affluent consumerism.[36]

As I walked through the arcade, water sloshing over my sandals, I saw several familiar shops. A pharmacy, two boutiques catering to older women, a greengrocer, a hardware store, a men's clothing store, a shop selling household goods. The old community-access radio station, FM Champla, was shuttered. The A&W Root Beer restaurant was gone, but it had been closed for years. A record store that was a branch of the larger Fukuhara Music across the street was also vacant.[37] Many shops had changed hands so many times that odd remnants of past identities still remained—a large, faded sign with a new, smaller one nailed over it; glass windows stenciled with advertisements for services that the business could not possibly provide. Stairs between stores led up to a nightclub but posters announcing events were months out of date. The only sign of real activity was in the small stalls of the market at one end of the arcade where a steady stream of customers bought fresh meat and produce, bulk tempura and prepared lunches, and at a new senior center at the intersection of two of the main passages. There were signs that families still lived in apartments above or behind businesses, and people came and went from the small houses in the alleys behind the arcade. Several bars and nightclubs had opened near the entrance to the arcade closest to Kadena Air Base. The wars in Afghanistan and Iraq—and perhaps elsewhere in Asia—still fueled business as they had during wars in Korea and Vietnam.

The girders that tied the buildings together, the decorative lamps that lit the arcade, the illuminated signs that advertised the local merchants association, the ornamental tiles beneath my feet—all are traces of a moment of transformation and a sense of hopefulness. If not hope in the present, perhaps a material reminder of a moment in the past when the dreams and desires of the community were oriented toward the future. The arcade was built from what was already there—the streets themselves predate its construction by decades. For Okinawa City is born out of war. The American military built their bases amid the ruins of villages and farms destroyed in the fighting. They directed Okinawans to rebuild their shattered communities in the spaces that remained. In these new base towns, they worked together to create a grid filled with hundreds of similar bars and hotels, tiny houses and cramped apartment buildings. The streets that brought Okinawan workers to the bases also carried American soldiers in the opposite direction to the pawn shops and clothing stores; the bars and dance halls; the brothels and hotels that existed among and within Okinawan houses. The appropriation of Okinawan communities was so thorough that residential space itself was drawn into the network of material and immaterial labor that supported the American occupation. For thousands of Okinawan women, the home also became a workshop for commodified sexual labor.[38] Higashi Mineo's novel *An Okinawan Boy* describes this in its crushing banality—a child grudgingly gives up his bed to a sex worker from his family's bar and the soldier who paid for her labor.[39] Production and consumption enmeshed in the wooden and ferroconcrete structures that made up the community. Of course, Okinawans were no strangers to the cycles of industrial capitalism. For generations, they have known how to work, to sacrifice, and to hope.

That is why the form of the arcade is particularly compelling. At the moment of Okinawa's reversion to Japanese sovereignty in 1972, it seemed that everything Okinawans had labored and hoped for was at hand. The arcade offered ordinary Okinawans a critical space to engage the occupation and its legacy of suffering and complicity, of political opposition, commercial support, and artistic creativity. It did so by appropriating the remains of a fading American colonial outpost, linking them together in something new. While it drew on the form of arcades popular in 1970s mainland Japan and articulated the desire for spaces that enabled pleasurable consumption, there are echoes of earlier practices of transformation. Like *senkotsu* (the practice of washing the bones of the dead), the remnants of a seemingly exhausted form of life were beautified, reassembled, and transformed. Okinawans would continue to live and work there, but they would also be among those for whom these spaces were intended. The pieces of a world that they had built for others would be remade into a place for them. They could stroll together, shop together, eat and drink together with their fellow Japanese consumers—in the same way that they could now travel unfettered and enjoy similar spaces across Japan.

For a time, the promise of the arcade was fulfilled, and the area prospered. However, distance from the conventional tourist destinations that were developed after Reversion and changing patterns of consumption spelled the end to its success. Visitors were drawn to coastal resorts. American military personnel were constrained by curfews and long absences, as well as captured by increased commercial development on base. It seemed that Okinawans themselves could no longer see the future in the shops and passages of the arcade. As they turned to the sprawling shopping centers built near the beaches or in newer, more attractive urban developments, the Ichibangai became an archive of the traces of uncomfortable dreams.

I was surprised to find one new, brightly lit shop in a particularly desolate corridor. Its glass doors were propped open and a desk stood near the entrance. There were chairs on each side as if customers were expected. On the wall, several large charts displayed information about the Chinese zodiac; to the side, three doors were built into a temporary divider. An elderly woman dozed behind the desk. A large sign read *uranai* (fortune telling) and a number of pamphlets testified to the importance and efficacy of their services.

1.2. Fortune tellers in the arcade.

It wasn't surprising to find that this new shop was run by an *uranaishi* (fortune teller). Japan was in the midst of a fortune-telling boom, grounded in long-standing popular interest in divination.[40] Ordinary people regularly consulted specialized calendars to determine auspicious times for trips or important events. Magazines, almanacs, and radio broadcasts pass along the most current horoscopes. A late-night walk through any major city would show diviners holding consultations at tables near train stations, park entrances, or closed department stores.

However, there seemed to be a new intensity to its popularity. Friends told me that they felt pressured to consult popular *uranaishi* because it was so trendy. The long wait and the shockingly expensive fees charged by well-known diviners were an expected part of the experience, adding to their prestige when they told their friends about it. Digital media brought access to fortune tellers via phone services, web pages, and apps as well as a host of television shows that featured everything from celebrity readings to audience call-ins.

Okinawans were drawn into this resurgent interest in divination as much as anyone else. At the same time, Okinawa was mobilized in new and important ways. The tourist industry represented Okinawa as a space of intense spiritual awareness, and tourists—especially young mainland women—were urged to visit local "power spots." Most of these were sites associated with the Kingdom of Ryūkyū—castle ruins, the palace at Shuri, sacred groves.[41]

Nationally televised historical dramas such as *Tenpesuto* (The tempest) romanticized the supernatural powers of women such as the Kikoe Ōgimi—the chief priestess of the Kingdom of Ryūkyū—while novels, chat shows, and self-help books sought to create an uncanny aura around ordinary Okinawan women, particularly the elderly *obā*, wise grandmothers who regularly appear in nationally televised family dramas. This has also generated a fascination with *yuta* (shamans). Okinawan performers have told me that their mainland collaborators often ask to consult with a *yuta* during visits to Okinawa. Several elderly *yuta* complained to me that they are beset by mainland tourists who hope for some insight into their problems but will not follow the solutions they offer them. Conventional fortune tellers have also benefitted from this focus on Okinawan spirituality. A well-known *uranaishi* in Urasoe had become wildly popular as a result of his nationwide television appearances. Within minutes of opening his appointment line, he would be booked solid for the month. Clients paid exorbitant rates. As I drove along the streets at night, I came to expect the violet glow of the neon character *uranai*, beckoning customers, or the sight of several diviners working at small tables set up outside theaters and popular shopping centers. These places and practitioners, tokens of a Ryūkyūan past, have been converted to a common cultural resource to be experienced by Japanese tourists.

Perhaps it is inevitable that divination would be appropriated by Japan's highly integrated culture industry. The past is fodder for endless media representations, marketing strategies, and tourist campaigns. Difference is appropriated, mediated, commodified, effaced, and reconstructed in complex practices and networks.[42] And yet, there is something about divination that differs from the experience of reconstructed samurai villages, romanticized folkcraft centers, or resuscitated traditional festivals and performances. For Theodor Adorno, divination yielded insight into contemporary responses to crisis. It taps into the anxiety experienced by ordinary people in a world where the future is in question.[43] This feeling is exacerbated by the same networks of media that deliver divination to consumers—a complexly articulated ideological system. Nonetheless, the crises that anxiety references are all too real. The threat of China or North Korea, the ambivalence of US occupation, economic uncertainty, political disempowerment, and social injustice—all of these have material conse-quences for Okinawans.

And yet, as Ernst Bloch observed, it is easy for subjects to conflate their apprehension of the conditions of an objective crisis, generated by the con-tradictions of contemporary capitalist society, with a more ideological in-timation that a future that had been promised to them by the past was now foreclosed.[44] It is this disjuncture that divination exploits, "expecting from the transfigured shape of society misplaced in the skies an answer that only a study of real society can give."[45]

Divination validates the perception of crisis, while absolving people from the possibility—indeed the necessity—of working through this by any kind of practical, political action. For Adorno, it suggests that this ideological formation is underpinned by the subject's own death drive, the sense that this endless cycle is being staged by an actor who enjoys the anticipation of their own impending destruction.

Okinawans certainly experience the anxiety of life on the uneven periph-ery of Japanese prosperity. Dwelling among the ruins of colonial domination and wartime sacrifice, they are caught between a military occupation that extends endlessly into the future and the complex form of Japanese industrial capitalism that relentlessly reconfigures the built environment—highways, dams, resorts, commercial zones, and urban centers—only to abandon the space it transformed in another paroxysm of destruction and reconstruc-tion. Even if their lives were lived in the kind of bad faith that Adorno sug-gests, who could blame them?

And yet, I feel as if their experience with practitioners such as *uranaishi* or *yuta* are much more creative and productive. Divination reveals a pos-sibility that the world is structured by something other than the endless cycle of labor within the spatiotemporality of the Japanese nation. Through attentiveness to certain signs—the time and place of their birth, the char-acters of their name, the features of their face—they can discern another way of being, a totality in which they already have a place. What's more, they already have some intimation of that world from stories told by their families and friends, and in memories of earlier encounters. The *uranai-shi*'s neon sign and the shop in the arcade may be symptoms of impending economic catastrophe. However, they are also signals that disclose another set of possibilities. What *uranaishi* offer is not simply a consultation but an awakening to a set of relationships and network of practices within which one is already imbricated. It only takes a moment of remembrance, a mo-ment of action, to take advantage of it.

At the same time, this encounter discloses more than a choice to be made. These possibilities also contain obligations. You are not simply connected to the motion of the stars as they cycle through the heavens or the half-forgotten sacred spaces of Ryūkyū that lie behind modern facades. You are also called to your place in an endless network of living consociates, ancestral spirits, and local deities. You must confront a future charged with powerful elements of the past. To move forward toward one requires moving toward the other as well. *Yuimāru* describes being bound as much as binding.

I think back to my friend Hiroshi's story about his brother's wife and her complicated consultations with the *yuta*. Her prayers unanswered, her problems unresolved, she found that she had yet another set of responsibilities to bear. However, simply abstracting a moment in a newly rediscovered set of reciprocal relations does little to expose the dense network of obligation and care that the *yuta* illuminated. Looking at the *uranaishi*'s shop, I thought that customers might discover something other than a life lived alone, and that powerful networks that could be awakened in this modest storefront. I remembered an earlier conversation with Adaniya Kyōko, an elderly *yuta* much concerned with these issues.

On a rainy summer afternoon, we sat together drinking tea. Her small house was on a quiet street, not far from the arcade. The room was filled with the memories of a busy life. Individual photos and family portraits were displayed along the walls, as well as her husband's certificates for loyal service in the construction industry. The family altar was open: fresh fruit, bright flowers, and glasses of water offered to the ancestral spirits. Boxes of sweets and other gifts were arranged neatly, presents from grateful clients. Next to the altar, an orderly stack of photo albums chronicled her long service to her deities.

Her life, lived in the aftermath of the war, had not been easy. Now in her eighties, she moved with difficulty, her hands rough and knobby, her features worn. Perhaps an unseen toll taken by a lifetime of devotion. And yet, she still seemed to crackle with energy, laughing, enthusiastically telling stories. Dignity and confidence too, whether she spoke about the dark, difficult postwar years that nearly destroyed her before she was summoned to service, or her pride in her grandchildren and her concern for her clients and colleagues.

She remained active, a steady stream of consultants seeking her assistance. She was well known in Okinawa, respected for her power and insight. Rejecting the stereotype of the solitary and secretive shaman, she was involved in efforts to bring *yuta* together to share their ideas. Along with local ethnologists and psychoanalysts, they met regularly to explore their abilities and share their experiences. She was an innovative and energetic collaborator, reaching out to mainland *itako* (spirit mediums most often associated with northeastern Japan), as well as Native American spiritual practitioners and scholars from around the world.

She had been talking to me about the autochthonous beings that made Ryūkyū home long before human beings arrived. She said that they continue to dwell in their native places, unseen by people caught up in their daily routines. "Of course they're still here. If we try to become aware of them, we'll see that they are already interested in us. Recognize them, be kind to them, and they will help you to understand the world around you. There are things that they know, things that they can do, that are beyond our abilities. But they appreciate our interest and are happy to do things for us too."

Mrs. Adaniya smiled quietly and sipped her tea before setting it down on the low table. She paused for a moment, her casual manner shifting to a stiff formality, her eyes distant. In a quiet, tremulous voice, she began to sing, her hands softly clapping to the rhythm of her song. It was not a mystical invocation but a simple children's song, "Tinsagu nu Hana" (The balsam flower), perhaps the most well-known song in Okinawa.

> Like fingernails dyed with the balsam flower
> My heart is painted with my parent's teachings.
> I can count the stars in the sky,
> But I can never add up what I learned from my parents.
> Like ships that steer their course by the North Star,
> I am guided by my parents watching over me.
> Why hold a beautiful treasure if you don't take care of it?
> If you care for your body you will live a wonderful life.
> If you live with sincerity, your way will be true
> And you'll prosper.
> You can do anything if you try.
> You won't amount to anything if you don't.[46]

Finishing her song, she folded her hands on her lap and laughed. "Everyone knows this song. But do they understand it? I shouldn't have to explain it, but it's important. We have already benefitted from the love of our parents, our families, and our ancestors. There is a long line of people who have cared about us. We need to hear their voices, acknowledge their gifts, and do our part for them. It should be easy, but we face so many problems and difficulties. And we are drawn to other things. That's when we forget to show our gratitude to those who have done so much for us."[47]

A simple song, charged with a history of complex and contradictory ideologies, with questions that demand critical consideration. Like the image of the hand, at once multiple and undivided. It is grounded in a Confucian-inspired ideology, one crafted by Ryūkyūan philosophers and statesmen like Sai On in the seventeenth century to centralize authority under a single monarch, to suppress conflict, and to articulate the kingdom with household organization.[48] It is also a record of the cunning use of this ideology—in part by those like the *yuta* who were initially threatened by it—and its transformation into an ethos of care and kindness. However, *yuta* were not the only ones to recognize the power of these formations: although it eliminated the Ryūkyūan monarchy, the Meiji state appropriated its ideological underpinnings, contributing to the frenzy of imperial murder and self-sacrifice in World War II.

Perhaps this is related to the anxiety that Okinawans experience. They have powerful resources available to them, ones that could transform their daily lives. At the same time, they face discrimination if they identify themselves too closely with a dangerously non-Japanese subjectivity. They know that their practices can be distorted and the consequences of this appropriation can be catastrophic. They are also attracted to other things, drawn away from the attitude that Mrs. Adaniya described. The Okinawan proletarian poet Yamanokuchi Baku captured this conflict in his poem, "The Ritual of Parting." The narrator, an Okinawan laborer living in prewar Tokyo, dies suddenly. After a perfunctory funeral marked by the desultory prayers and offerings of his acquaintances, he finds himself in the land of the dead:

> When I got to the other world
> There was my oldest son
> Waiting for me
> With a sullen expression on his face.
> When I asked him why he looked so sour
> He complained that
> Even when it was Obon[49]
> We never made any good offerings to him.
> I gently stroked his head
> That son of mine.[50]

In that moment, he realizes that he has never reciprocated for the gifts of the dead. The suffering caused by his selfish, indolent ways does not end at the door of the tomb. Desire remains, the need for care persists.

> When you think that
> Even the enlightened spirits of the dead
> Want things that cost money
> Then it's just like being alive on earth.
> This world
> And that world
> Aren't any different.[51]

In the time of the poem, recognition comes too late for the narrator. But in the time of the world, as the reader pauses during her daily routine to consider these short lines? Perhaps this is the possibility that divination offers. In the chance visit by a young woman, a family's decision to consult a *yuta* about their father's estate, a student seeking advice about his examinations, a politician asking for help with an impending election. They are not recognizing the traces of an obligation fixed in the past. They can no longer take comfort in unreflexively believing that things will follow their natural course. They are not like prophets or critical thinkers who anticipate a moment to come. Instead, they have uncovered a moment that is at hand. A moment that requires their action to be transformed.

To be accurate, that is not all it takes. One must be prepared to invest in this choice. A *uranaishi* will ask ¥1,000 for an introduction to the invisible powers; an initial consultation with a *yuta* might be ¥3,000 or more. As Matt Allen writes, it could even cost ¥50,000 to put the appropriate forces in motion.[52] In the end, we are brought back to the heterogeneity of the moment, the peril of decisiveness. Everything costs something.

The Okinawan *manzai* duo Surimu Kurabu capture the ambiguity and fragility of everyday life in their work.[53] In a series of short videos, Maeda Ken and Uchima Masanari take a trio of young mainland comedians who, like them, are represented by the entertainment agency Yoshimoto Kōgyō, on a performative tour of the contradictions of Okinawan society.[54] They want to introduce their stablemates to the form of Okinawan *dāku aruaru* comedy that they practice, a genre that depends on the resonance of their grim observations with the experiences of their audience.

[*Uchima knocks at the door.*]

MAEDA Ah, it's you. What is it this time?

UCHIMA Well, can you lend me some money?

MAEDA What, again? You're always coming to borrow something. Now what?

UCHIMA It's my wife. She's really fallen in with this *yuta* . . .

MAEDA Are you OK? How are you going to pay me back?

UCHIMA *Kisetsu de kaesu kara.* . . . I'll pay it back by seasonal [labor] up in the mainland.

How bitterly ironic that the cost of discovering the path to happiness might entail the loss of any possibility of benefiting from that knowledge. I turned to the north, walking back through the arcade to Parumaira Dōri (Palmyra Avenue). As I stepped into the open street, the vibrant murals and fresh paving tiles seemed out of place after the grim arcade, like a fresh green shoot growing from a gnarled trunk.

Parumaira Dōri is home to one of the most fascinating sites in a city of creative spaces. A group of historians working for the municipal government—the same scholars who published a series of critical texts focusing on important aspects of life in Okinawa City—had constructed a small museum called Hisutorīto, woven from the terms "history" and "street." Hisutorīto occupied a space in which visitors could explore the history of Koza—the aftermath of war, American occupation, the political struggles of the people who live here—in the fragments and debris of everyday life. In their earlier work, Onga Takashi and his colleagues argued that the history of Okinawa was made in these streets through the actions of ordinary people. With the museum, they appropriated a form that instantiated and expressed this conviction.[55]

Hisutorīto had been created in two vacant storefronts. The museum's interior and exterior spaces were assembled to preserve the feeling of the old shops. Window displays were filled with objects associated with postwar consumer culture: rows of bottles, cameras, and other commodities. Their artless presentation seemed deliberate. Like a thrift shop—dusty, hastily arranged, things that had been used before being redeployed to some new end. While a sign above the door announced the museum's name in jaunty

1.3.   Hisutorīto Museum.

katakana script, a distinctive structure bearing the words New Koza St. stood next to the entrance.[56] This was a replica of a sign that marked the first permanent district of bars, restaurants, and brothels for GIs on liberty in Koza.[57]

I waved to Onga himself, who was busy with a group of high school students visiting from the mainland. Hovering between the domestic and the foreign, mainland students experienced an Okinawa that was both a popular tourist destination and an archive of battlefields and ruins, a site where young men and women could think about the consequences of war and oppression while enjoying the sun and the beach.[58] With shouts and gestures, we made plans to meet later. Stepping inside, the interior was dark and surprisingly cool. A docent stood behind a counter, explaining objects on display to a fashionably dressed mainland Japanese couple.

To the left, a collection of texts. Worn, cloth-covered books, faded paperbacks, well-thumbed manga. Alongside these stood copies of new publications from the municipal government. A history of postwar intern-ment camps, interviews with Vietnam-era musicians, translated American documents related to the Koza Uprising of 1970, a monograph about *eisā*. With a small desk in the center of the display, it seemed like a recreation of a long-neglected scholar's office or a used bookstore.

The next exhibit focused on the material organization of everyday life, fragmented reconstructions of the things that gave that life its form. A radio, a television, a case of school badges. A set of children's clothes sewn from used Marine combat uniforms. Overhead an arch of corrugated metal sug-gested an occupation-era Quonset hut.

Across from this, laminated photographs and printed cards recounted life in the refugee camps that housed Okinawans before the construction of urban Koza. Most arresting, the blurred image of an American-style cemetery where the Okinawan dead were interred in closely packed rows. Forbidden the solace of their family tombs, even the dead had to comply with the military structuration of everyday life.

Beyond this, a space that held traces of the postwar explosion of mass entertainment. While the *kankara sanshin* has come to signify cultural resilience, these objects spoke to adaptation, desire, and the cunning of those who, having survived unimaginable horrors, were determined to live.[59] Radios, jukeboxes, records, more televisions, neon signs. Photos of performances by the bands Murasaki and Condition Green, the dance floor jammed with American GIs, Okinawan women, and Okinawan men. A riot of bodies, their actions arrested, suggestive and unknowable. A moment of artistic production, initially driven by the American occupation, expressing both pleasure and oppression.[60]

In the opposite corner, an alcove lined with text and images gave shape and context to the other things on display. Black-and-white photographs, assembled from the work of both famous photographers and unknown amateurs. Iconic images of moments such as the Koza Uprising alongside anonymous shots of sun-bleached, empty streets and nightclubs shimmer-ing with neon light. The clarity of the images distorted by enlargement, their aesthetic presentation dulled by lamination, their intentionality obscured by juxtaposition with so many others. It was a space charged with urgency and excess. As I walked from image to image, I became aware of an insistent theme of collective action. Scenes of young politicians celebrating the suc-cess, however limited, of their demands for self-governance; the struggle to have stockpiles of chemical weapons removed from military storehouses; the furious clash of unionized base workers and students with armored police

1.4.   The A-sign bar in Hisutorīto.

and soldiers; cars burning in the streets during the Koza Uprising. Inter-
spersed with these, images of Okinawans and Americans dancing, drinking, talking together. A complex constellation, ambiguous and powerful.

All of these objects and images were arranged around a counter built at
the center of the space. While it served as an information desk, it was a fully
reconstructed A-sign bar. I couldn't imagine a more overdetermined form
to provoke a reconsideration of the relationship between Okinawans and
Americans. A space where Okinawan bartenders served drinks to soldiers
about to leave for Korea or Vietnam, where young Okinawan women negotiated the price of their sexual labor with GIs returning from combat. Where
Okinawans and Americans drank together in enmity and in friendship. It
is a space in which fortunes were made and lives were ruined and created.

Behind the bar, rows of liquor bottles: Old Parr, Bacardi, Jack Daniels. A
pair of signs bearing the capital letter *A* certifying that military authorities

approved the use of this space by American servicemen. Above those bottles, the wall was plastered with dollar bills, each with a signature scrawled across its face.

Money is a strange thing. For Okinawans, its particular form indexes successive modalities of exchange, conflicts, and occupations in the Okinawan past: Ryūkyūan coins and Chinese cash speak to a time when Okinawan diplomats and merchants acted as mediators in trade between China and the rest of East and Southeast Asia; prewar and postwar Japanese yen recall different moments in the loss of Okinawan autonomy and the difficult incorporation of the islands into the Japanese state; the heterodox A yen and B yen produced by the US occupation and, finally, the US dollar point to the uneasy persistence of a temporary American military occupation. Yellow embossed sheets of *uchikabi* (the money of the dead) evoke complex relationships that must be negotiated across the boundaries of this world and the next. A shifting, contingent collection of signs that represent the constantly changing terrain of valuation, the instability and uncertainty of power and authority, the unreliable guarantor that stands behind the commodity that insists on its permanence.

The American dollar bills displayed are more compelling, knowing, as we do, that the value of money is only realized in circulation, moving from hand to hand, replacing other objects. Perhaps inhering here and there, flotsam in a torrent of exchange.[61] Here, they are detached from that temporality, frozen, marked with the signatures of those who drew them out of their final circuit. Each dollar a token of existence, of the fact that at a certain time, in a certain place, a person—an American soldier—was alive and able to sign his own name to its face.[62] And with that signature, a human dimension overwrites the impersonal presence of the state that otherwise guarantees the value of the bill.[63] A single dollar, the lowest denomination—both anonymous and specific—marking the horizon between presence and absence, perhaps between life and death. Collectively, they represent an accumulation of sacrifice as, one after another, soldiers sign and post them and are gone: gone to the mountains of Korea; the jungles of Indochina; the desert plains, rocky highlands, dense urban neighborhoods and broken villages of Iraq or Afghanistan. I doubt that Okinawans are surprised by this collective remembrance. Okinawan space is laden with sites for the counting of the dead. The Cornerstone of Peace, the massive monument to all who died in the Battle of Okinawa that stands surrounded by rank after rank of silent Imperial memorials. The *irei no tō* (monuments to the war dead) that have been built in communities throughout the islands. The tombs in every neighborhood that bear family names and the altars in virtually every home that hold tablets recording the ancestral dead. Perhaps Okinawans wonder at the alienation of these soldiers who, with no one else to memorialize them, must write their own names on the wall. Okinawans are crucial partners in this material memoration. They built the walls where the bills are displayed, trade with the soldiers who sat at the bar, and maintain these graphic traces once the soldiers left en route to their fate.

Onga Takashi has written that Hisutorīto is a space crafted to encourage visitors to remember, to reassemble a sense of the past from the fragments that have been made available to them, and to do so among the streets and buildings where the remains of the past lie so deep.[64] What kind of past does it conjure? Does it repeat the work of a *lieu de memoire* like Yasukuni Shrine in Tokyo, where a distorted Shinto formalism binds countless spirits of the dead to the crippled remains of fascist militarism? Is it no more than a tableau that invites consideration of the colonial labor produced here, the military occupation executed, the complex patterns of exploitation and sacrifice? The images give the clue—this is not simply a space where Americans purchased commodified forms of Okinawan labor. It is a place where Okinawans made fortunes, where they perished, where they experienced relationships both satisfying and humiliating, where they gathered for purposes entirely of their own. With the construction of Hisutorīto, these spaces are not simply preserved: they are appropriated, once again, as a site to reflect and to act on the past and the future. As the Okinawan activist and folksinger Sadoyama Yutaka sang in "Duchuimuni," his critical yet hopeful ode to Koza, the dynamic and resilient community where he grew up:

> People who only act cool
> Don't understand anything else.
> If you have that kind of power,
> Use it to accomplish something for yourselves![65]

The poet Takara Ben once told me that the events now represented here in the museum were also produced in spaces just like it. On a winter night in 1970, he said, the Koza Uprising was given form in the bars that lined the neighboring streets. Before that, innumerable actions had been organized in union halls and community centers, university classrooms and the offices of political parties, in the streets and parks of Okinawa. But the Koza Uprising is remembered as being something very different—American cars left ruined in the streets, soldiers beaten, the fence around Kadena Air

Base breached and buildings burned. How did places like these bars and clubs figure in the uprising? Friends who experienced the uprising, who participated in it, laughed when I asked them about that. It was too easy an answer, they said. People drank in Koza every night, but the uprising was something different. Takara had a different response. The bars and restaurants were filled with activists who had come from a rally in Misato that afternoon. Tensions were high following the dismissal of charges against an American soldier accused of killing an Okinawan woman in Itoman while driving drunk.[66] These events had happened many times before, but now something would be different. On the evening of December 20, scores of *moai* (mutual aid organizations) were holding their monthly meetings in the bars and restaurants of Koza. A writer calling themselves Okinawashi Jieigyōsha (Okinawa City self-employed laborer) in *Jinmin no Hoshi*, the journal of the Maoist left wing of the Japanese Communist Party, described their experiences: "On that day, my classmates and some older friends were having a moai at my friend's house in Nakanomachi [across the street from the arcade]. The riot happened right in front of my friend's house, so everybody rushed out into the street. The bars in Nakanomachi were full of the people who had led the movement to force the Americans to remove chemical weapons from Okinawa and these guys were turning cars over and burning them."[67] In the complex networks of obligation and forbearance, care and accountability, that are spun out by the *moai*, something fanned the spark of hope into a flame.

The Moai, December 1997

I stepped out of the driving winter rain into the crowded *izakaya*, not far from the arcade. A popular bar district during the occupation, the *izakaya* depended on business from the neighborhood now. "Sonda Youth Group Meeting—2F" was written on a blackboard by the door, so I went upstairs. Two parallel rows of tables ran the length of a tatami room, and sixty people or so were already there. Everyone had changed from the work clothes and company uniforms that made up the everyday attire of most of the members. Women were dressed in 1970s retro fashion that was popular; men in patterned sweaters, polo shirts and slacks, tracksuits. The officers of the youth group were the exception: all in sharp suits. Women with fashionable hairstyles, younger men with hair slick with pomade, veteran members sporting crew cuts and tight *punchipāma* (a closely-curled men's hairstyle). Tables were lined with bottles of beer and *awamori* (distilled rice liquor), trays of hors d'oeuvres and sashimi, glasses, plates, and chopsticks. Most of the younger members of the youth group were seated around the far table, with the officers at the head and the women at the foot.

As I took off my shoes and stepped up onto the tatami floor, a couple of my friends seated at the closer table grabbed me and, laughing, pulled me down onto an empty cushion between them. Virtually everyone at the table was a former community leader or a distinguished performing artist.

The party was both a Shinnenkai (New Year's party) and a Seinennokai (celebration of adulthood) for four younger members who were entering their twentieth year. Although their names were written on the banner that stretched across the front wall, none of them were actually present. One was already doing *dekasegi* (itinerant labor) in Yokohama, two working distant construction projects elsewhere in Okinawa, another bartending nearby. While the leader of the youth group introduced the evening's master of ceremonies, another very different performance began to unfold.

Yamashiro Masamichi had been a former officer in the youth group. Although he was working as an electrical contractor, he was also something of a local fixer—someone who could always be counted on to organize a bus for a group trip, find a private dining room for a party, or get you a table at a popular club. Tonight, he was serving as the record keeper for the *moai* made up of the OBs or "old boys"—older members who no longer danced with the youth group. He was busy moving back and forth among the guests at our table, a small ledger and pen in hand and a bank envelope under his arm. He sat next to each guest in turn, taking the crisp ¥10,000 note that they proffered and slipping it into the growing stack of bills in his envelope.[68] Then, he opened the ledger on his lap and entered the member's name and the date of the payment. Finally, he sat down next to the head of the community association—the parent organization of the youth group—and they whispered together for a moment. As the emcee continued his witty banter, the head of the association looked down the table and raised his eyebrows. Laughing, the members looked at each other, some making tentative gestures as if they were going to raise their hands. Finally, Aragaki Shūhei, a veteran member laughed and thrust his hand into the air with the mock formality of a schoolboy.[69] He had agreed to be the winner for the month. While the waitresses brought steaming platters of Okinawan dishes, Yamashiro knelt next to me and passed a long white envelope across the table to the winner. Aragaki raised himself up to a kneeling position and accepted it, lifting it with both hands above his head, grinning and nodding to everyone along the table. "This will go a long way to paying the bills—you know how things are at the end of the year!" he laughed. As he slid the overstuffed envelope into his handbag, the two men sitting next to him finished tuning their *sanshin* and launched into an enthusiastic performance of "Medetai Bushi," a famous celebratory folksong.

When I first read about Japanese cooperative loan organizations in *Suye Mura*, John Embree's brilliant ethnography of prewar life in rural Kyushu, I assumed them to be a historical form of village sociality.[70] During my first weeks of fieldwork in Okinawa in 1996, the members of the traditional musical ensemble that I was interviewing surprised me by negotiating their biweekly *moai* while we spoke. I soon realized that *moai* remained vital in Okinawa. Okinawan journalists and scholars alike write of them as a unique and important element of Okinawan social life. Although most Okinawans now live in urban communities, they are proud to maintain a connection with agrarian cooperativism and they often evoke its roots in the Ryūkyūan past. References to the *moai* in the media inevitably turn to the legendary statesman Sai On and the edicts he issued creating an emergency fund. Many of my friends pick up on this connection. Most of them claim descent from the disestablished Ryūkyūan nobility—their neighborhood had its origin in a *yādui*, a hamlet of déclassé samurai that lies ruined beneath Kadena Air Base—and they reminisce about the *moai* that supported their ancestors. Through cooperative arrangements made primarily through networks of kin, relief funds were established in order to enable these nobles to survive the difficult transition to a working life in rural Okinawa.[71]

My friends were quick to qualify any claims to uniqueness. It was not that they believed that cooperative credit associations only existed in Okinawa. Reports in Okinawan media about *moai* would regularly cite their similarity to other forms of cooperativism found across Asia. *Moai* were often compared with practices of shared agricultural labor in Indonesia or mutual aid societies in rural China. Inevitably, there would be a comment about cooperative organizations in the Japanese mainland. The work of scholars such as Sakurai Tokutarō have shown that associations for mutual assistance referred to as *mujinkō* (circles of endless reciprocity) have existed in Japan since the Heian era, and that by the fifteenth century they had already assumed economic functions similar to those I noted in the *moai*.[72] Tetsuo Najita has written that these cooperative associations were particularly resilient and continued to grow well into the twentieth century, enmeshed in both the practices of everyday life and the communitarian ideologies of figures such as Miura Baien and Ninomiya Sontoku. Najita cites Yanagita Kunio's discussion of cooperatives in his study of Japanese customary practices: "There is almost no town or village in Japan that does not have the cooperative organization called the kō, which is composed of persons who contributed to a mutual fund intended for a variety of purposes. In recent years the number of kō has declined, but in the Meiji period they still existed in abundance."[73]

It was the direct intervention of the Japanese state that caused this decline. During this period, authorities launched a series of actions against *mujinkō*, seeking to divert the capital circulating in them to state-sanctioned banks and credit associations.[74] Although those that survived state interference played important roles in local postwar reconstruction projects, their numbers continued to dwindle. Najita has suggested that they persist primarily in the influence that their ethos exerted on other forms of commercial organization.[75] Their traces also remain in popular representation. Across contemporary Japan, there has been a tremendous proliferation of commercial credit institutions whose practices have colonized the spaces where *mujinkō* once provided mutual assistance. The consumer loan company Acom (*akomu*) once parodied the term *mujinkō*, using a cute mascot named *mujin-kun*, a smiling cartoonish bodhisattva who invites people to take out high-interest personal loans, available from their nationwide system of automated cash points. Predatory lending disguised in an image of self-sacrifice.

Perhaps the uniqueness that Okinawans invoke is the continued vitality of their *moai*. After Okinawa's colonization by Japan, the prefectural government was also active in regulating *moai*, but not to the same degree of intervention in the mainland. They remained important sources of capital throughout Okinawa's difficult incorporation into the Japanese state and the brutal prewar depression. During the postwar years, *moai* maintained an anomalous status, excluded from the regulation of banks and cooperative savings associations and exempted from sanctions directed at pyramid schemes and the like. Although banks, credit unions, and commercial credit institutions have as many offices in Okinawa as anywhere else in Japan, *moai* also remain profoundly important. Studies within the past decade suggest that as many as 60 percent of prefectural residents participate in *moai*. My own experience has been that most adults belong to several, ranging from family cooperatives to associations of friends or coworkers to highly speculative syndicates.

When I asked one of my friends why he belonged to the *seinenkai* (youth group) *moai*, he answered that he was inspired by the spirit of *yuimāru*. "We take care of one another like people did back when they helped each other in the fields." And yet, participation is more than an exercise in nostalgia. The utility of the *moai* and the capital it provides is crucial in Japan's poorest prefecture, a place that remains riven by crisis and indebtedness. The smoldering anger and the sense of injustice that has driven opposition to US bases for decades is always grounded in the remembrance of famine, death, and abandonment.

In this respect, Okinawa is not unlike much of the world subject to the predation of Western hegemony and finance capital. Maurizio Lazzarato's critique resonates painfully with the experience of many Okinawans.

> The debt economy has deprived the immense majority of Europeans of political power, which had already been diminished through the concessions of representative democracy. It has deprived them of a growing share of the wealth that past struggles had wrested from capitalist accumulation. And, above all, it has deprived them of the future, that is, of time, time as decision-making, choice and possibility. The series of financial crises has violently revealed a subjective figure that, while already present, now occupies the entirety of public space: the "indebted man." The subjective achievements neoliberalism has promised ("everyone a shareholder, everyone an owner, everyone an entrepreneur") have plunged us into the existential condition of the indebted man, at once responsible and guilty for his particular fate.[76]

The *moai* has given Okinawans an instrument to contest the exploitation that Lazzarato describes. Okinawans who take their place in a *moai* find themselves immersed in a dense network of practices charged with the ethos of *yuimāru*, of binding care. Their actions produce a moment charged with shared possibility. Like forms of collective assistance once popular across Japan, *moai* offer Okinawans the opportunity to stand together against economic hardship, orienting their actions to care for their fellow members and to receive kindness and consideration in return.[77] To be sure, the accumulation and distribution of capital over time is critical to the project of the *moai*. Working together, they are able to accomplish projects that otherwise would be difficult or impossible for them to pursue. Like my friend in the narrative above, they can meet payroll expenses when work is scarce. They can pay for repairs to their home or improvements to their workplace. The money they receive can be put toward the expenses of a daughter's wedding or college education, or the cost of a parent's funeral. *Moai* create an opportunity for pleasure and personal development. Members can take a vacation, buy a new television, or call a loved one working in the mainland home for a visit. And yet, the importance that Okinawans place on the feeling of friendship that the *moai* creates and reinforces cannot be ignored.[78]

But what of life itself? Does the *moai* offer protection against guilt that diminishes the self, the qualities of the *mabui*? Does it provide relief from the political costs that Lazzarato describes? Would Okinawan citizens and local authorities tolerate military occupation and the unevenness of daily life if they were not so heavily indebted? Do *moai* encourage compliance and accommodation, protecting the existing order as much as it does their perilous lives? Most Okinawans know that *moai* can be inadequate to the challenges that threaten the everyday. The *moai* itself can even become an oppressive mechanism in which exploitative relationships are reproduced and renewed. Every Okinawan knows stories about *moai* that have careened out of control, demanding increasing contributions from their members until many broke under the weight of impossible financial obligation. Some became speculative, vehicles for the valorization of capital rather than mutual support. Others collapsed as members proved themselves untrustworthy, slipping away with their winnings and breaking the cycle of reciprocity. In the early 1980s, a *moai* organized among shopkeepers in the very arcade where I stood collapsed, leaving ¥300 million in unsettled debt, shattered relationships, unfulfilled promises and economic ruination in its wake.[79] Surimu Kurabu takes up this fear and uncertainty in another of their bitterly painful sketches.

[*Two men walking bump into one another on a crowded street.*]

MAEDA Hey, it's you! Where've you been? You took off with all the money from the *moai*!

UCHIMA Ah, I'm so sorry! *Kisetsu de kaesu kara.* . . . I'll pay it back by seasonal [labor] up in the mainland.

After Yamashiro presented the winner with his envelope of cash at the *seinen-kai moai*, he sat down with us again. As the singing continued, he handed me his ledger. It was unremarkable in size and shape, not much different than a student's paperback notebook. A traditional Ryūkyūan fabric pattern was printed on the cover: small clusters of pine and bamboo, a spray of plum blossoms separated by the elongated swirls of stylized clouds. Conventional signs of celebration and plenty. Instead of the vibrant colors of most festive kimono, it was printed in the subdued browns and grays of the *bashōfu* (woven banana fiber) textiles of rural Ryūkyū, lending the image a surprising unity of high and low.[80] On the cover, there were spaces provided to record the date that the record was opened and closed, as well as the name and address of the *moai's* scribe.

In the center of the cover, printed in black script as if written by hand, was the phrase *Dushigwā Moaichō*. With the exception of *chō* (the character for "record"), the inscription is written in the phonetic script called *hiragana*, a form of graphic representation usually reserved for Japanese terms and valorized as the pure form of Japanese native expression that existed prior to the distorting appropriation of the ideographic system of Chinese representation. This is significant because the nominal modifier of the character *chō* is an Okinawan, not a Japanese utterance. *Dushigwā Moai*—the mutual aid organization of friends. In mainland academic and popular writing, Okinawan terms are often expressed in *katakana*, a parallel syllabary most commonly associated with the representation of non-Japanese terms. For Okinawans, raised under the Japanese state educational system and socialized into its representational practices, the experience of writing what they feel to be their own language in the script reserved for foreign words can be disorienting and unpleasant. How can we be Japanese and yet our own words cannot be expressed as Japanese speech?[81] Here, the use of *hiragana* appropriates the phrase as an utterance legible to native speakers across Japan yet with a meaning that perhaps only Okinawans can understand.[82] It is their narrative practice, not that of their colonial rulers, that is exclusive.

The use of the diminutive *gwā* is also compelling. It is often appended to an utterance to suggest that the referent is small or insignificant. And yet, in this case, the effect is to both minimize or seek to obscure its object while, in so doing, also emphasizing its importance. I think of the storyteller Teruya Rinsuke who once told me why Okinawan parents gave their daughters names like Kamado (rice pot), Kame (turtle), and Ushi (cow). The humble term hides something of great worth. The form must disguise its content, or the deities would want it for themselves. It is nothing, they say, but of course it is everything. In the same way, the inscription *dushigwā moaichō* make the text seem trivial and unimportant, hiding in plain sight a record of real value. Disguise and disclosure intertwined in a visible manifold.

The text opens with a formal document: *moai kiyaku*, the cooperative contract that binds members together—again, resonating with the ethos of *yuimāru*. It carefully enumerates the rules for participation: time and place of meeting, the amount to be paid by each member at each meeting, the

1.5.   The cover of a *moai* record book.

requirement for regular attendance, strictures against absences or early resignation.[83] It indicates who will be responsible for the conduct of the *moai*
and who will keep its records.[84] Most importantly, it sets forth the reason
for these friends to gather together. The first line of the contract explains
that the *moai* is established so that members can help one another. Because
of that, they agree to be bound by the regulations that follow. Members
ratify this collective compact with individual contracts bound in the back
of the booklet. Each member fills one out with their name, along with the
names of two other members who will join together to assume responsibility for one another. In practice, they will make sure that their partners come
to every session and bring their contribution. Generally, only one member
will win at each meeting, so it is essential for those members, and every
other member, to make all of their payments so that the *moai* can meet its

obligations to everyone. The primary member affixes their registered seal to the contract, obligating themselves to abide by the terms of the initial agreement and agreeing to accept sanctions should they violate its terms.[85] By signing their own contracts, the guarantors assume responsibility for obligations not met by the other members of their group.

Yamashiro paused and said that, in spite of everyone's efforts, people sometimes default. He couldn't remember the last time it happened in this *moai*, but he would occasionally hear about problems at work. Someone wins early in the *moai* and disappears with the money, leaving everyone in the lurch. He turned to the contracts in the back of the record book and pointed to his own. "See—if something happens to me, Mīchū and Kattchan [his cosignatories] will take care of my debt. The truth is, they'll try to make sure that it would never happen in the first place. If they're worried about me, they'll call me before the *moai*, help me figure out what to do and make sure I show up. And I'd do the same for them."[86]

Yamashiro flipped to the pages between the collective and individual contracts. Each member's name was carefully written in a space at the bottom of the page.[87] Above it, columns of small blocks recorded the date each contribution was made—¥10,000 toward the ¥240,000 collective loan and an additional ¥3,000 to pay for the food and drink that everyone shared. This is not an insignificant amount of money in a working-class neighborhood—at the time, according to prefectural statistics, the average annual income in Okinawa was only ¥2.2 million.[88]

Alongside the dates, here and there I could see a notation from Yamashiro to show that a member had received a loan for a particular session, transforming them from creditor to debtor for the duration of the cycle. Column after column, page after page, a graphic record of the meetings held, loans extended and repaid. Most *moai* are repeated again and again—many Okinawans say that their *moai* have been meeting for fifteen years or more. The repetition becomes blurred—without a record, most members aren't sure where they stand in terms of debt and credit, just whether or not they have won in the current arc of the *moai*. What's more, unlike cooperatives organized by contract or speculation, there are no indications of the valorization of capital in the loans made and received, no reflux to trace who benefits and who does not.

This detailed accounting was compelling, but the text represents more than what has gone before. The blank squares hold the promise of completion, a space to record exchanges not yet made. The contracts introduce the anticipation of the future, of a duration to be filled, a sequence to be completed.

What's more, they provide an ethical orientation that will shape a member's action. Obligations will be met, mutual care and kindness will be extended. Like a musical score, it creates a space for the possibility of what is to come based on what has (and has not) been.

In the streets beyond the *izakaya* where the *moai* met, in the neighborhoods beyond the arcade, the everyday pulses with rhythm. The repetitive cadences of capital and conflict, work and leisure, life and death. The political inscribed in the rhythms of daily life. The *moai* beats with its own rhythm against the teeth-gritting harmony of the everyday. It appears as a regular cadence, promised by the markers of time and place, the seals affixed to the contracts; measured in the gathering and departure of the same number of members at the same time each month; in the collection of the same amount of yen in monthly contributions, in the distribution of the same in loans extended and repaid. It is counted out in the movement of ten-thousand-yen notes, the largest denomination of paper currency in existence in Japan, a flashy marker of contemporary Japanese prosperity. Out and back they go, no interest clinging to them as they move, unchanged by any of the valorization that one expects from a loan. The cadence of the repetition captures, as Gilles Deleuze wrote, "a regular division of time, an isochronic recurrence of idealized elements."[89]

And yet, the punctual beat marked out by the recurrence of the *moai* is far from a perfect repetition. A tremendous amount of effort is necessary to recreate it, to ensure that the members are all present each month. They must not allow the working day to expand and encompass the time set aside for their gathering of friends. They must discipline themselves to use the form of credit as something other than an opportunity to valorize capital. They must struggle against the other demands of the everyday—to spend more time with their families, to play, to sleep. They must endure the alienation of labor and the anxiety of idleness, the pressure to follow the possibilities of the labor market to Japan, to Hawaii, to Latin America. The ten-thousand-yen notes collected each month might reflect the same amount of value in exchange, but they also index widely different sacrifices among workers who plan and save carefully to bring them each month. Once again, disclosure and disguise.

It is important to consider how this moment of repetition is experienced from within, and think about why so much effort is invested in recreating it each time the *moai* meets. Free of utopian excess, it is anchored in the pleasurable repetition of familiar activities. In the creation and recreation of a moment in the here and now. Month after month, each meeting with commensal feasting, members' formal speeches in praise of one another and their shared goals, quiet discussions between friends, laughter and music, negotiation of the loans to be extended and repaid. Since *moai* are often constituted out of already existing collectives, meetings are also powerful vehicles for remembrance. Members reminisce about the past, look back on the young men and women that they once were, reinscribing something of the social order of days gone by in the present. While a *moai* like the one I have just described might not create oppressive distinctions, they are certainly not purely egalitarian. Complex negotiations are in play, mobilizing remembered patterns shot through with past hegemonies against hierarchies recognized in the present. At the same time, these collectivities are committed, formally and in practice, to a shared ethic of mutual support. The effort expended to bind one another together in the spirit of *yuimāru* is inflected with the goals and objectives that they once shared as dancers, musicians, comedians, students, or revolutionary activists, and brought up against those they feel in the world beyond their gathering. Okinawans labor to clear the space for that moment in the present, to experience a now that is otherwise threatened by the times of nations, the onslaught of capital, the pressure of the everyday. As the *yuta* told my friend Hiroshi's sister-in-law, everything that matters is here right now. It is up to you to act.

In the course of a *moai*, very little time is actually spent organizing and distributing the loan. And yet, the affect that this exchange produces is profoundly important. In the dense network of payments made and received, members are both debtors and creditors, experiencing a manifold of obligation and benevolence. As they sit together, laughing, eating, and drinking, they are attentive to the hopes and dreams of their fellow members. They are reminded to be deferential to those in greater need, humble in their contributions to others, and grateful for the consideration they receive. They reflect the shared goals and experiences before the *moai* was founded, but they also repeat the kindness extended, time and time again, in the *moai*. A member of the Sonda *moai*, a young fisherman struggling to maintain the family business in the depths of Japan's lost decade, once explained to me what the *moai* taught him about being human: "In order to be a person, you have to be concerned about others. You have to learn about them and open up about yourself. You must give of yourself if you expect anything in return. If you don't do this, you treat other people like things, not people. Then, you're no longer a human being—you're just like the rest of the Japanese today." As they make whatever sacrifices they need to make and come together to recreate the *moai*, as they share this deceptively ordinary moment together, they experience once more the pain, the pride, and the pleasure in that act. As they look to each of the moments that extend into the past, they know what they can hope for in the future. To be known and valued, to be in the company of those upon whom they can rely. They seize the opportunity to remember who they have been, to experience who they are and what they can do, to make the most of this moment—of all moments. And yet, the ethical orientation of the *moai*, the care that they demonstrate for one another, is not enough to do more than repeat the moment. There must be more. As I think about my friends at the Sonda *moai*, enjoying the pleasure of each other's company, I know that their commitment to one another is profound. But is it enough for them to take to the streets together on a night like that of the Koza Uprising?[90]

After a final look at the recreated bar at the center of the museum, I turned and stepped out into the street. Behind the smudged plate-glass windows alongside the door, I looked at the rows of dusty soda bottles again. They were certainly a token of the effects of a consumer culture fostered by American occupation and inflamed by reincorporation into Japan. And yet, as I reflected on my tour of the museum, they were more than that. In the hands of the groups of young Okinawans who took to the street during the Koza Uprising, furious at the callous insensitivity and casual brutality of their occupiers, carried down the street to the Caltex service station and filled with gasoline, they became weapons of rebellion.

As I stood for a moment looking at the bottles and photos on display, an elderly man stepped up beside me. For a moment we stood there quietly, side by side. He reached out and tapped the glass, pointing at a black-and-white photograph that showed young men and women hurrying down the street toward the camera. Their faces wore expressions of happiness and expectation. There were no captions to indicate where they were going or where they had been.

"See that?" he said, tapping the glass again. He gestured with his head to the street behind us. "That's here."

Iphigenia in the China Sea   2

CONFRONTING THE MEMORY OF SACRIFICE

The determination of incompleteness is idealistic if completeness is not comprised within it. Past injustice has occurred and is completed. The slain are really slain.

Max Horkheimer, letter to Walter Benjamin, March 16, 1937,
in "Convolute N," *The Arcades Project* (2002)

The artistic work of memory is that which accords everyone the dignity of fiction.

Jacques Rancière, "Jacques Rancière and Interdisciplinarity" (2007)

Message from the Society for the Dissemination of Historical Fact, December 2015

The message arrived unbidden. Sent from Japan on December 10, 2015, it appeared in my mailbox a day earlier. It addressed me directly, my full name in boldface. And yet, the greeting seemed to be an afterthought, two commas following my surname as if whoever prepared the message was not entirely familiar with the mail merge function used to personalize a mass-mailing. This uncertainty carried over to the body of the letter, which opened with a declaration centered at the top of the text: "Alliance for the Truth About

Comfort Women Concludes that the Anti-Japanese Comfort Women Accusation is Totally Vacuous." The message was not simply addressed to me: it also took me as its object. I was a signatory of what the authors characterized as an accusation, a public letter signed by 187 scholars urging the then prime minister, Abe Shinzo, to acknowledge Japanese aggression during the Pacific War and seek reconciliation with those who suffered from those acts.[1] It also identified the addresser: a collective of revisionists organized around the Shijitsu o sekai ni hasshin suru kai, or Society for the Dissemination of Historical Fact (SDHF). Embedded in the body of the text, a series of links that led to additional polemics that took up, both broadly and in detail, the letter to Abe and its statements about the Japanese past.[2]

The revisionist project operates at the intersection of revelation and repression, of remembrance and forgetting. It is grounded in the avoidance of a difficult past: the shamed silence of survivors; the institutional suppression of historical criticism; the experience of daily life in a world bombarded with mass-mediated distractions. And yet, far from attempting to efface the past in social memory, it continues to recollect and transform it within the field of mass communication. Pierre Vidal-Naquet once wrote that televised European depictions of the Holocaust converted the genocidal event into spectacle, inscribing it in language and constructing it as an object of mass consumption.[3] In part, the SDHF attempts to do the same, working across social media to disseminate their work, collaborating with Japanese media institutions such as Dentsū and Fujisankei for translation and distribution.[4] In doing so, they appropriate academic methods and technologies, a tactical decision to conflate events with their representations. They attempt to confine historical critique to the text, refusing to extend their consideration to events in the world and their material traces. They are not concerned with the event itself, a moment guaranteed by ontological certainty even when it has not been representationally expressed. The practices of memory related to war and the Imperial past in Japan have important differences from those of the European and American memoration of the Holocaust. However, it is important to follow Vidal-Naquet in highlighting the interplay between the gaps and silences that one might expect in traumatic or proscribed remembrances with the excess of powerfully mediated mass representations and the scholarly voices chosen to narrate them. At this nexus, we can see the project of those who struggle to communicate what they believe to be tokens of the past, vital to the nation, to those who either disbelieve or dismiss their act and its object as unimportant.

Their tactics and the objects they denounce are predictable. They deny sexual slavery and the Nanjing Massacre, and they reject any criticism of Yasukuni Shrine.[5] They attack the credibility of their critics and the existence of their evidence. Their polemic valorizes mediated representations, or at least those that support their claims: a single American War Office document, the report of a Japanese commission to compensate former sex slaves, the memoir of a lone survivor.[6] It is an argument constructed in a world in which every text is equal, and no determinations of ostensive reference can be used to judge truth. Evaluation is aesthetic, selecting new pieces to complete an anticipated pattern. Scholars such as Jordan Sand have published thoughtful responses to the revisionist attacks, and I will not repeat them here.[7] Instead, I want to consider how narratives such as the letter mentioned above represent other experiences of space and time, expose obscured ontological certainties, and reclaim forgotten kinds of affect. An intimation of this effect appears early in the message: "We do, however, possess the right to preserve the honor of the Japanese people in the face of unfounded accusations and unreasonable demands. Beyond that right is a moral, sacred obligation to our ancestors and descendants to refute those accusations and oppose those demands."[8] Although the message is written in fluent, idiomatic English, this passage indexes a dialogic disjuncture, an affective gap between addresser and addressee. Rather than laying the groundwork for scholarly argumentation to follow, it embraces the language of ancestral obligation, patriotic duty, and national spirit. I recall reading these lines with surprise. How could the authors imagine that this ideological justification could convince the American scholars that they address?

Their project became clearer to me as I read the supporting documents linked in the message. There, they write that the American scholars who accused them have yet to respond to their challenges. At the same time, they claim to have learned that some of the signatories to the letter never gave permission for their names to be added. Others told them that they didn't believe the historical arguments, but they wanted to express disapproval of the policy of the Abe administration and show their solidarity with Japanese colleagues. No names are given, no references provided, all recorded as indirect speech.[9]

Michele de Certeau has written that "narrative infiltrates a non-narrative discourse."[10] Here, it is a different narrative that takes shape within the manifest form of the letter. I had been distracted by the seeming completeness of the message addressed to me, drawn in by familiar rhetorical devices. However, that which I took to be the whole was only a part constituting a more complex genre. Responding to the letter would be pointless when that moment had already been consigned to the past by its authors. The message belonged to a different act of storytelling, one where I functioned only as a character.

That letter and its links were material evidence of a riposte, a strike by the SDHF against those who challenged Japan's imperial past. It addresses fellow revisionists and, more importantly, a broader, imagined group of Japanese readers who might come to their site seeking the truth of the Japanese past. This narrative takes a familiar form, grounded in the appropriation of iconic narratives of loyalty against all odds. From wartime reimaginings of Ōishi Kuranosuke and the loyal retainers or the selfless sacrifice of Kusunoki Masashige, to contemporary accounts of beleaguered infantrymen fighting to the death or pilots giving their lives in defense of the emperor and the homeland, fascist cultural forms have been saturated with those accounts.[11] It is not a coincidence that the near-weekly messages that I continued to receive for many years often contained excerpts from Albert Axell and Kase Hideaki's *Kamikaze: Japan's Suicide Gods*—a polemic cowritten by Kase, a former chairman of the SDHF.[12]

In telling this story, the authors present a subject position for themselves as successors to these courageous predecessors. They write with humility: they are just ordinary men and women who have kept faith with their emperor, their nation, and their ancestral spirits. And yet, they are unafraid of imperious Americans or disloyal Japanese. They cannot be swayed by foreign ideologies, by deceptive academic rhetoric, by the shame imposed on them by wartime defeat and forced assimilation into the postwar world.

At the same time, the relationship between Japan and the United States is depicted as not entirely antagonistic, evoking memories of intimacy as well as anger at surprising betrayals by an ally. Does no one remember the Cold War, when Japan was recast and recast itself as a base of action for US imperial incursions in Korea, Indochina, and the Middle East? As a practical and ideological ally containing the Soviet Union and China? The authors demand equivalence in remembrance: hasn't the United States done everything that it accuses Japan of doing? They also remonstrate with the United States for unearthing these accusations again after earlier investigations found nothing. Their aggrieved conclusion is that the United States approves of Japanese conduct until it becomes expedient for them to do otherwise.

Here they demonstrate their commitment. The SDHF has not simply endured American criticism. It has been waiting, prepared to act decisively when the opportunity arises. The historians' letter in the *Asahi Shimbun* provided the moment. The strike that they launched, their refutation of the historians' assertions, speaks as if their actions are grounded in a deep reserve of memory, an archive of beliefs and experiences shared by their colleagues and by their fellow Japanese citizens. Their website both records and instantiates this operation, the traces of the story told. Not the English-language website to which the messages I receive link back: that is but another graphic trace of their riposte. This is the Japanese-language website of the Shijitsu o sekai ni hasshin suru kai.[13] Here, the story is constructed in the constellation of archived messages written in English that have been dispatched to their interlocutors, as well as the Japanese translations rendering them legible to their countrymen. Viewers can find a mission statement outlining the organizations' patriotic objectives. A collection of digitalized texts points the reader to memories of the past that must be defended. An interface allows viewers to sign up for the organization's newsletter, joining this community of remembrance and action. As viewers immerse themselves in the site, they can work their way through these documents, constructing the narrative for themselves. In doing so, they encounter the affect that organizes the SDHF's website as much as the presentation of a historical argument, feelings immanent in the poetics of the texts. Disdain for the historians who criticized that which they hold dear; respect and admiration for politicians such as Abe Shinzo; contempt for former Japanese colonial subjects of Imperial Japan (leavened by a feeling of fellowship for those who share their Imperial nostalgia); their own feelings of pride and resentment; and their overwhelming devotion to the emperor, their ancestors, and those who sacrificed themselves for the Imperial cause. In their caustic reminders that Americans have not only tolerated past Japanese behavior but committed many of the same actions themselves, they evoke a duration during which the United States and Japan shared comparable objectives, actions, and sentiments. Memories of the Japanese Empire are interlaced with those of the Cold War era during which Japan and the United States stood together as allies.

The SDHF website is continually operated upon as a site of memory, reworked with each message sent, each text posted.[14] In a subsequent message, Acting Chairman Moteki Hiromichi shapes a powerful dimension of this shared past: the ways in which the war dead who sacrificed themselves for the emperor and the state are remembered.[15] He embeds another selection from Axell and Kase's *Kamikaze*, a revisionist favorite. Adding another layer to this construction, their narrative is itself assembled from citations.

Writing of the deaths of more than 10,000 soldiers killed in the defense of Pelileu, they quote the American military commander Chester Nimitz:

> Out of admiration for the bravery of Japan's soldiers, Fleet Admiral Nimitz himself composed a poem which is today engraved on a stone monument on the island of Peleliu: "Tourists from every country who visit this island should be told how courageous and patriotic were the Japanese soldiers who all died defending this island." Pacific Fleet Command Chief (USA) C. W. Nimitz[16]

Axell and Kase then turn to the work of Columbia University literary scholar Donald Keene to illustrate the intentionality of sacrifice.

> Professor Donald Keene wrote in his book, *Meeting with Japan*: "As I read the diaries of men who were suffering such hardships, it was impossible not to be moved. By contrast, the letters of the American sailors I had to censor once a week revealed no ideals, and certainly no suffering, but only their reiterated desire to return to their former lives. Throughout the war this contrast haunted me—the consecration of the Japanese to their cause and the total indifference of most Americans to anything except returning home. I could not help but feel admiration for the ordinary Japanese soldiers, and in the end I came to believe that the Japanese really deserved to win the war."[17]

With Moteki's post, the site of memory is subtly shaped and transformed. To the graphic traces recording the heroism of the dead are added fragments of the duration of intimacy between Japan and the United States. The respectful words of a former enemy, the admiration of an American scholar. While committed to a certain kind of recollection, it is also a redoubt against remembrance, a site of forgetting. The constellation of materials linked through the SDHF website represent a challenge to history as it is conventionally understood. For the revisionists, no amount of empirical evidence can authorize a critical rethinking of a past that they know to be true. They do not simply argue for a different historical narrative; rather, they question the methodological and ontological foundations of history itself. Their understanding of the past is not, as Ricœur might have it, the dialectic engagement with a narrative of concordant discordance.[18] They are not interested in working from text to text, constructing an increasingly comprehensive and critical set of interpretations. Instead, their polemics expose the unreliability of the world of the everyday that ordinary people rely on as the ground for understanding the past they remember, the events they experience, and the actions they undertake. Once the certainty of that milieu is broken, the tools of historical argumentation are useless: textbooks, critical monographs, investigative journalism, and juridical records cannot help to make a meaningful judgment. And yet, unlike scholars of postmodern fragmentation who theorize this as a new conjuncture, revisionists move in the opposite direction. Readers must consciously clear away the daily life that has been presented to them and be attentive to a truth of being that lies beyond scholarly or judicial arguments. They must look for, listen for, the moments that irrupt into the everyday, intimations of that which lies beyond daily life.

This is the domain of nativism and the reactionary field of custom. Harry Harootunian has characterized it as the return to archaism, a strategy deployed throughout the history of modern Japan.[19] And yet, the qualities that the SDHF struggle to recover from oblivion are not those of a romanticized agrarian lifeworld, the ideological formation that native ethnologists have struggled to reanimate for decades.[20] They do not exist on the spatial or narrative margins of Japan, spectral traces hovering on the verge of disappearance.[21] What revisionists seek to expose are the enduring qualities of the Japanese people once objectified in the practices of loyal Imperial soldiers. They must be rediscovered, recollected from the interior places where they are overlain with a false and inauthentic sediment of the traces of other words and deeds. Those who open themselves to the revisionists' project will recognize that the narrative presented to them is not what is of primary importance. Rather, it is the hidden immanence that they can discover within themselves once they become attentive. In uncovering it, it can once again become a schema for orienting action.

And yet, there is something troubling to the SDHF's appropriation of the forms of scholarly practice. Perhaps it is no more than a discursive strategy, the appropriation of a narrative form associated with authority, judgment, and reliability. It is not difficult to imagine that it might also contain a parodic element. I have written elsewhere about Okinawan performers such as Teruya Rinsuke and Tamaki Mitsuru who appear as scholars, both evoking and destabilizing academic authority. That is certainly possible. Is there a more traumatic dimension to their selection of scholarly forms of narration and debate? Dominick LaCapra has argued that unreflexive engagement can lead scholars to a repetition of the problems that they initially sought to investigate.[22] Eelco Runia has expanded on this, suggesting that parallel processes may be as important to understanding historiography as they are to psychoanalysis. Pervasive identification and absence of reflection create a moment in which "historians may be the playing of their objects."[23] Might there be something like that at work here? The determination of the SDHF and their collaborators to speak authoritatively about the Japanese past, about the ontological qualities of the Japanese lifeworld, lead them to choose what they believe to be adequate forms of understanding and representation. However, these choices regularly return their discourses to the fields that they are attempting to appropriate and subvert. Arguments that are, in the terms of these genres, poorly conceived and constructed, are continually brought to the attention of the scholars best equipped to dispute them. The conflicts that erupt from these cycles of repetition both satisfy and frustrate the revisionists.

Readers of the revisionists' project will find that they are called upon to acknowledge many qualities of self and society that might otherwise pass unnoticed. They are always reminded of the importance of sacrifice—an act both archaic and contemporary. And, like Iphigenia in Euripides' *Iphigenia at Aulis*, they learn that the actions of both sacrificer and those to be sacrificed must be voluntary. When Agamemnon's daughter Iphigenia was told that she would be sacrificed to Artemis so that the becalmed Greek ships would be free to sail to Troy, she reacted with horror. Over the course of the performance, Agamemnon, Menelaus, Achilles, and even Iphigenia herself move between the commitment to duty and honor demanded by their roles, and their much more human expressions of sympathy, fear, and self-interest. In the end, Iphigenia chooses duty. She embraces her role as sacrifice, loyal to her deity and creating a historical image of bravery that will transcend the moment.

> All Greece turns her eyes to me, to me only, great Greece in her might. Through me alone is sailing for the fleet, through me the sack and overthrow of Troy. Because of me, never more will barbarians wrong and ravish Greek women, drag them from happiness and their homes in Hellas. The penalty will be paid fully for Paris' rape of Helen. And all these things, all of them, my death will achieve and accomplish. I, savior of Greece, will win honor and my name shall be blessed.[24]

Perhaps Artemis, in her mercy, spirits Iphigenia away to safety, replacing her sacrifice with that of a stag.[25] Perhaps Iphigenia dies under the priest's knife. The distinction is irrelevant: she has chosen to act. The Greeks, drawing on their history of sacrificial relations with their deities, hope that Artemis will recognize the magnitude of their offering and grant them the gift of winds to fill their sails. And yet, Iphigenia's act is not simply a moment in a history of prestations and counter-prestations. The immediate consequence of her action has been the restoration of a state of harmony between the Argives and their deities—the "making sacred" to which the practice refers. In the performance, viewers see a representation of the immanence of her will toward sacrifice, her resolution to embrace her own death with courage and dignity, with a sense of a world that it constitutes and a future that it creates. Unlike the Akedah, when Abraham remains committed to sacrificing his only son, it is the experience of the sacrifice that the viewer experiences.[26]

Why is this distinction critical? What is the relationship of these narratives of sacrifice to the world beyond the text?[27] How do they address ordinary people, those who serve rather than those who rule? Can contemporary readers come to grips with the weight of shared feelings and beliefs that these narratives of courageous sacrifice recall? Will they experience the revisionists' work as ideological attempts to reciprocally construct a field as their narrative emerges, investing it with the impression of a vast, chthonic world of memory? Or do they feel no more than a rustling as it passes, an intimation of a melancholy tale whispered to a legion of ghosts?

In Yogi Park, July 2011

I parked in the public lot at the prefectural library in Naha. I could see the police sentry on duty in front of the governor's official residence as I turned toward the library.[28] I was early, so I decided to walk through Yogi Park before going to the Naha Shimin Kaikan (Naha Civic Hall), the large municipal theater on the edge of the park. I was happy to be back in Okinawa after a month in the mainland. Tokyo seemed very distant, with its rainy, airless streets and its still, dimly lit public spaces. Guilty but relieved to be away from the melancholy discussions of the dead in Tōhoku, the anxiety that surged with every new tremor, every demonstration, every unexpected stop on the train, every rumor about contaminated food or radiation spikes. Away from whatever it was that lay burning beneath the Fukushima reactors, wrapped in uncertainty and silence.[29]

Of course, I was not truly away from it. The same sacrifices that had freshly marked the landscape surrounding Fukushima had been inscribed in every dimension of Okinawan social space for more than a century. Their traces are found in every barbed wire and chain-link fence that surrounded an American military base, in every run-down bar district clustered around their gates, in every group of young men or women boarding a flight or a ferry for seasonal labor in Osaka or Tokyo, in every elementary school textbook recounting wartime genocide, in the faces of every young clerk at every fast food restaurant, department store, and resort hotel. I still felt uneasy as I reached the edge of the park, the sunlight intense, the air thick and humid. I had both escaped and returned. Returned to a place where the mediations of time and space protected me physically but lay bare my own responsibility for the world that surrounded me.

The arc of the Gābugawa traced the northern boundary of Yogi Park. If you stood alongside it in early spring, looking at the cherry trees blossoming on either bank or watching the river quietly flowing in its concrete bed before disappearing under a nearby highway, you could be in a park anywhere in Japan. That impression would fade when you saw the row of palm trees that rose up behind the cherries along the southern bank. Those cherry trees, the national symbol par excellence, had lost their blossoms months earlier; now they were in full leaf.[30] The same was true of the *deigo* trees that burst into flame-like flower every spring on the anniversary of the battle of Okinawa. Along the sidewalks, clusters of flowers bloomed in carefully tended arrangements, a formal counterpart to the riotous vitality of the *gajumaru* trees densely planted across the park. Yogi Park was the first of fifteen sites set aside as parks in 1956. A decade after the destruction of Naha in the Battle of Okinawa, the site represented a space of possibility for citizens whose lives were still profoundly difficult. The city and prefectural libraries were built, as well as an outdoor amphitheater and a *hiroba*, an open space, that could accommodate large gatherings. In 1970, the Shimin Kaikan opened, a modern complex of public performance spaces and meeting rooms. The city of Naha enfolds the park, giving it its shape. It is a complexly heterogeneous space in which a contemporary Japanese provincial city and a complex of American military bases are integrated in an uneasy spatialized division of labor, in which fragments of the colonial city and the Ryūkyūan capital that came before continues to emerge into the present. Yogi Park appears to provide a respite from these contradictions, a pleasant open space where friends and family can gather, where leisure displaces labor and political anxiety.

I knew Yogi Park well. For many years, I passed through it while doing research at the prefectural library. Over the past two years, I'd been a more regular visitor. During the week, I would stop when distributing food with the Promise Keepers. Starting early in the morning, several of us took the church van, visiting the unhomed and unemployed men and women who spent their days in city parks. Along the way, Gibo, once the president of a small construction company, pointed out interesting sites to me: an apartment house that his crew had built; a lot where he had once had a temporary office; a warren of small bars where, he said with a laugh, his money, his business, and his old life had disappeared into the tills. We brought rice balls and bottled juice or water to distribute to anyone who might be hungry.

Our pace was slow. At every stop, we'd sit under the trees and talk, passing the time. As people gathered, someone might bring a sack of chilled cans of Orion beer from one of the local convenience stores. They were careful not to offer any to my companions, a silent acknowledgment of their struggles with sobriety. However, they always lifted them up in a toast, right hand around the can, left formally supporting it, slightly bowing in gratitude to their visitors. Gratitude for the gifts that they brought, but also for a quiet companionship that engaged them as fellow human beings. As neighbors who could, if only for a moment, here on a concrete bench or in a circle of cinder blocks, receive guests. Conversations were casual—many Promise Keepers had lived with them in these same parks. The topics we discussed were inconsequential: the weather, perhaps something that happened when last we met. I never heard any mention of religion, but we would always leave printed invitations and a map of directions to Sunday services and lunch at the House of the Rising Sun.

On Saturdays, Reverend Yamauchi and his parishioners would return to Yogi Park. They set up an outdoor kitchen under a couple of brightly colored tents. Several elderly members of the church played *sanshin* and sang, sometimes familiar *minyō* (folk songs), sometimes Christian versions of the same. Occasionally, Yamauchi took the opportunity to say a few words to the crowd, reminding them that everyone was always welcome at his church. He would repeat this in a warm, friendly voice, like a teacher patiently emphasizing an important point to his students. He had a simple message for them, he would say. One that came from Jesus—someone who was not just the God of Western people:

> If you have a sickness from which you cannot recover, Jesus will
> heal you.
> If you are lonely, Jesus will comfort you.
> If you are sad, Jesus will comfort you too.
> If you are homeless, Jesus will make a place for you (*ibasho*).[31]

After this, they served steaming bowls of curry rice to everyone: the homeless, the elderly, even children playing in the park. The same printed invitations were passed around. Then we cleaned up, folded the tents, and left.

Once a year, the Promise Keepers organized a revival in the park amphitheater. For two days, hundreds of people gathered to enjoy the performances of *minyō* artists, gospel singers, *eisā* dancers, and church choirs. There were games for children, food and drink. Yamauchi's group accepted donations, but everything was free. Local nonprofits passed out pamphlets or held information sessions. While the bands played, municipal counselors described the resources available for people in need. Older members of the Promise Keepers explained to unhomed people that there was space for them in one of their group homes.

It had only been a couple of weeks since the last time I was here, just before my trip to Tokyo. The sensation of travel still clung to me and I felt a strange, temporal dislocation as I stopped and stood in the plaza between the library and the river. The park was crowded as usual. Elderly men and women sat in groups, enjoying the late afternoon sun. Most of the women were wearing brightly colored, patterned blouses with dark or khaki pants; men in neatly pressed short sleeved shirts and trousers, a few wearing utility vests covered in pockets. Some of the women were wearing sunglasses and bonnets in protection against the waning rays of the sun; all of the men wore hats. Some groups had brought plastic tables and chairs, while others sat along low ornamental brick walls or on tarps spread out on the lawn. There was a low buzz of conversation, and I heard Okinawan folksongs from a portable radio on the other side of the plaza. Looking at them, I tried to see the young men and women who once gathered for *moashibi* (illicit parties) in rural villages or danced in occupation-era nightclubs.[32] In the here and now, the tempo of everything seemed so slow. It was as if the urgency and the passion of those early years—singing and dancing, drinking, making love—had been worn down to a languid companionability. The old *minyō* songs on the radio like a message from the past. Or perhaps that was all my own imagination, my romantic appropriation of the scene.

Packs of children ran past, heading to the field that lay beyond the trees. To my left, I saw the memorial to the great proletarian poet, Yamanokuchi Baku. Three middle-aged men sat together in the open space in front of the monument. They wore light windbreakers despite the heat, and one had a farmer's wide-brimmed straw hat. Several small packs and sleeping bags were stacked neatly beside them as they unfolded a blue vinyl tarp. I

2.1.   The Yamanokuchi Baku memorial.

didn't recognize them, but I could see that they were preparing to spend the night in the park.

The Baku memorial was one of several in Yogi Park, one of countless others on an island bristling with monuments.[33] The memorials that weigh so heavily on the island are like pieces arranged in an endless game of strategy. They bear traces of contemporary political conflicts; at the same time, they also index other actions that took place in the past. The objective in this game is the nation: its acknowledgment, its instantiation, its contestation, its transformation. Pierre Nora has written of this uneven production of space: "We might oppose, for example, dominant and dominated lieux de mémoire. The first, spectacular and triumphant, imposing and, generally, imposed—either by a national authority or by an established interest, but always from above—characteristically have the coldness and solemnity of official ceremonies. One attends rather than visits them. The second are places of refuge, sanctuaries of spontaneous devotion and silent pilgrimage, where one finds the living heart of memory."[34]

Although the pasts that led to their construction are different, these broad characterizations illuminate important distinctions. In the Okinawa Prefectural Peace Memorial Park south of Itoman, set in the ruins of the final wartime battlefield, mainland veterans' groups built memorials to the Imperial Japanese units that fought—and were destroyed—on Okinawa. Constructed by the heirs to a defeated army, in the space of their loss and surrender, they built monuments to loyalty and honor atop the bones of the dead. In the forms that they are given, in the graphic traces that they bear on their surfaces, there is no space for equivocation or remorse, let alone critical reflection on the cruelty and violence that their shapes obscure.[35]

At the same time, there are many other monuments that represent the oppression of the Okinawan people, a duration of exploitation that extends back into the prewar past and extends forward into the future. The Hime-yuri memorial, commemorating the lives of young nurses conscripted from patriotic Okinawan elite families and slaughtered in the waning days of the war. The stone monument that records their names stands over a yawning pit, a still-open wound, that leads to the subterranean hospital where many of them were killed or took their own lives.[36] Kinjō Minoru's statue outside the caverns at Chibichirigama in Yomitan is even more temporally complex. A dreamlike installation—a musician playing the *sanshin* sits atop rows of statues representing the Okinawan villagers who were murdered or forced to commit suicide in the caves below. The statue itself bears the marks of attacks by Japanese fascist gangs in the late 1980s, angered by the attention that it focused on the crimes that took place in Chibichirigama. Now it is surrounded by a protective barrier, but it also points to a second assemblage nearby. Here, Kinjō built a one-hundred-meter-long frieze in the ruins of an American airfield, synchronically representing a duration of violence: from the brutalization of Okinawan civilians and the murder of Korean conscripts in 1945, to the violent postwar appropriation of village land by American soldiers, to the continued exclusion of Okinawans from their land by US bases and Japanese law. Complex remembrances, made visible in images of stone.

There is a formal similarity to the majority of Okinawan memorials.[37] At their most simple, an inscribed stone marker is mounted on a base. Some are shaped to appear natural, as if a thick slice had been cut from a boulder.

Others are cut in sharply defined, rectilinear forms, their faces polished. Perhaps they remind viewers of the eroded outcroppings of limestone that ring the island, stone masses balanced atop narrow bases. Or perhaps they draw inspiration from the *sekihi* or stelae that stand on the grounds of Shuri Castle. Imposing and seemingly durable, these monuments bear information about the benevolence of a Ryūkyūan monarch who ruled hundreds of years ago, carrying it from the moment of inscription into the future.[38] They are also inspired by cosmopolitan memorative forms that have been mobilized across Japan since the beginning of the modern era. Some are more clearly iconic in form: a polished stone shaped like an artillery shell commemorating a unit of the Japanese Imperial Army at the Okinawa Peace Park. Others are organized around more abstract forms. Virtually every community has a stone monument inscribed with a commemorative phrase, flanked with rectangular tablets recording their own war dead. The Cornerstone of Peace (Heiwa no Ishiji) at the Okinawa Prefectural Peace Memorial Park is the most elaborate form of this model, surrounded by concentric rings of stone tablets inscribed with the names of everyone who died—soldier or civilian, ally or enemy—in the battle. There is a painful referentiality to these memorials, each a locus in a mise en abyme that calls the viewer back to the awful violence and suffering experienced by Okinawans during the war.

While Nora's distinctions are productive, the experience of memorials is much more convoluted. As he suggests, there are ceremonies organized around dominant sites, and dominated sites that are visited with devotion. And yet, the will to remember—a will that is always anchored in the moment, that always addresses the future—comes into play in complex and contradictory ways. Dominant sites are appropriated in ways that the authorities never envisioned. Memorials "have a capacity for metamorphosis, and endless recycling of their meaning, an unpredictable proliferation of their ramifications. Understanding returns to them, an arabesque in the deforming mirror that is its truth."[39]

I recall the bronze statue of the Meiji emperor in the courtyard at Naminoue Shrine in Naha. Dressed in Western military attire, the characters *kokka* (nation-state) in bold relief on its base, the statue materially instantiates the interlaced logics of modern imperial Japan. The commanding leader of a powerful modern state; the paternal head of the nation as family; the primary deity of a national spiritual order. When I first saw it, I assumed that it commemorated both the prewar enshrinement of the deity that the emperor became when he shed his material form, and the reconstruction of

Naminoue after its destruction in the war. Enshrinement of the Meiji emperor or another member of the royal family was a routine practice across the Japanese colonial empire, investing a fragment of an imperial deity—one that was at the same time equivalent to the whole—to incorporate a colonial space into the body of the nation. It seemed to recall Okinawa's initial integration into the prewar Japanese state, and its enduring place in the nation, despite an American occupation that held it apart for decades.[40]

However, this image of the Meiji emperor, mottled with verdigris, is not a relic of the Japanese colonial era that somehow survived Naha's wartime destruction. The Meiji emperor is not even enshrined at Naminoue. By the time the practice of installing imperial deities in Shinto shrines across the growing empire was established, Naminoue already bore traces of the manifold attempts to integrate Ryūkyūan and Japanese monarchies and polities, after both the Satsuma invasion and the Ryūkyū Shobun. This statue was not installed until 1970, commemorating the centenary of the emperor's birth and indexing the desire of Okinawans for reincorporation into the Japanese state. A symbol of Japanese colonial domination, of ethnic discrimination, and cultural subordination, could be reconfigured as a sign of the struggle against American imperialism and the insistence on political self-determination. Or all of those things at once.[41]

At the Okinawa Prefectural Peace Memorial Park, members of patriotic veterans' organizations mingle with groups of peace activists, and those who come to mourn lost family members or wonder about their own survival. All around them, busloads of mainland high school students visiting the battlefield during school trips to Okinawa. The lectures and films presented at the museum, the narration offered by guides or recorded in brochures, the conversations among visitors, the lives they led up until this moment—all shape their experiences. And so, a service staged by the national government so that Prime Minister Abe can join US Ambassador Kennedy in expressing their respect to the dead and their survivors, thanking them for their sacrifices on behalf of the nation goes terribly wrong. Okinawans shout insults at him—Warmonger! Go home!—and video of the event goes viral on YouTube.[42]

At the same time, dominated sites—like the statue at Chibichirigama—become places of repetition, where the violence of the original act is mimetically reproduced on the surface of the memorial. In the traces of the artist's hand in the shaping of the monument, and in the traces of the blows struck against it, we can see an intimation of the difficulty and shame in acknowledging the event, of the conflicted experiences that have moved and divided the surrounding community at every moment since the war.

And yet, these memorial spaces lie far from the everyday lives of most Okinawans. Mainland tourists regularly go to see the battlefield memorials; Okinawan war survivors and antiwar activists may visit on Irei no Hi, the annual commemoration of the end of the fighting on Okinawa on June 23, 1945. However, most Okinawans I know avoid the memorial park. Many are tired of the constant discussion of war; more than a few are concerned about the inconsolable ghosts who roam those fields. Most are simply too busy with the struggle of everyday life. Even community monuments become neglected and forgotten. They stand like eddies of remembrance, graphic traces at a distance from the rhythms of everyday life. A chance encounter could bring someone to them, an unexpected diversion from the route usually followed. They might be encountered in representation and remembrance: a newspaper article on the anniversary of invasion or surrender; a conversation on the death of an elderly neighbor; a television commercial advertising a war movie; a line or shape that catches the eye, the cool weight of stone and metal beneath the hand.

Although I could only see the largest part of Baku's monument from where I stood, I remembered it as an assemblage of objects, each drawing on the conventions of material commemoration. Behind it, a short rectangular post bore an inscription that indicated that this was the Baku memorial. Next to it, the sloping face of a concrete cube was inlaid with two photographs of Baku and short descriptions of his life in Japanese and English. The memorial was a dark slab of stone as tall as a person and perhaps twice as wide. Its surface was rough, discolored with blotches of lichen, etched with the poem "Zabuton," Baku's painful representation of rootlessness.

I remembered looking for it on a moonlit night in 1998, drunk and exuberant, after a concert dedicated to Baku's work. At Takara Ben's encouragement, I read a collection of Baku's poetry the year before, and I was moved by the economy of his artistry, wit, and melancholy. The concert gave new form to his work. Each of the well-known musicians appearing played one or two of their own songs, as well as something that they had crafted from Baku's poetry. More collaborations between the living and the dead. Picking out laconic blues lines on his guitar, Ishigaki Katsuji told stories about growing up in Koza, playing in bands, working in restaurants and bars. After a quiet, unaccompanied performance of the song that he and Takada Wataru had crafted from Baku's poem "Omocha" (Toys), he spoke to the audience again. He had inherited some land from his father, he said, and he supported his slowly failing businesses and musical career by selling it off, piece by piece. To cover the expenses of a life that never quite came together. With a wistful laugh, he wondered what he would do when the last bit of land was gone. Katsuji was followed by Kadekaru Rinji, son of the legendary Kadekaru Rinshō. He opened his set with virtuoso performances of two classic *minyō* before turning to his collaboration with Baku. "Kokubetsushiki" (A funeral, lit. the ritual of parting) was driven by a powerful, rhythmic *sanshin* figure, poignantly sung in the shadow of Rinji's father's terminal illness.[43]

Sadoyama Yutaka took the stage next. Perhaps the most famous Okinawan folk musician of the 1970s, he performed with the energy and humility that distinguishes his work. He chose "Kaiwa," Baku's famous poem that seems to recount an Okinawan man's painful discussion with his mainland Japanese lover, struggling to make her see that he can embody the difference and mystery that she fears and still be the man she loves.[44] Sadoyama was followed by Daiku Tetsuhiro. Daiku foregrounded the strange whorl of temporalities brought together in this performance: lyrics written by Baku in the 1930s and 1940s; music grounded in the very different experiences of protest movements that he and Takada Wataru had in the 1960s and 1970s; created, recorded, and performed at this moment of violence and possibility in the 1990s. Daiku reappropriated the song that inspired this collaboration: Takada Wataru's 1960s setting of Baku's poem "Seikatsu no Gara" (The pattern of life) to music. Joined on stage by an accordionist, he wove together the *jinta* stylings of prewar labor and protest music with the distinctive techniques of musicians from Yaeyama, the Okinawan islands clustered north of Taiwan. Takada Wataru himself closed the concert. One of the most famous folk musicians in Japan, his presence was quietly commanding. His more sardonic wit seemed to capture the spirit of Baku's work. Songs of death, memory, the possibility of something more. Everyday poverty, horror, and action.[45]

As I stood there in the plaza, I thought about the complex manifold of time that came together in the production of that concert, that sent me here twenty years ago to find Baku's memorial. I was transformed again as I watched the three men spreading out their tarp for the night.

> On top of the ground, there's a floor
> On top of the floor, there's tatami[46]
> On top of the tatami, there's a zabuton[47]

On top of that, you can say that there's comfort
On top of comfort, there probably isn't anything else
The sadness, when I'm told, "Please sit down"
As if I'm looking down on the world below,
The sadness of a world where I can never get used to living.[48]

The hard, monumental permanence of the stone pulls together uncomfortable contrasts. The uncertainty of a life like that lived by Baku, remembered in accounts of sleeping in other people's houses, in mainland parks like this. The alienation of an Okinawan living anywhere in modern Japan. The moment of its utterance, a flash of words spoken or sung, now carved into a duration of stone. In his critique of European commemorative practice, Eelco Runia notes that there was a shift in the 1970s from efforts to remember the Holocaust to the struggle not to forget.[49] Perhaps the latter impulse organizes this monument, reminding the Okinawans who live in the affluent neighborhoods that surround the park not to forget Okinawa's history of poverty and exploitation. Of course, the homeless men and women who spend their days in the park need no reminder. And yet, they might find other meanings in its inscription. Beyond its narrative of alienation and desire, it uses the space of commemoration to give form to the temporality of refusal. In doing so, it instantiates the consequences of Baku's rejection of the conventional life that was presented to him as a Japanese citizen: trading the security of wage labor for the chance to write a poem. For the poet who produced it and for those who read and appreciate it, it is a powerful, material record of the determination of Okinawans to create, as well as their demand to be seen as creative and critical artists.[50]

Turning from the Baku memorial, I thought of other spaces scattered through the park. On the opposite side, near the entrance to the auditorium, there was a metal plaque mounted on two steel posts. I discovered it several years earlier, killing time on a summer afternoon while waiting for a friend to finish work at the nursing college across the street. On its face, images and narrative passages combined to describe the Okinawa Kenritsu Nōji Shikenjo, an experimental farm that once occupied the same fields. Until World War II, state agronomists experimented here with sugarcane, rice, barley, tobacco, indigo, palm, and turmeric. They also worked to modify agricultural technology, mechanizing the small cane presses that dominated Okinawan sugar production. After the war, experiments focused on potatoes and ornamental flowers, as well as livestock such as pigs, cattle, and goats.

A trace that juxtaposed the now of a site of relaxation and leisure, of escape from work, with its place in an earlier partition of the division of labor and distribution of knowledge in the Japanese colonial empire and the American military occupation.

The representation of these two moments do not simply mark two points in the ongoing subsumption of Okinawan labor. Prewar experiments with sugarcane cultivation, wet rice, and tobacco point to the powerful transformation that Okinawa underwent after its incorporation into the Japanese state. It was integrated into a program of national and colonial economic development that touched every aspect of everyday life. Cane production yielded short-term benefits for Okinawan farmers until the end of World War I; in the recession that followed, it brought catastrophe. Having decisively shifted to sugar cultivation, Okinawan farmers were unable to produce the food needed to survive. During Sotetsu Jigoku, the hellish famine that followed, many Okinawans were reduced to boiling the poisonous fruit of the sago palm, leeching the toxins so that they could eat its flesh.[51] Cane production also marks a site of struggle against mainland agribusiness and the prefectural government's efforts to establish plantation economies in the islands. Wendy Matsumura argues that Okinawans resisted these efforts in unexpected ways. She writes of the coordinated effort of small landowners, cooperative cane refineries, local bureaucrats, and Marxist organizers to fight against the industrialization of Okinawan agriculture and the incursions of mainland capital. This turbulent transformation is also deeply enmeshed in the movement of Okinawans into wider labor markets: as agricultural laborers working for wages at home or supported by their families and communities in the absence of effective social welfare programs; as unemployed laborers seeking work in mainland Japanese industries; and as workers in new colonial enterprises in Taiwan, mainland China, and islands across the South Pacific.[52]

With Japanese defeat at the end of the Pacific War, the commercial network that connected Okinawa with the rest of the empire was shattered. Okinawan farmers, policy makers, and agricultural researchers were forced to reevaluate and recreate their practices. Under the influence of American authorities and planners, Okinawans turned to the cultivation of potatoes to satisfy their basic needs for subsistence, a renewed period of immiseration represented in popular music as the *nmu nu jidai* (the time of the potato).[53] At the same time, they experimented with producing pork and cattle that might be sold to their meat-hungry occupiers, as well as ornamental flowers that new and efficient forms of distribution might bring to mainland Japanese markets.

The replacement of the colonial experimental agricultural station and transition from a site of labor to a place of recreation parallels the hopes that many Okinawans have for new spatial transformations. While occasional base reorganization has freed some land, much remains under American military control. Those who own it are still denied its use. Parks and bases could be described as spatial inversions of one another: while both are supported by taxes paid by citizens, the park provides a site for ludic, imaginative practices, while the bases can only be the object of the same.

There are other memorials in the park: a steam locomotive offers a glimpse of the infrastructure that connects the rest of contemporary Japan, or reminds elderly Okinawans and antiquarians of the narrow-gage railroad that once ran here during the colonial era. It also provides a strange contrast to the monorail that crosses Route 330 just north of the park, material manifestation of Japanese policies that use massive infusions of state capital as a consolation for enduring the continued presence of military bases. Elsewhere in the park, two twisted columns of stone testify to Okinawa's status as a city that cares for the disabled—an important declaration considering the horrific wartime injuries that many still bear. The city and prefectural libraries are also exhaustive reserves of memory in graphic form. Their holdings are extensive: from local publications to the work of mainland and international presses; from the private papers of seminal Okinawan intellectuals and full series of important prewar journals, to contemporary works of science, technology, and Okinawan fiction. Open to all, these libraries exist in important and dynamic relationships with every other act of Okinawan remembrance.

As I continued on to the Shimin Kaikan, I passed another monument that echoed the form of the Okinawan war memorials. A large, polished black stone bearing the inscription Kōkyū Heiwa pinned an event of more evanescent duration to the present—that of eternal peace. Not the calm that followed wartime genocide as Marine Corps infantry crossed these same fields in pursuit of retreating imperial soldiers. Not the not-violence, the muted fragments of everyday life that appeared here as survivors sought escape from their ruined homes. Eternal peace here indexes the intersection of multiple temporalities: that of postwar Japan and that of Okinawa, once it escaped from American occupation. On its face, the inscription directly quotes Article IX of Japan's postwar constitution:

Aspiring sincerely to an international peace based on justice and order, the Japanese people forever renounce war as a sovereign right of the nation and the threat or use of force as means of settling international disputes.

In order to accomplish the aim of the preceding paragraph, land, sea, and air forces, as well as other war potential, will never be maintained. The right of belligerency of the state will not be recognized.[54]

Beneath that, a smaller plaque has been affixed to the base of the monument. A thin, uneven seam of cement shows around its edge, as if it is a later addition. Dated Showa 60 (1985), it cites Oyadomari Kōsei, then mayor of Naha, on the importance of Article IX. "We cannot forget that we have finally reached a turning point in our history, forty years after the end of the terrible Pacific War. The permanent peace that the Constitution has set forth as its objective is finally taking hold. So that we will never again be enraged at the calamity of war, we erect this monument as a symbol of the establishment of Naha as a City of Peace."

In order to see this as something more than a valorization of peace, it is crucial to understand the temporalities that it weaves together. There is the Japanese national time referenced in the larger memorial, a duration that begins with the establishment of the constitution in 1947 and continues on into the future, affording every Japanese citizen the protection of this binding renunciation of war.[55] There is the moment of Reversion in 1972, when Okinawans hoped that their return to Japanese sovereignty would enfold them in that same protection. Oyadomari's commentary qualifies that reincorporation. For Okinawa, the postwar period had been a struggle, and activists fought to make "renunciation of war" more than just a performative included in the constitution. Finally, after forty years, he believes that there is hope that the promised duration of perpetual pacifism can be fully realized. And beneath all of this is the temporality of war—darkening the past, its negative potential shading the present. Standing before the monument, reading both inscriptions, looking out at the fields beyond, I think about the presences that must come together for this constellation of temporalities to appear, at the possibility of standing at this point and seeing these things in the same frame. Nancy Munn writes of space and the phenomenology of remembrance: "In London, where landmark places have longer lives, one can, in effect, center within one's own bodily field of action and be centered by and within places that give concrete spatial presence to the past bodily orientation of known historical figures."[56]

Perhaps someone standing at this place could do the same. They might imagine Oyadomari Kōsei supervising the crew mounting his commentary on the base of the memorial, reading the inscription from Article IX, looking out at the open space of Yogi Park beyond. It is a compelling moment, extending Munn's provocative theorization of manifold space-times even further. Actions at that moment give material presence to complex representations of space. Meetings in municipal buildings across the city; library research; university conferences; site surveys; reviews of forms of memorial design; experimentation with writing styles for possible inscriptions; selection of materials; sketches and models at an architect's studio. And, at the moment that the plaque is mounted, it becomes part of the representational space of the city. A material object that cannot disclose itself, cannot tell its story of citizenship and social justice unless it is intelligible to the people who pass by it on their way to play with their friends in the *hiroba* beyond, to borrow books from the library, to meet fellow base landlords at a local *izakaya*, to attend a performance or a class at the Shimin Kaikan, to stand up against military occupation in the park. It must articulate in some way what they already know and expect, reinforcing their understandings, angering them, shocking them with the force of the unexpected. Or, perhaps it falls victim to disinterest or distraction. And, at that moment, it becomes part of their spatial practice: from men and women walking through the park or picnicking with their friends, to Oyadomari and the architects, politicians, and laborers who accompanied him.

And yet, Oyadomari's perspective might not be necessary to express the kind of identification that Munn describes. Perhaps what viewers imagine as they confront the field of action that passes from this point, through the moments represented in the memorial and into the fields beyond, is the position of ordinary people just like them who have passed through this space. And they feel some intimation of a reciprocal field of action that begins out there, out in the *hiroba*, running through the memorial until it reaches them, calling on them to respond. The field of activists and demonstrators who have gathered there, again and again over the years, whose actions form a powerful practical constellation with the peace memorial and its commentary.[57]

I first saw this monument on a winter evening in 1996, when I stopped to collect myself after a clash between anti-base demonstrators and a heavily armored detachment of riot police. I had initially joined the demonstration in Naha Chūō Kōen (Naha Central Park). Riot policemen in full gear were already deployed at the entrance. They were dressed in deep blue from head to foot, helmet with segmented neckpiece and clear visor, forearm and hand armor, thickly padded fatigues (probably covering some kind of body armor) and tall, gleaming black boots. They carried a meter-long shield, grey with a crimson and gold *shīsā* painted on it.[58] Their commander wore similar equipment, but carried a thick staff instead of a shield.

A dozen plainclothes policemen moved around the demonstrators. Several were dressed like businessmen: dark suits, white shirts, subdued ties. The rest wore jeans, warm-up jackets, ball caps and—in the twilight—sunglasses. They all carried cameras, many equipped with handheld radios and microphones. Several wrote in pocket notebooks, while the rest took photographs.

Inside the park, a small stage had been set up and a portable sound system was in place. A truck and sedan with top-mounted speakers were parked to the rear of the stage. The demonstrators were sitting cross-legged on the ground while various speakers addressed them from the stage. Several members in ball caps, jackets, and surgical masks circled the proceedings, taking their own photos and video of both the event and the police surrounding them.

The seated demonstrators differed from their leaders in much the same way as did the riot police. They were wearing hardhats with *tenugui* (small white towels) wrapped around their faces, white vests, and a few wore sunglasses. Their vests were overwritten with various antiwar, anti-base, anti-ANPO slogans, and their helmets bore the name of their organization in block *kanji* (Chinese characters).[59] One carried a thick staff, about a meter long. A dozen demonstrators stood around the seated members, holding large flags that snapped in the evening breeze. Like their helmets, these bore the names of their student organization: the University of the Ryūkyūs, Okinawa International University, and Okinawa University. There were also banners from mainland schools such as Waseda, Osaka, and Yokohama National University. A large banner proclaiming their support for *hansen jinushi*—the anti-base landowners compelled to lease their land to the Japanese government for military use.

One after another, speakers from local student and labor organizations as well as a student activist organizer from mainland Japan spoke to the audience. Their manner of address was all the same: short phrases, relying heavily on almost ritualized rhetoric, shouted into the microphone. Loudly amplified, the speeches were often almost unintelligible. Since there were only about one hundred and twenty demonstrators gathered, there was no practical reason to use the sound system. However, it must have irritated workers still in the surrounding offices (to say nothing of the neighbors), and it did seem to recreate the form of earlier activism.

The speakers attacked both Japanese and American imperialism and denounced the national leaderships of both countries. They criticized the American military presence and increasing Japanese militarism. They demanded that Japan follow the constitutional imperatives of peace and non-militarization. They warned about Japan's increasing expansion into East, Southeast, and South Asia. They declared that they would not tolerate Okinawa as a *kichi no shima*, island of military bases. They called for students and labor to stand together and fight to the end. In doing so, they recapitulated themes of many larger demonstrations of the past year, including the *kenmin taikai* (prefectural citizens assembly), with the addition of overt denunciations of the Japanese state.

When the speeches ended, the demonstrators organized themselves into three closely-packed columns. The leader with the staff stepped forward and used it to link the first people in each of the three files. These three grasped the staff in an underhand carry, as if they were cradling a baby. Those behind them wrapped their arms around the waist of the person directly in front of them. They immediately began chanting anti-ANPO slogans and snaking back and forth through the park. Once the banner carriers had assembled in front, they began marching. By this time, the police detail had grown. Now, there were two detachments of riot police, three armored buses with screened windows, and a Land Cruiser with a platform and speakers on the roof. There were also several police cars, marked and unmarked. The two groups—rioters and police—integrated into a single formation as they took to the street. A marked police car led the way, lights flashing, followed by one bus and the Land Cruiser with four riot police on the roof. To their rear marched more police, shields at the ready. Their commander rapped them on their helmets with his white baton as he called out orders. Behind them came the demonstrators' flag bearers. Then the column of protestors. Another group of riot police, waiting in a single file, deployed themselves on one side of the demonstrators' column, forming a fourth file separating the demonstrators from the oncoming lane of traffic. To their rear came the remainder of the riot police, two more armored buses, and an unmarked patrol car. On the sidewalk on the left side of the column, the plainclothes policemen jockeyed with the activist leaders to photograph and videotape the march. I moved along in this group.

Keeping to the left side of the street, the marchers turned away from the park, toward downtown Naha. They would briefly march at a comfortable walking pace, unkinking their arms from the demonstrator in front of them. Then, at a command from their leaders, they would relink and, moving at a sort of half-step, resume their chanting. When this happened, the police became particularly aggressive. As they were crossing a busy intersection, police struck them with shields all along the column, as if herding unruly animals. The police also struck any demonstrators who moved out of formation. Baton-wielding police clubbed the demo leaders videotaping the march whenever they felt that they were encroaching on the formation, and clearly tried to knock the cameras from their hands.

Marchers wound their way through residential streets before emerging in downtown Naha. Tourists and shoppers watched from the sidewalks. Children in apartments above rushed to windows or onto balconies to watch the parade below. As we passed through the bar district in Kumoji, startled salarymen speculated among themselves about what was happening. Hostesses stood in front of their clubs watching the marchers and occasionally clapping. Finally, the column halted in front of the Ministry of Defense offices, where activists delivered a virulent attack through the loudspeakers of their van. The column continued on, past the Chinese gardens in Kume, before stopping in a small park.

The police once again established a cordon around them. One of the leaders of the march delivered brief remarks about cooperation and perseverance. Then, they linked arms and sang "The Internationale," swaying side to side, their voices hushed. After this, the demonstrators collected their helmets and divided up into smaller groups, filing out into the evening darkness. The riot police and their plainclothes colleagues boarded their buses and were gone.

And yet, in the moment of their departure, something remained. In the remembered images of the demonstrators' confident movement through the streets of the city, their shared objectives expressed in speech, in song, in motion. As surely as *eisā* dancers lay claim to their neighborhood streets during Obon, dancing together with passion and conviction, these demonstrators—Okinawans and mainland Japanese, men and women—asserted their right to the city. Their claims were echoed, validated, given form in the presence of the police who marched alongside and against them. A moment when the politics of intention and opposition became visible.

Alone, in the darkness, I realized that I had left my car in a lot near Yogi Park. As I crossed the park, I decided to stop and sit on a bench for a while, drink a bottle of tea and make some notes. It was then that I discovered the monument to Article IX. A poignant reminder of the struggle of Okinawans to free themselves from a seemingly endless American military occupation, even at the cost of reverting to Japanese sovereignty. Rejoining the state that had brought the promise of cosmopolitanism and modernization as well as the reality of exploitation and death. A decade after the mayor of Naha added his postscript to the memorial, I wondered if Okinawa had truly reached a turning point.

At the Shimin Kaikan

I continued toward the Shimin Kaikan, Naha's civic hall. On the sidewalk ahead of me, an elderly man paused as if something blocked his path. He staggered forward before slowly crumpling to the ground. I pushed my messenger bag around to my back and ran to him. By the time I reached him, he was already struggling to his feet. I put my arm around his shoulders and encouraged him to lie back down. Several other people had gathered around, and I asked someone to go the park *kōban* (police box) and get help. Smiling with embarrassment, the old man told us not to bother—he was fine. He said that the heat had been a little too much for him and he was just going to go back to his house on the other side of the park. Waving off any offers to help, he straightened his neatly pressed shirt and bowed apologetically. I watched him as he slowly walked toward the Kanehide supermarket beyond the plaza. Although I felt that I should have done more, I turned and continued on my way.

More than forty years after its construction, the Naha Shimin Kaikan remained an impressive space. Designed by the groundbreaking Okinawan architect Kinjō Nobuyoshi, it represents a benchmark in the creation of Okinawan vernacular style. Kinjō fused traditional elements of Okinawan household architecture and social space with a clean, functional, modernist aesthetic. He did so metonymically, exuberantly enfolding the whole of the contemporary project in a single distinct feature of remembered design. The simple, concrete rectilinear volume that contains performance spaces and offices is completely wrapped in a red-tiled mansard roof. The effect of this is to visually recall Okinawan farmhouses with their heavy roofs and surrounding *amahaji* (verandas). At the same time, its tightly fitted, angled masonry surface, broken only by a wide, arched entrance approached by broad stairs, evokes the battlements of Ryūkyūan *gusuku* or *gushiku* (castles). The hall also incorporates other traditional spatial features, such as surrounding walls made of fitted stone, and *hinpun* (defensive barriers) that can be used as protection against thieves, restless spirits, and other dangerous intruders.

2.2.   A gathering in Yogi Park.

Like both traditional Ryūkyūan homes and castles, it is built so that the length of the space falls along an east-west axis, facing south. The impact of Kinjō's work on Okinawan regional design was profound.[60]

The Shimin Kaikan was part of a movement to redefine the form of public space in Reversion-era Okinawa. Against the ideological and functional spaces of the Japanese colonial era or the postwar American occupation, spaces such as this join historical forms of domestic and sovereign spaces in ways that are experimental, playful, and deeply political. For example, its performance spaces are located in its eastern side. According to the dispositions of a traditional home, this would be the site of the intersection of the domestic space of the household with public space. It is here that the deities and ancestral spirits would be venerated, it is here that guests would be welcomed. In a *gusuku*, the spaces surrounded by the castle walls are where governance and spiritual practices come together, an interrelationship debated by historians and archaeologists of Ryūkyū, and reflected in mainland nativist insistence on the identity between politics and religion.[61]

The Shimin Kaikan is a powerful token of spatial and temporal transformation, of the subjective passage from American occupation to

2.3.   The Naha Shimin Kaikan.

reincorporation into the Japanese nation. It is defined by creative appropriation, not passive acceptance. It is also a space of action. From the remains of
an experimental agricultural station, it reclaims moments of earlier spatialized modes of production. Sites of labor and exploitation are refigured as
spaces of play, of study, of dissent, of change. It was here on May 15, 1972, that
Yara Chōbyō, the about-to-be governor of Okinawa, waited to receive official
notification of the reversion to Japanese sovereignty. Nearly a thousand miles
away in Tokyo, US Vice President Spiro Agnew, Prime Minister Sato, and
the Showa emperor met to formalize the decision. As tens of thousands of
Okinawans stood together in the rain in the Yogi Park *hiroba*, bureaucratic
rituals transformed them from their ambiguous state as Ryūkyūans in an
American-occupied territory to Japanese citizens.

Yogi Park carries other, more ambiguous, traces of years of political action. The *hiroba* had been the site of mass protests by students, union members, and ordinary citizens against the ANPO accords, American military
and Japanese self-defense force occupation, nuclear and chemical weaponry,
and the exploitation of Okinawan social space. Thousands of Zengunrō—the
union of base workers—met there to strike against their American rulers
and employers. Only the day before Yara's ceremony, a coalition of activist
groups gathered there after voting to reject reunification because their
demands for demilitarization had been ignored. Other groups accepted

Reversion, but the ambivalence and contingency of the moment set the tone for the future. Even Yara's speech recognized this: the qualified success of a movement that formally ended American military occupation but left the American military presence largely unchanged. As activists acknowledged the moment of Reversion, they planned to continue the struggle against American military imperialism, mainland marginalization, and exploitation that continues into the present. A duration broken and reconfigured. While new spaces for public assembly such as the Ginowan Marine Park have been built, Yogi Park remains an important site, representational traces scattered across media and memory, continually engaged in practice. A strange convergence then, of the site of *bokoku fukki*, the space where Okinawa returned to the motherland, and the performance of *Kikoku*, a play written and staged by Kuramoto Sō in which it is the spirits of the war dead who come home again.

I followed the arriving crowd up the concrete ramps and stairs until we reached the entrance hall that cut across the center of the building. It was open at the roof, crossed with evenly spaced girders. The waning sun cast bands of shadow across the floor.

Weeks ago, I had bought tickets for *Kikoku*. Performed in this place, the title seemed provocative—the return to the motherland—and I thought that any performance about the consequences of the Pacific War would resonate with my work. I knew Kuramoto from nostalgic television dramas like *Kita no kuni kara* (From a northern country), and I had heard that there had been a television production of *Kikoku* starring Beat Takeshi (Kitano Takeshi). Beyond that, I had no idea about what to expect.[62]

I checked the seating chart in the lobby before finding my seat in the second row, near the center. The theater was nearly full. Around me sat well-dressed older couples, with a few groups of young women and parents with little children. I took a moment to review the brochure that I received when I presented my ticket before the lights dimmed.

The curtain rose and the play began. A battalion of Imperial Japanese soldiers killed in combat is given leave to return home for the first time since their deaths. They arrive during Obon, the festival of the dead. They are carried by a ghostly train that comes to a halt at an empty platform in Tokyo Station. As the bugler sounds assembly, the soldiers quickly file out of the cars and form up on the platform. Very little special effects are used to create a spectral appearance—a smooth layer of makeup that evokes the conventional ghosts of family television programs. The actors are also dressed in the most ordinary manner. Their green blouses and trousers

2.4. Poster for the play *Kikoku*.

are faded and worn, puttees wound haphazardly around their legs. Wounds are visible through holes in their clothing, and some lean on their comrades for support. Their equipment is irregular, but their field caps are set squarely on their heads and they carry their rifles with a weary formality.

The inspiration for these ghostly representations seems to be popular theater or television dramas rather than the grotesqueries of the experimental stage or contemporary horror films. They do not look like the remains of Japanese soldiers that I have seen in the present, their bones polished and transformed by burial or exposure, their uniforms reduced to scraps and fragments. There are no traces of decades of immersion in the sea. They have not been captured in the moment of their death: their wounds have been staunched, their dismembered bodies reconstructed. Like the manifold temporalities represented in the park outside, they are vigorous soldiers, dead heroes, and handsome young actors, all at once. The viewer must collaborate in the performance, acknowledging one representation or another, thinking through the contradictions of the uneasy whole. I thought again of Kinjō Nobuyoshi's design of the performance space, of the audience gathered to listen to this tale of revenants unfold, much as I have sat in countless living rooms with my friends as we spoke of ghosts and the dead.

A staff officer named Tachibana Saburō, wearing a worn fatigue uniform, without weapons or equipment, meets them on the platform. A junior officer quickly takes roll and presents the formation to their commanding officer.

"At ease!"

Major Akiyoshi Daisaku stands before them, dressed in the same weathered fatigues but wearing high leather boots, his left hand lightly gripping the scabbard of the sword slung at his hip. "Listen up. It is now August 15 of the eighty-fifth year of the Showa era.[63] The time is now 00:15. Our current location is Tokyo Station. Sixty-five years ago today. Our motherland Japan . . ."

With a commanding voice, the lieutenant who organized the formation now calls the soldiers to attention, and Akiyoshi continues:

". . . having received with great awe the divine edict of our emperor, swallowed ten thousand tears, unable to avoid unconditional surrender."

The lieutenant shouts again:

"At ease!" Then

Akiyoshi resumes:

> Sixty-five years have flowed by. These sixty-five years. We imperial soldiers who bear the blame for defeat have been spirits floating in the southern seas, unable to look upon the faces of our family, friends, and relations. And yet. We have heard our mother country has been so completely reconstructed that it has become the pride of the world, the peaceful country that we all worked to make. The purpose of our return is to look upon this peace and to report back to the multitudes of drowned souls still floating in the ocean so that they may rest in peace.
>
> As of now, you may act on your own initiative. However, you must conduct yourselves so that you take seriously your responsibilities as a soldier. You must not inconvenience any citizens, and you must not allow yourselves to be seen.
>
> We will reassemble here at 04:05. Uphold our military standards! In the brief period of time available to you, explore freely.

The presence of these revenants at Tokyo Station indexes a complex and contradictory nexus of temporalities. They are aware of the defeat that followed their deaths; they know of recovery and reconstruction. And yet, while they manifest themselves in the now of contemporary Japan, they are still bound to the duration of an earlier era and loyal to a long dead emperor. A familiar feeling for the Okinawans sitting around me. They were torn from the duration of Showa while the emperor still lived, forced to live in the space and time imposed on them by the authorities of the US military occupation until reversion in 1972.

The spirits of the dead set off to learn about this Japan that has risen from the ruins of war. As the dead are wont to do, they visit the places they knew in life, and seek out their surviving friends, family, and lovers. As they explore the city, the soldiers observe the practices of the living. When they encounter stylish and attractive young women, they are shocked and excited by their scanty clothing and puzzled by their preoccupation with mobile phones and social media. In discos, they are caught up in the unfamiliar music and dancing. Several meet before the main gate at the Yasukuni Shrine. There, they find the specter of Shimura Kazuhiko, a soldier haunting the space around the shrine, the rope that he used to hang himself still dangling from his scarred neck. Like the lone member of a mad chorus, Shimura speaks only in excerpts from letters that he and his comrades wrote before their deaths. Here, they discover that they are barred from the shrine and the government no longer offers them the prayers that they were promised in exchange for the sacrifice of their lives.

It is a grim evocation of imperial ideology and the promise of Yasukuni that unfolds on stage. For many Okinawans, these subjects remain painful and divisive. In the spring of 1945, nearly 150,000 Okinawan civilians and conscripts were killed in the final land battle of the Pacific War, survivors' lives shattered, the landscape a blasted ruin. Then, the state and the emperor abandoned them to the American occupation. Many Okinawan families found that the catastrophe continued. Work was scarce; homes, businesses, and fields were destroyed; the wounded continued to die and diseases such as malaria spread; community support was exhausted. When the Japanese government, with the consent of the United States Civil Administration of the Ryūkyūs, offered Okinawans the opportunity to receive pensions as bereaved survivors of war dead, many chose this over an uncertain future. Survivors had to submit themselves to bureaucratic reassessment. More than 50,000 cases were recategorized at the survivors' request. Families killed in American artillery barrages were determined to have given their lives supporting Japanese military action. Those conscripted and forced to act as messengers or nurses became heroic volunteers. Those killed by Japanese soldiers charged with their protection were said to have died fighting at their side.

While I know many Okinawans who remain enraged by their families' treatment by Japanese soldiers and bureaucrats, they've also told me that these pensions saved them from starvation, or made the difference between mere survival and rebuilding their lives. I have heard friends speak with passion and conviction about Japanese colonialism and genocide, only to tell me that they are active in veterans' groups and regularly attend ceremonies at Okinawaken Gokoku Jinja, a shrine in Naha.[64] Some even travel to Tokyo for commemorative events at Yasukuni Shrine and Budōkan.

In 2008, this issue erupted in acrimonious debate. Five Okinawan plaintiffs filed a lawsuit charging that the Law for Protection of War Victims and Bereaved Families allowed Yasukuni Shrine to falsely confine the spirits of their relatives in Yasukuni and perpetuated lies about the Battle of Okinawa. Although the lawsuit had been dismissed in a Naha court the previous summer, it often came up in interviews and in discussions with friends. Feelings remained raw. And yet, as I glanced at the faces of those sitting around me, I could see no intimation of this—only rapt attention.

As the performance progressed, I began to think about these representations of the dead. Like the dead themselves, characters were able to travel more quickly than their corporeal counterparts: in the four hours or so allotted to them in Tokyo, they swiftly traversed the city, moving from Tokyo Station to Ueno, Shibuya, Asakusa, and Kudanshita (where Yasukuni is located) and back again. Temporally overdetermined, they could represent their younger, living selves or the spirits of the dead as they are today, shifting from one to the other with a gesture while never entirely leaving the other behind. This allowed the director to use the figure of the revenant to blur the distinction between intentional action, memory, and the past to which it refers, suggesting that past, present, and future are open to one another in complex and transformational ways.

Kuramoto's script and direction also emphasizes the modernity and creativity of his protagonists. The vignettes in which memories of the prewar past are recreated, the encounters with former comrades and lovers in the present, all demonstrate their artistry. The soldiers portrayed have been musicians and composers, painters, writers, stage actors, baseball players. They work in genres of Western classical music, representational art, contemporary theater. The hard-working farmer, backbone of much nativist discourse, is absent. Their creativity is not simply measured in the objects they produced: the paintings, the musical compositions, the indelible memories of expert performance. It extends to the social worlds that they constructed through their collaborative actions. It leaves its traces inscribed in memory, in the abiding loyalty of a friend, in the enduring love of a survivor.

When they volunteer or are conscripted, this creativity is transferred to work on the nation and the emperor. Their actions now call the national community into being. This too, is a relationship of care and concern, to an object that encompasses and exceeds the interpersonal relationships that had once been their focus. And yet, there are significant changes. The atelier gives way to the parade ground, the concert hall to the battlefield. Their hours and days are no longer filled with artistic expression or play. They march, they shoot, they learn unquestioning obedience to orders. They train to kill. With that, brutality creeps into their actions. And yet, these new practices are also said to be done under the sign of love, devotion, and care.

The soldiers' actions are oriented by a sense of obligation that remains very familiar to the Okinawans seated around me in the theater. They also understand indebtedness to ancestors who worked tirelessly to build the world that they, the living, have received. They feel the spirits of the dead around them, sharing their world, watching and evaluating their actions. They know that the dead depend upon them for offerings of prayers, incense, and food. They also know that these ancestral spirits will watch over them and do what they can to add to their good fortune. Like the members of the *moai* discussed in chapter 1, they know what it is like to bear an obligation handed down from the past that must be discharged in the production of the future, on behalf of a collective composed by the dead, the living, and the not-yet-born.

At the same time, I wonder what they make of the sacrificial dimension of this obligation? If the actions necessary to care for the self, for the household, and for the nation coincide, one can take pleasure meeting those commitments. What happens when they do not? What happens when the decision to fulfill one obligation means that all others will be neglected?[65] This question of sacrifice shades the remembrances enacted on the stage. And this conflict between serving one obligation or the other resolves itself in the rhythms of daily life. Although confronted by the immanent possibility of their own deaths, the soldiers behave as if it were simply a question of a duration shaped by their actions. As one lieutenant tells his fiancée, he will return to her after the war and they will build their own life together. After his actions served the state, he could return to those closest to him. I am reminded of Terence Turner's exploration of long durations of sacrifice, of exploitation, in noncapitalist social formations. Young men are willing to allow their labor power to be appropriated by their wives' fathers because they know that one day they will assume the leadership of the multigenerational household and make similar use of the labor of their daughters' husbands.[66]

And yet, as the performance directs us to the soldiers' remembrances, we learn that these durations of sacrifice for the nation never ended. They never returned to their homes, their families, their vocations—their sacrifice continues. While the memory of wartime sacrifice often emphasizes the willingness to die—heavy as a mountain, light as a feather—this suggests that it is more complex than that momentary resolution.[67] As Emiko Ohnuki-Tierney made clear, the objective of the kamikaze was not simply to die; it was to continue the attack.[68] The lesson to be learned from the men of *Kikoku* is not their twilight existence, trapped by the consequences of their actions and the inattentiveness of the nation—and the emperor—who promised them solace. Rather, it is to the idea that the burden of obligation must still be borne, that sacrifice must be resolute and continuous. In part, this is due to the incalculability inherent in understanding the magnitude of sacrifice. In balance, we have the emperor—the absolute measure of value, the "dignity," in Michael Lambek's citation of Kant, that is beyond all notion of equivalence.[69] This is the standard against which the remembrance of Japanese actions must be understood: the impossibility of establishing any adequate equivalence drives its continuous performance.

And so, the understanding of their sacrifice turns on its temporality. Given all the other ways in which they could creatively and usefully be expending their energy over time, they have chosen to act in service of the nation and the emperor. However, this is not measured in the duration of their lives nor in the tragedy of their deaths. It is weighed in the value not created, the millions of other acts unperformed. It is counted in paintings unpainted; concertos not composed and not performed; plays never staged; games never played; lovers unloved, families abandoned, generations never brought into being. The things that go undone become the negative magnitude of the value of their acts, the endless duration that frames the enormity of their sacrifice. In a sense, it is the negative figure of the extraction of absolute value. The time of sacrifice has expanded to the entirety of the day, that day and every other, forever. The nightmarish conjoining of quantia and qualia—absolute commitment, endless performance, by every subject. That is the standard to which remembrance gestures.[70]

This also points to subtle distinctions among the spirits of the dead, a hierarchy laid out under Kuramoto's direction. The ghostly soldiers that arrive at Tokyo Station are all initially referred to as *eirei*, heroic spirits of the war dead. This emphasizes their positive status as subjects, brave entities who exist and act. It distinguishes them from once-living humans whose state has been transformed by the actions of others: *reikon* (spirits of the dead), *shibōsha* (those who have been killed), *senshisha* or *senshi no mono* (those killed in combat).[71] It also stands in contrast to *gunshin* (war gods), a category that Emiko Ohnuki-Tierney has shown was often used throughout the modern era. It seems to me that the distinction here is that *gunshin* locates the entity more directly in a field of relationships composed by both the living and the dead, an entity that must be situated with other marked and unmarked categories of *kami* (which could include ancestral spirit, household and local deities) and which the living must treat with loyalty, respect, and obedience. While a high level of status is accorded to *gunshin*, there is little to suggest distinctions within the category. Every dead soldier is *gunshin*.

However, it becomes clear that not all the dead soldiers who appear are *eirei* (heroic spirits). In conversation, Tachibana, the staff officer who greeted them, casually reveals that he is *bōrei* (simply, spirit of the deceased), an unmarked category at best. The same holds true for wraithlike Shimura, who haunts the boundary of Yasukuni Shrine. In both cases, it is the nature of their subjective transformation from life to death that accounts for their categorization. Shimura was a replacement draft, previously discharged from military service and deemed unfit for duty, but recalled for the final defense of Okinawa. However, training proved to be too severe. Bullied by his fellow soldiers, he died by suicide before the battalion shipped out. In the case of Tachibana, he confesses that he lost his nerve as his unit was about to launch an attack in Okinawa. Lifting up his blouse to reveal a gaping wound in his abdomen, he explains that he was shot as he attempted to flee.

In contrast, all of the other soldiers—all of the *eirei*—died as *gyokusai* (shattered jewels). This is not to say that they died in combat. In fact, most of them were killed in transit from Kagoshima to Okinawa when American aircraft sank their troopships. As a consequence, young recruits who never heard a shot fired in anger are *eirei*, while Tachibana, a veteran of combat in Rangoon and New Guinea who died on the battlefield, is a mere *bōrei*. While the fact of their death is important—this is, after all, a performance about the spirits of the war dead—it is their resolution to continue their sacrificial acts, even across the horizon of death, that distinguishes one from the other. The *eirei* continue to prosecute their attack to its limit, allowing nothing to interrupt the action before it reaches its objective. That the battalion was destroyed by aerial bombardment before it reached the battlefield in no way diminishes their accomplishment. They never hesitated of their own volition; their resolve never weakened. On the other hand, the valor of experienced soldiers is negated by a single moment's hesitation.

It also becomes clear that, in the lifeworld conjured by the performance, the dead cannot enter Yasukuni Shrine. Okinawan activists often speak of the indignity of Yasukuni enshrinement, that the imperial state could continue to lay claim to the souls of its citizens. This appropriation of the dead has also been highlighted in critical scholarship and media. Of course, the entire diegesis for *Kikoku* would have to be reimagined if the war dead had been properly enshrined—why would they need to return to the mother country if they were already safely held in its embrace?

Perhaps their exclusion is related to distinctions among them. There is a kind of perverse patriotic logic to the lonely exile that the mad Shimura experiences, consigned to the grounds outside the shrine. As he took his own life just before entering the combat zone, it seems that he must spend eternity on the spatiotemporal margins. He lingers on the edge of Yasukuni's grounds, reading the final letters that he and his fellow soldiers wrote as if they were incantations. Again, this is telling—even the dead substitute the representation of death for its experience. This is also true of their guide Tachibana. His final, perhaps involuntary hesitation at the moment of decision leads him to an eternity of bureaucratic accountability. Like a staff officer tasked with writing an interminable after-action report, he constantly questions the returned spirits about their impressions of contemporary Japan. And so, there is a logic to the exclusion of *bōrei*. And yet, this is a distinction that would not be immediately intelligible to the living. Without any way to know of the loss of resolve at the moment of death, how could the living know that the war dead are not *eirei*? Unaware of their melancholy exclusion, they would go about the routine tasks of memoration, making offerings at the household altar and the tomb, perhaps visiting local shrines or traveling to Yasukuni for solemn commemorative ceremonies.

However, even *eirei* themselves are barred from the grounds of the shrine. When several try to visit, they can only bow down before the Imperial seals set in the massive gates. If these *eirei* have been called back from the depths of the southern seas on a mission to evaluate the conditions of contemporary Japan, perhaps this is the intelligence gathered by their recon-naissance: even the dead who never faltered in their voluntary self-sacrifice are excluded. Yasukuni, a mechanism designed to propitiate the spirits of the dead, is not working. It becomes a material sign of the ways in which the contemporary state and citizens have abandoned their responsibilities. Soldiers were promised that their sacrifices would be recognized. Should they give their lives for their company and their emperor, their reward would be more than mere remembrance. The emperor would lead the services to enshrine them at Yasukuni, and the spirits of dead would remain there for eternity. However, Akiko Takenaka has written that, during the war, shrine authorities were only able to complete the formal enshrinement of 251,135 *eirei*; the final ceremony conducted by the emperor was conducted in March/ April 1945. The deaths of Akiyoshi and his men had yet to be reported, and they were not included. Along with the remainder of the more than two million Japanese combatants who were killed, they have been stranded somewhere in the continuum of between life and death.[72]

The endless duration of sacrifice is at the heart of *Kikoku*, and the story of Sgt. Ōmiya and his nephew illustrates the critique of voluntary sacrifice made by Kuramoto as author and director.[73] Ōmiya had been inordinately proud of his younger sister, an aspiring dancer. They moved to Tokyo from their farm in Iwate, and they remained together while he eked out a living on the mean streets of Asakusa. When he was conscripted, she was still a popular dancer at one of the most famous dance halls there. On his return, Ōmiya was delighted to learn that she still lived, but shocked at the course her life had taken. In the aftermath of war, responsible for a son born of her relationship with yet another soldier killed in combat, she became a mistress to an occupying American soldier. When that relationship ended, she became a stripper. Despite this, she raised her son and sent him to the University of Tokyo. Her selfless labor was rewarded: her son was now a successful university professor and prominent economic analyst. However, he had also become emblematic of modern spiritual collapse. Obsessed with material accomplishment and social mobility, he paid little attention to his mother. Her death in hospital was another inconvenient chore to be delegated to his subordinates.

Enraged at this ingratitude, Ōmiya takes physical form and stabs his nephew to death. This act is doubly transgressive: a breach of military dis-cipline in violating his commanding officer's orders, and disregard for the familial obligation he bears to his sister's son. And yet, what seem to be viola-tions of the powerful logics of descent and alliance do not directly index the magnitude of Ōmiya's crimes. Rather, they provide a point of comparison as the viewers try to understand what is at stake here. In the moment, his murderous act is not only justified but is the correct choice. Later on, the ghost of Ōmiya's murdered nephew affirms the justice of his uncle's actions as their ghosts meet before the gates of Yasukuni Shrine. There, he tearfully apologizes to his uncle and begs forgiveness. If any questions remain, they are dispelled in another conversation between the commander Akiyoshi and the guide Tachibana, in which they consider the current state of affairs in Japan, wondering sadly at the moral degeneration of the populace despite their material wealth.

As the performance moves to its conclusion, it becomes clear that it is less about the valorous acts of sacrifice that were offered in the past than the way that they must be redeemed in the present. This is the field of shared memory that the revisionists struggle to recover or, more importantly, to create. Akiyoshi and Ōmiya, both manifestly figures of authority, intervene to offer the viewers a critical guide to how they must understand and respond.

As Ōmiya stands above the body of his nephew, he delivers a speech that makes this clear. He recalls the daily indignities and routine beatings that he experienced in military training. After this suffering, he was sent to the battlefield. Like his comrades, he was thrown into the sea when his ship was destroyed. However, he was a hard man, and he lived on for six days, adrift in the ocean. If the horizon of life is the moment of death, this moment was intensified over a duration that he lived like no other time in his life. He reflected on his act of sacrifice, a temporality as exceptional as the moment in which he now recounts it. And in those moments, all he could think of was his sister. He had no regrets for acts done on her behalf.

He addresses the corpse of his nephew: "Why couldn't you recognize the material traces of her sacrifice for you in the wrinkles that marked her once-beautiful face? Why couldn't you do for her what we did for you?" Dying, he dreamed of all these things. What you do must be done for someone else. This, he says, is a commitment that is forgotten in modern Japan. The country may be peaceful, but it is also *zankoku* (inhumane).

Kuramoto resolves any questions as to how the Japanese people must act in the sharp exchange between Tachibana, a figure who exists only to record, and Akiyoshi, a figure whose creative powers have always been given form in leadership. As the detachment is about to board the train that will carry them back to the ocean depths, Tachibana presses the commander for his final judgment about contemporary Japan. Akiyoshi responds by questioning Japanese affluence. How have ordinary people responded to it? Why do they put so much stock in *benri* (convenience)? Akiyoshi is disgusted with the laziness he sees everywhere, and the disdain for physical labor. In case the audience might miss the importance of Akiyoshi's summation, Tachibana's behavior underlines it as he writes furiously to record the commander's words in his notebook. "Do you know the word *hinkō*? It's a word made up of the characters for poor and happy. Nobody wants to be poor or in a desperate situation. But you can be poor and still live a happy life. That's what our lives were like. My grandfather used to say that all the time."

Remembering his family, Akiyoshi suddenly seems to tire of Tachibana's persistence. With resignation, Akiyoshi notes that he and his men didn't give their lives to make Japan into the pathetic place that they found on their return. He orders his men to board the train and prepare to depart. And yet, Tachibana pushes him to continue his evaluation of contemporary Japan.

Although Akiyoshi begins by acknowledging the importance of peace, he wonders what it means to show as much concern over a single death as the media has for Ōmiya's nephew. Does this same indignation continue with more and more deaths, or do people, bored and distracted, begin to dismiss them as mere numbers? Here, he returns to the heroic dead: "There are three hundred thousand *eirei* still abandoned at the bottom of the ocean. Three hundred thousand huddled together, here and there, lost in the depths. Forgotten. We lie in the icy waters at the bottom of the ocean."

He tells Tachibana that they occasionally rise to the surface on moonlit nights to look at the skies and think of their loved ones far away. "And sometimes, we think back on the unhappy past. Does anyone still remember us with gratitude, our generation who died for them?" Akiyoshi doubts that they do. Forgotten by family and friends, they still remain steadfast in the depths of the ocean, "praying for the happiness of their homeland." A lonely, unappreciated vigil; a solitary, unrequited love. With that, Akiyoshi breaks off the discussion. Amid bugle calls, boots stomping, clashing of rifles, the soldiers board the train and are gone.

The performance returns to Ōmiya, left behind in punishment. A kind of exemplary dialogue between the past and present, both immanent in the moment, emerges in the final scene between Ōmiya and his nephew at the gates to Yasukuni. His nephew wonders aloud where he went wrong. There was a time when he did everything for his mother, to repay his great debt to her. When did that change? When did he become caught up in the instrumentality of capitalist labor, focused on the means, forgetting the ends?

Ōmiya responds obliquely, asking his nephew if he had ever been struck. When he replies that he hasn't, Ōmiya begins to beat him. This is his lesson to his nephew, the culmination of *Kikoku*'s narrative. Today's Japanese don't know true pain or suffering. They do not know how to sacrifice themselves. For his part, his nephew thanks him and asks to be beaten more. At that moment, the ghost of his sister intercedes. Not on behalf of her son, but to thank her brother for his sacrifice.

Earlier, Akiyoshi had argued that contemporary Japanese people no longer understand the concept *yutaka*. It speaks to bounty or plenty, but he insists that it once represented pleasure in living in a world where people had just enough. Now everyone wants more than enough—they demand excess. What's more, they want to do as little as possible to have as much as possible.

Akiyoshi insists that Japanese people recall and remember the spirit of earlier times. They must recalibrate the equilibrium between giving and receiving; they must want less and give more. Happiness comes from having just enough. His argument is grounded in the historical moment in which he lived, deeply embedded in the ideology of the Showa era, in the romanticization of diligence and frugality.[74] At the same time, Akiyoshi doesn't hesitate to extend his convictions as to the appropriate way to be and to act as an imperial subject and soldier, to a judgment about contemporary Japanese society. It is telling that Akiyoshi and Ōmiya are not concerned with building military discipline: Ōmiya's nephew is not criticized for being a capitalist rather than a soldier. Instead, it is for working to accumulate more for himself, rather than discharging his debt to those who have gone before. Work more and accept less. In this way, the story of Ōmiya's nephew and the conclusions that Akiyoshi draws from it defines *Kikoku*. Kuramoto's diegesis equates the particular to the general. This move has its parallel in the earlier relationship constructed between concrete forms of practice and the abstract logic of sacrificial action that was used to mobilize them. Clearly there is a formal equivalence between the two. The authority to determine how a subject must act resides, not with the subject themselves, but is broadly invested in the community and articulated by the state. If the state as sacrifier makes no claim on their actions, they are still not free to live their lives, to sell their labor as they will. Or, rather, they cannot seek any particular advantage in doing so. The possibility, the anticipation of sacrifice, shadows their every moment.[75]

In the same way, Akiyoshi and Ōmiya's insistence that Japanese people must make it their priority to care for one another is nothing new. The logic of *yuimāru* and the ethos of mutual assistance is an important dimension of everyday life in Okinawa, its practices subject to valorization in Japanese popular media and scholarship. And yet, it is important to remember that these practices were created and sustained because ordinary people had little else available to them. Cooperative credit associations did not just instantiate some abstract quality of the folk. They were not enacted in order to realize a fundamental dimension of Okinawan (or, for that matter, Japanese) community organization. They were ways in which people who were already entangled in relationships of kinship or collaboration could support one another in times of crisis. As Okinawans became caught up in broader networks of capitalist production, whether in their own agrarian or urban communities, or in mainland industrial centers or colonial agricultural projects, these practices were mobilized to address their privation. If fewer Okinawan workers were needed in the factories of Kawasaki, Yokohama, or Osaka, they could return home to their native villages—conditions that are as true today as they were during the Japanese colonial era or postwar American rule. The logic of *yuimāru* could be relied upon to sustain them until production increased again—or at least to lure them home to suffer in places distant from the metropolitan centers.[76] In that sense, the repetition of these practices discloses histories of exploitation that culminate in contemporary forms of precarious labor.[77]

The performance of *Kikoku* has opened a moment to intervene in the organization of Okinawan everyday life. It does so by enacting and describing a chronotope, positing a constellation of space and time that already exists, perhaps unseen and unacknowledged, but already bonded to Japanese industrial modernity.[78] The specters of Japanese soldiers do not appear in the interstices of the modern city, haunting spaces or engaging in practices that expose the presence of a fragment of Edo or the timeless countryside beyond the city's edge. They travel by train, walk streets busy with automobiles. They visit nightclubs, galleries, universities, hospitals, the Western-style housing of the elite, the shrine at Yasukuni. All places that any Tokyoite would know today. When their time in the city ends, they are not sent off with rituals and gifts, as the visiting dead would be at the end of Obon. They are not driven off by incantations and carefully executed gestures, like the uneasy spirits that wander inconsolably or the predatory dead that try to commandeer the bodies of the living. Instead, they respond to military command and board a military transport, as they would have done in life. Even the place to which they return is framed by modernity. Not a cemetery or cave, not an ancient temple or a devil-haunted mountain. They return to a space on the contested boundaries of the Imperial state, along the lines of communication that led to the battlefield. When they sink beneath the sea, it is to drift among the wreckage of troop ships and military aircraft, not to find solace in the undersea kingdom of the Dragon King.

The chronotope that they have created is durable, speaking to the power of those who invested it with their strength and resolution. Its presence is reinforced in the aphorisms that are constantly repeated by the performers in their guise as spectral soldiers. Valorize wartime discipline. Accept less, give more. Embrace hardship. Be prepared to join in an eternity of endless sacrifice.

In the heterogeneous temporality of the performance, it is captured under the sign of Showa, instantiated in the daily practices of those soldiers for whom the war remains practically and experientially immanent, an unbroken sequence of actions unfolding in an endless present of action, conflict, and sacrifice. Until Ōmiya's murder, until Akiyoshi's meditation on difference, it had been something created, and experienced in the now. Only then, only when narrated and reflected on in comparison with this visit, of a contemporary Japanese ethos made known to the soldiers in their travels around Tokyo, could it be contained in a duration, an interval called back from a newly created past that now begins to slip away from them.[79]

And yet, it is also fragile, spun off from the totality of modern life by the inattention, the faithlessness, the desire for convenience, the aversion to labor and the fear of pain. Of a state in defeat that abandoned those who had sacrificed so much, of a nation willing to passively accept anything. It is also marked by the intimation—never uttered—of a monarch who failed his subjects, accepting the terms of a defeat that, however ignominious, preserved his life while consigning them to a faithless oblivion. And, perhaps more cynically, allowing them to persist in this state, a kind of reserve to be recalled and remembered at some point in the future, in service of some new patriotic project as yet unimagined. The endless conscription of sacrifice.

My head spun as I thought about the ideology expressed in Kuramoto's play: the weight of the dead brought to bear to shape the actions of the living. I suppose it was unsurprising that these revenants were chosen to open up this moment. Bataille has argued that, in the modern world, men and women discover the possibility of community in the mute presence of death. It is in the silence and the absence (the nonpresence) of the dead, the incommunicability of the sacrifice, that the living can recognize love and friendship, that they can imagine the possibility of something beyond their own isolated existences.[80] Taking up Bataille's argument, Maurice Blanchot is more direct in asserting that this absence, this negativity, structures life:

Now the "basis of communication" is not necessarily speech, or even the silence that is its foundation and punctuation, but the exposure to death, no longer my own exposure, but someone else's, whose living and closest presence is already the eternal and unbearable absence, an absence that the travail of deepest mourning does not diminish. And it is in life itself that the absence of someone else has to be met. It is with that absence—its uncanny presence, always under the prior threat of a disappearance—that friendship is brought into play and lost at each moment, a relation without relation or without relation other than the incommensurable. . . . Such is, such would be the friendship that discovers the unknown we ourselves are, and the meeting of our own solitude which, precisely, we cannot be alone to experience.[81]

Kuramoto appropriates the painful memory of wartime sacrifice and death shared by the Japanese people, and yet he does not trust in the power of the absence and the silence of the dead. The revenants portrayed in *Kikoku* are vocal and reflexive, capable of both physically reminding the living of their absence as well as narrating and reenacting their past actions as sacrifice. It is a theater of overdetermination, one that replaces melancholy remembrance with speaking and acting subjects.[82] In doing so, it discounts the dialogic, experiential practice of constructing community that Bataille and Blanchot proposed. Instead, the terms of the community are clearly expressed by the dead: the living must simply accept them and incorporate them into their own practices.

At that moment, Akiyoshi's army of ghosts appear once again. The stage is swirling in fog, skeletons and wreckage appearing on back-projected screens. The soldiers march at a slow, funereal pace to the front of the stage. They present arms, then face about, marching back into the fog. The audience erupts in applause and cheers. A screen drops and a plaintive ballad plays while a photomontage of highlights from the performance flashes by.[83] The aural and visual unity of their presence is torn apart, ghosts on the stage and their mediated remembrances on screen. Three curtain calls follow, wild applause and cheers from the audience.

The play ends and I gather my belongings in silence. As I walk back down the broad concrete staircase to the street below, the audience flows around me. Couples, heads together, animatedly discussing the performance. An elderly man, absently touching his grandchild on the shoulder, the head, gently keeping him close as they walk off into the night. I think of the melancholy spirits of the dead and their call for sacrifice. How can I make sense of that when refugees still sit in school gymnasiums and community centers in Tōhoku, when the broken reactors in Fukushima still smolder, when the newly dead still float in the ocean off the coast? When, here in Okinawa, people settle into their homes as the night patrol takes off from runways at Kadena and Futenma? When demonstrators at Takae and Henoko make their plans for tomorrow?

How can I understand the pleasure that the audience took in the performance? Certainly, there is enjoyment in seeing an expertly staged production created by a popular and respected director. Most Okinawans cannot regularly travel to Tokyo or Osaka to see performances like this, and those that I've seen staged by traveling companies are always well received. Perhaps it also resonated with the earlier televised version and its lead performance by Kitano Takeshi, who has certainly romanticized Okinawa in his work as an actor and director. At the same time, it might remind Okinawans of the time after the war when dozens of theaters across central Okinawa staged performances of the *uchinā shibai*, or Okinawan popular theater.

There is an undeniable nostalgia for the past in Okinawa. Mainland Japanese were not the only ones who submitted themselves to military discipline, who buttoned their creative and particular selves into the uniform of the nation. Okinawans are also proud of their patriotic service, as well as that of their fathers and grandfathers. But what about all the things that were lost as a result of that service? In their willing or unwilling acts of sacrifice, the island was destroyed, thousands and thousands of Okinawans died in agony, others consigned to lives as miserable as that of Ōmiya's sister.

What has been proffered in this performance, to Okinawan audiences as well as those in mainland Japan, is the chance to recognize that they already belong to the sacrificial community of the nation, and to accept the ethos that it demands. And yet, as willing as the characters are to call on the audience to join them, much is left unsaid. It is not enough to describe the sacrifice of these soldiers as some kind of move from the particular—their lives as painters, as musicians, as athletes, as actors, as artisans—to the general. The concrete form of their sacrifice must be taken into account. What does it mean for this sacrifice to be performed as soldiers who not only adhere to the ascetic life extolled by Akiyoshi, but who behave with Ōmiya's cruelty and violence? What kind of ethical judgment accepts the equivalence between the acts of a painter and a soldier, or the objects that they produce?

This is the contradiction at the heart of sacrificial practice. What does it mean to take a life in exchange for another? What does it mean to voluntarily offer up your own life if others will suffer as a consequence of your actions, even if your objective is accomplished? What is the process of evaluation that determines which lives can be sacrificed and which lives must be saved? And what of the loss of the ascetic commitment that Akiyoshi bemoans? How much of the Okinawan past must be explained away if everyone is to agree to the life of *hinkō*, the happy poverty that he commends? Should they forget generations of struggle for fair treatment as laborers in mainland factories? As workers on American bases? As citizens of the Japanese state? As workers supporting wars in a nation constitutionally committed to peace? Kuramoto's company avoids engaging these complicated questions. Akiyoshi and his men have not spent the decades since the war pondering the moral consequences of their actions, working through guilt over the lives they took or the families they abandoned. Neither have they been admitted to the grounds at Yasukuni where they would presumably be cheered by the gift of Imperial prayers and whatever immaterial portions of offerings they might claim. Still bound by their respect for authority, they can't even muster a direct criticism of the emperor and the state apparatus that consigned them to the depths of the ocean forever. Instead, we are left with a perverse romanticization of an eternity that resembles nothing so much as the lives led by soldiers in garrison, engaged in the same repetitive routines, mooning over their loved ones far away, and grousing about the comfortable lives lived by those who benefitted from their sacrifice. Marking time at the bottom of the sea until their service is required again.

Behind us, in the theater, the crew is already at work striking the scenery and packing up their equipment onto trucks waiting in the parking lot. The actors are wiping the makeup from their faces, hanging up their costumes. It's still early enough for them to explore the restaurants and bars of Naha. As I look back up the stairs, I see again the evocations of Ryūkyūan domestic architecture, and I think of the thousands of Okinawan homes destroyed in the Battle of Okinawa or cleared away by the forces of the American occupation. In the traces of the hearth and the Okinawan theater, I see the displacement of these traditional forms and the new possibilities of contemporary Japanese entertainment that have taken their place—cinemas, karaoke boxes, living rooms illuminated by the glow of massive flat-screen televisions, video games dancing on laptop monitors and cellphone screens. In the suggestion of *gusuku* (castle) walls, I think of the rule of Okinawan monarchs disrupted by the Satsuma invasion and

2.5.   The *hiroba* or meeting area in Yogi Park.

destroyed forever by Japanese colonization and incorporation into the modern nation. I think of the auditorium that I have just left, and I recall the ambiguous promise of return to Japanese sovereignty and the more than forty years of American military occupation that have followed. And in the critical and inventive traces of Kinjō's purposeful appropriation and transformation of vernacular style and modern formalism, clearing a hopeful space toward the future.

Yogi Park is dark and quiet. I see only shadows as a few people move along its paths. The monuments are out there, still and heavy in the darkness. Beyond the dark silhouette of trees, I can glimpse the *hiroba*, illuminated by the light of the rising moon and the glow from streetlights surrounding a distant parking lot. The audience, leaving the theater, flows out into that darkness, carrying with them the memories of the duration of sound and vision that they experienced. And, as they move further from the fleeting moment that emerged in that space, the memories of that experience come up against the memories and experiences of everyday life. Can the stories told, the promises made, the commands issued by Kuramoto's characters, survive that interaction? Can the marching of ghostly Imperial soldiers transform that of anti-base demonstrators, or the hurried steps of a student, a dancer, or a stockbroker, as they rush off to work? Can they believe that the capacity to join a community of sacrifice underlies all of their actions, a potential for a pleasurable and catastrophic repetitive rhythm awaiting their recognition? Or will they side with history, a history that stands against the pernicious effects of any feeling that seeks to insert itself into the space of memory and tradition, a parasite that is ideology in the guise of remembrance, a reminder of a need that they do not feel.

When morning comes again to Naha, Kuramoto's troupe will have moved on. Few material traces of their visit will remain: trash from their dressing rooms to be taken to the dumpster, a few posters tacked to bulletin boards or stacked in the lobby. Children will play in the *hiroba*, elderly men and women will return to the tables and benches that surround the plaza. Busloads of anti-base activists heading to Henoko might stop. And perhaps those activists will read the lines of Yamanokuchi Baku's poem cut into the face of his memorial. Families attending a benefit concert for the homeless may pause to consider Mayor Oyadomari's commentary on the Japanese constitutional refusal of war. A young, aspiring poet visiting Baku's memorial could find herself listening to the impassioned words of a speaker addressing union workers sitting at the *hiroba*. In the months to come, more workers will gather at times such as the May Day demonstrations. It may be that they will encounter a true revenant, one of the elderly survivors of the Battle of Okinawa that sit together listening to *minyō* around the plaza. Perhaps they will even meet the shade of a Japanese soldier or Okinawan civilian who lost their life when the park was a killing field. And these experiences will be carried along as people move to other places, other moments.

In the morning, the sun will wake the three men sleeping in front of Baku's memorial. A uniformed patrolman might remind them that it's time to move along. Groups of schoolchildren rushing off to school will pass by. The men will fold up their blue tarps, tie them to their packs, and begin another day.

Unburying the Future

3

OKAMOTO TARŌ AND THE DIALECTICS OF SACRIFICE

Despite the televisions, the electric stoves, the washing machines, I have never felt so close to prehistory as amid these coppices, these rocks, these caves, these natural wells, these springs, which for the people of the Ryūkyūs are the only expression of the sacred.

Claude Lévi-Strauss, "Herodotus in the China Sea" (1983)

It is sad to see how a large, muddy current is fed from springs situated at a considerable altitude.

Walter Benjamin, on Roger Caillois's *L'aridité* (1938)

A Coffee Shop, July 2011

The sun was beginning to set as I drove north on Route 58 to Chatan. Outside, the humid air was dense, almost visible. It was as if my car had been wrapped in a fine curtain. To my left, stores and restaurants shimmered with light. The rush of business commuters and daytime tourists had begun to taper off as the island turned toward night. To my right, steel chain-link fences ran along the road, sharply marking off the American bases that stretched inland to the east. Beyond the fence, I could see rows of military vehicles and equipment painted desert camouflage. I wondered if they had been returned from Iraq or Afghanistan, or were waiting to be sent to some distant battlefield. The base streetlights hadn't been turned on yet, but the fortified gates were brightly lit. With a desultory wave, an Okinawan security guard directed a few cars with Y license plates into the slow-moving stream of traffic on the highway, as the last Marines and sailors headed home after work. As always, the strangeness and familiarity of these two intertwined worlds caught at me. With some effort, I turned my attention back to the road that lay between them.

The noisy air conditioning in my tiny Nissan did little to push back the clinging heat, but at least the blast of air kept me awake. Since dawn I had been working with a group from Promise Keepers, clearing brush in their fields in Nishihara. I knew that I should go home, take a shower, and rest, but I wasn't ready for an evening alone in my tiny, bare apartment. Tired, behind in my work, I still needed to catch up on my fieldnotes and prepare for the Okamoto Tarō retrospective that had just opened at the Okinawa Prefectural Museum. Since I had my laptop and some books with me, I decided to stop at the Starbucks along Route 58. As I pulled into the parking lot, the concrete wall of a Coco convenience store blocked my view of the ocean off to the west, but I could see the lights of the American Village shopping center against the darkening sky.

I took my computer bag out of the trunk and went inside. The shop was one of several new Starbucks in Chatan, a bright, open space of glass and blond wood. It was crowded: groups of young Marines in civilian clothes on their way to the American Village shopping mall; several soldiers from the Japanese Self-Defense Force, the Jieitai, also out of uniform, waiting with shopping bags for a bus to take them back to their base to the north in Onna; a pair of mainland tourists planning their travels for the following day; several well-dressed elderly Okinawan women talking over their drinks. I sat down with a cup of coffee to reread some of the passages from Okamoto's *Okinawa Bunkaron* (Theories of Okinawan culture), the collected accounts of his Okinawan travels. For several weeks, the young Okinawan academics that I knew had been looking forward to the opening symposium. It came up in discussions in Tokyo and here in Okinawa. I wanted to be ready for the debates that they expected.

The exhibition was a culmination of years of preparation and was part of a nationwide set of events timed to coincide with the centenary of Okamoto's birth. There was a series of exhibits at other prominent museums across Japan; critics and celebrities reevaluated his work in journals and television specials. Tourist campaigns urged travelers to visit sites related to his work, particularly the *Tower of the Sun* in Osaka and the Okamoto Tarō Museum in Kawasaki. The Japanese national broadcasting company NHK even presented *Tarō no Tō* (Tarō's tower), a serialized drama about his life. For a month, the galleries of the fortress-like Okinawan Prefectural Museum were filled with his paintings, sketches, and a wide variety of objects. However, the centerpiece of the exhibition was a collection of photographic images of Okinawa that he produced in 1959 and 1966.

As Nariai Hajime, one of the curators, told me, it can be difficult for Japanese people to remember Okamoto as a figure of artistic or intellectual importance rather than one who was simply famous. For many years, it has seemed that artists and critics could only disparage or dismiss his work. Despite the ubiquity of the *Tower of the Sun* and the plaza that he and the renowned Japanese architect Tange Kenzō designed for Expo '70, popular memory seemed unable to reach beyond images of his chat show appearances and television commercials to the pathbreaking artist and public intellectual that he once was. His aphorism "art is an explosion" is remembered more as a popular catchphrase than a call to experience the violent creative power of unresolved dialectic tension. Bypassed by Japanese artists who demanded a more confrontational and transformative relationship between aesthetics and politics, he seemed to respond by further embracing his position in the mass media. Until his recent popular and critical resurgence, many simply remembered him as yet another eccentric *talento* (media personality). All this has served to obscure genealogies that lead to an artist who was instrumental in creating the Japanese postwar avant-garde.[1]

The book that I held in my hands was the more recent *bunkobon* (a pocket-sized paperback) published by Chūkōbunko, a small compendium that contained the original account of Okamoto's 1959 travels, *Wasurerareta Nihon: Okinawa Bunkaron* (Forgotten Japan: Theories of Okinawan culture). It also included "Kamigami no Shima" (Island of the deities), a brief essay about his subsequent visit to Okinawa in 1966 titled "Hondo Fukki ni Atatte" (In the time of Reversion to the main islands), a letter addressed to the Okinawan people, urging them to reject plans to reunify with the Japanese state in 1972, and "'Hitotsu no Koi' no Shōgensha to site" (As a witness to 'a kind of love'), a short commentary by Okamoto Toshiko, Okamoto Tarō's adopted daughter, companion, and amanuensis.[2] It was a book about voyages: the manifest record of his two trips to Okinawa and a polemic based on his remembrances. At the same time, it was an account of a man profoundly transformed by movement. A young man who sailed to Europe in the company of his complex family—father Ippei, mother Kanoko, and her lovers—

3.1.　Poster for the Okamoto Tarō exhibit at the Okinawa Prefectural Museum and Art Museum.

and chose to remain there.[3] An aspiring artist and intellectual who sought out new and established artists and scholars in the classrooms and ateliers of Paris—Kurt Seligmann, Pablo Picasso, Alexandre Kojève, Marcel Mauss. His flight from Paris as the invading German army closed on the city. There are also intimations of Okamoto's long march as a Japanese soldier during the Pacific War and his return to a ruined and defeated Tokyo to find his studio and his archive destroyed. If these were the only tropes mobilized in Okamoto's work, they would still resonate with familiar themes. A young man of privilege overcomes hardship to realize himself. An apprentice labors to master his art, to create something new. A traveler, long absent, returns home at the moment of greatest need and most profound loss.

There were other voyages that exerted influence on Okamoto's project. The seeker who made his way through the darkened, wintery streets of Paris to dusty bookshops and attic apartments, driven by the realization that the catastrophe at hand cannot be halted by conventional notions of art, scholarship, or critique. A cataclysm that could overcome even the most innovative forms of expression. And so, it is also a record of his search for new travelers' tales from which to learn, new forms of knowledge and action. In Michel Leiris's ethnography and Marcel Mauss's ethnology. In essays and monographs compiled by native ethnologists like Yanagita Kunio and Orikuchi Shinobu. In Watsuji Tetsurō's memoir of visits to Japanese temples, and in his philosophical meditations on the relationship of place and life. In Rudolf Otto's and Mircea Eliade's speculative excavations of the authentic world that lies beneath the mundane. In tales told by Georges Bataille, Roger Caillois, and Pierre Klossowski. In the furtive movement through the woods at twilight, in moments of awe and terror spent in a torchlit clearing in the Forest of Marly, surrounding a tree split by lightning, enacting now-forgotten rituals. Hoping for—what?

The records of these earlier travels—by foot, by ship, by eye—come together in the pages of *Okinawa Bunkaron*. And yet, the heart of the text remains his reflections on his voyages to Okinawa. This project, the desire and determination that carried him there, resonates with Jacques Rancière's *Short Voyages to the Lands of the People*: "The questions we will pose here will concern, first, the signs by which a gaze—curious, nonchalant, or impassioned—comes to recognize reality as exemplary of the idea; and second, the way in which thought comes to incarnate itself."[4]

It is an account of an expedition to discover that which Okamoto already knows, to confirm the pieces that came to him through his travels in books, ateliers, and battlefields. And, as a record of the very journey that he longs to begin, it gives form to his anticipation. Okamoto himself stands at the center of this process: an archaeologist of everyday life, committed to uncover that which he knows lies buried. To remember that which he knows to be forgotten. A cosmopolitan modern, attuned to the ravages of industrial capital, the alienation of everyday life, and the quotidian horror of fascism and war. A psychonaut, whose intuition and experience had convinced him that the voyage into the past follows a path excavated in the self as much as any trail that leads through broken ruins or dense jungle. A geometer, in Bourdieu's terms, whose embodied experience will drive the project. An artist prepared, entitled, perhaps obligated to act on what he discovers.[5]

While Okamoto is attuned to that which he expects to find, he is also attentive to the unexpected, the unnoticed, the unseen. It is this interplay between confirmation and surprise that adds depth and complexity to the text.

After an hour or so of reading, I realized that one of the baristas had come around to my table and was standing across from me. Catching my attention, she shyly pointed at my copy of Okamoto's book and asked me what I thought of it. I told her that I'd been familiar with Okamoto for a long time, but I had only just started to think seriously about his work. She replied that he had been an important influence when she was growing up. As an elementary school student in Koza, she discovered a book in the school library that contained a collection of images of his paintings and sculpture. Something about Okamoto's aesthetic vision enthralled her. As she got older, she became interested in his essays. *Okinawa Bunkaron* was the most inspiring, a text that encouraged her to see the value of the everyday practices she had always taken for granted. Reading, she told me, gave her new pride in being Okinawan.

Although she was now a student at Ryūkyū Daigaku (University of the Ryūkyūs), she said that she had no interest in following Okamoto's lead to become an ethnologist, artist, or critic. Even so, she believed that lessons learned from his work have helped her to see herself as a strong, creative Okinawan woman regardless of what career she chooses. The popularity of the Okamoto retrospective at the Okinawa Prefectural Museum suggests that her interest in his work is widely shared in Okinawa. It is not difficult to understand his appeal, despite the debate about his actions on the island of Kudaka that would erupt during the symposium. The success of the retrospective, built on a smaller exhibition in Naha a decade earlier, made it clear that many people take pleasure in the attention of an artist of Okamoto's stature, and enjoy the experience of his work and his insights into Okinawan culture.

And yet, this exhibition, intended to celebrate his Okinawan work, stirred old memories of his desecration of rural tombs, reopening debates about colonial authority and the collaboration of local elites in the appropriation of representations of the Okinawan everyday.

Symposium, Okinawa Prefectural Museum, June 2011

Sukiyabashi Park in Ginza, Tokyo's stylish business and fashion district, the day before Christmas, 1966.[6] It was sunny and windy, the temperature warm. Okamoto Tarō arrived in a rush. In front of him stood a tower, perhaps eight meters high. The *Wakai tokeidai* (Youth's time tower).[7] His tower. Reaching up from the ground to the sky, the sun surmounting it by day, the moon by night, a face, a clock. Like a ferroconcrete tree, thick at its base and tapering as it rises, its design made it seem even taller. Perhaps he was concerned about its popular reception, or if his patrons at Shichizun tokei kabushikigaisha, the Citizen Watch Company, or the Ginza and Sukiyabashi Park Lions Clubs, would appreciate it. Perhaps he was distracted, his thoughts on a temporality beyond Ginza.

A series of limbs emerged from the trunk of the tower, thick at their base, narrowing to points at their end—silver, blue, green, and gold. Like tentacles, or branches from an austere tree. Okamoto called them horns—perhaps recalling the minotaur, that uneasy fusion of man and beast, culture and nature, reason and passion.[8] Some were short, as if they had just erupted from the body of the tower. Others were long, one even curving back on itself. They seemed to arrest motion, a duration of action captured in concrete and metal. On the face of the clock, simple black hands swept the time, the canonical hours marked on the dial. The word "Citizen" was written across it in the company's familiar black font. Beneath that, the author's signature—Tarō—dashed off in dramatic roman letters.

And yet, it was far from a conventional clock. The hours were inscribed as bands on the body of a serpentine form that curled across the face, thick and rounded at its highest point, tapering to almost nothing as it spiraled back to where it began. The impression was of a snake, a comet, a *hitodama* (in Japanese folklore, a comet-shaped ball of fire representing a spirit of the dead) rising up from the depths of the dial and winding around it in a counterclockwise direction. An impossible ouroboros, its head and tail seemingly on different planes, yet meeting at the top of the disk. This motif was echoed in two golden forms, another pair of *hitodama* that circled the clock as if they were drawn to it. It was chronotope as much as chronometer, an aesthetic materialization of the immanence of past, present, and future.[9] The clock endlessly measuring the passage of the time of the city, of work, of everyday life. The remainder of the tower holding another temporality in place, pointing to another way of being.

As darkness fell, spotlights illuminated the base of the tower. Soft light began to shine at the root of each horn, yellow, green, and red. The form swirling around the dial was illuminated in red, the hours marked on its back in blue—the colors reversed on its obverse. On either side of the face, two large round discs glowed, like eyes peering out of the mask-like visage. The timekeeper, watching those whose actions create the time of the world, as they look to it for guidance. Manifold temporalities represented in its features. The hands, moving constantly, picked out the succession of moments, one after another. Spiraling backward, the comet bore all of

3.2.   The *Wakai tokeidai* during the day.

the hours in itself, a duration with no beginning and no end, buried in the future, rising up into the past. Endlessly present. The limbs too, moment after moment of growth and movement, spatialized accretions present in the now. However, Okamoto, the artist who had conceived it, who had supervised its construction, who had stood before it as it began to condense the progressive measurement of time into a figure of presence, who had made visible the invisible, was no longer there. By the time the lights in the tower began to glow, Okamoto was stepping off a plane on the tarmac in American-occupied Okinawa. Christmas Eve.[10]

Several prominent Okinawans had invited Okamoto to attend a ritual on Kudaka Island. The island, a mile or so off the east coast of the main island of Okinawa, had long been valorized as a site where the ancient Japanese past persisted in an otherwise neglected and impoverished corner of contemporary Japan. The ritual—an initiation ceremony for the women of the island known as Izaihō—was important to Okinawans themselves, but also central to Japanese ethnographies and romantic fantasies that appropriated Okinawa for nativist projects.[11]

Okamoto writes of his fascination with the tension between the harsh and impoverished everyday life that he found on Kudaka and the intensity of the initiation practices that were maintained in the face of those material constraints, the demand and the desire for migration away from Kudaka, and the challenge and lure of the American occupation. As a part of a group of folklorists, teachers, reporters, and bureaucrats, he described his intense curiosity as he watched the ritual. The initiates hid themselves away in a ceremonial house, emerging to dance ecstatically before the observers. He wrote:

> In Kudaka, the island said to be the holiest in Okinawa, the ritual known as Izaihō takes place once every twelve years, in the year of the horse. At that time, island women from the age of thirty to forty participate in a strict trial (and sacrifice/rite). By so doing, they all become *kaminchū* [those with powers to communicate with and serve the island's deities and ancestral spirits]. For three days, they are cloistered in a hut known as *nanatsuya* that's built in a forbidden grove called Mt. Izai. While chanting Iffai, iffai they cross the Nanatsubashi [a low bridge]. It is said that any woman who has committed an injustice will fall from the bridge and die, her blood gushing from her wounds. Curiosity is incited by rumors of tests of virtue and the like, but the women who participate are absolutely earnest.[12]

On the third day of the festival, Okamoto decided to explore the rest of the island. It may be that he had completed his research, or perhaps he was inspired to seek out other ritual spaces. Okamoto had written that there were many places on Kudaka that he longed to visit, but he had avoided them in the past, fearing that outsiders were forbidden access. Emboldened by the presence of a number of other Okinawan and mainland photographers, he walked to a valley known as Gusō ("after life," a term regularly used to describe the place of the no longer living), a space where islanders believed that the quotidian world intersected with the world of the dead.[13] After photographing remains at the mouth of the valley, bones that had been cleaned, prepared, and placed into ceramic funerary urns by their families, he went deeper to a place where the newly dead were exposed to the elements.[14] "This is the primitive style of burial that has been a mystery to me for so long," he wrote.[15] There is some controversy about what happened next. Many believe that Okamoto pushed the lid back on one of the small wooden caskets, rearranged the remains within, and photographed them. He wrote of the image: "Around its knees, a scrap of crosshatched cloth fluttered, unexpectedly conjuring a vivid memory of the dead. There is something pure about the image, in spite of its cruelty. This is a world of obligation. And yet, I felt that it was better to fade away, exposed to the depths of eternal time, than to be cremated or hastily buried."[16] This photograph, along with several others that he took during his visit, was published in his column "Taiyō no Me" in the next issue of the popular weekly magazine *Shūkan Asahi*.[17] Its publication had an immediate effect on village life on Kudaka. Travelers descended on the tiny island, while scholars renewed their efforts to see everything for themselves. In time, a crematorium was built and the forms of death that fascinated Okamoto were sealed up in concrete. Half a century of Okinawan critical debates followed. In Okinawa, if nowhere else, the memories of this moment remain.

The 2011 Okinawan retrospective recalled his earlier visits, the works they inspired, and the popular interest he brought to these neglected, American-occupied islands. It also recalled the debates, often acrimonious, that they generated. At the same time, there seemed to be a desire to reach back to the Okamoto who had engaged Okinawa, to call up his words, to demand some kind of long-deferred accountability to those in this moment. This feeling was particularly strong at the opening symposium.[18] The auditorium was packed, with listeners sitting along the aisles and standing in the back. The keynote speaker was Akasaka Norio, a respected mainland scholar known for his ethnographies of Tōhoku, his comparative studies of Okinawa, and his longstanding engagement with Okamoto Tarō's work. Only weeks after the catastrophe of March 2011 in Japan's main islands, Akasaka was still deeply affected by the earthquake, tsunami, and nuclear disaster. Having come directly to the conference from a ravaged village in Tōhoku, his remarks lingered on the death and destruction he had seen. Communities where he had worked for decades had been swept away, his friends and collaborators lost. Shaken by what he had seen, he turned to *Okinawa Bunkaron* for solace, to collect his thoughts, to find the link between that moment and this that he intuited. Like Okamoto before him, he said that he now realized that Okinawa and Tōhoku are still Japanese colonies—oppressed, ignored, and exploited. The Okinawan audience listened politely. Some pleased, some indifferent, some angered that he finally recognized in Okamoto's words what they have known every moment of their lives.

When I walked through the museum's cold white galleries, I often saw patrons searching for the photograph or asking if it was exhibited. It was not.[19] And yet it exerted a powerful force in its absence. Once the speakers had finished, the discussion inevitably turned to the image. After pressing Akasaka to comment on the insensitivity that allowed Okamoto to ignore the island's customs and publish the photograph, the Okinawan poet and critic Takara Ben angrily said that Okinawan journalists, schoolteachers, and local elites were just as guilty of thoughtlessly disregarding local tradition and violating Kudaka's taboos.[20]

Takara's use of the category *taboo* is important. While he is a poet, a political activist, and a chemist, he is also a sophisticated student of ethnology and used the word quite deliberately. If we think of taboo as the generative principle of social distinction, there is something in Okamoto's photograph that disrupts the comfortable, expected dispositions of everyday life and exposes the unstated—but changing—realities of the social world.[21] A site like Gusō and subjects like the dead are incorporated in and productive of a certain kind of space and time. In Okinawa, access to places like this is regulated by convention, both articulated and unspoken. There are times when the living and the dead are expected to come together: to exchange gifts at the household altar or share a meal around the dining table, to converse at the tomb, to dance together in a clearing in the forest or along a city street. There are also times when the dead are left in solitude in the altar, the tomb, in places known only to them. When the living and the dead meet in a place like Gusō, they move through its space-time in familiar rhythms. There are those who take the lead, those who happily follow, those who uncomfortably accept the duties allotted to them. There can even be a place for guests like Okamoto.

What's more, photographic representation of the dead can be permitted.[22] Most Okinawans would agree that the dead do not need the media of film to speak. They can do so in their own way, and through their own network of intermediaries: in dreams and in signs that appear in everyday life, as apparitions, as subjectivities spatialized in household altars and family tombs, and through the mediation of *yuta* (shamans), priestesses, and still-living members of their household. However photographs also have their place. A solemn black-and-white image of the deceased can be made the focus of memoration at a funeral.[23] Sometimes the living and the dead collaborate in the production of new images. Local artists and photographers work on the faded school photographs or military snapshots of men who died in combat, crafting commemorative images of weddings or family gatherings that they never attended in life. When I walk past photography studios in Koza's shopping arcades, I often see their solemn faces staring out from these tableaux, stately in the dark suits or formal kimono that artists have fashioned for them.

The living respond to the call of the dead. They prepare a place for them—beautiful, stable, enduring—a carefully framed household altar, an ornate funerary urn, a hand-painted family photograph, a magnificent tomb, a community war memorial of polished stone. In doing so, they shape and organize the spatial field of these ancestral spirits, helping them to resume their material engagement with the social world.

Okamoto's image disclosed the dead in an intermediate form—that of the decaying corpse—through which it was not yet ready to engage the world. It should have been left in seclusion in Gusō until decay had worn away the physical body and the time came to make it beautiful once again. Okamoto's image was an interruption to the expected development of these relationships and an affront to both the living and the dead. It revealed and represented the dead, repeating and circulating its image thousands of times, to newsstands, living rooms, libraries, and museums across Japan. Throughout his career, Okamoto often referred to himself as "a shaman with a camera." If, like a shaman, he believed that he was a mediator between worlds, perhaps he should have stopped himself before throwing the unprepared remains of the dead back into this one.

Okinawans have grown accustomed to the appropriation of their landscape and practices by mainland Japanese nativists such as Okamoto. They are all too aware of the ways in which the Japanese valorization of a putative Okinawan primitiveness, even when done in the name of respect for a place that still values what modern Japan has lost, consigns the Okinawans to the Japanese past and stigmatizes them as backward and in need of development. However Takara's critique does more than expose an insensitive violation of sacred space, an interruption of an important ritual, or a betrayal of confidentiality. His intervention makes visible a system of social relationships in which Okamoto's act was permissible. It demonstrates the ways in which many Okinawans were willing to allow fragments of their past to be used to construct a national history rather than represent the particularity of their experiences. They have collaborated in effacing the everyday in which these images were once situated, obscuring a past of exploitation and privation that resulted from decades of American military occupation and Japanese colonization. Okamoto's image explicitly indexes the field of doxic regulation, disclosing a hegemonic network in which Okinawans have contributed to their own subordination. That is why, five decades later, Okinawans like Takara are still driven by their commitment to critique and to action.

And yet, I would like to remain with Okamoto Tarō for a while, to think more about his voyage to Kudaka. The urgency that brought him to Okinawa was evident in his hasty departure from the ceremonies in Ginza, in his absence from Tokyo during the busy final weeks of the year. What did he hope to find? Is it enough to say that he came to see Izaihō? His interest in the ritual itself was uneven. Although he produced some striking photographic images, his published discussion of the ceremony in *Shūkan Asahi* was little different than what he recorded in 1959, a year that Izaihō was not even performed. Even that seems to be largely drawn from the famous ethnologist Orikuchi Shinobu's research. Perhaps that which he sought was really in Gusō, among the remains of the dead. Something in that place, something that inspired awe and horror. Something that spoke to absence and presence, weakness and strength, memory and action. Some trace of sacrifice, presence, and creativity.[24]

Brief Notes on the South Seas: Okamoto Tarō in Okinawa

Jacques Rancière's critical reading of the travel narratives of artists and poets in *Short Voyages to the Land of the People* remains with me, his observation that their experiences reveal to them that which they knew all along. They find the ideas that compel them already located in these new spaces; careful reading discloses the ways in which thought instantiates itself in the landscapes they find before them. And yet, that is not the entirety of Rancière's understanding of the work of those who go out to unfamiliar places. How could anyone sustain interest in the work of a traveler, a scholar, an artist, who can do nothing more than project what they already knew into a space as yet unexperienced? Instead, he urges us to look to the moments in which their curiosity sustains them, and their interest takes them beyond the easy and expected agreement between the image and the word, between the event and its representation.

> The poet who put together the words and images uniting the play of light and cloud with the sensible certainties of politics revolts against the impoverishment of the image, takes back his words,

takes his place in the gap between images and any promise of common happiness.

Thus diverge two paths: that of one who continues to recognize in the land he crosses the words and places of the book, and the path of one who takes back his words and figures, engraves the flower in the hardness of stone or in a poem, in the rediscovered foreignness of the work [oeuvre].[25]

My challenge is to follow the traces of Okamoto's path through his essays. We know of his desire to discover "that which had been a mystery for me for so long," the image for which words, gestures, techniques have been prepared. Once he arrived in Okinawa, was that enough? Was he satisfied to locate that which he expected in the streets of Naha, the markets of Ishigaki, the sacred groves of Kudaka? Or were these patterns, experienced against the texture of everyday life, the inspiration for new discoveries and new creations?

There are ways in which Okamoto's work anticipates Rancière's critique. His struggle to make sense of the catastrophes that have scarred the Okinawan landscape makes him skeptical of the everyday life that he experiences in the streets of Naha and Koza, and apprehensive of the future to which paths pieced together from the fragments of American and Japanese worlds might lead. At the same time, he is alive with anticipation of the possibilities that are buried all around him, a past that he longs to conjure into the present, unseen presences that he hopes to reveal.

In order to construct the narrative remainder of the text, he plays with what Marc Augé calls forms of oblivion: exemplary patterns that structure anthropological texts in order to experientially and narratively express the relationship between past, present, and future. In particular, Okamoto mobilizes a figure that Augé calls "The Return"—a moment in which actors, or the scholars who interpret their actions, clear aside the present and more recent experience in order to open themselves to the deeper past. For Augé, the figure of spirit possession is what most represents anthropologists' concern with this type of temporal displacement: the reappearance, in his telling, of the ancestors in the embodied present.[26] It is a form that would be familiar to Okamoto, resonating with Michel Leiris's manifold account of his experience with Zar spirit possession, and his remorseless project of self-discovery as he crossed Africa with Marcel Griaule's Dakar-Djibouti expedition.[27] Certainly, it bears the mark of his powerful preoccupation with Rudolf Otto's and Mircea Eliade's work on the numinous, the traditional sacred hidden in the profane present.[28] And yet, if Okamoto's

3.3.   Okamoto Tarō photographing travelers boarding a ship in Okinawa.

interest in Eliade's work on shamanism gives us any indication, perhaps he felt that it was the shaman on which this narrative figure of return depends. More importantly, it could be a role he incorporated into his own practice.

For Okamoto, the shaman does not surrender his body to another, be they ancestor or deity or any other entity. He does not try to fully efface or obscure the recent past. He does not want to make one present at the risk of excluding the others. Instead, he moves back and forth, calling each in order to create the complex narrative that both serves his project and represents his own alternative formation of space and time, one in which all that has happened, all that has to occur, can be uncovered in the moment.

I am reminded that Akasaka referred to Okamoto as a "shaman with a camera" in his remarks at the symposium. He was not alone in speaking of Okamoto in those terms. It is a phrase often used to describe him, evocative of his efforts to bring together the signs of difference in the material practices of representation. In an introduction to a collection of Okamoto's Tōhoku photography, the photographer Iizawa Kōtarō noted: "Whenever he ran into a dynamically moving subject, Tarō continued to click the shutter, already transformed into a shaman with a camera."[29] The promotional literature for an exhibition entitled *Shāmanizumu* (Shamanism), held at the

Tarō Okamoto Museum of Art in Kawasaki, moved beyond euphemism. "While Okamoto Tarō was a clearly logical person, he was also a shaman who could seize hold of the forces of chaos that lie deep within himself and be faithful to those sacred mysteries."[30] Perhaps the most direct characterization comes from Okamoto Toshiko: "Sometimes, all of a sudden, he would become a shaman."[31]

Okamoto as artist, as ethnographer, as shaman. Is that so difficult to imagine? There is much to add to his friends' ambiguous description. Since his return from France, from the war in China, he had sought out the same places in which Japanese native ethnologists discovered the porous boundaries between seen and unseen worlds: dimly lit museum halls, the mountainous villages of Tōhoku (a region of the island of Honshu, northeast Japan), and the island communities of Okinawa.[32] He had studied those who had learned to cross these lines. He wrote with a conviction that these were not spaces where weird remainders persisted, but places where forgotten practices and possibilities could again become familiar. His fascination with things from the Jōmon period (ca. 14,000 to 300 BCE) was not simply to elicit a rough, powerful form that could stand against the elitist, derivative aesthetics that he despised. Jonathan Reynolds has written that Okamoto believed that Jōmon pottery instantiated a dimension of "a mysterious spiritual world based on magic that Okamoto's contemporaries theorized was so central to the life of hunting-based societies."[33] These ceramic objects served as an index of a moment in which visible and invisible worlds coexisted, in which entities were not confined by their material forms, in which magic was a necessary practice in human life. Reynolds notes that Okamoto would go on to link art and magic more explicitly, arguing that the artist was a "magician who acted as an intermediary between his community and the mysterious forces unleashed through the creative process."[34]

Given the ways in which the spaces that interested him have been shaped by state development projects, economic marginalization, rural depopulation, colonial rule and its intendent practices of repression and prohibition, the genocide of war, and American military occupation, there is a resonance with the approaches that contemporary anthropologists have also brought to the question of shamanism.[35] Manuela Carneiro da Cunha frames the shaman as a kind of Benjaminian translator:

> What is the shaman's labor in the Amazon today? More generally, how should one account for the expansion of shamanism and its clientele in colonial situations since the sixteenth century? Which

shamanic power hierarchies and competences and which specific forms correspond to different political systems and to each kind of nexus between the local and the global? The shaman is, by his very trade, a translator. It is suggested here that translation should be understood in its strong, Benjaminian sense, as a search for resonances and reverberations between different codes and systems, and as a totalization of partial perspectives.[36]

Okamoto's project goes beyond producing an image of the past in a way that would be intelligible to moderns. He was determined to break down the barrier that confines these possibilities to a category so distanced from us as the past, to grasp them and use them in the moment. It is a project, a vocation, an art, for which he had been preparing himself for decades. As a student, he likely attended Anatole Lewitsky's lectures on shamanism at the Collège de Sociologie in 1937, exposing him to these problems and practices more than two decades before his first visit to Okinawa.[37] It is a subject that he returned to again and again in his work: in his essays about Tōhoku and Okinawa, in his reflections on his life in Paris, in his equation of art and magic, and in a whole sequence of paintings and sculpture created in the postwar era. His studies with Lewitsky, Mauss, and Kojève; his fascination with Otto and Eliade, point the way. At the center of it all is his relationship with Georges Bataille and the work that they did together.

Arriving in Paris in 1929, barely eighteen, he immersed himself in artistic practice. After several years working with artists such as Kurt Seligmann, then involved in the group Abstraction-Création, he began to be recognized. André Breton wrote approvingly of his exhibition of *Itamashiki ude* (Wounded arm) in Salon des Surindépendants, and he became more involved with the surrealists. However, he was still dissatisfied. Troubled by social fragmentation, the rise of fascism, and the possibility of war, he began to search for a new direction. He started to explore the relationship between art and the occult. Then, as he wrote in his memoirs, a chance invitation on a cold evening in 1936 by Max Ernst and Patrick Waldberg changed his life. He joined them at a gathering of Contre Attaque in Jean-Louis Barrault's studio in Paris— Okamoto remembered it as the place where Picasso had painted *Guernica*. Speakers like André Breton and Maurice Heine denounced a totalitarianism that they believed would destroy humanity, and bureaucratization that would crush all creative activity. And yet, it was Bataille, speaking late in the evening, who entranced Okamoto. In his halting words, in the project that he briefly sketched, Okamoto felt that he had discovered a kindred spirit.[38]

Bataille spoke of the danger of the moment and his frustration at what he perceived to be the inability of any initiative such as Contre Attaque to effect change. His concern went beyond the failure to respond to the ascendance of the Right. He was infuriated by the fascist appropriation of Nietzschean thought and committed himself to recover the radical potential of Nietzsche's work. This would be a political revolution effected by a withdrawal from conventional politics; an immersion in an ecstatic, creative practice that sought spiritual transformation in a world free of the weighty shadow of God. "We are ferociously religious and insofar as our existence amounts to the condemnation of everything that is known today, an inner necessity demands that we be equally unyielding. What we are starting is a war."[39] With these words in the inaugural issue of *Acéphale* in April 1936, Bataille initiated what he called a sacred conspiracy. By this time, he and Okamoto had met, and he brought Okamoto into that collaboration.[40] In their work together, Okamoto heard the call to ecstatic and critical practice, to the exploration of the hidden and the sacred, the renunciation of reason and calculation, the embrace of fate and chance. He discovered the similarity between the sorcerer's apprentice and the shaman. Their plan to reinvent the social sciences and reinvigorate art and literature was grounded in their determination to liberate the forces of the self that society had shackled with morality and convention. This was the idea behind the organization of the Collège de Sociologie, the public face of the project, and *Acéphale*, the private.

> If you really want to accomplish something in a place like Europe or in today's managed society, you need a kind of painless revolution. You have to get people to take it in without noticing the pain. Then it will be like cancer—spreading out until it permeates [society] in its entirety. That is the kind of perfect understanding Bataille had.
>
> This was the primary purpose of our secret society. It was a hidden group, united by a secret ceremonial vow, and bound up in all the ways that our research organization could spread the movement throughout society. I can't write clearly about it here, but there were rituals that took place, in the depths of the night, in the forest of Saint-Germain outside Paris. I threw myself, body and soul, into this Janus-faced movement. I felt as though I had an intense awakening.[41]

The practice of ethnology was crucial for the group—Mauss's students Leiris, Caillois, and Lewitsky were each deeply involved; Bataille, who was neither ethnologist nor student of Mauss, had nonetheless been inspired by his own heterodox reading of Mauss's work. Their meetings were often organized around lectures and discussions. Leiris and Caillois spoke on the sacred and the quotidian, Caillois on festivals, and Bataille on sacrifice. Klossowski lectured on Sade, and Kojève on Hegel. Walter Benjamin attended regularly, although a planned session devoted to his essay on Baudelaire came to nothing.[42]

At the same time, they collaborated in *Acéphale*, both the private collective and the published journal, to integrate theory and practice, a radical project of research and self-exploration that opened up ways to transform themselves and the world around them. Members were sworn to secrecy—perhaps Okamoto was remembering the strictures of their oath when he wrote of the fate that initiates at the Izaihō might suffer if they bore any hidden sins. Somehow this bond was kept: across the years, very little has been told of what the members did in their clandestine gatherings. They were encouraged to meditate and as consciously reflect on the lectures they attended. It has been said that there were quotidian rituals to be observed, such as the refusal to shake hands with anti-Semites. There might also have been a secret ritual to commemorate the execution of Louis XVI, that most acephalous of public ceremonies. More mysteriously, there were rumors of sacrifice. Some say that a gibbon had been offered, although Michel Surya dismisses that as a misreading of Bataille's fiction. Others say that a human sacrifice was planned, that Bataille himself had volunteered to be the offering, but no one would serve as sacrificer.[43] Okamoto intimates other ecstatic practices—the most mysterious, that dance by firelight in the forest at Marly. It is not difficult to imagine that this was an inspiration for his postwar painting *Yoru* (Night), in which a woman clad in a plain white dress stands before a menacing, undulating tree, a death's head hidden in its branches, a knife concealed behind her back.[44]

The form that these transgressions took remains unclear. Surely nothing compares with their experiences in the war to come. Still, it is not necessary to have a precise record of the events staged by *Acéphale* to understand their efforts. The public project of social research was not a cover for the outré. The two were integral parts of a critical and experiential whole. Their intertwined objectives were to develop an understanding of a kind of Maussian totality so that they could penetrate to its essence. However, unlike ethnologists and sociologists, the principle expressions of their work would not be monographs, lectures, or museum exhibitions. Rather, they would plunge into their discoveries, effacing the distinction between subject and object in their own practice. The counterpoint between the figures of the practical sacred and the academic profane are crucial here. The objective was to embrace excess, to be immersed in horror, to engage in actions that exceeded the boundaries of convention. To do so would require one to abandon oneself to the experience of death and decay that lies at the heart of all life, but to do so supplemented by a scholarly perspective that allows one to recognize a field that goes beyond human experience, for which the experience of death is incommunicable. Only then could they bring about a total transformation of the self. Bataille wrote:

> From now on, your joy will debase and trample underfoot your repose, your sleep, and even your suffering. Remember that truth is not stable ground but the ceaseless movement that destroys all that you are and all that you see.
>
> REMEMBER THAT IN WAR IS TRUTH
>
> You will not cease before you recognize yourself as a man who carries within him a hope great enough to demand all sacrifices.
>
> This Memento will remind you that from this moment you can no longer expect any peace from yourself.[45]

As Okamoto recalled in his memoir of his work with Bataille, he committed himself to the project of breaking through the limitations imposed by contemporary norms and morals, discovering a reserve of energy within himself that could transform the world. However, he also began to feel doubt about the direction taken under Bataille's charismatic leadership, something that went beyond conventional disagreements and clashes of personality that marked many prewar radical movements.

> And yet, I somehow began to feel an undefinable contradiction. In the final analysis, there is always the "will to power," even in this kind of pure and spiritual moment. In their single-minded efforts to reach this will to power, I began to feel a gap that I could not accept. Isn't there a path with a more humane existence? I questioned whether we could impose our will upon others. At the same time and with equal intensity, I began to feel something within me that I did not want to acknowledge. It's something that I've felt in the depths of my heart since I was a child, but now I was made conscious of it. If I were to be

understood, to be accepted, if that were to be resolved, my authentic existence would disappear. I want to make people accept me but, at the same time I don't. I won't let them do it. Isn't that the real dialectic of human existence?[46]

Okamoto acknowledges his discomfort with being completely known and understood, the regularity and limitations that recognition would impose on him, even if acceptance by his friends depends upon it. He links this to the fundamental dilemma that he faced in the political mobilization of the Nietzschean, ecstatic capacity that Bataille and his collaborators were determined to wrest from fascism. If he could find this capacity within himself, it must exist among others as well. How could he impose his will on others, even if his intention was to liberate their own creative capacities?

Okamoto was not alone in his reservations about the direction that their project had taken. Mauss famously denounced Bataille's group in a letter to Caillois, after his shocked reading of the dissertation that would become *Le mythe et l'homme.*

What I believe is a general derailment—of which you yourself are a victim—is the sort of absolute irrationalism with which you conclude in the name of a modern myth: the labyrinth and Paris. But I believe that, right now, all you are probably under the influence of Heidegger, a Bergsonian held back by Hitlerism, legitimizing a Hitlerism infatuated with irrationalism. And, above all, it's the political philosophy of sorts that you try to draw from it, in the name of poetry and vague sentimentality. As persuaded as I am that poets and men of great eloquence can sometimes establish the rhythms of social life, so too am I skeptical of the capacities of a philosophy of any kind, and especially of a philosophy of Paris, to establish the rhythms of anything at all.[47]

The attack also came from critical theory. Benjamin's association, while it served his own purposes, also reflected those of his colleagues in Frankfurt. For many years, the Institüt für Sozialforschung (Institute for Social Research) had followed the activities of critics and scholars in Paris, attentive to the possibilities of a collaboration as they established a base of operations for the institute in France. Max Horkheimer and Theodor Adorno carefully read the work of "the *Acéphale* circle," with Horkheimer visiting them in Paris. However, it was Benjamin who grew closest to them. During his time in

Paris, he became intimate enough with Bataille to entrust his papers to him before his death. Intellectually, his response was more ambivalent. He was an enthusiastic reader of Leiris's work, and there are a number of citations of Caillois in the manuscripts for the Arcades Project.[48] And yet, Benjamin was deeply critical of what he saw as their overall ideological orientation. His greatest reservations seemed to be around their emphasis on stance—the embodied instantiation of ideology—and he worried that their analysis of fascism risked recapitulating its structure.[49] It is not difficult to see this possibility. Caillois's foundational essay "The Winter Wind"—included with Bataille's "Sorcerer's Apprentice" and Leiris's "Essay on Everyday Life" in the first issue of *Acéphale*—valorizes the performance of confident masculinity against what he sees as a directionless bourgeois individualism. Here, he further elaborates a position that he first articulated in earlier texts that called for a life of voluntary servitude.[50]

Benjamin responded to Caillois's position in an essay published under the pseudonym J. E. Mabinn: "[Pathological cruelty] represents now the necessary basis for the revelation of the 'superior meaning' immanent to the praxis of monopolistic capital, which prefers to use its means 'for destruction, instead of using them for utility and happiness.' When he says: 'one works for the liberation of beings that one wants to have serve and that one hopes to see obedient only toward oneself' so he has with great simplicity characterized fascist praxis."[51]

Beyond the question of stance, Horkheimer and Adorno felt that the entire project was constructed on a flawed intellectual framework. They were dismissive of the revolutionary possibilities of a form of critical theory built upon Kojève's notion of the dialectic, which they found to be technically competent but ungrounded in materialist praxis and unquestioningly pro-Soviet. Moreover, they saw the members of the circle as overreaching, avocational scholars, whose conversant understanding of philosophy was characterized by endless description without critique.

Okamoto's concerns both intersect with and diverge from those of these skeptics. Bataille's insights presented Okamoto with a dilemma: he wants to open himself to the possibilities that the experience of the secular (or perhaps the resacralized) sacred might present so that he can develop his own capacities. However, he does not wish to impose his own discipline on others; nor does he want to be subjected to theirs. Unable to reconcile his convictions with his work in *Acéphale*, Okamoto wrote to Bataille, expressing these sentiments, and he withdrew from the activities of Bataille's collective.[52] He seems to have remained on good terms with Bataille, and he spent his remaining time in Paris creating art and immersed in Maussian ethnology.

Although he had distanced himself from the projects of *Acéphale* and the Collège de Sociologie, Okamoto returned to these concerns in his postwar exploration of mainland Japan, and in his essays on the essence of Japanese being. In the narrative account of these travels, we can learn more about that which he carried with him, the expectations and desires that would organize his project. Of course, we cannot see the memories of his studies, but we brush against its traces in the books that he kept. In 2011, Sasaki Hidenori curated an exhibition at the Okamoto Tarō Museum of the most frequently read books from Okamoto's personal library, a constellation that perhaps inspired his voyages and shaped his work upon his return. Familiar texts by Mauss and Kojève, and an extensive selection of Bataille's writing, stood alongside a wide-ranging collection of postwar works by Claude Lévi-Strauss and Mircea Eliade. Of these, Sakaki writes, the most heavily annotated was Eliade's *Le chamanisme*, published in 1951. These were all books that Okamoto acquired after the war: his original collection was destroyed in the American firebombing of Tokyo.[53]

The influence of the native ethnologist Yanagita Kunio's Okinawan work on Okamoto's project are manifestly clear as well.[54] For both men, the turn to Okinawa represents a search of the southern islands for an analog to the knowledge and practices produced in the mountains of mainland Japan, a reserve of difference gathered against the transformations of modernity. It is no accident that Okamoto's voyage from island to island follows closely in the wake of Yanagita's own travels. Alan Christy has suggested that the narrative structure of Yanagita's collection—like Lévi-Strauss's *Tristes Tropiques*, which stood on Okamoto's bedside bookshelf—instantiates a deliberate conflation of time and space, a movement into a shared past as Yanagita sailed further into the southern islands.[55] While the relationship of narrative to temporality carries over to Okamoto's work, the chronotope that he crafts is much more heterogeneous. The industrial and the agricultural, the rural and the urban, the place of silent spirits and the world of American imperialism are all gathered together in an uneven totality in Okamoto's text. What's more, he presents himself as one capable of detecting these different space-times, and of navigating from one to the other. Cosmopolitan Okinawan artists and professionals might take him to a performance or to a rural shrine, priestesses might speak to him of their deities, struggling workers might confess their frustrations with industrial capitalism or rural idiocy, but it is Okamoto who can experience each of these moments in their own terms, as well as interpret them for his readers. And, perhaps, he can do something more than that.

His ambitions emerge in his introduction, a moment that evokes Yanagita's preface to *Kainan Shōki*. In that passage, Yanagita recounts his visit to Geneva several years after completing the travels narrated in the text. The wintery city echoes the chill reception he received in his attempts to meet with the foundational scholar of modern Japan, Basil Hall Chamberlain, who had moved to Switzerland a decade earlier. Although Chamberlain rebuffs his efforts, Yanagita still acknowledges the love that animated Chamberlain's project, and avows his commitment to assume the mantle of native ethnology, advancing the objectives set by his predecessor while rectifying his errors—explicating the deep sameness that unites both Okinawa and Japan.[56] As we will see, Okamoto appropriates the form as well as the critique. However, it is Okamoto who will succeed Yanagita, much as Yanagita replaced Chamberlain.

In the text, I can also feel intimations of Leiris's *L'Afrique fantôme*, his account of the Dakar-Djibouti expedition.[57] Okamoto does not attempt to sustain the immediacy of Leiris's narrative or its reliance on the contemporary record of his dreams and experiences. As I have said: Okamoto is too committed to calling together different times and different possibilities to restrict himself. Even so, they seem to share an ambiguous mix of desire, respect, and condescension toward the Other that they encounter. Beyond Leiris's responsibilities as secretary to Marcel Griaule, the expedition leader, he hoped that the scientific promise of ethnology could establish a reflexive account of the distortions created by the unrecognized racial ideology that configures the perceptions and conceptions of white European colonizers. At the same time, he acknowledged his own racial fantasies, noting that his project, however critical its objectives, was driven by his attentiveness to "the singular attraction—at once mystical and erotic—exerted by the black race on those that comprehend it."[58]

The traces of this tension—to discover something that is prefigured by the negation of the known, while still acknowledging the fantasy that underwrites the project—can also be found in Okamoto's work. In his introductory chapter to *Okinawa Bunkaron*, he writes a passionate indictment of modern narratives that not only obscure memories of a Japanese colonial regime that stripped Okinawans of their very language, prohibited their performing arts, and drove them to their deaths, but also offers callous critiques of Okinawan compliance and mindless loyalty. Filled with a sense of empathy that allows him to "taste their misery," he entreats his readers to restore freedom to these occupied and impoverished islands; not the false freedom of reversion to Japanese rule, but one that allows its true possibilities to be realized. Still, in the span of a few pages, he can write: "I love Okinawans. Dark colored, bright eyes, hairy bodies—thick and strong. And yet, they are gentle."[59] Dismayed at the ways in which Okinawan women rebuff his efforts to photograph them, turning away each time he presses the shutter, he cannot imagine that they are responding to his lack of restraint, his imposition upon them. Instead, he naturalizes their behavior: they turn away from him "like the way that a plant just naturally closes its leaves when a typhoon is coming." In one metaphor, Okamoto reveals the discovery of that which he expects, as well as the political critique that exceeds his own observation. As Leiris's own memoir intimates, the recognition of the humanity of the Other, and the desire for—and right to—that alterity, are deeply imbricated in one another.

Okamoto's organization of the text also seems to find a sly inspiration in the form of narratives such as Watsuji Tetsurō's *Kōji Junrei* (A pilgrimage to ancient temples). Both begin with overdetermined figures of modernist movement and transformation into archaic or forgotten worlds: Okamoto sets out by plane, freighter, and car; Watsuji by train. Watsuji announces his intention to explore significant sites of representation, forms that he argues will allow the reader to experience the determinate categories of Japanese aesthetics. And yet, before he departs, he visits a friend living closer to home who has invited him to contemplate a reproduction of the famous Ajanta wall paintings in his private collection. Watsuji uses this opportunity to set out his argument about the ways in which the environmental specificity of India configures the forms of representation reproduced in the work, to tease out the presence and absence of Greek influences, and explore his own response to viewing these reproductions, an experience that is both critical and affective. This introduction lays the groundwork for his project of viewing of Buddhist iconography in the travels to follow.[60]

Okamoto had already critiqued projects such as this. His *Nihon no Dentō* began with a response to this popular genre of narrative, which recount the respectful visits that pedantic scholars made to valorized sites of antiquity.[61] He wrote of his distaste for any search for the origins of Japanese culture that was bound and distorted by a sterile academic reliance on aesthetic theory, or a genealogy that gives undue reverence to elaborate foreign inspirations. While Watsuji wrote about ancient influences from classical Greece that he detected in the work of unnamed temple craftsmen in Kyōtō, Okamoto conceived of a project that was concerned with a world that was at once more archaic and more immediate. A project that he believed demonstrated how seen and unseen worlds could be brought together by one who had the attentiveness, vision, and artistry to do so. As Okamoto wrote, reflecting on the terrible fire that caused extensive damage to Hōryūji temple in 1949: "It's OK to burn Hōryūji, as long as you can be Hōryūji."[62]

And yet, the object that he considers as he begins his account of his travels to Okinawa is every bit as overdetermined as Adjanta murals or famous temples. While the title of Okamoto's introductory chapter—"Okinawa no hatazawari" (Feeling Okinawan on my skin)—raises expectations for an account of the sensuous embodied experience of the southern islands, it immediately defers those reminiscences for something closer at hand. As Yanagita Kunio sought out Chamberlain, his flawed literary ancestor, and as Watsuji contemplates an archaic mural, Okamoto effects a similar move, turning to Yanagita's own account of a horrific event in rural Gifu:

> A story of a charcoal maker in his late fifties living in Mino. His wife had died, so he was left with only his thirteen-year-old son. Wondering what he should do, he adopted a little girl of about the same age. And so they lived together in his tiny charcoal maker's hut in the mountains. For some reason, he just couldn't sell any charcoal and, whenever he went down into the village, he had a hard time earning enough for just one *gō* of rice. Even on that last day, he came back empty handed. It was too painful for him to see the tiny starving faces of the children, so he just slept the day away in the back of the hut. When he woke up, the late afternoon sun was shining through his doorway. It was the end of autumn.
>
> His children were crouching down in the illuminated doorway, working seriously at something. When he looked to see what they were doing, he could tell that they were working as hard as they could to sharpen the edge of his great axe. They said, "Please kill us with this!" Using the timber that was stacked by the door as a pillow, they lay down on their backs. Seeing that, with no thought for the consequences, he giddily took off their heads with the axe.[63]

This is one of the most famous passages in Yanagita Kunio's work, originally published in 1926 in the book *Yama no Jinsei*, and is widely read and often reproduced.[64] In *Overcome by Modernity*, Harry Harootunian argued that this narrative instantiates a signal dimension of the work of the native ethologist: the incredible act of memory necessary to remember the experience of this obscure and inarticulate charcoal maker. Locating himself at the end of "an unbroken chain of signification" that authorized the construction of these accounts, there is a deeply melancholy quality to Yanagita's project.[65] And yet, there is more to Yanagita's account than the pessimism of witnessing and postmemory, a sense that the difficult lives lived on the margins of capitalist modernity become increasingly inaccessible to cosmopolitan moderns.[66] Against this material loss, something new is coming into being. In Yanagita's narrative of rural suffering and inescapable, violent death, something else has emerged. Marilyn Ivy has written of this as a foundational characteristic of native ethnology: the necessary disappearance of the object that allows its ghostly reappearance through an authoritatively rendered text. However, Okamoto's ambitions exceed the material boundaries of the essay and of disciplinary practice.[67]

While Akasaka Norio has argued that Okamoto's citation of Yanagita is crucial to understanding *Okinawa Bunkaron*, he draws an important distinction between the popular reception of the charcoal maker's account as an indictment of rural poverty and human abjection, and Okamoto's own interpretation.[68] By his own admission, Okamoto eschewed conventional politics and resisted involving himself in any kind of direct action. He was not sympathetic to the humanistic projects of scholars such as the ethnographer Miyamoto Tsuneichi, who had also reproduced Yanagita's famous passage in his *Nihon Zankoku Monogatari* (A tale of Japanese poverty)—the collection where Okamoto first read of the charcoal maker.[69] After Kojève, he understands that all history is tragic, that the modern world is propelled forward by struggle and by war.[70] Okamoto also evinced little interest in the textual strategies that have attracted many folklorists to this particular passage in Yanagita's work, and that have been thoughtfully critiqued.[71] In any case, a critique of his text would have to take into account the complex productive relationships in which his narratives were assembled from notes and dictation by Okamoto Toshiko.

And yet, there is something terrifying about Okamoto's retelling this tale in an introduction to his reflections on life in Okinawa. Regardless of what Yanagita might have intended when he wrote the account in 1926, how could Okamoto not see the story as an allegory for the ideology that compelled Okinawan wartime sacrifice? The gentle, hard-working father as a model of the emperor; the loyal, self-sacrificing children as his subjects. The act, a beautiful performance offered out of love and accepted with love and gratitude. Perhaps the adopted daughter could even be read as standing for Okinawa or for colonies written more broadly: feminized, rescued from elsewhere, eager to do her part but following the lead of her elder brother.

In spite of all of this, something in the narrative resonated with Okamoto in a way that the accounts of a thousand other deaths in a thousand other villages did not. Something that penetrated the numbing routine of an everyday life that otherwise allowed the modern Japanese to keep both the horror and the possibilities of another way of being at bay.[72]

Okamoto's retelling of his initial encounter with Yanagita's narrative captures his intimation of something beyond the political indictment of rural poverty and death. He has discovered a kind of Nietzschean elsewhere, a place beyond conventional politics.

> I had never felt shock like this before. The beauty on the edge (*giri-giri no utsukushisa*) of human life. At first glance, this might seem to be a miserable conclusion, but this is the transparent flow of life. More than any other kind of nature, it is fresh and indomitable. It is also tremblingly symbolic of but a single moment in the eternal struggle of human beings to survive. Like [the feeling of] the texture of silk stockings, it isn't an experience that you can capture through humanism or ethics. By contemporary moral standards, surely it would be considered in a negative light. But what of its cruel beauty, its strength, its innocence?[73]

Okamoto acknowledges that his interpretation of this experience runs counter to that which contemporary moral standards would impose. He responds, not to the searing critique of rural devastation and the indifference of the Japanese state that characterizes most readings of the story of the charcoal maker—particularly in Miyamoto's appropriation of the account—but to a sensation, a feeling that arises in him, a moment of communion with some ineffable dimension of the world opened by Yanagita's narrative. In doing so he reveals another form of movement, one that allows him to touch this invisible world.

Okamoto's text is informed by the temporal interventions of native ethnologists; and yet, his project differs in important ways. Having reproduced Yanagita's account of the charcoal maker, the narrative reverses time to the moment before the axe falls, and to the beauty of that most minimal act.

That first cruel story that I chose: against the backdrop of a blazing sunset, in the doorway of a starving charcoal maker's hut, children are sharpening an axe. In their hands, the blade glitters brightly. And in that brightness, eternity presents itself. It is a world without hesitation. In this way, it moves and completes itself—in and of itself, both cause and effect. It is neither weak nor strong. There is no morality nor immorality to it. It is impossible that the fate of Japan and the world around us is not related to this fundamental duration of time. It is a different problem altogether to ask whether or not this is good for the Okinawan people. But if we look at ourselves, the present is somehow incomplete and there is nothing we can do about our own feelings of emptiness.[74]

It is productive to understand this episode from *Yama no Jinsei* as an appropriation of nativist tropes, inflecting Yanagita Kunio's melancholy project with the understanding of transformational practice that Okamoto and his collaborators developed during their studies with Kojève, particularly in his lectures on Hegel and death. Okinawans are not the only ones capable of a transvaluation of value—Okamoto himself effects a parallel move.

In the child's preparation of the axe, Okamoto presents us with a moment in which a subject reflexively discovers itself, separates itself out from its being in nature. Kojève serves as inspiration here, writing, "In order to *be* human and in order to manifest himself or appear as such, that Man must be able to die and must know how to risk his life."[75] The children may or may not be attempting to sacrifice themselves so that their father might survive. That point, as well as any consideration of how long they might have survived if they had not been killed, is unimportant to an argument grounded in this Kojèvean critical exploration of death. All possibilities lead to tragedy. But in that moment, the children rejected servility—the helplessness and misery of rural abjection—and humanized themselves, an act that was acknowledged by the recognition accorded to them by their father. More than that, they recognized him—the sacrifices he had made, the abjection he had endured on their behalf. Inspired by their actions, their example, the gift of their acknowledgment, he also acted. It is a practice that captures the important points of Kojève's reading of Hegel: the negative of the being that is man, the struggle that creates actual men, the labor that creates the cultural world.[76]

These considerations are central to Bataille's work on sacrifice during his collaboration with Okamoto in *Acéphale*; they are foundational to the critical project that led to his theory of the economy of excess in *The Accursed Share*, a Maussian-inspired exploration of the ways in which people go beyond the carefully calibrated exchanges of Lévi-Strauss, capturing the mad, joyful, Nietzschean expression of the will, the creation of an autonomous self in the moment, without regard for the future. It is clear that Okamoto and Bataille shared this interest in blood and sacrifice. In 1972, Okamoto writes of his first exposure to images of Aztec ritual, something that he almost certainly explored with Bataille in the 1930s. He recounts a mythic narrative of sacrifice, deities willingly hurling themselves into a raging bonfire in order to be transformed into a higher order—the sun, the moon. He recalls the ecstatic dance of warriors who tore themselves to pieces in festivals of renewal, and the icy courage of sacrificial victims who unhesitatingly offered themselves up to the priests' stone blades. Thrilled, horrified, excited by this stunningly unfamiliar practice, he writes of the excess of blood offered to reply to the gods for the unrepayable gift of life. "Blood spilled at this dignified yet harsh sanctuary is proof of an existence residing within chaos and functions as a pivot on which the universe acts as balance."[77] It is possible that Okamoto's travels in Okinawa, along with his oft-repeated revulsion at war and ruminations about human sacrifice, could have inspired a critique of the wartime slaughter of Japanese soldiers and Okinawan civilians that concluded the Battle of Okinawa. Perhaps he could make sense of the act of a people similarly indebted to their god-emperor when given the opportunity to spill an excess of blood. Perhaps, in that moment of convergence between sacrificer and sacrifice, when soldiers willingly extended their attacks beyond any fixed point in space and time, victory or defeat; when soldiers and civilians alike showed the "extraordinary courage" to kill their loved ones and take their own lives, Okamoto could have crafted a new form of critique.

However, Okamoto's argument takes a different turn. Rather than focusing on the excess of violence and death on the battlefield, he chooses instead to vilify the Japanese commanders who led Okinawans to their senseless deaths. Instead of exploring the logic of mad joyous violence that includes Okinawans as well as mainland Japanese, he focuses on ideology and forms of domination. In responding to a Japanese critic who characterized the Okinawans who fought and died in the war as having "the loyalty of an animal," Okamoto wrote in their defense:

You can say that there were systems of military and bureaucratic oppression. There is nothing animalistic about it. We must make that point clear. . . . I've heard what prewar politicians and bureaucrats thought of Okinawans. I've had it with the governmental and educational programs that were put in place after the disestablishment of the *han* system in order to subjugate the Okinawan people. The Okinawan people were not allowed to live in their islands as themselves. Under the disagreeable sign of Kōminka [becoming imperial subjects], Okinawans were treated like savages and disciplined by their immersion in a system of standardization that compelled conformity.[78]

It is not for lack of evidence that Okamoto defers any deeper consideration. While a new era of remembrance was ignited by the critical oral histories published by the two main newspapers and publishers in Okinawa, the *Okinawa Times* and the *Ryūkyū Shimpo*, in the 1990s, important work had already been done. In 1950, the *Okinawa Times* published *Tetsu no Bōfū* (Violent storm of steel), a detailed exploration of the wartime experiences of ordinary Okinawans.[79] By the time of his first visit, a cosmopolitan traveler like Okamoto could have had access to a significant amount of critical literature, from pamphlets and newspaper editorials to plays and novels. Okinawa was alive with debates over American occupation and militarism, the possibility of social and political transformation through independence, and the desirability and dangers of a return to the Japanese state.[80] He is attentive to its material traces—as he tours the battlefields, as he walks the streets of occupied Naha, as he notes the destruction of Kudaka and impact of war in Ishigaki. And yet, he makes little effort to represent his discussions about the war. His banter with a young waitress at his Naha hotel gives him an occasion to reflect on the Okinawan character, but he never considers the fact that she would have been a child during the war and its aftermath. Instead, he writes as if he had arrived in Okinawa with his feelings about war fully developed. Perhaps he feels a painful resonance with his own memories: two years before this visit to Okinawa, he had written that he still bore the traces of his service, scars across the knuckles of his hand and deeper marks within.[81]

On his return from Europe, Okamoto was conscripted into the Imperial army, serving in a motorized rifle regiment in China until his unit surrendered. As a soldier in a colonial army, he had an opportunity to witness brutality and violence in every possible configuration. He would see it on the battlefield and in the occupation of the Chinese communities through which they passed, although he maintained that he never fired a shot. He personally experienced the arrogance that he ascribed to military officers, and he remembered the callous ignorance with which he was treated by his fellow soldiers. Surely, he remembered the year that he spent in China after defeat and demobilization—a year driving trucks and doing odd jobs as a prisoner. Finally, I wonder if he is speaking in terms of his own identification with the Okinawan people, rather than with the Imperial army. Perhaps he remembers the ways in which the Nietzschean will to power that he had discovered and cultivated in France had been crushed by military discipline. As a soldier, he was not free to express himself as he chose. He was forced to do nothing; when he was given an opportunity to create something, it was to make representational art at the whim of his superiors. He was only free to live his life as a soldier.[82]

His reflections on the war unresolved, he leaves the tourist-haunted battlefields and the dense, urban spaces of Naha and Koza, teeming with American soldiers, behind. After his initial frustration, he seems to surrender himself to the pleasures of repetition, to a voyage into the past guided by Yanagita Kunio's earlier example. With a kind of mimetic magic, he turns to the south, moving his body and his text like an incantation. Conjuring the essence of Okinawa. Finding airline charter services to Ishigaki and Miyako suspended, Okamoto, like Yanagita decades earlier, boards a ship bound for the islands. However, his nativist reveries are complicated when a flight of American jets swoop across the bows. Okamoto embraces the fragmentary, uneven texture of the voyage. As he explores a village in Ishigaki, he recounts his dreamlike sense of moving through the darkened streets of a medieval Japanese castle town; he also describes his contingent friendship with a jovial American lieutenant—the local commander of a three-man garrison of military occupiers—who drives him around the island in his jeep and drinks with him at an inn at this intersection of disparate times and places. The Ishigaki that he finds is not a space isolated from the present—it is subject to wars of destruction and development that keep it in a state of unevenness poised on the edge of catastrophe.[83]

Although the dissonance that Okamoto experienced in Naha between the rhythms of the modern world and the pace of Okinawan daily life persist, it is transformed again as the impact of Japanese and Ryūkyūan colonization and American occupation seem to diminish. More of the buried practices that compel him appear, and he is able to explore the tensions that he first identified in Naha. Although Kudaka lies no more than 250 miles from the airport in Naha, efforts to articulate the small communities he visits with larger networks of capitalist production and exchange seem absurd. Okamoto notes that, despite its natural beauty, the climate and weather are a threat to any notion of progress. Villages, many resettled from the main island, struggle in absolute poverty to rebuild their meager homesteads, destroyed by the typhoon that had just swept through the islands. Nearby, he finds the graves of thousands of Japanese soldiers, killed by malaria during the war, a disease that raged through the islands until American public health efforts brought it under control. Okamoto also writes of a small village where he discovered piles of desiccated peanuts. He learns that the villagers had grown them as a possible cash crop but left them to rot when they realized that the market price was too low to cover their transportation costs. Okinawans can grow a wide variety of fruits and vegetables in their gardens, they eat a diet far more varied and interesting than residents of Naha, but their fields lie too far beyond the space-time of contemporary commerce for them to do more than enjoy them as part of their traditional lifestyles.[84]

Outside intervention seems no more successful. He writes about a recent project to develop the local agricultural base by shifting to pineapple production. With mainland Japanese capital investment, people planted fields and built a cannery. However, production outstripped demand and the aspiring entrepreneurs were left with an excess of three thousand tons of pineapple that simply rotted. In Okamoto's words, "human effort and mechanical production were all wasted."[85] The pessimism with which he writes leaves the reader with a depressing awareness of the futility of any effort to bring together what must be kept apart. Amid this destitution, the pleasure that one might already experience in Naha—*izakaya*, cabarets, cinema, brothels, hotels, bathhouses, restaurants—are totally absent. Only two transistor radios mark the time of recreation in the village. Their days may be structured by the endless labor of clearing fields, rebuilding and repairing their homesteads, growing crops, and fishing, but the modern circuits of consumption interlaced with production are almost entirely absent. There is only the endless repetition of work and rest. Like the mythical traveler Urashima Tarō in the southern seas, he finds a group of bored children amusing themselves by tipping over a tortoise and laughing as it struggles.[86] In many ways these remembrances are politically compelling: he writes with an almost Clastres-like rejection of the state, dismissing every institution from the Kingdom of Ryūkyū to the American military occupation.[87]

In the case of war and occupation, it seems that Okinawan subjectivity and creativity are irrelevant. The forms that interest Okamoto can only be found elsewhere. It is when writing of the margins of Okinawa—Ishigaki, Kudaka, Ōgimi—that he discovers them. He seemingly inverts Bataille's emphasis on excess, presenting instead an act of symmetrical reduction: the minimal beauty of lives and practices almost incapable of producing any kind of surplus rather than those of grand gesture. In fact, it actually parallels Bataille's argument in *The Accursed Share*: it is simply that the excess that Okinawans offer with courage, joy, and abandon is so small. Here, the manifest form of Yanagita Kunio's tale of the charcoal maker is central to what will be the theme of Okamoto's book: the aesthetics of a people whose lives are so precarious that even the smallest surplus cannot be taken for granted.

> It's not strange to consider people, stone walls, baskets and ships without differentiating them. All of them are manifestations of the existence that breathes in this place. They are expressions of the same value, the same quality. They are all beautiful, but this is not the beauty of something that was intentionally made beautiful. There is no more to the line than that which is necessary for everyday life. It is something that appears in the constant repetition and repetition of a pattern in which nothing goes beyond the necessary.[88]

His essay invests Okinawa with a powerful sense of difference and power, one that is explicitly at odds with the late 1950s and early 1960s valorization of Japan as a nation emerging from social and economic catastrophe through the herculean efforts of its people, drawing on its traditional values to create a modern ideal of production and consumption. Okamoto argues that the power of Okinawa lies in precisely the opposite direction. It is only when the trappings of consumer society and the pleasures of excess are stripped away that the true power and beauty of everyday life can be experienced. Okamoto's Okinawans tread a fine line between a nativist ontology of sameness and repetition, and a modern society of endless transformation driven by the logic of capital. He finds both beauty and purity in their efforts to transform themselves, but he rejects any actions that would reflexively build on that transformation to ethically create a new society. They can act creatively, but only to a certain degree, always falling short of escaping the repetition of sameness.

The forms of unevenness that Okamoto records in his brief travels through Okinawa are worth considering. He does not see these as signs of Okinawa's violent and painful integration into a capitalist system, its struggle with persisting Japanese colonial institutions, and the embrace of the expanding American empire. By evoking the determinations of climate, he suggests that Okinawans can't be fully modern: failed peanut and pineapple ventures, labor migration from the mainland, distance to markets and cost of transportation, a climate more dangerous than the main island. And yet, this narrative of the past often distracts him from critical resolution of the immanent contradictions that he perceptively notes.[89] His limited encounter with the Okinawan everyday becomes the occasion to foreground the relationship between the mnestic and the graphic—embodied memory and text.

In doing so, he does not see that the tentative attempts of Okinawans to articulate their own practices with the central Japanese economy were but the most recent skirmishes in a century-long struggle. In staging their efforts in a seemingly unfamiliar network of modern production, he makes no mention of a century of capitalist development that preceded Okamoto's voyage and the contested industrialization of agriculture in these very islands.[90] He ignores decades of intensive exploitation of the labor power of workers born and raised here, and sucked into factories in Osaka, Kawasaki, and Yokohama; of the same workers that were cast back to their native villages when work became scarce, forced to rely on the resources of family and community.[91] Instead, he pushes back to an earlier past, to a time in which both Satsuma (the domain in western Japan that controlled Ryūkyū during the Tokugawa era) and Shuri exploited the villagers as forced workers, shattering their families and their communities, moving them from island to island as their plans demanded, making men servile and women concubines. His encounter with failed forms of industrial capitalism on Ishigaki Island inspires a long rumination on the work of native ethnologists like Yanagita Kunio and Orikuchi Shinobu, recalling the abjection of local people by their Ryūkyūan or Satsuma overlords centuries before. While Okamoto does not quite grasp the continuity, he notes that bored young men await the opportunity to escape—surplus laborers from the main island are shipped in to replace them as they go.

As attentive as he is to their abjection, he rarely acknowledges their manifest political activity. Okinawans contested the inequity of capitalist modernization on the basis of alternate plans to more reasonably accomplish the same objectives; they fought against exploitation on the basis of clearly defined political positions and socioeconomic critique; they resisted on grounds all of their own. Okamoto did not need to be expert in the rural sociology of the Miyako Islands or the origins of the mainland industrial proletariat in order to understand this dimension of Okinawan political subjectivity. Three years before his visit, Okinawa had erupted in violent rebellion over the continued appropriation of land for American military use and the efforts of American officials to interfere with the election of Senaga Kamejiro, a communist and vociferous anti-base activist, as the mayor of Naha. He makes no mention of the work of smugglers to connect the Okinawan islands that he visited with a thriving covert East Asian market, and he hears nothing of the struggles of local men and women to establish a socialist experiment in Ishigaki itself. It was all there to be seen, and it could be found in the streets of Koza and the council rooms of Naha as easily as it could be located in Yaeyama. "I'll pay it back thorough seasonal labor," went the punchline to so many of the bitterly comic dialogs by the duo Surimu Kurabu that I discussed in chapter 1. The painful experiences that ground their performances have deep roots in the Okinawan past.[92]

Even so, in Okinawa, Okamoto sees something more than islands of idyllic rural villages and archaic custom that have somehow survived the furious onslaught of fascist imperialism, war, and capitalist modernity. It is more than just the "ancient living in the modern." "Kamagami to shima" (Gods and the island), the essay describing his visit to Kudaka, bears the traces of this project: intimations of a cruel, austere aesthetic, and a desire to experience it so intense that he made his way among the dead in Gusō. And yet, it is still rural space in which the immediate referent of *girigiri no utsukushisa*—the faintest trace of beauty that suffuses a life from which all luxury, all surplus, has been and will be beyond reach—persists.[93]

Constrained by a history of deprivation, he believes that Okinawans create objects with only the most minimal ornamentation. In lives lacking any kind of surplus that would authorize leisure or comfort, everything must be functional or it will not be made. At the same time, there is an aesthetic to this life of austerity, a style that is difficult for the modern eye to discern. Where a contemporary Japanese critic or collector might see a kind of early expression of functional design, Okamoto argues that it is important to recognize that Okinawans themselves are working expressively with a palate limited by material constraint. Unless you are guided by a subtle observer, you might miss the faint traces of excess in their poverty.[94]

The aesthetic that he describes is not limited to a set of patterns developed at some time in the past and then remembered and redeployed. Because the conditions of oppression and scarcity to which Okinawans are subject are repeated ceaselessly and remorselessly, he argues that they never lose touch with these practices. It matters little if they are ruled by a distant king in Shuri, a brutal daimyo in Kyushu, an aloof emperor in Tokyo, or a disinterested American commissioner in Naha. The effects are the same.

These austere conditions are not simply the result of political exploitation. The aftermath of a typhoon in Ishigaki looks much the same as communities depopulated by malaria a century ago, or a village destroyed in the Battle of Okinawa a decade earlier. The traces of disaster are depressingly uniform.

Discovering Nothing

As the account of Okamoto's travels in *Okinawa Bunkaron* continues, the reader finds him making his first visit to the ethnologically overdetermined island of Kudaka nearly a decade before the visit that caused so much controversy at the symposium. He memorably sketches the poverty and isolation of the two small villages on the island, then turns to something else: the experience of the numinous, "that which has been a mystery to him for so long." The title of the chapter, "Kami to Ki to Ishi" (Gods and trees and stones), anticipates what follows. The description of his experience of the island is interwoven with an explication of his readings of Rudolf Otto and Mircea Eliade, and what he learned during his work with Bataille. Rather than a conventional ethnographic investigation of a certain practice at a particular place and time, his description of his walk around the island becomes a kind of Ricœurian interpretation of remembered texts.[95]

Despite his attentiveness to the consequences of war, and the enduring inequality of life under Japanese influence, he returns to the theme of an essential dimension of Okinawanness, one that continues to repeat itself in everyday practices and is instantiated in the organization of social space. Earlier, he described this as the vertiginous experience of nothingness, or "nani mo nai koto" no memai.

> What I felt, most of all, in the *utaki* (sacred grove)—unexpectedly, at that—was the absences of things and the way that they interfere with life. The *utaki*—that's what they call the place where a deity descends. This holy place was not built as a place of worship and there are no images or fetishes. It's just a little place in the woods—a space that isn't anything. If you were to happen upon it, you would only find a small, rough-hewn block of stone. I really admire that wonderful space of nothingness. It was a wonderful discovery and a question/problem for me.[96]

Okamoto begins by meeting an elderly *noro*—the chief priestess of one of the villages.[97] Although he memorably persuades her to let him photograph her at her home, creating the portrait that became iconic of his travels in Okinawa, he does not watch her carry out her duties. Instead, he and her son set out to explore the flat, arid island. They visit the site where Izaihō is held, but they do not observe it or any other rituals. Pushing through dense thickets of *adan* (screw pine), they stand on the rough coral shore at Ishiki-hama, remembered as the place where the deities gave the islanders the five grains that would be the foundation of Okinawan agriculture. Together they cross sparse fields where each farmer's plot is marked out in white stones, according to the archaic practice of the *jiwari seido*, the annual division of communal farmland. Later, they visit the home of the *sōrēganashi*, an elderly man who serves the Dragon God, offering daily sacrifices and asking the deity for its help in securing a successful day of fishing. Okamoto is fascinated by the tall pole that symbolizes the *sōrēganashi*'s relationship to the deity, an imago mundi in Eliade's terms that instantiates the linkage between the two worlds and anticipates the focus of the remainder of the chapter.

> After a time, we arrived at a forest. Her [the *noro*'s] son said that this is the road that leads to the *utaki*. And in we went.
>
> Walking with the trees arching overhead. There is, then there isn't, a trail. Finally we came to a small clearing. I was a little disappointed. I've seen many different kinds of *utaki* on the main island or in Yaeyama, but none this minimal. There are *kuba* and *māni* trees, but nothing like a God Tree [the tall trees that stand in the sanctuaries of Shinto shrines]. Nothing mysterious. The *noro*'s son noted that there had been a bad typhoon and there are downed trees and scattered leaves as a result. Usually the grove is better kept. But that still doesn't account for it. We walked thirty minutes just to get to this very ordinary looking space?
>
> Her son was quiet. . . . Right now, only women participated in ceremonies. They brought sake and food and offered it to the gods. They ate some themselves. Whatever was left, they took home and could eat themselves. Men can't touch anything. . . . Although he said that it's OK for men over fifty to eat.
>
> Minimally, *utaki* have a censer. They are usually not the kind where the ashes build up. Often they are just stone cut into a rectangular shape. Although it is used to make an offering to the deity, I didn't see that in here either. When I asked him about it, he pointed to three or four stones half buried in the ground. That's it, he said. They look like they'd just been thrown there. He didn't know if these

were special stones, or if they had been purposefully arranged. He's a man, so he doesn't know. Or perhaps he knows and won't tell me. Very possible that taboos would lead him to just talk around things. So without any response from him, I headed back to the village. A strange feeling came over my body, and I really wondered about things. *Nani mo nai* (nothingness) really became a theme for me. I kept returning to the idea that it was an austere, real object. Here again I had encountered the idea of nothingness. This time, I quietly experienced it with a deeply liberating sense of joy and delight.[98]

Okamoto writes of his attentiveness to the mood of the space. And yet, as attuned as he might be to the unseen forces that move through the grove, he enters with a casual disregard of local custom. I recall from my first visit to Kudaka that men are forbidden entry to the *ugwanju* (sacred grove)—even the king of Ryūkyū was compelled to disguise himself as a woman in order to receive the gift of *seji* or spiritual power from the deities that entered this world through the grove. I have seen the anxiety and embarrassment felt by villagers and ethnographers when tourists casually transgress the boundaries—I can't imagine it was different when Okamoto visited. Only that Okinawans bore this transgression in the hopes of pleasing an elite visitor. What concerns Okamoto is the numinous qualities that he experiences: he uses *zankoku* (cruel) to describe the sense of sacred terror that he feels in its space. In its emptiness, he discovers an Eliadesque hierophany, the emergence of the sacred in the everyday. Eliade's influence is strong in these pages, particularly in Okamoto's interpretation of the sacred grove.[99]

The axis mundi that Okamoto found in places like the *utaki* on Kudaka, the sacred spaces in which Okinawans communicate with their deities, is not just a place, a vertical line of descent that connects the world of the gods with that of men. It is a point around which the world is organized and invested with meaning. In that sense, this invisible line connecting the heavens and the earth creates the *ugwanju*; the *ugwanju* creates Kudaka; Kudaka and places like it give shape to Japan and to the world. The aestheticized forms that Okamoto despises are not necessary—no elaborate Chinese-influenced designs, no echoes of Japanese Imperial pageantry, no ostentatious detail funded by wealthy and powerful patrons. No massive trees, no pillars, no ropes, no bells constitute the axis mundi. He writes of nothingness as an austere, real object, but here he describes it as a duration in its Bergsonian sense—time filled with an endlessly repeated ensemble of practices of care and concern. Villagers tending to the grove, subtly trimming and clearing the sacred space. Artlessly organizing the simple stones that represent the point at which the axis connecting the unseen worlds intersects the earth. Day in and day out, making humble offerings. Subjects capable of interest and attentiveness, uninterrupted by the practical, temporal demands of capital and the nation that have reconstructed the mainland. In their practices of concern and care, they draw the interest of the deities back into the world.

In some ways, Okamoto's remembering precedes his initial experience of the space, the word before the act, the idea before reality, the concept instantiating itself in the landscape. Surely the awe that he experienced in these spaces of nothingness was prefigured by his studies in Paris, his experiences in the woods with the *Acéphale* group, his postwar turn to Eliade. His distaste for aestheticized and politicized sacred spaces. The moment he narrates was one of remembrance and discovery. The productive absence of material objects that he finds becomes the focal point of his text, organizing a long reflection on the relationship between material culture and everyday life in Okinawa. Okamoto argues that his visit to Kudaka has reminded him that there is something in the Japanese character that inclines them toward the sacred. Unlike Western moderns whose lives have been irrevocably transformed by labor and bureaucracy, and who bear the inescapable weight of their sins, Japanese people continue to nurse the spark of another life. Eliade wrote that profane existence is never found in its pure state, and Okamoto believes that the Japanese concern with purification and bathing shows that the possibility to kindle this ember remains.[100]

His narrative also recalls his work with *Acéphale*: a kind of ethnographic observation and interpretation intertwined with personal experience, the desire for awakening and self-transformation. Okamoto is determined to master the changes that he's experienced. "When a strong person has to endure the slippage of an era, he had better be able to overcome it," Okamoto wrote. If you are to rise above your time, you must be resolute and ignore the constant demands that fragment your life and diminish your intention. He is clear about the possibilities of escaping from the modern present, and living in "eternal time." He doesn't dream of slipping away from his life in Tokyo and fleeing, like Gaugin, to Okinawa. "At this late stage," he writes, "it's impossible to live according to Ryūkyūan rhythms."

> How can you capture the essence of two contradictory times and recover the satisfaction of eternity? Within the organizational time of organizational society, how can you incorporate that primitive feeling and hold onto it? It's an increasingly violent confrontation that must

be resolved. It isn't easy. Even if you are logical and progressive and are 100 percent convinced of the goodwill of human relations, that can't hold at bay the process of bureaucratization or the crisis that was fated to give birth to the colossal institution. On the far side of organization, a wicked devilishness is exposed.[101]

His encounter with the rhythms of Okinawa, the recognition that it stirs within him, has made him all the more attentive to the grating experience of the industrial cadences and managerial excesses of the world in which he lives. This experience, familiar yet distant, remains with him. Okamoto believes that he can draw upon something that he captured in order to create something new, something adequate to life in the modern world. Not the photographs that he took. Those were graphic representations, traces to remind him of that which he had experienced in the sacred groves and windswept fields of Okinawa, and to intimate his interest, his authority, and his creativity to his readers. Not even his essays, which only explicate his new understanding. For Okamoto, the possibilities reside in art. It is contemporary art that affords the opportunity to bring two disjunctive durations of time together. It can illuminate the transformation of everyday life in the modern world, indicating new practices of bourgeois lifestyles, and new strictures in accordance with the bureaucratization of a managed society. However, in recovering what he calls "lost time," he realizes that this moment he discovers is not equivalent to what a modern might consider freedom. Rather, the artist reaches for "a pure shape, having drawn it out of the primordial feeling of the darkness of human existence."[102] It is something other than freedom, something that is not constructed in opposition to modern forms of domination. It is a force that resides deep within the folk, the essence that lies beneath the modern Japanese. It is a relationship with unseen beings, powerful deities. It is beautiful and terrifying, and Okamoto's encounter with it, and its encounter with him, is deeply unsettling. Because it is so different, grounded in alterity and familiarity, Okamoto doubts that a contemporary artist can be confident in his ability to capture it. He can only try to draw on his experiences and to create something. Perhaps he will be successful, perhaps not. He can only be sure that he will have been irrevocably changed by the effort.

As I watched the waves splashing on the deep blue sea at noon, I had a constricting feeling in my throat—as if something I could not say. The purity that I felt, "It's the energy from the depths of the folk (*minzoku*)." But now it wasn't just energy. In order for it to become energy, it must be transformed. And now, it doesn't have the strength to advance this argument. Isn't it content to be covered up?

I've emphasized its beauty and toughness. However, it is also impure. Innocence is the cause of impurity.

After coming to Okinawa, instant after instant, the thing that has questioned me. Time that bears that strange weight.

Like something that has stuck out a long tongue.

By chance, I joined the campaign.

It was bitter. I had to bear that bitterness.

It was wide. Limitless.[103]

In his attunement to this experience of place, his attentiveness to the actions that are performed there and the deities that are called upon and call to the islanders, Okamoto works to construct a relationship between the space of the text and the world of the reader. Thinking of Benjamin's notion of the aura, I wonder about the discussion with the Collège de Sociologie of his essay on Baudelaire that never took place.[104] Okamoto has found something in Okinawa, something proper to that time and place, kept present by the actions of those who attend to the space. In one moment, his narrative makes it immediate, his simple, detailed descriptions bringing it close to the reader. In the next, he reminds the reader of their own distance, of their place elsewhere as modern and cosmopolitan. In this movement back and forth, spatial and temporal, closing the distance only to reestablish it, Okamoto again invokes the position of the shaman. Okinawa is in one place, the readers are in another. Without the play of his narrative, Okinawa would be obscured and readers would be uninformed. With this, Okamoto moves beyond a notion of representation inspired by his broad experience and transformed by his creative abilities. He has been recognized: not simply by the Okinawans who joke with him in bars or look away when he raises his camera. Not just the women whom he meets in markets, or the farmers and fishermen he passes as he drives through their villages. Not only the doctors and scholars who invite him into their homes, or the newspapermen who escort him to important sites and special events. Not the Okinawans who dwell in these spaces, but the deities who look back at him. Who recognize him. Who enlist him "in their campaign." This is the transformation that he anticipated in his account of the charcoal burner's family.[105]

In his narrative, he focuses on the point that ties together the distant and the present, that connects the earth and the heavens, the profane and the sacred. He explores it in his discussion of representations, the imago mundi—the image of the world—the *sōrēganashi*'s simple staff. He writes of it as material spaces, burial sites, and sacred groves, fixed in time and space. And it can be embodied by a person. The *noro* in her courtyard, the dancer on the stage, the fisherman-priest that he meets on a narrow path. And perhaps Okamoto himself. As he becomes attentive to the old ways, to the old entities stirring in the quiet groves, he knows that he, too, is different. He may have been trained as an artist, as an ethnologist, as a philosopher, as a pianist. But in his work with *Acéphale*, in his travels throughout Japan, he finds new ways to appropriate old forms. New skills to articulate with old powers. In Okinawa, those living the beautiful life of the last moment, of *girigiri no utsukushisa*, might be able to beckon the deities with simple prayers, with three artlessly arranged stones that complete the circuit between heaven and earth. For them, that is enough. What of Japanese moderns, hurrying from their prefabricated apartment blocks and detached tract housing, taking trains and buses and taxis to their monolithic office buildings or sprawling factories? In order to bring this experience to them, Okamoto draws on his artistic capacities to create an icon of the unseen. Evoking Benjamin's more subtle and complex notion of the aura from the Arcades Project: "To experience the aura of an object we look at means to invest it with the ability to look back at us."[106] The *Wakai tokeidai* that he has built in Ginza is not just a tree reaching to the heavens, but a mechanism that teaches its own use. Hence its explicitly chronotopic form. He restores the head to the acephalous and makes explicit that which others know unconsciously. He acknowledges their routine practices, recognizes and transforms them. He gives it a form indelibly shaped by his own immediately recognizable style. He creates the pathway for the deities to reach out to the modern era, adds to it a didactic dimension so that those who have forgotten can remember. This is not rescuing these deities from the past, although relationships were certainly differently mediated then. He creates—he is the bridge. It is both the imago mundi, representations of the world tree that Eliade recognizes and explains, and the axis mundi, the thing itself.

Sweets from a Stranger

By the time Okamoto's narrative reaches the final chapter, the figure of the return has collapsed upon itself. He no longer makes any attempt to locate his ethnographic presence in space and time. There are no chance encounters or visits to sacred sites that prompt his remembrance. He simply introduces the title—"Churakasa no dentō" (The tradition of beautiful blisters)—before recalling the famous ethnologist and novelist Orikuchi Shinobu:

> In Okinawa, there's an interesting phrase called "beautiful blisters." These are smallpox blisters. They occur at a time in the disease when it's no longer contagious. Why are these blisters seen as being beautiful?
>
> Orikuchi Shinobu has the answer.
>
> Even though it hurts, [Okinawans] learn to praise and welcome it (as coming from a deity from the other world) and to pass it along. Things that are sent from the farther shore are always seen and understood as something beautiful.[107]

From this point, Okamoto takes the possible, that which is contained in Orikuchi's words, and anchors it in his description of the material spaces that he visits, the practices that he has heard described. During an evening at the Officers' Club in occupied Naha, he watches a middle-aged Okinawan businessman charm American officials, acting as a subject that, despite his small stature and physical weakness, commands the respect and consideration of these battle-hardened soldiers. Okamoto writes that Okinawans have become used to subjugation. And, as such, they know how to endure without being overcome.[108]

Here again, in their creative action, we see the transvaluation of value, the conversion of brutality into beauty in the context of American empire. And yet, the limitations that Okamoto imposes on this creative action— the vertiginous experience of nothingness that gives shape to the "beauty on the edge" that he valorizes—consigns Okinawans to forever recreating this beauty while never experiencing substantial or ethical transformation. In that sense, Okinawans are also denied their history, the objectified form of a series of successful practices. Even Okamoto's language displaces them from the field of action; after all, he describes them as buried and forgotten. In what way can a handwoven kimono belonging to an elderly woman on Ishigaki, or a community ritual performed on Kudaka, be buried? Is it no different than an urn from the Jōmon era entombed in a mound or broken in a midden? Is it forgotten by the people who wear it each day, who still dance ecstatically with their neighbors when the moon is full?

While he can walk with them in the sacred grove or touch their homespun fabric with his skin, these things are not objects of unreflexive experience for him in the same way that they are for the Okinawans that he describes. He does not see them as material objects of use, taken up again and again with little critical thought in the rhythmic repetition of everyday life. Okamoto can see that they have a history as well as a presence, can extend their possibilities so that they can be taken up and used in new ways. These differences emerge most clearly in his exploration of the *utaki* on Kudaka, a hierophany in which gods and men can be together. In "Kami to ki to ishi" he wrote: "There is something of the primal circuit of exchange in the relationship between men and gods, natural trees, and natural stones. . . . The space around us is filled with the deities. The destiny, cool and clear, that gushes out from the stillness. They are there in that flow. They may be below the grass we have just tramped upon. I was captured by that fancy."[109] Here, in his description of the sacred grove, he is both attentive to the world around him and most inspired by the work of scholars such as Eliade. Shaken from the routine of his daily life, he finds his capacities awakening. As he unburies, uncovers the life forgotten by cosmopolitan Japanese, he recognizes his own capacity to participate in it. Not fully, not there, not forever. But he knows that he, too, has access to the things that Okinawans can feel, can do. That awakens in him the capacity, not simply to represent but to convey. To take them back to Japan, to his atelier, to inscribe them in his essays and shape them into his installations.

While Okamoto is entranced by the daily life that swirls around him, it is impossible to ignore the fact that he has staged each of these tableaux for his own experience. Like Horkheimer and Adorno's Odysseus, he goes from island to island, village to village, seeking out the remnants of mythic life—the strange creatures that have retreated to hidden islands and grottos.[110] If he were a native ethnologist, this would be a sign of his melancholy vocation to capture the experience of that which is on the verge of being lost—the vanishing that Marilyn Ivy so eloquently describes.[111] This is not the way in which Okamoto represents himself in his narratives. He shares something with the islanders and villagers he meets—something that makes him attentive to the old ways that they continue to practice, the old places where they continue to dwell. And yet, he seems to lack confidence in the vitality of the practices, the sites that he seeks. His destinations are always prefigured by the memory of texts, of representations of earlier travels, already mediated by the interpretations of Yanagita, Orikuchi, Watsuji, and Eliade. Like Lévi-Strauss, he is more comfortable with the consideration of a myth than the experience of a ritual. Perhaps his project is less a search for the past, or even its remnants, than the act of separating himself from the modern world, of setting aside his comfortable surroundings in order to experience a moment of self-transformation in a space that he has filled with his dreams and his desires.

By his own account, he was profoundly changed by his experiences. And yet, it is not a new critical perspective that he discovers, a result of his dialectic engagement with the world that he found in Okinawa. It comes as a feeling— he cannot comfortably slip back into the familiar, quotidian life of an artist and author that he finds waiting for him in Tokyo. When he looks at the newspapers, books, journals, and magazines that had piled up in his Tokyo atelier during his (ten-day) absence, he's stunned, unable to bring himself to read them, or to even deal with their presence.[112] Here he resembles that other famous Tarō—Urashima Tarō, the mythic adventurer who returned after a long sojourn beneath the sea in the Dragon King's palace. This is not simply a play on their names. Scholars such as Basil Hall Chamberlain and Yanagita Kunio have written of the palace of the Dragon King as having an origin in Okinawa, and popularly imagined to resemble the Ryūkyūan court. It is a place of magic and power, near to hand but immeasurably far away. Only one who had been summoned can discover it.[113]

Okamoto's narrative confirms that recognition, that summons. It acknowledges his capacities, his ability to be transformed, and his determination to act. This becomes apparent in his account of a performance of *kumiodori*, the dance of the Ryūkyūan court, at an exclusive restaurant in Naha. As he watches the dance, he writes that he is recognized—the dancer reaching out to him despite evading his gaze.[114] As Alfred Gell reminds us, a work of art can capture us in its visual field without any sense of the representation of its eyes engaging us directly.[115] Okamoto can then write authoritatively about the duration created during her performance, disregarding the interpretation of the accomplished Okinawan dancer who accompanied him. And, it is Okamoto who can mount the stage and dance with her.

Here the consequences become explicitly clear. The whole narrative of *Okinawa Bunkaron*, his reflections on his studies in Paris or his wartime experiences in China, the written and photographic traces that he leaves of a life lived in public—all this provides a material record, accessible to magazine readers and television viewers as much as critical thinkers and connoisseurs of fine art, of that which allows and compels him to create work like the *Wakai tokeidai*. Everything that he describes—the simple, artless devotion of the Okinawan people, the creativity that they show in their lives of privation, the mastery of art that he developed in France, his ability to experience and understand the lives of others, his spiritual and aesthetic exceptionality, his critique of modernity and his concern for his fellow Japanese—all is made explicit in the constellation of his work. They are indices to be discovered, learned, recognized. They provide the field into which the work of art itself can be suspended, the space prepared for it by his lifetime of action.

It is the representational dimension that is crucial here. He is not simply conjuring up the deity of an Okinawan *ugwanju* or a Tōhoku mountaintop in a plaza in metropolitan Tokyo. He is shaping it, giving it form, just as the Jōmon people who forged the unforgettable ceramics that captured his imagination might have done. He is creating a work of art that is adequate to all of this, and that is invested with the aura that he first sensed in Yanagita's account of the charcoal burner. In recognizing the presence of deities in places like Kudaka, Okamoto acknowledges that he has been transformed. In designing a representation such as the *Wakai tokeidai*, he creates the possibility that those who pass by, that those who find themselves in its presence, will feel its gaze upon them, will know all of the experiences that went into the making of Okamoto Tarō—his knowledge, prestige, authority, and ability—and can feel modern and the timeless bound up in it and its gaze. Submitted to that gaze, aware that something that binds together different planes of being have become aware of them, they have the opportunity to act on that recognition, to shake themselves loose from the demands of rhythm and routine that separate them from what they could be, what they could do.[116]

And yet, the rediscovery of the past in the present has consequences for the Okinawans who have kept company with Okamoto, who have been represented in his texts and his art. Having failed to engage the ways in which Okinawan creative action was also imbricated in the imperial ideology and the fascist genocide of the Pacific War, there is a danger in "the space around us [that] is filled with deities"—the gods who might have been found beneath the very blades of grass where they stood. Harry Harootunian reminds us of the work of the critic and scholar Takeuchi Yoshimi, who argues that contemporary Japan is marked as the place of "any number of miniature emperor systems," that could be found everywhere, in "every single blade of grass, in every tree's leaves." That is a reserve of possibility entirely different than that which Okamoto valorizes.

It is a failure of Okamoto's work that his experience of Okinawa has been so overlain with the texts and projects that brought him to its shores. Perhaps he is not interested in practices. He seems satisfied to stand in the place where actions occurred, to be in the places of power. Because of this, he doesn't find it necessary to understand the collaborative, commensal practices of the place itself. Okinawans also understand the beauty on the edge that the practices that he describes creates, but they have a sense of anticipation and timing that allows them to be in the moment with some future objective in mind. That creates a rhythm of offering, of waiting, of acting, of conflict, and of change.

Because of this, he shows little concern with the forces against which the beautiful negativity that he has identified has been deployed. He risks effacing the determinate historical conditions that engendered these practices, narratively imposing a kind of repetitive sameness upon them that a series of situated interpretations would not authorize. There are real political consequences to his conflation of the Ryūkyūan monarchy's callous exploitation of Miyako villagers with the suicidal genocide that swept across Okinawa during the Pacific War.

In fact, when Okamoto's appropriation of the story of Yanagita's woodsman is situated in the context of postwar Okinawan society, an Okinawa that has been shattered in the aftermath of its sacrifice by Japan and its sacrifice of itself, it becomes particularly noxious. While eschewing the more stereotypical forms of fascist imagery such as falling cherry blossoms or valiant samurai warriors, it trucks in images of patriarchal authority, indebtedness, sacrifice of the self, blood and violence.

At the same time, he ignores the historical specificity of sacrifice in Okinawa, organized around principles that run counter to the practices he valorizes in his essay. There are countless communities in Okinawa that have and continue to practice forms of animal sacrifice such as *shimakusarashi*, *kanki*, and *hamaēgutu* that are meant to protect and increase life.[117] What's more, there is a long history of efforts by central governments to regulate or suppress these practices. As early as 1600, the scholar-bureaucrat Sai On penned polemics against the wastefulness of rituals that demanded the sacrifice of cows, pigs, and chickens in order to maintain the harmony of the community with cosmological principles.[118] Maetakenishi Kazuma has argued that the modern Japanese state continues to interfere with these practices, imposing food sanitation policies that force many Okinawans to rely on commodified meat, depriving them of the freedom to commit the sacrificial act themselves.[119] And yet, this still-vibrant set of practices represents efforts to intervene in a trajectory of events that might lead to human catastrophe and enlist the action of nonhuman entities to serve as mediators with the deities to forestall these consequences. Postwar native ethnologists were already exploring these rituals in the towns and villages across Okinawa when Okamoto visited for the first time.

Harada Nobuo has described the history of the sacrifice of cattle, valuable co-laborers, in communities throughout central and northern Okinawa, perhaps those that Okamoto visited. An ox is brought up out of the fields where he draws the plow, unharnessed from the wagon he might pull, unbound from the cane press that he might turn at a small sugar mill. Separated out from the cycle of agrarian production, he is called upon to reset a far more important cycle. Led to a central place in the village, he is sacrificed. In other communities, one of the household pigs was chosen. I have written about the importance of the pig, an animal that (until efforts by Okinawans intent to modernize the dimensions of daily life that might be found ridiculous or primitive by their fellow Japanese) was quartered in the household toilet, for conserving the life force of the community, for allowing its productive reappropriation in the consumption of its flesh.[120] Other animals are also offered in sacrifice, such as chickens and goats. During a period of postwar scarcity, a community near Nago even substituted dolphin until cattle were available again.[121]

Often in *shimakusarashi*, the sacrificed animal was dismembered. The flesh of the sacrificed animal was prepared in a stew offered to the deities that safeguard the community. After they have taken their invisible shares, it became a commensal meal consumed by all who dwelt in the village. Humans and deities alike had their portions. Rope boundaries were strung across all the entrances of the community. Recognizable elements of now fragmented sacrifice—a shoulder blade, a jawbone, a foot—were hung from the ropes that stretched across village entrances. The sacrificial animal, its physical integrity broken in the act of sacrifice, is reconstructed in the material wholeness of the boundary that encompasses the community and the meal ingested by those who dwell there. The one is fragmented and made whole; the threatened community is restored. The practice is contingent and creative.[122]

Unlike the kinds of sacrifices that Rane Willerslev, Piers Vitebsky, and Anatoly Alekseyev have described—the objects of cunning that struggle to defer the demands of the deities by offering cleverly disguised substitutes: a reindeer for a human, a sausage for a reindeer, a stone for a sausage—these offerings are offerings of a terrifying honesty.[123] As Valerio Valeri—and Bataille before him—knew, the sacrifice becomes most like the sacrifier in the moment before that difference is forever reimposed.[124] This admission to the gods: we will offer you the thing most nearly us, but at all costs we want to preserve human life. And, despite the difficult lives that the villagers might lead, the conditions that might resonate with Okamoto's notion of *girigiri no utsukushisa*, the sacrifice is intended to preserve life and restore hope and totality, not valorize some sense of protracted crisis. A classic Okinawan folktale that I heard from friends captures this. It was said that during the reign of King Gihon, a twelfth-century ruler remembered as feckless and whose life was marked by catastrophe, a monstrous serpent troubled the farmers and fishermen in Chatan. A priestess told the monarch that the creature could only be appeased by the sacrifice of a young woman. To induce someone to step forward, Gihon promised that the sacrificed woman's family would be elevated to the nobility and live the rest of their lives in happiness and security. A young peasant woman volunteered immediately: What was her death to rescuing her loved ones from their lives of toil and privation? As soon as she offered herself up to the priestess in charge, a benevolent deity appeared, destroying the serpent and compelling the king to reward everyone. It was the desire to save and preserve, the concern with family and friends, that was to be rewarded. Not the offering of a life.

Moreover, Okamoto's insistence that the beauty of Okinawan life is that they remain in this state of near nothingness, always near death and ruin, excuses him from dealing with the consequences of sacrificial violence. He is not simply unconcerned with change: the beauty and creativity that he admires could not exist if there is some kind of dialectic resolution.

Okamoto's focus on the glint of steel on the head of the woodsman's broadaxe, his emphasis on the ineffable beauty of the act silences its material ground and consequences. This runs counter to a critical trend in art at the time, which emphasizes the corporeality of wartime sacrifice.[125] It also elides the most immediate wartime context in Okinawa, one that Okamoto surely understood quite clearly. There was a widely publicized effort at the time to publicly memorialize the civilians who were forcibly conscripted, ordered to commit suicide, or killed outright in battle. To refuse the martial valorization of genocide.[126] In fact, it is precisely this debate into which Okamoto intervened in his earlier dismissal of an unnamed critic, Ōya Sōichi, for describing the Okinawan people as docile and obedient, like animals. It may be that Ōya's choice of words was cruel and insensitive. However, his call for a critical inquiry into the ways in which the conditions of wartime murder and suicide were created seems to be what Okamoto avoids; his warning about the aestheticization of sacrifice is precisely what Okamoto does.[127] Finally, by imposing a categorical uniformity to this beauty on the edge that Okamoto finds, again and again, throughout

Okinawan history, he creates an objectified aesthetic that is wholly dependent on his representation.

At the same time, these ostensibly progressive objectives recall the reactionary implications of much of Japanese native ethnology. As Jacques Rancière wrote, in a scathing critique of Pierre Bourdieu and postwar French sociology:

> Through the historical naïveté of resorting to working-class "cultures" and "sociabilities," through the sophisticated sociological demystification of "distinguished culture," through the development of new discourses of identity as through old discourses of class struggle—I could hear through them all the same fundamental tone, the same valorization of the "bottom" against the "top." And behind the various forms of this "progressive" valorization, I could hear the same proposition of preserving the order of things, the proposition for which Plato established the formula once and for all: let all do their own business and develop the virtue specific to their condition.[128]

In Okamoto's work, the knowledge and practices that he locates in Okinawa are valuable as an alternative to the conditions of contemporary Japan. Yanagita once wrote that Okinawa was a mirror held up to reflect ancient Japan; for Okamoto, Okinawa was a mirror held up to the modern, disclosing possibilities that were otherwise lost.[129] However, this discovery risks the reproduction of a sense of absolute difference, one that leaves the modern Japanese on one side, and the Okinawans on the other. He actually writes an open letter to the Okinawan people on the eve of the end of American occupation, urging them to refuse their return to the Japanese state, reminding them of the beauty and power of their minimal aesthetic, of all that would be lost in joining modern Japan, while, at the same time, effacing the complexity, depth, and ferocity of the Reversion movement, or of Okinawan politics under American military colonization. Forget about *Hondonami*, he tells them, of the desire to catch up with the mainland. Instead, he urges mainland Japanese to embrace *Okinawanami*—to discover their own identity with Okinawans. This partition leads him to a kind of mimetic confusion, shifting from the valorization of Okinawan creative action to appropriating their repetitive production of marginal beauty for his own aesthetic and ethnographic practice. Okinawa as a mirror, consigned to being for someone else, never for itself.[130]

3.4.   The *Wakai tokeidai* at night.

Keeping Time: Ginza, August 2019

On a hot summer evening, I climbed up from the airless subway, crossed a busy intersection, and stood along the edge of Sukiyabashi Park in Ginza. The sun had set, but no evening breezes made it through the steel and concrete barriers of the city. The plaza was quiet, empty except for occasional couples that hurried to the nearby station, and an older man sleeping rough on a bench. There, in front of me, Okamoto's *Wakai tokeidai* still kept watch. Perhaps it still calls to the working men and women, to the shoppers and tourists who pass it each day, seen and unseen, its gaze alerting them to the more complete lives that they could lead. After decades of casual neglect, it has been recently renovated. The new paint on its trunk and its horns is smooth and undamaged, the lights at the base of its horns shine warmly. It remains a material trace of Okamoto's commitment to his mediational role in the transformation of value—a shaman working in concrete and metal, lights and motors and circuitry. New construction surrounded it, and a line of scaffolding and a public toilet obscured the view of the back of the tower, the tang of sewage in the air. An elderly sentry came out of the bathroom and sat on the footing surrounding the tower, quietly smoking a cigarette in its shadow.

I thought of the other public installations that Okamoto had created during the peak of his postwar activity. Many have disappeared, or have been gathered in his museum in Kawasaki, separated from the everyday life that once shaped their experience. I have explored their traces, their absences and presences, as I think about Okamoto's work in Okinawa. It has been a strange experience, taking me on bullet trains and subways, in dense urban neighborhoods and extravagant suburban parks across metropolitan Japan, far from the neighborhoods in Okinawa where I usually work. A week before, I climbed the *Tower of the Sun* in Osaka. It stands alone on a hill at the entrance to the Exposition Park, near the National Museum of Ethnology. If tourists were permitted to look out of the windows at the top of the tower, perhaps I could have seen the crowded neighborhoods along the waterfront to the south in Taisho-ku, where Okinawan laborers have lived and worked for generations. Outside the tower, small groups of tourists hurried along, heads bowed against the brutal heat, eager to reach the booths and vendors at a nearby summer festival where cold drinks and shaved ice offered some relief.

Once, decades ago, the tower seemed to burst forth from the center of the architect Tange Kenzō's modernist pavilion, in what Okamoto hoped would be a concrete space of ecstatic transformation in the midst of a state celebration of production and consumption. Beneath the floor of the pavilion, a vault filled with exhibitions designed and curated by Okamoto told of the history of life on Earth, the development of meaning and experience. Like the mechanism that his mentor Marcel Mauss described at the heart of Chukchi homes on the coasts of the Arctic Ocean, it stood at the center of the everyday world, promising a chance at a renewed, pleasurable relationship with the deities.[131] Now, Tange's pavilion is gone, and the exposition has been cleared away. The tower itself seemed more like an artifact of the optimism of the supercharged seventies, rather than a sign of possible futures or meaningful community/milieu. Along with the rest of Okamoto's paintings and objects that have been tidied away to museums, the remaining installations inside the tower are treated by staff and visitors with a kind of formalized reverence, and the project of recognition and transformation that Okamoto dreamt of goes unmentioned.

Considering techniques of memory in *The Genealogy of Morals*, Nietzsche wrote: "Man could never do without blood, torture, and sacrifices when he felt the need to create a memory for himself; the most dreadful sacrifices and pledges (sacrifices of the first born among them), the most repulsive mutilations (castration, for example), the cruelest rites of all the religious cults (and all religions are at the deepest level systems of cruelties)—all this has its origin in the instinct that realized that pain is the most powerful aid to mnemonics."[132] It would be easy to counterpose the casual neglect of Okamoto's project, its subsumption into the everyday, with a powerful field of action such as Yasukuni Shrine in nearby Kudanshita. As disdainful as he would feel, Okamoto himself would certainly recognize the dark magic of a massive gate forged in blackened steel, of the museum glorifying the endless sacrifice of war, of the stately Imperial Shinto architecture, and of the millions of souls enshrined within. Perhaps I could also contrast it with the fields, thick with memorials, in Okinawan battlefields. And yet, these places existed in Okamoto's day, blood-saturated sites in the construction of Imperial memory. However, these are not the places where Yanagita traveled to touch the *girigiri no utsukushisa*, to feel the vertiginous experience of nothingness. What of those places?

In Yaeyama, where he once listened to melancholy folksongs, explored failed development projects, and walked through timeless village streets, the occult powers of capital have muted the power of repetition and sacrifice. Until the pandemic, more than a million tourists arrived each year at the new international airport in Miyako or on luxurious ocean liners that tied up at the pier. There are still humble fisherman's houses to be found, but extravagant resorts line the beaches, and real estate prices rival that of Tokyo. At the same time, armed Japanese cutters patrol coastal waters in increasingly bellicose confrontations with Chinese fishermen and the Chinese navy, and a new Japanese amphibious brigade is training for future combat.

Generations later, the rhythms of Imperial sacrifice that Okamoto hoped he could disrupt with his magic remain strong. In Yanbaru, where Okamoto traveled in a failed effort to meet a famous dancer, the Japanese government defies local referendums to build a new base for occupying American soldiers. Police shipped down from Osaka, inspired by a different sense of archaic Okinawa, publicly ridicule Okinawan demonstrators, calling them *dojin* (primitives).[133] Young men, conservative activists from local communities, harass the elderly antiwar activists who survived wars with humility and courage. The flow of laborers to the mainland continues. And yet, the struggles that Okamoto had little interest in understanding continue. Perhaps the invisible forces, the grandeur of nothingness, the minimal power generated in a life of endless sacrifice still informs their daily lives.

What of the power that Okamoto hoped to bring back to the mainland? From the fragmented remains of his work, it is difficult to say when Okamoto was the traveler and when he created. When he was recording what he had seen, and when he was bringing something new into being. Movement and action—he was the work of art as much as his paintings and statues. One in the other. The mass of mediated indices into which he was woven, the icons of experience that he had worked into himself, and that could have once led people to understand, are still there somewhere. They emerge in a newly released theatrical documentary about his life, a serialized drama on television, new exhibitions and reprints of his essays, libraries full of books and journals. At the same time, they have been rendered obtuse by the turbulent waters of public culture. His tower that once limned the relationship between the heavens and the earth has been represented in popular comics as an unsettling, sinister monolith, and you can buy transformer-like action figures built around its form in hobby shops and online stores. As I stand in the darkened plaza, staring at the glowing face of the tower, I wonder about it. Is this visible icon of an invisible world still charged with the possibility that Okamoto sought to invest in it? Does it remain a space of hierophany, where the sacred forever erupts into the everyday? Perhaps the answer is not with the tower. Okamoto had the generosity to build it and to leave it, with no further directions about its use.[134] It is there to see, and to be seen. Like the woodsman who watched his children sharpening his axe, perhaps the responsibility remains with those who pass it each day, who may summon the interest and the courage to see it, and to be seen.

From Among the Dead

4

THE TRANSFORMATION OF SACRIFICE

He compares the thinker to an arrow shot by Nature that another thinker picks
up where it has fallen so that he can shoot it somewhere else.

Gilles Deleuze, *Nietzsche and Philosophy* (1962)

The living can assist the imagination of the dead.

William Butler Yeats, *A Vision* (1925)

Okinawa Prefectural Archives, Haebaru, August 1997

The Okinawa Prefectural Archives stand on a ridgeline to the east of Naha,
rising like a fortress above the city. It is a massive structure, built as if it were
intended to withstand another bombardment like those that scoured these
hills during the Battle of Okinawa. And yet there is modesty to the design
that runs counter to the sense of monumentality evoked by the scale of construction and the building materials, cut limestone and polished concrete.
With its cascading red-tiled roofs and its traditional courtyard gate, the
prefectural archives are a kind of palimpsest of remembered rural spaces, a
distillation of the forms of the rambling farmhouses, enclosed courtyards
and elevated storehouses that dominated the Okinawan countryside before
World War II.

It commands spectacular views of the surrounding area, stretching across densely developed neighborhoods and green hilltops, views I have rarely seen anyone enjoy. Visitors hurry from the parking lot to the entrance; inside, they sacrifice the panoramic vistas revealed by large banks of windows for the materials before them. It is the interior of the archives that creates a space for discovery and contemplation, among the carefully collected graphic traces of the Okinawan past.

As I gathered my gear from the back of my car on a late summer morning in 1997, I could already feel the weight of the sun pressing down on me. I was tired from a long season of fieldwork in Okinawa City. Hours of dancing each day and an intense schedule of festivals and performances had taken its toll. My back and my shoulder ached, the calluses on my hands had begun to painfully crack and peel. And yet, as I walked along the limestone-paved path that led to the archive, I found myself absently falling into step with unseen dancers, walking to the rhythm of a folksong that still echoed inside me. It was an unsettling experience. A moment of pride as I felt my work embodied in habit, shaded by the recognition that I walked with a rhythm that did not belong to me. I struggled to refocus my attention on the files that awaited me inside.

I paused for a moment on the threshold, my attention captured by an inscription etched into a sheet of polished granite mounted at the entrance. It was a reproduction of a verse in the handwriting of Ifa Fuyū, the first director of the old prefectural library and a brilliant linguist, historian, and social critic.

There is a monumental impulse at work here, in the weight of the tablet that fixes Ifa's words, the fluidity of his hand frozen in the graven surface of the stone. Much depends on capturing the moment of inscription, so that, beyond the desire of any reader to return to contemplate their meaning, the words themselves can be expected to endure, an epigraph to the encounter with the constellation of texts and materials awaiting the researcher in the archive beyond.

Who better than Ifa Fuyū to mark this crossing? At a moment in the 1960s, balanced between American occupation and Japanese sovereignty, Ifa assumed the role of an intellectual figure instantiating Okinawa's turbulent and conflicted past. The intellectual historian Kanō Masanao has suggested that, in place of the fiercely principled Jahana Noboru, who committed suicide rather than compromise his ideals, the more nuanced and ambivalent figure of Ifa articulated with the moment. Discourses were given material form: his reburial, scholarly conferences, and the publication of his selected

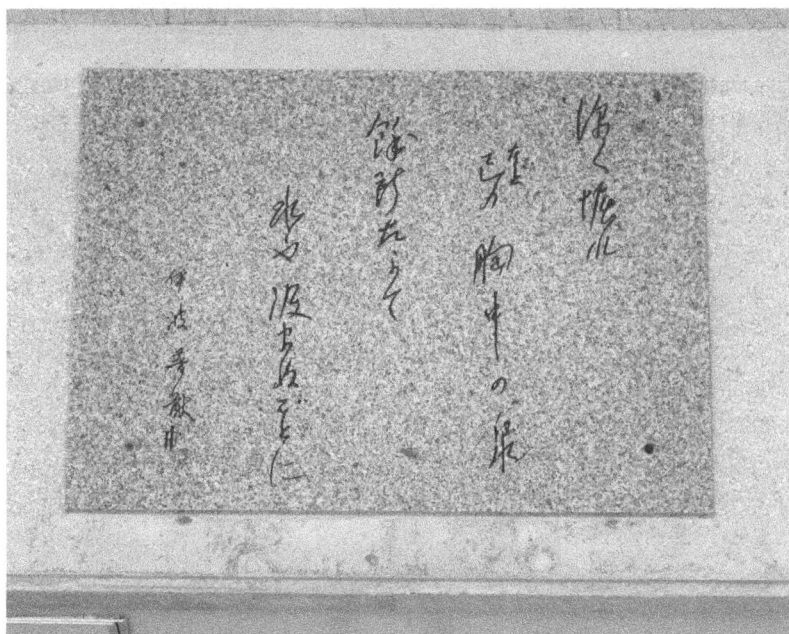

4.1.   Ifa Fuyū's inscription at the Okinawa Prefectural Archives.

works in 1962 and his collected works in 1972 fall at points in the struggle
to exchange American for Japanese rule.[1]

However, Ifa wrote the lines memorialized at the archive at an earlier moment, before he was burdened with the weight of identification as the father
of Okinawan studies. Still a young scholar, he was concerned with helping
his fellow Okinawans create a self-understanding that would allow them to
escape the burdens that they had endured during their era of Satsuma repression and thrive in the world of modern Japan. He probably first wrote
these words in his study at the newly established library while he prepared
Koryūkyū (Ancient Ryūkyū), his famous collection of essays on Okinawan
history and culture, for its second publication in 1916.

It was a time charged with possibility for Okinawans. The violence of
incorporation into the Japanese state now lay nearly four decades in the
past. The indignity of colonial rule and the transformation of the practices
of everyday life at every level were perhaps tempered by the possibilities of
participation in the modernizing Japanese state. The rhythms of practices
of assimilation into the time of the nation: the daily routine of schools regulated by national policies, the cadence of the Japanese language spoken and

heard, the regularity of Japanese dress, the cycles of labor in fields and in offices, were harmonized with those that beat across the growing empire. Of course, dramatic disparities in wealth and poverty still existed. Still, as the rhythms of the nation become more familiar and routinized, they could become less obtrusive. Soldiers and ethnographers withdrew to the background for a time, leaving an ideological commitment to becoming Japanese—good Japanese—behind them.

Okinawan harbors were busy with the shipping that connected the distant reaches of the new and growing empire. Aspiring workers boarded ships that ferried them to factory towns in mainland Japan and island plantations scattered across the southern seas. Merchants and farmers were excited by the possibilities afforded by the interruption of Western trade by World War I: perhaps the extensive and difficult transformation of Okinawan agriculture was worthwhile after all. Sugar was selling and there was money to be made. Engineers consulted their plans while surveyors charted the construction of a railroad that would connect Naha with Futenma to the north, like the railroads of any other prefecture. Enterprising bureaucrats in prefectural offices searched for likely local deities to install in a proposed shrine that would make use of the otherwise vacant castle at Shuri; the emperor and other state-sanctioned deities had already taken up their positions in community and household rituals.[2]

When Ifa sat at his desk in his office at the Okinawa Prefectural Library, could he have had an intimation of the catastrophe that was to come? Could he see that in another decade, Okinawa would be wracked by poverty and famine, and crushed by increasing labor migration? Could he imagine his fellow Okinawans lost in a national history and imperial ideology? Could he anticipate the horrific, genocidal Pacific War? I cannot say what hopes or fears occupied him as he edited *Koryūkyū* for republication, but the author's foreword closes with the following epigraph:

汝の立つ所に深く掘れ　其所には泉あり　　　　ニーチェ

Where you stand, dig deep and pry!　Down there is the well. Nietzsche.[3]

Scholars have been unable to determine with any degree of certainty how Ifa came to be familiar with Nietzsche's words. The full text of *Die Fröhliche Wissenschaft*, or *The Gay Science*, had yet to be fully translated, but Nietzsche's work was certainly in the air. Perhaps he encountered the German manuscript as a student in Tokyo; he may also have read it in one of the many books or journals he collected in Okinawa.[4] What is clear is that this aphorism was so important to him that friends remembered it as his personal motto. Ifa himself says as much in his introduction to the 1918 collection of essays on the history of Kunigami village by his friend Shimabukuro Gen'ichirō: "I'm very fond of citing Nietzsche's aphorism. In fact, if you will allow me to do so again, I will do it here. I think it's an exceptionally apt phrase to express the necessity of *kyōdo kenkyū*—studies of our own native places."[5]

The printed Japanese translation of Nietzsche's aphorism—perhaps done by Ifa himself—captures the formal construction of the original. The trope of difficult excavation is used to evoke a sense of painful self-evaluation. For Ifa, this act is of a piece with the rigorous study of local history and culture—the material that makes up *Koryūkyū*. And yet, regardless of the personal importance that these lines held for him, he was somehow moved to revise them in a handwritten note alongside the original inscription in the copy of the book that belonged to his friend Higa Shunchō.[6] Taking pen in hand, he rewrote it in the open margin—using the words now etched in granite at the prefectural archives.

深く掘れ 己の胸中の泉
余所たよて 水や汲まぬごとに

Dig deep in the spring that lies in the depths of your heart
If you rely on others, you will not draw up water.

Ifa's handwritten lines weaken Nietzsche's creative revaluation of Christian and pre-Christian tropes of human and demonic realms, and its emphasis on the intentional movement from above to below. At the same time, it makes explicit the metaphoric relationship of excavation to critique that was captured in the printed translation. What's more, in warning of the negative influence of others, it alludes to the second half of Nietzsche's original aphorism that had not been included in the printed epigraph:

Let the obscurantists cry:
"Down there's only—Hell!"[7]

Is this, in Walter Benjamin's terms, the translator's loss of nerve, an effort to grasp the meaning of Nietzsche's words by abandoning the attempt to reproduce its form? Does it signal Ifa's concern that his readers will not

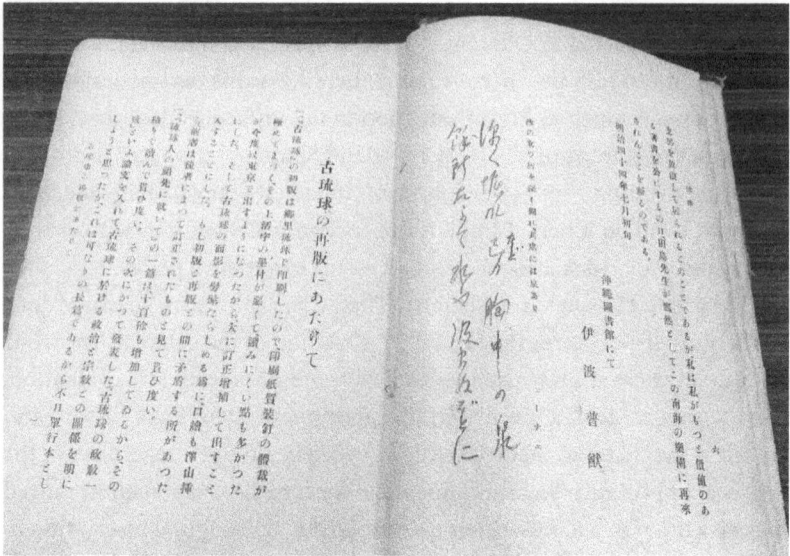

4.2.   Ifa Fuyū's handwritten inscription in *Koryūkyū*.

understand Nietzsche's transformational appropriation of elements of Western Christian symbolism or the subtleties of its message?

Because the printed translation is still present on the page, it might be more productive to read one against the other, to see Ifa's handwritten lines in a dialogue with the first epigraph. Written in standard Japanese, it appears to be a kind of brief explication of the original. The original metaphors are made didactically clear: explore the contents of your heart but do not rely on others. Certainly this is in keeping with influential discourses of the time that called for a commitment to self-improvement.[8]

However, as Deleuze cautions in his essay on Nietzsche, it would be a mistake to consider this an invitation to a kind of psychological introspection.[9] For Nietzsche, the act creates its agent and a much more collective subject is at stake. There is too much urgency in the moment for Ifa to simply urge his fellow Okinawans to be ambitious. I believe that Ifa's supplement is both subtler and more creative. The printed translation is left in place, a trace of his first effort to capture Nietzsche's command—his warning. In his revision, Ifa breaks it into fragments, building something new that links Nietzsche's injunction to the project of *Koryūkyū* itself. But what? Far more prosaic advice hastily sketched in everyday Japanese? My first intimation of a more complex interpretation of Ifa's act came one evening several years ago while I was having dinner with the historian and critic Hiyane Teruo, an influential interpreter of Ifa's work.

I had copied the inscription into my notebook during an earlier visit, and I took the opportunity to ask Hiyane—an important scholar of Ifa's work—about it. He took my notebook from me, looked at it and smiled, then handed it back.

"Read it," he said.

I paused for a moment and looked at the lines, perplexed. Was there something so obvious that I had missed it?

"Go ahead—read it out loud."

Nervous at this impromptu performance, I carefully recited the poem.

Hiyane laughed and shook his head. "Let me read it for you," he said. Without bothering to look at my notebook, he gave voice to Ifa's words. As I glanced at the lines I had written, I realized that Hiyane's recitation was not spoken in Japanese at all. He repeated the aphorism for a second time, careful to capture the rhythm of Ifa's utterance. I could hear his words resolving themselves into a *ryūka*—a classical Ryūkyūan poetic form organized in four successive lines, the first three of eight syllables, the last of six.

> *Hukaku huri, nadu nu*
> *Ṇ ni uchi nu ijun*
> *Yusu tayuti mijiya*
> *Kuma nu kuduni*

In this small space, Ifa appropriates both the formal framework of written Japanese and elements of Nietzsche's injunction to give shape to something of his own. He mobilizes fragments and absence to create something new. He gives voice to a song that can only be understood by those who know to listen for it, one that resonates with cunning and creativity.

Tomiyama Ichirō has written that Ifa was heartbroken by the limitations that Japanese imposed on his ability to know and express himself, and his anger at the violence of a national system that required him to adopt its own system of representation: "When one is compelled to represent and construct oneself by means of another's words and images, and one realizes that such expressive tools are insufficient to translate one's own inner self, then one has then reached a state in which one cannot possibly comprehend oneself."[10] That moment would come later, when he was overcome by disappointment and disillusioned by the results of his labor. However, when Ifa took up his pen to inscribe his friend's book, it seems as if he wrote with a sense of urgency and hopefulness. Standing before the archives, standing before the text in the place where Ifa had been as he wrote, the reader is invited to feel something similar. The epigraph gathered readers and prepared them for the text; the inscription does so for the archives. What comes next? All that is dependent upon the courage of the reader.

After Hiyane finished his recitation, he tapped my notebook with his forefinger.

"Give it another try."

Conical Hill, December 2011

The squall swept across the fields and pushed over the ridgeline, the sky and sea beyond a seamless, silver curtain of rain. From where I stood, the hill sloped down and away, the grass peeled back for hundreds of meters, the exposed earth red and wet. A dozen or so laborers slowly climbed out from under a white tent, trailing like a line of skirmishers across the broken and uneven ground. Blue *sagyōfuku* (work uniforms) and white hard hats. Here and there among the other volunteers, I saw the red vests of the Promise Keepers. A series of blue vinyl tarps traced lines along the field like ribbons, following furrows cut straight across the wet earth. More workers crested the hill behind me and cautiously picked their way down the slippery steps that had been built out of sandbags and fitted into the slope. Most of them were carrying vinyl buckets, brushes, and trowels, a few with folding stools to keep themselves out of the mud as they worked. Looking back, I saw Ishigaki from Gamafuyā, the nonprofit organization supervising the operation, standing at the top of the hill, his mobile phone at his ear.

I stretched my shoulders, muscles sore after days of digging. All morning, I had been cutting away at the face of the slope in front of me. Short strokes of the *katatekuwa* (a small handheld hoe) working from right to left, then back again. I tried to cut the soil into slices thin enough to disclose anything that might be embedded in it. Occasionally, I paused to clear away the soil piling up at my feet, or to wipe away the sweat streaming from under my helmet with the back of my work gloves. My neighbors kept up a steady pace, talking and laughing as they worked.

Taking advantage of our break time, I wiped my hands on my heavy twill trousers and slid my sketchbook out of its Ziploc bag. Checking the folded map that I'd tucked under the cover, I tried to orient my drawing to the ground. My Japanese map calls this, in English, Conical Hill. A name from the war that clings to the peaks like the thick forest we had just cut back, and the memories of death that remain intertwined. Once the fortified anchor at the eastern end of the Shuri Line, a system of military infrastructure that integrated the space and the people of central Okinawa into the logic of Imperial military strategy. And now? A space to be developed, to be brought into a new relationship with the world.

My partner stood next to me, retying the thin white towel around his neck. He was short and muscular, built like a boxer, dressed in a long-sleeved T-shirt, work pants, and rubber knee boots. When we met that morning, he told me that he and his wife were retired schoolteachers from Yonabaru. He said that about a third of the kids he grew up with were raised by their grandparents and perhaps another third by their widowed mothers. His wife, who was also from the area, was wounded by shrapnel in four places during the war. This is all very real to him. He thought that opening up this battlefield and reconsidering the war was as important as returning the remains. Looking over my shoulder, he nodded at my sketch. "That's good. Get it while it's all still here. I wonder what it's going to look like once the bypass goes through?"

Below where we stood, the Yonabaru Bypass stretched out in a wide, muddy arc slashed across the bottom of the thickly forested hillside, just past the edge of blocks of densely packed concrete houses. It had been imagined and planned as part of another massive Okinawan development project. Images depicted the new highway sweeping eastward from Naha, threading the interval between the Okinawa Country Club to the north, and Yonabaru and Nishihara to the south and east. Its advocates argued that it would reshape the southeastern coastal region, providing a modern and efficient high-speed link between Naha and the new centers of prefectural development along the east coast. New tourist and residential centers at the Marine Park in Nakagusuku; the academic and industrial sectors of Nishihara; the shopping and residential sections of Yonabaru. Government reports and media releases described it in the language of service, the shift of traffic from congested village streets to spaces less developed, giving the residents of these communities more convenient access to the rest of the island.

Beyond the efficient, accelerated circulation of people, vehicles, and commodities, the bypass would be an affordance for the sensory and narrative experience of a different kind of life.[11] Moving swiftly in a sleek sedan, drivers could feel the same speed and comfort as a Japanese commuter in the main islands, a life that they have seen in the media, or perhaps experienced themselves as a worker or a student. Even a villager who sees traffic streaming by on the highway or hears the sounds of cars rushing by in the

4.3.   Volunteers digging for the remains of the dead at Conical Hill/Untamamui.

night could experience something of that newness, bringing them closer to how they imagine life is lived in suburban mainland communities. The modern life of speed and action that has been valorized since the Meiji era, and promised to Okinawans again and again. An experience very different from the painfully slow crawl from town to town that has marked everyday life in Okinawa since the beginning of the American occupation. It might also spur an upsurge in consumption: automobility demands the glossy hybrids and mini MPVs that are displayed in the new dealerships along all of the highways in central Okinawa, and the fuel, parking fees, insurance, and long commutes that go with them.[12] Another moment in the seemingly endless cycle of dreams and efforts to be like Japan, to truly become Japanese, to grasp that which is always just beyond reach.

Long before ground was broken, the bypass appeared in the distant workings of the planners and designers at Kokudōkōtsūshō (Ministry of Land, Infrastructure, Transport, and Tourism) in Tokyo, and the Nambukokudōjimusho (South National Highways Office) in Naha, who imagined the highway transiting these spaces. It took form in the meetings and discussions of the bureaucrats and politicians in Naha, Yonabaru, Nishihara, and other municipalities who implemented their designs. It set commodities in motion: petroleum from the Gulf States; production at steel mills and refineries in Honshu and Kyushu; concrete and asphalt factories in Okinawa. It reorganized supply chains, starting the movement of commodities through highways, warehouses, harbor facilities, and across the sea. It shaped the deployment of American naval battle groups to protect distant sea lanes, and summoned coastal patrols from the Japanese Maritime Self-Defense Forces. It called to the engineers, the contractors, and the subcontractors who would cut a path through these mountains, weaving all of this into other rhythms of capital and the nation.

It also sparked the dissent of residents, reporters, and taxpayers, who questioned its environmental effects, its impact on everyday life, and its enormous cost. They complained that it was designed to shift massive amounts of state capital to the accounts of the contractors involved, a pattern of exploitation that has characterized much of postwar Okinawan history.[13] Local activists and politicians pushed back, arguing that this placed an unfair burden on the very citizens, local businesses, and municipal governments that it was intended to help, forcing redesigns and cost reductions. Construction was halted for many years.

When I had a chance to explore the bypass, it was still a broken line that ran along the base of the hillside. A long metal structure stood in the center of one segment, a frame to carry the elevated highway. In another, a rectangular space had been cleared so that the foundation could be built, but it was flooded with stagnant water. Past that, a smooth reinforced concrete pad had been poured to support the asphalt surface of the highway. Finally, two new paved access roads that would one day flank the bypass stood alongside a flat expanse of land covered in patchy weeds. Tall grass or scrubby trees still grew between each of these segments. Where it reached Route 329, a mass of black, cylindrical barriers blocked the entrance. This seemed to capture the manifold spatiotemporality of postwar Okinawa. An uneven juxtaposition of the no-longer and the not-yet, a place where the calculating ambition of bureaucrats and businessmen, the struggle of activists, and the dreams of ordinary people intersected in the fragments of a highway that has been already built but may never be completed. Where the promise of speed and mobility becomes intertwined with fragmentation and stagnation. A place of warning and inspiration.[14]

The space across which planners intended to construct the bypass might be represented as open on local maps or indeterminately under construction in files in the hard drives and cabinets of planning officials. And yet, it seemed to me that it was neither empty nor a ruin filled with the melancholy fragments of an exploited past and an unrealized future. Shaped as I was by my studies, I saw that a manifold of time and space, of rhythms of being and doing, already came together here.[15] There were chronotopes of farming, daily and seasonal, wet rice in the lowlands, vegetables, flowers and sugar cane as you move higher into the hills.[16] These are shaped and inflected by the rhythms of weather and the seasons, cycled by sales at markets and the availability of labor, and buoyed by government subsidies. Families maintain the rhythms of interaction with their dead when they visit the large tombs nestled in the hillside, during Shīmī, Obon, or at other times of sorrow, of need, or of love.[17] Higher on the slopes, far from the "power spots" that attract mainland tourists seeking spiritual renewal, small shrines show tokens of visits to the deities who reside there: coins, stones, and bundles of burned incense.[18] In the clearing at the top, discarded plastic bottles and crushed beer cans index the hikers, tourists, or history buffs who come and go, interrupting lives led elsewhere to climb to the heights and look out at the ocean beyond, perhaps thinking about the past. Tourists interested in military history might stop to see this old battlefield; American military officers from nearby bases pause training for wars underway elsewhere to walk the slopes in trace of their predecessors.[19] And survivors—are they ever far from these fields? They might travel to these hills with friends and family, looking for reminders of a past that they cannot forget, or the remains of the dead that they cannot fully mourn. Beyond the hillside, across the eastern slopes of the mountain and the coastal plain that runs down to the Pacific, the intertwined rhythms of business and leisure are paced out on the greens of a golf course. Other traffic runs on the roads that already crisscross the hills: laborers and businessmen heading to their own workplaces; families to shops or to school; commercial overland shipping running north and south, east and west. And finally, there is a longer rhythm, the rhythm of war—one that raged across these hillsides and valleys with an unbelievable ferocity in the spring of 1945 before falling silent. Perhaps ended, perhaps simply a sustained rest in a much longer pattern of repetition.

Were these the preoccupations of an anthropologist, as obsessed as Okamoto Tarō or Yanagita Kunio in their visits to Okinawa? Did planners and engineers feel anything? Did they wonder how their highway would cut across these spaces and times? The construction workers who follow us might be more concerned when they arrive at the *genba* (workplace) in the early morning darkness, apprehensive that their shovels will unearth the remains of the battlefield dead.[20] The farmers who have sold their land to the state and the neighbors who remain have their thoughts about that, having kept company with the dead for decades. The owner of a Family Mart convenience store at the base of the mountain told me as much one morning when I stopped for coffee and a sandwich before heading up to the excavation. "Make sure you take some time to explore Untamamui," he said, "but be careful that nothing follows you home." This is a sign of the other rhythms that resonate through these spaces, an intimation of the weird presences that exceed all of the others I've described.[21] Although my map shows it as Conical Hill, the people in the community and the people that I worked with call it Untamamui or Untama no mori. I could translate this as "the forest of the jewels of good fortune," but that misses its association with the legendary bandit Untamagirū, or simply Girū.

The figure of Untamagirū is at the center of a number of songs, folktales, novels, manga, television documentaries, and children's books. His heroic image was shaped in *Uchinā shibai*, a form of Okinawan popular theater. A staple in early Meiji, it remained popular until long after the Second World War.[22] Girū was said to be a peasant who lived in early eighteenth-century Ryūkyū. As a household servant to an *aji* (local warlord), he found himself in a position where each moment of his everyday life was appropriated and integrated into the rhythms of his master's household. From grooming the *aji*'s hair to sweeping the villa grounds, his work was intimately focused on satisfying his master's needs and desires. His life was like that of a tool, unobtrusively contributing to the efficient operation of the household, present yet unseen. And yet, he was more than that. He lived his own life in the homes and communities of the elite. Their villas, their gardens, the paths between their estates became as familiar to him as the farmhouse where he was born or the fields where he played as a child, yet he also knew the famine and misery that scratched at their gates. He came to share a feeling for their aesthetics, appreciate the luxurious experiences of their domestic life, and develop a sense of their notions of virtue and governance.[23] He dreamed of building on the capacities he could feel within himself, perhaps becoming a leader who could improve the lives of those around him. When he confided his hopes to the *aji* he served, he was stunned that the warlord callously dismissed them. The highest to which a farmer could aspire was nothing to a noble. Abandoning his hopes of service, Girū became an outlaw, refusing to sacrifice himself any longer to support his master's life of ease.

In this moment, he felt what Jacques Rancière has described as the "commensurability of incommensurables."[24] As hurt or humiliated as he might have been, his anger was not simply grounded in resentment. He had shared the courtiers' world and recognized that their imperiousness and cruelty did not align with the ethos of virtue and justice that they espoused. He also realized that the skills and abilities he had developed over a lifetime of work and experience, capacities he hoped to use on behalf of his community, were being appropriated to sustain an oppressive regime. It was a critique from within the same order, shaped by shared values. When he escaped from servitude and became an outlaw, the form that his rebellion took was also grounded in his experience. He continued to slip inside the rhythms of the lives of the nobility, moving unseen through their estates like the servant he once was. His care had created comfort, refinement, and leisure time for them, allowing them to live as artists, scholars, and statesmen; now it left them in a state of fear and uncertainty. The once-invisible servant had become more real to them, constantly in their thoughts, even when he was absent. His concern exposed their parasitic relationship to commoners, reversing patterns of exploitation and accumulation, returning money and fine things to those whose work had created them. He illuminated their real disregard for the lives of ordinary people, demonstrating their willingness to kill those who threaten their privilege. In the fastness of his stronghold in a mountaintop forest—in Untamamui—he defied the monarch and resisted the armies of the court. In return, the peasants and farmers from the surrounding villages concealed and protected him. He received the loyalty that custom and law dictated was the sovereign's due. Even when he was mortally wounded in a struggle with the king, the peasants hid his body. He was never captured, his death never confirmed.

Uchinā shibai became popular in the late nineteenth century, at the same time that the nobility was disbanded and Ryūkyū incorporated into the Japanese state. Given that, it is not difficult to imagine plays like *Untamagirū to Andakwībōjā* (Untamagirū and the Buddhist monk Andakwī) to be a critical allegory of Japanese colonization. The misery of peasant life depicted in the performance would certainly have resonated with the poverty and suffering that ordinary people experienced under Japanese rule, and with the anger and humiliation they suffered through their uneven transformation into imperial subjects.[25] When performance of *Uchinā shibai* resumed in the tents of postwar refugee camps or newly rebuilt theaters, the disdainful, callous courtiers could just as easily stand for the new American occupiers.

The Okinawan film director Takamine Gō once told me that his dream was to make a truly Okinawan film. It was not simply that the dialogue would be in Uchināguchi; it would be organized around the rhythms of everyday life and crafted from all of the genres of contemporary Okinawan performance. Starting with *Okinawa Dream Show* (1974), he began to experiment with *Uchinā shibai* and popular songs, courtly dance and community festivals, rock theatrics and stand-up comedy, folktales and relations with autochthonous deities, political protest, yakuza and experimental film, and avant-garde art. *Untamagirū*, filmed in the years after Okinawa's reversion to Japanese rule and the nominal end of American military occupation, gave Takamine the opportunity to playfully transform earlier tellings of the story.[26] In this space of capitalist labor, American military colonialism, and memories of wartime genocide, Takamine composes a Benjaminian allegory in which the moments created and the capacities developed in one domain could inform the possibilities for action in another. At the same time, his work is intensely personal, recalling the forms that he experienced as a boy and as a young man. This intimacy is manifestly clear in films such as *Kadekaru Rinshō: Uta to Katari* (Kadekaru Rinshō: Song and narrative). Takamine himself regularly appears in the frame, directing the performance or displaying his sketches and paintings of the scene, storyboards constructed in the midst of the shoot, his struggle to represent an imagined form against that which has already been committed to film.[27]

Untamagirū disrupts viewer's expectations, both playfully and seriously, shifting from genre to genre. Takamine seems to have little interest in working toward the kind of transparency that could close the gap between everyday life and representation. In their daily lives, Okinawans may be familiar with each of the genres that have inspired Takamine; however, unless they are cinephiles, they are not likely to expect them to be juxtaposed with one another in a popular film. For many of my Okinawan friends, Takamine's direction creates an almost sublime experience, as if they have just discovered something that has been familiar to them since they were children. Others, even friends who are performers, find his films to be distractingly pretentious and complain about the jumbled references and forms of expression that follow, one after another. Takamine's film foregrounds this unsettling assemblage, embedding a community play inside a theatrical review inside the film itself.

Untamagirū begins with an outdoor performance by the popular Okinawan musician, comedian, and ethnographer Teruya Rinsuke—here called Terurin the Barber. For Okinawans and mainland Japanese familiar with Okinawan popular culture, it is a pleasurable moment of recognition—like a faithful member of the audience might feel at *Uchinā shibai* or in a nightclub when a favorite performer takes the stage.[28] The nostalgic form of the rural village is also presented, yet it is a strange and unexpected space—a barber shop and theatrical stage incorporated in a farmhouse built in a historical theme park. A real and identifiable place, yet one materially associated with memory and play. And, as Terurin welcomes his audience to the *Watabū shō*, his famous postwar theatrical review restaged for the film, singing a folksong about the American occupation, the narrative begins to unfold like a contemporary retelling of the popular drama, *Untamagirū*.

Like the stagebound play, the space of the film is compressed: the village, a beach, a glimpse of the high commissioner's villa, an enchanted forest on its margins. If the performance has any relationship to the time of the world, it seems to take place shortly before Okinawa's reversion to Japanese sovereignty in 1972. The characters pass through these same spaces, again and again. Once more, Girū is caught up in the rhythms of work: now commodified labor rather than of archaic servitude. The possibilities of modernization squandered—once again—on the creation of luxury for the elite. Girū works at a small sugar factory under the harsh supervision of his *oyakata*, the leader of his village. His labor is so devalued that he replaces a water buffalo, his days spent driving a motorized tricycle in circles, turning the arm of the factory's sugarcane press. The speed and mobility promised by modernity distorted into grinding repetition. For Girū, daily life is a tight cycle of working, eating, and sleeping. And yet, despite the demands on his body and on his time, he creates moments in which he can imagine—and live, however briefly—another life. In hours stolen from sleep, he cares for his sister, who works in a local brothel, and for his invalid mother. He carries out his own scientific research into the lives of ants, looking for ways to alleviate the suffering of others. He shares his meager rations with a *kijimunā*, a forest spirit living near his village. And he dreams. Waking and sleeping, his dreams give form to his desire for Marē, the *oyakata*'s shapeshifting ward. An entity that sometimes appears as a mortal woman, sometimes a pig, she pushes the sacrificial resemblance between the two to the point of identity. The *oyakata* intends to present her to a local deity, who anticipates receiving her as his consort. A sacrifice binding the deity to the community, his gratitude bringing good fortune in return to the *oyakata*. The film creates a parallel in the demands of the American high commissioner, who insists upon his own offerings from Okinawans, whether by taking Girū's sister as his mistress or draining the blood of animals. Here, the sacrifice is different: the duration of its offering is endlessly distended while no indebtedness is ever acknowledged or repaid. A model of colonial sacrifice that enfolds and exceeds the traditional.

Girū's dissatisfaction takes shape much like that of Untamagirū in the *Uchinā shibai*, at the intersection of feeling and knowledge. The discontent that he feels in his life opens him to the critique of colonialism and capitalist exploitation that is everywhere in Okinawa, and he finds parallels in the appropriation of his labor and the rejection of his ambitions. His rebellion against the conditions of everyday life begins with his refusal to work and his determination to act on his dreams. Instead of reporting for his daily shift at the sugar refinery, he takes Marē to a *moashibi*, where they make love. *Moashibi*—illicit outdoor parties where young men and women, outside state and community regulation, showed that they could choose their own sexual partners—are practices that Okinawans have long associated with moments of freedom and self-determination.[29] Girū's actions challenge the *oyakata*'s authority to sacrifice his lover. By interfering with this, he claims equivalence to the sacrifier, the local deity who expected to receive the gift of Marē's affections. And yet, the form of the *moashibi* is critical here: in the end, his rebellion is not about his right to give or to receive the gift of a woman. It is about their mutual right to freedom, to choose to be with one another, regardless of convention or consequence.

In that moment, Girū also becomes a bandit, recognizing that he has powers beyond those exploited in labor. In repayment, the *kijimunā* has taught him to fly and protect himself against dark forces. He joins the struggle of the Ryūkyū Liberation Army to overthrow American occupiers and create a truly free Okinawa. Terurin appears again, now within the story that he had been telling, encouraging Girū to play the theatrical Untamagirū in a performance that he will be staging at a summer festival in the village. It is a moment of anticipation and uncertainty. Anticipation, in that the predictability of repetition becomes clear to anyone who has seen *Untamagirū* performed. Actors and audience alike know that there is room to improvise, to color the role of Untamagirū with qualities associated with the actor. Still, the performance must ultimately end with the bandit's fatal confrontation with the king. This is the weird excess of theatrical performance: Girū himself recognizes the uncanny parallel between his abilities and intentions, and those of the character of Untamagirū in Terurin's play. Hope and catastrophe intertwine in his movement toward a future that can only be reached through something immanent in text and memory. What's more, he takes this on with irony and playfulness: his identification with the role seems to come down to the play of chance, rather than the constraints of fate—or Takamine's own script.[30]

The consequences of this uncertain *amor fati* are confirmed as the film continues to unfold. Girū expects to portray the bandit Untamagirū's rebellion, his experience of power, of fame, and of care for his fellow farmers, knowing that all of this will come to an end when he is run through by the king's spear. But the narrative shifts unexpectedly and he does not complete the anticipated mimetic arc. The *oyakata*, angry and jealous, throws his own spear from the audience to the stage, striking Girū at the very moment he is reveling in his powers of flight, pinning the actor Girū into the character Untamagirū. And yet, unlike the legendary hero, this Girū does not die; he stumbles from the stage to a beach, his head skewered by the *oyakata*'s weapon.

Takamine shifts the frame again. The actor who has portrayed Girū awakens from a hasty afternoon nap at the sugar factory. He is now called Sanrā—not only a popular character name in *Uchinā shibai* but the Okinawan cognate for the name "third son" in Japanese. With that, a third cycle of repetition begins: the Girū of the *Uchinā shibai*, the Girū of the American occupation, and this. For a moment, a flash of confidence crosses Sanrā's face, as if he now has command of all that he has done, of all that he has been. Informed by this experience, he seems about to act. However, the *oyakata* arrives before he can do anything. Speaking Japanese for the first time in the film, the *oyakata* announces that they must all continue to labor as before because Okinawa is now—again—Japan. With that, he steps down from his sedan, grabs a nearby stick of dynamite, and blows up the factory where they all labor. He kills himself and the shapeshifting Marē in a stunning moment of repetition, recreating the suicidal violence and the intentional destruction of the Pacific War. The performance ends without Girū's mastery of his powers or his freedom from exploitation: his rebellion remains contained within the film. As Benjamin has written, "life within the magic circle of eternal return makes for an existence that never emerges from the auratic."[31] And yet, perhaps the faintest possibility for an allegorical understanding remains, as Girū demonstrates the courage to inhabit the moment, knowing full well that only catastrophe awaits.

All around me, the volunteers are moving. There is work to be done, bodies to be disinterred. What kind of possibilities inhere in this moment, in the roles that we will occupy as we pick up our shovels and our buckets and climb down again into the mud? Overhead, the sky began to clear, bands of cloud casting dark lines across the field. Out at sea, everything remains hidden in the rain.[32]

Gushiken Takamatsu and the Search for the Dead, August 2010

I walked along the street in Makabi, a neighborhood lodged on the northern edge of Naha, below Shuri's hills. Once this was the anchor of the western flank of the Shuri Line, across the island from Untamamui, where I would dig for the remains of the dead in another year. Seventy years earlier, the staff of the Japanese Thirty-Second Army conducted a defense in depth in this space, drawing the advancing US Army into a war of attrition in the mountains and coastal plains of central Okinawa. They traded space for time, hoping that fierce fighting and heavy casualties in treacherous terrain and crowded villages would make American strategic planners hesitate before invading the home islands. It was to be a massive, bloody sacrifice. One that preserved the Japanese monarchy and the state and allowed the American military to consolidate their victory and their influence in East Asia, building their homes in these fields and remaining for decades to come.

My walk took me across a grid overgrown with weeds and marred by patches of hard, gravelly soil. Twilight muted the sharp lines of twisted rebar and broken concrete that surrounded me, the fragments of homes and businesses that had been thrown up in the rush of reconstruction after the war, then taken down again to make room for something else. Something new. Empty apartment blocks stood against the sky, the darkness of their windows flat and unrevealing. It was impossible to tell what was new and what was old. To my east, shadows pushed across the baseball diamond behind Makabi Elementary School, a shuttered taxi stand, a wooded neighborhood park, the low silhouettes of tombs. To my south, beyond the school, a line ran across the darkness, black against black. A cut in which the Naha Central Ring Road has been built, a road that was not a ring at all, but an asphalt corridor linking Shuri with the western coast. Traffic might have been moving somewhere below, but the ground obscured my view.

The evening was warm, the dusty smell of rain and earth in the air. Above me, the sky was dark with clouds, the hard light of stars emerging around the edge. I imagined this image mirrored in the city spreading out around me, an uneven pool of shadow traced with a corona of lights. I felt very alone. Mark Fisher has written of other similar spaces, places that consist mostly of absence.[33] Not ruins, or even rubble. Both of those imply the awareness of a duration, an unavoidable presence in the landscape of unevenness and disjunction. Here, absence is glimpsed in the moment, a brief pause.[34] It is as if a truck might return at any time to remove the last fragments of the buildings that once stood all around me, and that surveyors, designers, and construction workers would set to work again, replacing them with new spaces of work, leisure, and rest.

A hundred meters or so to the west, beyond the modernist silhouette of the monorail station, most of that work had already been done. Shintoshin—the New Heart of the City—stretched out toward the harbor at Tomari. This was not simply the renovation of a crumbling residential neighborhood in the interstices of a colonial city. Instead, it was a massive urban development project that would be the radiant center of Naha, Okinawa's capital, in the new millennium. Construction had been underway for several years, a new space built to fill the void once occupied by an American base. Machinato (later Makiminato) had been an Eisenhower-era suburb of ranch-style houses, schools, shopping centers, and sports fields, cut off from the rest of Okinawa by the 1952 Treaty of San Francisco, by the Status of Forces Agreement, and by a chain-link fence reinforced with warning signs in Japanese and English. Shintoshin reproduced the remembered shape of those spaces of American occupation, an eerie appropriation of the form of the demolished base community.[35]

Intensive capital investment; long negotiations between bureaucrats, landowners, and speculators; the coordinated labor of public and private designers and engineers—all came together to imagine and create a site of integrated private, commercial, and governmental spaces. It was a design intended to make a statement about the future—a city, rather than a public building like a municipal office or community center. An axis of green spaces, parks, and recreational areas intersected a wide boulevard lined with hotels, the southern office of the Bank of Japan, the Okinawa Development Corporation, broadcast and print media offices, a shopping mall, and an extravagant duty-free store. At the center, the new prefectural museum of art and history. The museum was a sprawling complex of courtyards and buildings, shaped from polished white limestone. Its award-winning design drew the image of a reef-encircled island into that of the walled courtyards and fortifications of a Ryūkyūan *gusuku* (castle). Like the *gusukus* that have been restored and preserved across Okinawa, it does not resemble a fully reconstructed citadel.[36] The lines of the walls and courtyards are sharp and clean, but none of the buildings that would have once stood in a castle's grounds have been built. Organized around the same logic of representation as Kinjō Nobuyoshi's Naha Shimin Kaikan (Naha Civic Hall), the battlements have become metonymic for the whole. The ceremonial spaces, the exhibition halls, the rooms for research and performance have been embedded in the base, as if protected within. They are subterranean, like crypts, like the caverns that lie beneath Ryūkyūan castles and shrines. The transient places of ritual and governance give way to the immanence of the past, of the dead, of the deities. Crafted with a modern curatorial logic that echoes the archaic. There is a sense of weight and permanence to this new, gleaming white, fortress-like structure. The qualia of monumentality resonates in a place where there has been so much violence and destruction, suffering and uncertainty.[37]

Extending out from this, there were blocks of restaurants and hotels, chic condominiums, and neighborhoods of upscale homes that blended traditional architectural motifs with luxurious modern amenities. From its station, the monorail could whisk tourists and residents to the international airport south of Naha; eventually, it would run north to Urasoe. As Nitta Susumu, the director of the public corporation that designed and managed the construction of the community, once explained to me, Shintoshin was an example of what Okinawa might look like in a future free of American bases. In spite of generations of violence, exploitation, and frustrated expectations, it awakened the hope that Okinawans could transform the spaces that had been denied to them for so long, and dwell in peace and prosperity.

At the same time, not everyone was convinced of the wisdom, or even the possibility, of embracing intensive development of the space. Okinawans were right to be skeptical of an island without bases. Aquapolis, the ambitious Metabolist floating city that the architect Kikutake Kiyonori had designed for Expo '75 in Nago as well as the imagined possibilities of a future Okinawa, had long since been towed away to Shanghai and cut up for scrap.[38] Ōshiro Tatsuhiro, the Akutagawa Prize–winning novelist, published a prescient story in 2006—*Tennyo no Yūrei* (The ghost of the celestial maiden)—in which he explored the fragmentation of daily life of which a project like the Shintoshin development would be both indexical and iconic. "Fushigi na kūkan ni natta na," muses a character as he looks out across the construction sites from the veranda of a new condominium—"It's become a strange space, hasn't it?"[39] The development was unsettled, the shimmer of the commodity that sparked across the polished floors of stylish boutiques and the bright facades of new homes darkening in the bare, open fields where fragments of bone and coral pushed up through the ground. It was not enough that the machines, the picks and sledges of workers, had shattered the remnants of this American colonial station. They would continue to tear through the fabric of Okinawan social space, the fields and villages that lay beneath the base. All to build something new—the old places would never be restored.

And yet, could the past ever be obliterated? Ōshiro writes of rumors of a *yūrei* that appears among the new places. A *yūrei* is a ghost, perhaps, but not always a revenant. It can also be a remainder, an entity that persists in a place despite its own transformations, despite the changes in the world around it, despite the forgetting that allows residents and tourists to go about their daily lives. Ōshiro's characters ask if it might be a spirit of one of the dead Okinawans who had been entombed in the graves at Mekaru, just behind the new museum. Could they have been disturbed by the movement of their remains to a modern cemetery in Naha, the destruction of small farming villages like Mekaru or Uchinoya that were scattered across the rolling hills, or the fields between them that grew crops for markets? Readers might wonder if it is a spirit of a dead American or Japanese soldier who was killed in these fields in April 1945, during a horrifically violent week in which the living were torn and blasted from their fortifications in the slopes of the hills still remembered as Horseshoe, Half Moon, and Sugarloaf, the dying left buried in the rubble or scattered on the ground. Could it have even been a bomb dropped or a grenade thrown decades earlier, waiting to complete its distended, deadly trajectory? Or was it the ghost of an activist who protested, year after year, before the gates of the American base that once stood in these fields; a household servant or groundskeeper who labored in the American neighborhood; a woman who married into the occupying army, living out her life and dying a world away from her relatives and her ancestors?[40]

In Ōshiro's novella, it was rumored to be the ghost of a celestial maiden, her story retold in *Mekarushi*, the famous Okinawan *kumiodori* (courtly dance). An entity that once spent a lifetime as a mortal woman, bound to the husband who had stripped her of her feathered cloak. She lost her ability to fly, the beauty of her appearance, everything associated with her divinity. Instead, she became a human woman. She worked and lived in one of the farming villages that once stood in these fields. She bore Mekarushi a son and daughter, and labored in his household. Despite the diminution of her powers and the loss of her freedom, she loved her children. When, by chance, she found her feathered cloak and returned to the world of the deities, she was heartbroken to be separated from them. And yet, performances pass over this sadness to valorize the filial piety of her children, who faithfully continued to search for their mother.[41] A poignant image of Okinawan sacrifice: both the act and its representation appropriated by others.

If the *yūrei* was that celestial maiden, she did not linger in the ruins of her home; neither did she bathe at the well where she had been captured. Her appearance—if indeed she appeared—was wrapped in mystery. One *yuta* insisted that she spoke to her, commanding Okinawans to abandon their plans to build new homes or create new businesses in spaces that she insisted remain untouched. Skeptical observers suspected that there was no *yūrei* at all, only the efforts of a yuta to earn a higher fee for quieting the spirit of an exceptional entity like a celestial maiden. Another younger *yuta* found herself unable to intercede for the living with the deity, unable to hear her silent call, to call her by her true name, to feel her in the spaces where she might walk. The world was in disarray.[42]

I continued on, following a barricade that led to a field next to the school. Ahead of me, I saw a small van parked alongside a steel cabin. Gushiken Takamatsu crouched there in the growing darkness, speaking quietly into his mobile phone. He was short and lithe, built with economy. Gushiken was an electrical contractor.[43] He was also an author and lecturer, a critic, an activist, and a visionary. A man who searched for the dead. His white button-down shirt and khaki work pants were neatly pressed, and his sleeves were precisely rolled above his elbows. The ball cap he wore was turned backward on his head, giving him a surprisingly youthful appearance although I knew that he was several years older than me. As I approached, he finished his call and slipped the phone into his trouser pocket. With practiced care, he lit the mantle of a camping lantern, his hard, weathered hands adjusting the flow of fuel. The gas flared, yellow and bright, before setting down to a cold, white hiss.

With a smile and a nod, he motioned for me to enter the building ahead of him. It was a prefabricated metal cabin, like those temporarily set up on construction or industrial sites in Japan. It was the kind of space where the planners and designers responsible for the transformation of communities like this could imagine the future that they would bring into being, creating plans on shimmering computer screens, spreading detailed charts out on tabletops. It was a place where projects could be discussed; orders issued; supervisors could meet with subordinates, contractors, vendors, and their own leaders; budgets managed and supply chains engaged. It was a place where leaders could retreat to reflect on their progress. It was a *genba* within a *genba*: a place where work is done that will enable other work to be done.[44] Buildings like this probably dotted the landscape in the immediate postwar period, as new construction replaced the cities that had been destroyed, as new dwellings were made to house those who would serve the occupying Americans and their bases, as those bases themselves were constructed atop battlefields and villages and the remnants of Japanese installations. For the past several years, they have returned to these neighborhoods, centers for projects of reconstruction and gentrification.

However, the work done in this cabin was very different. It is a space where the things that are unearthed during the violent transformation of the landscape, where the remains of another way of life and death,

4.4.   Gushiken Takamatsu at his workshop.

can be collected and sorted. It is the field office of Gamafuyā, a volunteer organization created to carry out *ikotsu shūshū*, the recovery of the remains of the war dead. Their work focused on both the subjects of the Japanese Empire and the soldiers who fought them, bringing them back from the spaces of death that dominate the Okinawan landscape. Like the offices in the prefabricated cabins that I discussed above, planning also takes place in this space. Site surveys are examined, plans for excavations are developed, records kept, visitors entertained. The building was also filled with the remains of these excavations. It is as if the contents of the soil, the deposits of the past, unburied from the places where they had lain for decades, had to be brought into new relationships with the living—considered, evaluated, understood. The building was lined with metal shelving, and every surface was covered with the carefully arranged remains of a battle that began more than half a century earlier. Fragments of military uniforms, folded and labeled. Helmets, battered and pierced. Pieces of boots, identification tags and amulets, the cap of a fountain pen. Everything arranged with care and artless precision. The surviving metal assembly of an American M1 Garand, its wooden stock broken and decomposed, its once-sleek form encrusted with dirt and rust. A Japanese Nambu machine gun that looked like it had been made of coral and clay. Dishes of bullets, scored and blunted, fired in the heat of battle. There were far more bullets of American manufacture than Japanese, more a sign of the ruthlessness of industrial dominance in the waning months of the war than an index of rounds fired and rounds received. Although the traces of war are virtually invisible in the surrounding streets and parks, it is as if the presence of that excess must be acknowledged somewhere.

And yet, the dead in their material form are absent. Where were the thousands of American Marines and sailors, Japanese soldiers, and Okinawan conscripts who had died on these hillsides? Even before the battle had ended, the Americans had begun to gather up their dead to return them to the United States. Few Okinawans from the surrounding villages had been killed here—most fled before fighting started. And the Japanese Army? Soldiers retreating under fire have little choice but to leave their casualties behind, and dealing with them was not a priority for the Americans. However, they were not forgotten. Although efforts to recover them immediately after the war were halting and inconsistent, a complicated network of veterans and survivors groups, national politicians and local officials, Buddhist priests, peace activists, imperial apologists and militarists, city and regional planners, Shintō religious centers, and national parks gradually came together to remember their deaths.[45] Networks of community monuments have been built: memorials, columbaria, museums, scholarly and popular literature, media installations, film, television, research institutes, group and individual projects. The rhythm of daily life has been altered by annual commemorations such as Irei no Hi, a practice that articulates in complex ways with moments of national mourning like the bombing of Hiroshima and the date of surrender. And yet, there always seems to be an inexhaustible supply of death to excavate and repatriate, an unending number of corpses and bone fragments. It is a strange and melancholy division of labor—the efforts devoted to the remembrance of loss overwhelm any actions to find the dead and bring them home.

Gushiken's life has always been intertwined with patterns of remembering and forgetting. Since he was young, he had been confronted with the ambiguous presence of the dead in the world around him. This is what organized our discussions during my fieldwork, the public lectures he would give across Okinawa, and his concise, urgent memoir.[46] As a boy, he and his friends had explored the caves that honeycombed the hillsides around Naha, spaces where soldiers and civilians had taken shelter during the war, where fragments of equipment, spent bullets, unexploded ordnance could be found everywhere. They scraped out the residue from old shells and made their own fireworks, watching them flash up against the sky as if they were at a summer festival. However, the bones, shattered and abandoned, were different. Here, their parents drew the line. "Leave them alone. They belong to someone else. Perhaps those people will return for them some day."

Years later, the dead intruded again. As a young Boy Scout leader, he met several scoutmasters from mainland Japan who were also involved in the search for Okinawan battlefield remains. Moved by their sadness and uncertainty, he joined them on their next visit. As they searched clearings and caverns in half-remembered battlefields, he discovered that the dead had withdrawn even further. At first, they only found traces of equipment and clothing. It was not until he crouched down and ran his fingers through the fragments of coral at his feet that the dead appeared to him. A smooth knob of bone among the jagged shards. It broke to the surface and clung to his fingertips, a moment of intimacy after decades of abandonment and solitude.

At that moment, he told me that he realized that the reverent visits of veterans and survivors could never complete the recovery of the dead. No matter how many volunteers joined in, the practices of decades past were not enough. It was too late to simply retrace the route that the dead might have marched along or visit the battlefield where they might have been killed. Returning year by year to a task without end kept the image of heroic sacrifice alive in remembrance, but the loss could never be finalized. A prayer could be offered, the remains that they found could be sent to a national ossuary, but the searchers' tread would push the remaining fragments deeper into Okinawan soil. The broader attitudes of Japanese society also fixed these events in the past, sacrifice and loss that resonated with the present but was beyond contemporary actions. These visits could only yield endless repetition, the construction of what Walter Benjamin has called "stance," the embodied performance of dutiful patriotism and familial melancholy.[47] The past had to be excavated, brought back into the here and now. It would take time and effort. It would demand intimacy, bringing the dead back into the hands of the living. It had to be done by an Okinawan like Gushiken.[48]

He began to spend weekends searching for places where the dead might remain. He read critical histories and memoirs. He spoke to those who survived, and the families of those who did not. He collected rumors and stories. He explored the cities and the countryside. He learned to follow a map like a historian and read terrain like a soldier. He developed a sense for the landscape, feeling changes in the soil as he dug, searching for soft spots that might indicate a collapsed tunnel, probing to find an open space below ground that could be a forgotten bunker.

But why? What—beyond empathy with the families of those who were killed and abandoned—inspired him? When he studied memoirs that could lead him to the dead, when he searched for their remains in old battlefields, when he wrote and lectured about his work, he was not gathering evidence for war crimes prosecutions or to advance claims for restorative justice. Although he was actively engaged in his own research projects about the past, it was not to challenge narratives of wartime responsibility. Instead, he confidently cited the historian Hayashi Hirofumi's conclusion that Okinawans were ordered to their deaths by the Japanese authorities.[49]

Gushiken is concerned with a history that is imbricated in the lived moment. This becomes much clearer as he explains what interests him in accounts of the war. He writes that it was the intention of the Japanese high command—perhaps on orders from Tokyo—to weave Okinawan civilians into the battle to the death that they planned to wage. In the face of certain defeat, Japanese soldiers and Okinawan civilians were united in sacrifice as a demonstration to the Americans. The all-consuming *gyokusai*—the sacrificial collective of shattered, jewel-like bodies—was intentional.[50] In order to make the consequences of this policy clear, he turns to the directive that preceded it. "Okinawan civilians," it read "were to live together with Japanese soldiers as if they were a single, unified family."[51] This uncovers the horrifying, quotidian dimension of Japanese strategy. It was not enough that Okinawans were mobilized as Japanese citizens in a state of emergency. It was not enough that they provided material and emotional support to the soldiers who garrisoned the island. The Japanese Army penetrated civil society, transforming the very structure of the family, and integrating domestic forms into the nation and the state. In his memoir, Gushiken explains that Okinawan civilians were ordered to flee to the precise place where the Japanese Army intended to make their stand. The fight to the death would be intentionally waged on a battlefield in which the army was integrated with conscripted Okinawans and unarmed, untrained civilians.[52] Decades earlier, when Ōta Chofu wrote of Okinawan assimilation that they should even learn to sneeze like the mainland Japanese, could he have imagined this moment? Now, the differences that had been the basis for decades of prejudice against Okinawans, the humiliating and contested history of efforts at assimilation, could be effaced by a single command. The national community that many Okinawans had dreamed of their entire lives would be offered in a narrative of deadly fusion that would continue to be repeated until the present.[53] I am reminded of what Valerio Valeri wrote in another context. "There are sacrifices that even include struggles between animals, as in Toraja [Sulawesi, Indonesia] where water buffaloes are made to fight before they are slaughtered."[54] After that, those who participated in the ritual can speak of the strength and aggressiveness of the buffaloes—who could say otherwise? When history is written by the sacrifiers—those who benefit from the act—they can always impose the qualities that they desire on their sacrifice.

Gushiken often spoke of the discovery of the dead in Shintoshin as a turning point for him. However, his memoir describes two earlier experiences that offer important insight into his project. The first took place in a concealed bunker that he and his friends located near the harbor in Itoman City. As they began to dig into the underground position, they found the fragments of the US grenade that caused the entrance and part of the ceiling to collapse.

> Beneath the fallen dirt and rocks, we discovered the remains of three Japanese soldiers. At the back of the tunnel, where the space remained open, there was a body curled up, holding its knees. We found a button on the ground near these remains. It wasn't something that went with military issue clothing. It was stamped with the insignia of the prefectural middle school. We realized that he had been a child soldier in the Tekketsu Kinnōtai [the Iron and Blood Imperial Corps—a group of children who had been conscripted to serve in the Japanese Army].
>
> Because of his cramped position, we originally thought that he had been a casualty who had been laid down back there by his fellow soldiers. As time passed, we realized that he might have survived, left alone in the back of the bunker after the three soldiers were killed in the attack. In that narrow underground space, unlighted, with no

exit, with no one to rescue him, left all alone. What a situation of unbelievable horror and hopelessness. I wonder if he had food or water? I wonder how many days he lived in that miasma of decay? I felt as if my heart would be crushed.[55]

Gushiken's second account begins with the wartime memoir of an elderly survivor. The author and his family had been forced to take shelter in a large cave near Itoman, a space that had once been reserved for burials and encounters with autochthonous deities. Several other displaced families from the community joined them. A detachment of Japanese soldiers driven south by the advancing American army occupied the cave themselves. Soldiers had taken Okinawans' food, confiscated their homes, conscripted them to perform their labor. Now they even followed them into the tomb, displacing them in those places of death.[56]

Most of those Japanese soldiers were killed in a failed raid on a nearby American position. US soldiers pursued the survivors back to the cavern, detonating a large explosive charge above it. Many soldiers and civilians were crushed as the cavern collapsed. The author's family survived, following a group of soldiers through a small tunnel in the rubble. As they were scrambling out, he heard a faint voice calling. Stopping to light a match, he found a wounded Okinawan conscript pinned beneath a large rock. The conscript asked him to get word to his family so that they would know how he died. After the war, he kept his promise, but the soldier's family refused to believe the account, insisting that he died in combat.[57]

Gushiken used the author's description to locate the cave in the hills outside Itoman. After he and a friend cleared the entrance, they found a space filled with human remains.

> We discovered what looked like a body, half buried by the collapse. It was still pinned beneath the rocks. If we were able to do a DNA analysis, we might have been able to prove that it was the Okinawan conscript.[58] When we searched the area around his upper body, we found a number of empty cans of canned food, an alarm clock, and a grenade that he was supposed to use as a last resort. However, when we spoke with the survivor who had written about it, he told us that the soldier didn't have any supplies with him when they spoke. Someone must have given them to him after that. When we found him, the cans were all empty. I think that he opened them himself and ate them. I suppose that the sound of the alarm clock's ticking

would have been comforting for someone left behind in the silent depths of that black cavern. The people that gave him the clock must have known that they couldn't help him. Even so, they might have told him that they would come back to help. I can't imagine that.

From the grenade that was left for him to use as a last resort, I can picture the injured soldier's last moments there in the darkness. Without food or water, he would get weaker and weaker. Someone might have given him that grenade so that he could take his own life. But he didn't use it. He didn't kill himself.

I've seen so many remains of those who killed themselves in the caves. One thing I can say from that experience is that, to keep living until the end without choosing death—that refusal requires courage, endurance, and hard work (endeavor). Whenever I think about that broken clock, I wonder which came first: did the clock stop running, or did he draw his final breath?[59]

The army that should have protected this young Okinawan conscript abandoned him. The empire that was to bring prosperity and enlightenment offered him suffering and death. And, recalling the theme of Kuramoto's *Kikoku* (discussed in chapter 2), the state and Shintō institutions that should have cared for his remains and enshrined his spirit have built narratives of loyalty and patriotic sacrifice while leaving him, alone and neglected, beneath a rock in a forgotten cavern.

These discoveries compelled Gushiken to move beyond conventional memoration of the past. He was unconvinced by state ideologies, figured by the constant repetition of narratives of valorized sacrifice that fix the dead firmly in the past and remind the living of their obligation to those who sacrificed themselves. At the same time, he has lost confidence in the endlessly prolonged, unsatisfying search for intimacy with the patriotic dead in the present that nonetheless sustains the production of auratic distance.[60] Instead, he and his collaborators have learned to listen for the call of the dead themselves, for what he calls their "voiceless scream."[61] These cries have been drawn out for decades, always in danger of being lost in the representational excess of patriotic loss. By answering their call, Gushiken and his friends challenge the past as something retained only in memory. In its place, they discover a duration that intersects with the present, and a space in which the effects of actions performed long ago persist.[62] It is like Okamoto Tarō's vision of the sacred: buried but awaiting the hands of those who know where to look and how to uncover it. It is a duration of action, a chronotope organized around the work of the dead. The members of Gamafuyā find it in the fragments at their feet—a scattering of empty cans, a jacket button, an unexploded grenade, remains in a certain position, bones unbroken by explosion—and a constellation begins to take shape. They recognize its relationship to the actions and experiences of other soldiers—those who abandoned the dying as they carried out their own acts of sacrifice, their own deaths; those who offered them grenades, platitudes, encouragement, insults, and solitude. The bodies that they discover have composed themselves into a material utterance that will run counter to narratives of murder and suicide, of loyal sacrifice. Their presence materializes more than their refusal. It gives shape to new and different actions.

This commitment was not the decision of a moment. Their determination not to kill—not to take another's life, not to take their own—continued. The young cadet sat alone in the back of the fighting position until he died. The conscript, his legs pinned under a rock, measured out his remaining days in the cans of food that he ate and the ticking of his alarm clock. They did not use their grenades or any of their other weapons. Surely, they recognized the inevitability of their own deaths. They simply would not kill in order to make it happen. Instead, they decided to wait. Not for rescuers or a relief force—they knew that no one would come for them while the battle raged. They waited for those whose arrival could only be anticipated.

Waiting is a powerful theme in Okinawan literature and performance. *Hanauri no En*, the famous *kumiodori* (courtly dance), tells the story of an impoverished samurai and his family who are kept apart for years until a chance meeting reunites them.[63] Their only hope comes from their confidence in *en*, the perduring relationships that bind them together.[64] In *Okinawa Bunkaron*, Okamoto Tarō writes of the figure of Nuzugema, a beautiful woman from Yaeyama, who appears as a character in a number of folktales and songs. Kept as a concubine by a Ryūkyūan courtier, she is separated from her commoner lover for the rest of her life. She imagines that a tree will one day grow from her grave, perhaps to be harvested and crafted into a ship—a servant even in death, made to ferry her masters from island to island. And yet, all of that would be worthwhile if, one day, her lover would also be carried home on its deck.[65] The popular song "Jūku no Haru" (The nineteenth spring) tells of a working man separated from his lover since they were together in American-occupied Koza during the spring of their nineteenth year.[66] Although he knows that she made a life with a wealthy man and there's no chance of their reunion, he still waits for the return of spring and the feeling of hope it brings. The idea of expectant waiting is also an important dimension of everyday life. *Machikantī* (I can't wait) is a common phrase in Okinawa, a feeling charged with pleasurable anticipation.[67] Okinawans wait for many things. For students and seasonal laborers to come home from the mainland. For land confiscated by American occupiers to be returned. For a local job to finally open, or for a new development project to be funded. For the discrimination they experience as Okinawans to come to an end. For justice, after generations of American exploitation.

And so, the soldiers that Gushiken found remained hidden, waiting for the arrival of their rescuers, men and women who would not even be born until long after their death. Despite the uncertainty of war, their arrival was anticipated in the promise of *yuimāru*, the bonds of intimacy, affection, and obligation that the soldiers knew would persist across time. They waited for those who were able to recognize what it is that they had done, so that they could experience together the possibility of a life beyond sacrifice and death. Their death was not a sacrifice; their waiting was a gift.

There is something about the tableau that they excavated that reminds me of the account of the charcoal maker that inspired both Yanagita Kunio and Okamoto Tarō. And yet, the *girigiri no utsukushisa* experienced here—the beauty of life on the edge, of life on the horizon of death—is very different. If not free of the moral ambiguity that charged Okamoto's project, the distinctions are clearer. They found soldiers who resisted calls to suicide and threats of violence. They refused the command to kill, to sacrifice. These are not Okinawans who fought alongside Japanese soldiers and killed on command or out of the necessity of the moment—or if they are, they have put that behind them. They are not the villagers who followed the commands of military commanders, community and family leaders, killing their families and themselves. They did not die at the hands of either American or Japanese soldiers. There was no last-minute cessation of hostilities, no narrow escapes, no merciful soldiers who saved them from death. They made their choices, they held their ground, and they died. In doing so, they transformed that space where they abided, creating something more than a place of murder and violence. But what?

Writing on the ethics of sacrifice, Webb Keane builds on the work of Bhrigupati Singh and Naisargi Dave to suggest that the ability to perform the act demonstrates a mastery over the prohibitions against the taking of life. It is a challenging capacity to develop, one that is built incrementally and against powerful prohibitions.[68] And yet, as Brad Weiss argues in his discussion of butchering meat, it is "a violation of the moral order in order to affirm the truth of a wider moral universe." The expectation of a better world to come reflexively sanctions the transgressions.[69] The soldiers recovered by Gamafuyā emphatically reject this logic. They have been subject to powerful ideological interventions to instill in them the capacity to kill others and take their own lives. To valorize violence and brutality, to aestheticize sacrifice and death. To accept with pleasure the value of an imperial institution that demands both the disciplined perfection of the self and the offering of their lives—of all lives—as its due. To know that they are embedded in complex and interrelated networks of relationships: family, community, the nation and the state, loyal imperial subjects, *gyokusai*. Like the seekers of refuge that the historian Amino Yoshihiko wrote of in *Zōho Muen, Kugai, Raku*, they have put these relationships aside. And they have done so without the benefit of the established and acknowledged spaces of sanctuary—the Buddhist temples and open marketplaces—that Amino described. Instead, they created their own places in the tomb, in the battlefield, at the center of spaces of death.

Here is where the intervention of Gushiken and his collaborators becomes so important. Together with the dead, they draw on the logic of *yuimāru*—practices of mutual assistance that are both liberating and binding. As they uncover the remains of the dead and record their actions, they draw them out of one world, the world of war and brutality, and reincorporate them into another. This is the rescue that never came during life. They recognize the courage of the dead and acknowledge their refusal to kill or sacrifice. And, in this encounter with the battlefield dead, they find life. The space and time between the living and the dead is transformed. False histories, melancholy presents are disrupted. As the distance between Gushiken's collaborators and the dead of a distant war collapses, a different interval emerges. This one is grounded in the moment of decision indexed by the dead, and by the question that it entitles them to pose: "I did not give in to an ideology of death. What about you?"

The time that the volunteers from Gamafuyā and the dead spend together is limited. After the initial moment of discovery and the dialogue that grows out of that encounter, there is work that must be done. They systematically search the area. Material conditions are recorded: the position of the bodies, their uniforms, weapons, documents, and personal effects. Great care is taken to locate any unexploded ordnance or other dangerous conditions. Photographs are taken, notes and sketches made. Police are notified, confirming that these are war dead and not the victims of other violent crimes. Beyond that, they contact representatives from the national ossuary in Itoman, workers from municipal and prefecture cultural resource offices, staff from the local university medical center, members of local and national veterans groups, newspaper and television reporters, artists and activists. And finally the remains of the dead are carefully prepared for delivery to the national ossuary. When the remains leave their company, they are free to become the settled dead: interred in the tomb; remembered at local and national memorials and in periodic public ceremonies; perhaps engaged at a household altar. In most cases, the dead remain anonymous. Without any evidence to identify them—even now, a genetic database program is in its infancy—there will be no way to connect them with relatives who do not know that they have been discovered. Perhaps there are no descendants left to be notified. In that case, they will go to wherever it is that the forgotten dead dwell, remembered by Gushiken and his friends.

And yet, the dead whose call Gushiken answers can never be fully free from the traces of sacrifice. There are too many spaces, too many texts, too many practices associated with the remembrance of wartime death. The Yūshūkan, the revisionist military museum at Yasukuni Shrine, the patriotic memorials that fill the fields in Itoman, the meetings of veterans groups, the narratives that appear in revisionist textbooks, patriotic novels, manga, and film. Against that, collections of accounts of wartime genocide—enforced suicides, murder by Japanese soldiers—antiwar documentaries, lectures by war survivors in local schools, regular statements by prefectural and municipal politicians, performances by artists and musicians. The pervasiveness of these accounts makes it impossible to escape their influences, and for the concrete examples of these lives to have a significant impact on the abstract categories of sacrifice or of victimhood. Because they have already been defined by countless ideological narratives and practices, their social transformation, their misrepresentation, remains with them, regardless of any historical actuality that Gushiken has revealed. If a play like Kuramoto Sō's *Kikoku* warns that the status of *eirei*, the heroic dead, is precarious, Gushiken's work asserts that it is much more durable.[70] And so, the effect of their valorization as heroic, self-sacrificing soldiers—as *gyokusai*, as *eirei*—enters into a manifold with the other pasts that have been exposed. They have already been acknowledged as heroes, and no one disputes that. They are destined to be buried in a national ossuary, to be remembered at Yasukuni Shrine. The empirical fact that they refused to kill or refused to be sacrificed does not change that. Instead, it intertwines with the knowledge of their heroism, and they become something more. This is why they can be powerful symbols for all kinds of political projects on both the Left and the Right.

The members of Gamafuyā have also been changed by their encounter. The experience of locating and recognizing the dead, the lessons learned, the determination to do more. Gushiken constantly evokes these themes in his lectures, his interviews, and in his memoirs. The dead taught him lessons that he cannot forget. "Do not kill. Do not tolerate killing. Do not kill yourself." These principles are what drive the members of Gamafuyā to continue the work that will allow them to expose others to the same experiences.

There are also more subtle changes—perhaps not visible at first. Here, it is useful to consider Gushiken's experiences in Shintoshin. He read a notice in a local newspaper that fragments of bones had been discovered as construction cut into the north-facing slope of Sugarloaf Hill. This had been the site of significant Japanese fortifications on the western flank of the Shuri Line. Gushiken contacted Naha municipal authorities, offering to search the construction sites on weekends for remains of the dead. Naha bureaucrats ignored him; when he persisted, they rejected his offer. Concern with the dead could not be allowed to stop construction of the new city, the infusion of capital into the landscape. When public opinion finally pushed local authorities to do something about the remains that were being uncovered, authorities treated their recovery as another industrial process. Contractors were hired, and they used a power shovel to excavate the site. The mass of soil and remains was dumped on a conveyor belt, and contractors recovered what they could. There was no effort to sort or to identify anything. No attempt to find a piece of equipment, a *hanko* (personal seal), a fountain pen that might bear a name that could lead to identification—that is to say, to locate the remains that belong to an individual soldier rather than just one of the mass of the loyal, patriotic dead. No encounter between the living and the dead that might allow them to speak—their silent scream to be heard.

Gushiken was angry and frustrated that the state could, at all levels, neglect its responsibility to the dead. He redoubled his efforts to be involved in *ikotsu shūshū* at Shintoshin. As he did so, he realized that his reputation for his commitment to the dead was growing. Cultural resource staff from other municipal governments consulted him when they heard stories of possible buried remains, or when they had a chance to conduct their own excavations. Media reports enthusiastically described his work. Itokazu Keiko, the progressive Okinawan member of the House of Councilors, offered her support. Masuzoe Yōichi, then the Minister of Health, Labor and Welfare, a member of the conservative Liberal Democratic Party, met with him and offered to fund a large-scale project. Eventually, he was awarded the Yoshikawa Eiji Prize, recognizing the contributions that Gamafuyā has made to contemporary society. However, it was the meeting with Masuzoe that set Gamafuyā on a new path.[71]

Gushiken felt that the state was materially accountable for the dead. This went beyond appropriating them for patriotic discourses or contracting out their responsibilities. If the state intended to pay someone else to care for the dead, then that money should be put to work in doing other things that the state failed to do. Instead of simply diverting capital to state allies in the construction industry, it should go to those who deserved support. Those who could not work any longer, who had lost their jobs and their homes. He had heard about Yamauchi Masayoshi and his ministry to the unhoused and the unemployed at the Bethany Church in Urasoe. He wondered if recovering the remains of the dead could give new hope to them. He reached out to Yamauchi and they began to plan a new collaboration between Gamafuyā and the Promise Keepers. It would bring these formerly unhoused laborers into the same contact with the dead that he and his friends had experienced. And the dead themselves? Perhaps there would be those like he described to me—those who refused to kill. And yet, there would certainly be others. The patriotic dead who sacrificed their lives in the service of the emperor and the state.[72]

And what of the relationships that these practices bring into being? They are far from the community of murderous fusion that wartime sacrifice conjures. Neither are they an established alternative, the kind of traditional network of communal care and support that nativists and ethnologists are constantly reminding preoccupied moderns once structured everyday life. It is not even the impulse to discover the faint traces of some new and novel form in the interstices of everyday life—the kind of network that anthropologists like Ryo Morimoto have disclosed in the ruins of Fukushima.[73] Instead, they speak to their confidence in *yuimāru*. Here, the act of binding together draws on deep practical familiarity and a comforting sense of custom, as well as the creative and contingent desire to create something new, something grounded in the needs and conditions of the moment.

Higa Toyomitsu and the Voices of the Dead

> In that instant, goosebumps stood up on my skin and my body froze. My hand holding the camera probably trembled. The first photos that I took weren't intentionally blurry and out of focus.[74] Here, in this

place where the Battle of Okinawa had taken place sixty-five years ago, a brain had appeared from among the fragments of bone that had been gathered. I can't forget the shock that I felt in that moment.

On March 21, 2010, Gushiken Takamatsu, of the volunteer group recovering remains from the Battle of Okinawa, and a woman from Kyoto had been washing clean the fragments of bone that had been collected. As I was recording a video, something like a lump of dirt or a shard of steel slipped out of the muddy skull. I focused in on it to see what it was. The three of us exchanged glances and, without thinking, the word escaped from someone: *brain*. We could see its clearly defined wrinkles and folds. Suddenly, I came to my senses, put down my video camera, and started taking still photos of the brain. The photos I took in that state of excitement were badly composed. Later that day, I set aside some time and calmly reshot them.[75]

"Have you seen Higa Toyomitsu's exhibit? Are you going to the symposium?" To be an anthropologist is always to be out of step, out of time. I had just met Gushiken Takamatsu and learned about the *ikotsu shūshū* projects that he had been doing with the Promise Keepers. I was busy with interviews, transcriptions, and my first excavation with Gamafuyā. It was all new to me, but Okinawans had been living with these discoveries for months. There had been news stories, lectures, critiques and debates on television, in magazines, journals, newspapers, and in classrooms, bars, auditoriums, galleries, and homes. The photographer Higa Toyomitsu had already staged an exhibition of images that he had taken during excavations, and he organized a symposium for activists, academics, and critics to discuss his project. The journal *Sekai* published a collection of photographs and essays that came out of these events in its September 2010 issue. Now, I discovered that Higa and his collaborators were about to revisit everything with a new exhibit at the Sakima Art Museum. A vertiginous swirl of action, representations, and critiques, all at once.

Higa Toyomitsu is a powerful presence in Okinawa, as a photographer, writer, and public intellectual. The first time I saw his work in person was in 2004 at an exhibition at MoMA PS1 in New York titled *The Perpetual Moment: Visions from Okinawa and Korea*. Since then, I had been following his critical interventions in Okinawan newspapers and journals, but I had never met him or heard about his involvement with *ikotsu shūshū*. When my friend, the anthropologist Maetakenishi Kazuma, suggested that we go to the exhibition and symposium at the Sakima Art Museum, I eagerly agreed. The images were so provocative that I returned a couple of days later to spend more time with them, looking, sketching, and thinking. Later that week, I transcribed my recordings and pored over the issue of *Sekai*. As soon as I could, I made an appointment to meet Higa.

On an autumn morning a week later, I was standing at the dead end of a narrow street in Sobe, Yomitan. I parked my car in the lot of a small apartment building nearby. Several cars alongside mine had the Y license plates of American military personnel, and I saw a *De Oppresso Liber* sticker in the rear window of one. To free the oppressed—the motto of US Special Forces, assigned to Torii Station, the army base that dominates much of the southern coastal area of Yomitan. Higa's house was between the parking lot and the sea. A flat-roofed, single-story concrete building, it looked like a *beigun jutaku*—a style of postwar residential construction that had been designed for American soldiers and their families so that they could efficiently and securely begin their occupation of Okinawa. While Okinawan architects like Ōshiro Ryūtarō and Kinjō Nobuyoshi experimented with a fusion of cosmopolitan and vernacular styles in their designs for municipal buildings, the American occupation imposed its own style into the space of everyday life. *Beigun jutaku* reshaped the functional form of the ranch homes that were spreading across postwar America into a durable, easy-to-produce concrete box. While they might remind servicemen and their families of an idealized life back home, they were also a material token of the early years of an intractable war of occupation. I have no idea if Higa's house had been part of an older base housing area, or if it had been built from the same plans and materials for an Okinawan family—perhaps Higa's—living in the neighborhood.[76] There was a small doghouse near the front door. I paused next to it for a moment to collect my thoughts for our meeting. I looked out across the beach to the sea, empty except for a distant freighter sailing south, the sky clear and bright. Despite my focus on our meeting—or perhaps because of it—I couldn't help imagining the ocean beyond the breakers thick with warships, wave after wave of Marines running out of landing craft to the shore around us, bombardments scouring these beaches and the fields inland. This is where the land invasion of Okinawa began in April 1945. Even here, in the place of an artist and activist whose life has been shaped by that war and what came next, who has devoted himself to the representation of that experience, it was hard for me to escape the force of commonplace cinematic images: *The Pacific*; *Saving Private Ryan*; *Letters from Iwo Jima*. And beneath it all, the remains of my long-ago training as a Marine, moods and memories that remain with me,

4.5.   Higa Toyomitsu (*far right*).

never far from the moment. I resettled those thoughts, straightened my shirt, and knocked on the door.

Hours later, the afternoon sun streamed through the windows facing the sea, spilling bottle green through the glass teapot on the table between us. We were sitting together in the front room. The walls around us were lined with shelves, stacked with papers, binders, a fax machine, extensive collections of photography magazines like *Asahi Kamera*, *Nihon Kamera*, and *Video Salon*.[77] A scuffed white riot helmet and folded towel had been left by the door, as if someone might rush out to a demonstration at any moment. Higa was across from me, his face fixed in an intense expression. We had been talking for hours, the cups in front of us filled and emptied several times over. The table between us was covered with notebooks, open binders of proof sheets, negatives, photobooks, the remote for the video monitor we'd been using to watch films. Like the helmet by the door, there was something about Higa that made the fragments of the past seem vital, as if they might also be the weapons necessary to clear a path to the future. His conversation unfolded in complex rhythms—silences and stillness, tentative comments, sudden action, long intervals of intense narration.

Our discussion followed a genealogical line, his concern with the representation of the dead leading me through a history of his career. We started off with his experiences as a student, a member of the influential Ryūdai Photo Club, learning to use a Pentax camera bought with money earned as a cashier on an American base.[78] Studying art and expression in the midst of the struggle over Okinawa's return to Japanese rule.[79] Higa would interrupt himself to show me a set of photos or point to a passage in a book. We watched a newly reedited version of the *Shimakutuba de Kataru Ikusayū* collection, his elderly neighbors from Sobe recounting their war experiences in the language of their native place. I sat entranced by the dreamlike video footage from *Nanamui*, Higa's deeply immersive recording of women's rituals in a village three hundred miles to the south on the island of Miyako.

Then he turned to this moment.

Higa told me that he had been summoned. *Sashindāri*, he called it. Summoned to photograph. It was like *kandāri*, to be called by a deity or the spirits of the dead, to be commanded to serve. Most Okinawans are familiar with the insistence of this call. It can shatter the expected patterns of everyday life. A child falls into a trance, awakening his family to the presence of the anguished ghost of an old man who died alone and unmourned in their house many years earlier. A young woman fears that she will be driven mad by the relentless voice of a deity who demands service, regardless of her obligations to her family and her work. An infant, his body wracked by sickness and pain, leads his parents on a search to find forgotten ancestors who are starving for offerings from their descendants. Okinawans believe that the dead watch over them and bring them good fortune. However, these relationships require constant attention—the living must always be answerable to the dead, to those other beings who dwell among them.

I was not surprised that the dead chose Higa to photograph them. He is one of the most respected Okinawan artists of his generation. His work has always been political: he was involved in radical action as a student and gained recognition for his provocative collection of images documenting the final year of official American military occupation. He has been relentlessly experimental, beginning with his early work without a viewfinder, using fixed focus and exposure, and for his participatory work with Ishikawa Mao that foregrounded the photographer's gaze as well as the subjectivity of their object. His recent work remains challenging—hallucinatory films of half-glimpsed rituals and harrowing documentary interviews with Okinawan war survivors. He is committed to efforts that shatter the boundaries between the aesthetic, the documentary, and the political. He is a constant critic of Japanese exploitation and oppression, a relentless opponent of American military occupation, an advocate for the use of the Ryūkyūan languages in everyday life, a dedicated local historian, and an activist in the movement for Okinawan autonomy.[80]

Writing in an introduction to the collection of photographs and essays that Higa published as part of his *Nanamui* project, the famous Japanese photographer Tōmatsu Shōmei recalled his early impression of Higa's student work. In a review of a 1972 exhibition of Ryūdai photographers for *Nihon Kamera*, Tōmatsu might have been expected to situate Higa's work as a record of the uneasy transition from contested American colonial rule to the sovereignty of the Japanese state. The images easily could be read to tell that story. Nearly every photograph in the collection shows some number of Okinawans or Americans going about their daily lives in the days leading up to Reversion. A child urinating into a ditch; two soldiers, shirtless, staring at the camera through a chain link fence; an elderly woman sweeping the street in front of a bar. Those that do not follow this pattern capture an object—a horse-drawn cart, a radar dish, an abandoned bus—that is part of that same everyday. Some images are carefully composed; some unaimed and hastily shot from a moving vehicle. A photographer and critic with Tōmatsu's technical mastery, aesthetic sensibility, and political commitments could find much to say.

Instead, writing as someone attentive to the expression of Okinawan artists and the exploitation of the Okinawan people, as well as an outsider from mainland Japan, his comments were tentative and disturbed. In the sequence of images, he could not see an intelligible, comforting interpretation or a comprehensive account of Okinawan history. He saw fragments thrown down before the viewer. Even when a new image in the sequence negated the one that preceded it, no narrative emerged. It was all scraps. "It is a philosophy of silence," he wrote, "narrated in confusion."[81]

Tōmatsu's review anticipates Jacques Rancière's later critique of the narrative and aesthetic dimensions of photography. The disorder of the image, of the constellation of images, and the disorientation of the viewer are deeply imbricated. The narrative of occupation, of revolt, of hope and ruination that a viewer might expect is subverted. At the same time, Tōmatsu does not discover a knowable alterity in the collection, an auratic distance that his critique can penetrate. As he concludes his essay on Higa's work, he recognizes that Higa may be a photographer, an essayist, and a historian, but he is also an Okinawan. His practice, like those of the men and women represented, is instantiated in the materiality of the image. In both the photographer and his photographic subjects, Tōmatsu sees an intimation of something that discursively and interpretively escapes him. He recognizes the ability of characters to play with the image of their being, and of an Okinawan photographer to be their collaborator. Again, Rancière: "But this theoretical *coup de force* would not be possible if the art of photography today was not already the bearer of this tendency to break the historical complicity between the art of the photographer and the aesthetic capacity of his subjects."[82] Tōmatsu's critique asks what might be accomplished when the photographer can do more than stand in a fraught, mediational space between viewer and subject, sharing some things with both, their final alliance unclear. What can emerge in a more reflexive collaboration? Where does this leave a viewer?

In an essay reflecting on Higa's career, the critic Nakazato Isao takes up Tōmatsu's characterization of silence and confusion. He does so by asking how Higa should be understood in the context of postwar Okinawan photography. He carefully explores the effect that collaborations and associations with Tōmatsu, Taira Kōshichi, Ishikawa Mao, and Higa Yasuo had on Higa Toyomitsu's work. While he saw all of them as important, he is most interested in contrasting his work with that of Higa Yasuo—an award-winning Okinawan photographer with whom Higa Toyomitsu shared many concerns. Nakazato argues that Higa Yasuo's famous work on festivals is suffused with a sense of awe, which grounded his shocked recognition that other forms of life remained vital and present in these places and times. Nakazato focuses on the auratic materiality of Higa Yasuo's representations, his efforts to photograph the exceptional, sacred spaces and practices, obscure yet enduring, that are otherwise excluded from postwar quotidian space and time in Okinawa, and to come to grips with the dislocation that he feels when he returns to everyday life after personally experiencing what he describes as the happiness of those other communities.[83]

And yet, if there is a sense of a vertically organized order instantiated in the distinction between sacred and mundane in Higa Yasuo's work, Nakazato finds an intimation of horizontality in Higa Toyomitsu's images. Recognizing that these dichotomies are too crude, Nakazato qualifies his analysis. It is not that Higa Toyomitsu is without awe, he writes, but that he enters the production of an image from a different point.[84]

For Nakazato, Higa Toyomitsu's experimentation with images shot from moving vehicles, from inside the ranks of a demonstration, from within a ritual from which he might otherwise be excluded, from an intimate dialogue with neighbors recounting their most horrific experiences, creates a space for images that reject conventional notions of meaning and continuity. They are about the discovery—the representation—of an Okinawa that continues its fragmented emergence as the constellation of images grows. An Okinawa that contains the artist as well as the objects of their work, challenging and transforming their differences, their commonalities. Nakazato makes an explicit connection to the work of the director Takamine Gō: "They both love anonymity and are inspired by the randomness that does not grant any kind of privilege—a sense of equivalence that doesn't give a special emphasis to the landscape."[85]

As he reflects on Higa's work, Nakazato returns to the experience of silence and confusion that Tōmatsu described. And yet, his critique diverges in important ways. Having engaged Higa's work for decades, what Nakazato experiences is not silence. Instead, he hears a murmur. Somewhere below the threshold of hearing there is a repetition that continues to build, vague yet insistent. In that inchoate murmur, Nakazato hears what might be multiple Okinawas taking shape.[86]

The summoning that Higa experiences indexes a shift in the pattern of emergence for those Okinawas. It might be that something new is taking shape. Or there is an older, obscured dimension erupting. Or perhaps what is building goes beyond conventional notions of new and old, past and present. Higa himself feels these effects. He has been hailed, subject to a call that is relentless and demanding. It upends his understanding of life in contemporary Okinawa and his place in it, forcing him to reconsider the meaning of the work he has done, the work he has yet to do. He has been dislocated and must make sense of the world as he now experiences and understands it. This is very much the way that *yuta* describe their calling, their entry into a radically new space and time, with its own forms of doing and being.

Higa told me that the first indication of this summons came after reading a short newspaper article about Gushiken Takamatsu. As I noted earlier, after construction workers found human remains when they broke ground for the Shintoshin project, Gushiken received government authorization to conduct *ikotsu shūshū* in the area. At that time, Higa thought that something about the reporter's description of the dead captured his imagination: Japanese soldiers killed in the Battle of Okinawa. The fate of dead soldiers from the mainland had never interested him before. Higa felt compelled to ask Gushiken if he could observe their work. One visit led to another, and he ended up spending months photographing the dead.

When discussing his current project, Higa often says *"honetachi ga kataru,"* "the bones speak." It should not be surprising that the dead can speak. My friends say that the dead often appear in dreams or in signs on their bodies. There are countless household and community rituals to mediate the communication between the living and the dead, and *yuta* are always available if these relationships become difficult or unclear. In some cases, communication moves beyond the quotidian. *Yuta* have told me of the plaintive calls of the dead that they hear from old battlefields; workers involved in *ikotsu shūshū* say that apparitions would sometimes stand before them, leading them to their places where their remains could be found. It is not surprising that they can speak, but things change when they do.

And yet, I am also surprised that these dead soldiers—mainlanders who volunteered or were conscripted—can speak for themselves. Long ago, the state and its apparatuses had claimed the right to do so on their behalf. The very institutions that required their sacrifices and appropriated their self-consuming labor were those that produced powerful representations of the outcome of their acts. Patriotic funerals in the homes of the bereaved, solemn ceremonies at national ossuaries and local memorials, martial pageantry at Yasukuni Shrine, all sought to ensure that narratives of their lives and their deaths were controlled. *Manga* (comics) that depict their final, heroic actions on the field of battle, films that show intrepid pilots climbing into the cockpit of the plane for one last flight, speeches by conservative politicians that subsume each particular life and death into a heroic collective. Walls at Yūshūkan, the war museum at Yasukuni Shrine, covered in row after row of individual portraits of earnest young men soon to sacrifice their lives. Whatever material forms their actions once took have been lost in a cascade of cherry blossoms.[87]

These are the dead soldiers that found their voices and called out to Higa Toyomitsu. Answering them, he threw himself into this new project. The excavation was exhausting. He worked alongside the volunteers during the day and his nights were troubled by the voices of the dead. Digital imaging helped him to keep pace with the number of remains that were uncovered, and he left many rolls of film undeveloped, preferring to print daily proofs from his digital camera and review the video that he recorded. He was so consumed by his work that he was shocked when the recovery project came to an end. And yet, there was more to be done. In the passage that begins this section, Higa describes the moment on the final day of the project when a brain appeared from the skull that they were cleaning.

> I wonder if the conflict above ground isn't what has summoned the bones that had been below? In the subject of the photograph and in the landscape, something is called back and appears in the *genba*. When the bones are the subject of a photograph, in being photographed, it symbolized that they had been living here as the dead, but they have no *ibasho*—no place of their own.[88] When the brain appeared, I felt that it had exceeded the capacity of words or images to give meaning to something.[89]

Higa's description is provocative. For most volunteers, the *genba* is clearly demarcated in space and time. It is a construction site, an archaeological dig, a forensic excavation. Temporary barriers separate it from the surrounding community. Volunteers are dressed in work clothes and hard hats when they enter. Tents, metal cabins, and excavation equipment are placed across the space. When the recovery project ends, the space will be returned to the rhythms of everyday life. And yet, the war dead are not just below the surface of this field—they could emerge anywhere. If, as Higa has written, they have no place of their own, they are waiting in all of the spaces across Okinawa where they lived and died. As a photographer, Higa's *genba* articulates with this possibility. It is wherever he brings forth an image. It is where he has been called to photograph.

The call that brought him to Gushiken's *genba* intensified. He told me that the dead soldier whose skull they discovered on the final day of excavation began to speak to him, calling to him every night in his dreams. In the intensity of this summons, he realized that the dead were asking for his help to once again address the living. That, after seventy years beneath the red Okinawan soil, they had something urgent to say.

The thousands of photographs and hours of video that he produced led to the exhibition *Hone no Ikusayu* (Bones of a world at war). The exhibition was staged at the Okinawa Prefectural Museum (the same space that would host the Okamoto Tarō retrospective the following summer), the Sakima Art Museum in Okinawa, and Meiji University in Tokyo. Higa also organized public symposia held on the anniversary of the end of the Battle of Okinawa and the Japanese surrender, locating his project in cyclic temporalities imbricated with history, memory, and death.[90] Many Okinawans were troubled by the exhibitions, and the symposia were marked by their struggle to reconcile a history of brutal Japanese exploitation with these recent images of Japanese soldiers who suffered. As one of the participants at the Sakima Art Museum symposium asked: Could one be both murderer and victim? What obligations and relationships were indexed by the images? Why now?

On a rainy October day, I met Higa at the entrance to his exhibition at Meiji University in Tokyo and we talked as visitors filed past us.[91] Higa was concerned that Typhoon Chaba, then approaching the city, would disrupt the symposium scheduled for the following day. Event sponsors had reserved a room at Ami, a club near the university, in case the campus was forced to close. A storm couldn't be allowed to disrupt something this important.

Higa showed me the booklet that Iwanami Shoten had published for the exhibition, an offprint of images and essays from the earlier issue of *Sekai*.[92] He was excited that the images would continue to circulate across Japan, but he was angered that his editors had covered the pamphlet with a wrapper that equated the recovered bones with the continual threat of unexploded wartime bombs in the Okinawan landscape. "I want the bones to speak for themselves," he said. "They don't need anyone else telling you what to think when you see them." It is not that Higa rejects interpretation or dissensus. The symposia and the *Sekai* collection include contrasting voices, and discussions at these events often become quite heated. What upset him was the concise, textual certainty of an editorial voice that overwhelms the call of the dead, presenting interpretation as an objective dimension of the project.

He told me that members of *izokukai* (war survivors associations) would attend the symposium the following day. He said that he wasn't really interested in the gratitude of the descendants of veterans who were able to use his images to identify departed soldiers, insisting again that the exhibition was about the words of the dead, not the living.[93]

I left Higa discussing the upcoming events with organizers from Meiji University and followed a well-dressed elderly couple as they walked through the exhibit. To our right, two parallel rows of paired images were mounted on a long glass panel. I remembered many of the small images from the exhibition at the Sakima Art Museum. Shards of a teacup, an engraved fountain pen, buttons and military insignia—the material traces of soldiers' lives. The crumpled fragments of a boot, pale bones visible within. An intact skull in profile, wrapped in a clear plastic bag.

At the end of the panel, a group of men and women sat on folding chairs surrounding a monitor. A short video played in a loop, Higa and Gushiken Takamatsu of Gamafuyā cleaning a human skull. The surface of the bone had been dyed a deep mahogany, steeped for decades in red Okinawan clay. The two men spoke quietly as they carefully washed the skull with a hose and gently scraped out its eye sockets with a set of wooden chopsticks. This is the moment that affected Higa so profoundly. I watched the recording play through two or three times.

I turned to a column of glass panels that led back to the entrance, perpendicular to the long display that I had followed into the interior of the exhibition space. A group of visitors stood in front of the first panel, staring silently at an image of horror. The bones of a soldier sprawled alongside *jīshigāmi* (funerary urns) in the tomb where he had sought refuge. The formally composed photograph had been divided neatly in half. To the left stood three urns, surprisingly intact. To the right, a skeleton, fragments of a hand resting on a broken hip, its jaw thrown open as if laughing. Their forms stood out against the red clay in which they had been entombed, the careful strokes of the workers' tools still visible on the ground, the faint lines of brush strokes on bone and ceramic. I tried to look beyond the abjection of his crushed form and the grim irony of a Japanese soldier sheltering himself among the Okinawan dead. I found myself comparing one side with the other. On the left, the Okinawan remains had been cleaned and organized, made beautiful and whole, each installed in a ceramic vessel. Subjects once more able to take their places in a community of the living and the dead. The Japanese soldier to the right was broken and alone. Abandoned by his comrades, the emperor and the nation he served and protected, he lies discarded in a place where others had been kept with care, tiny fragments of buttons and badges scattered across him. The entire tableau hidden away by the American occupation until brought to light by laborers' hands and Higa's camera.[94]

We moved together to another image, even more striking in its brutality. It had the intimacy of a portrait, but the lone figure was awkwardly tipped to the side. Only bones remained. The soldier's spine described a segmented line stretching diagonally from left to right across the red clay floor of the tomb. His face blown off, his ribs shattered and missing, his pelvis crushed. The images captured him after he fell backward, arched across the rusted remains of his helmet, an instant after exploding a grenade in his own lap. Again, thoughts of *gyokusai*, that wartime expression conjured from classical

Chinese references: precious jewels, cultivated only to be broken. A subject that has struggled to be perfect and beautiful, only to sacrifice itself.

The image is devoid of the personal details that mark the portraits displayed in a place like Yasukuni Shrine, details that suggest difference in a field already defined by sameness through its inclusion.[95] There is nothing in his stripped bones to give any sentimental intimation of the individual life he led before his death. The earlier evocative photos of teacups, watches, fountain pens, boots, and personal seals have been left on the other side of the barrier. I can see none of the details that could be used to construct a collective subject subordinate to the emperor. Nothing remains of his intention. There are no traces of intense patriotism or of pride in the discharge of familial obligation. No signs of remorse at the slaughter in which he participated or regret at the future he would never live to experience. Only the physical remains of an act: sitting formally, a grenade in hand, waiting five seconds or so for the fuse to detonate. In its stark simplicity, Higa's photograph captures something of this moment of the soldier's decisive action.[96] It is a portrait of a soldier, a sacrifice, a dweller in this place who has waited for decades. Waiting to emerge, to be photographed. At the same time, it is framed by Higa's intervention in the excavation and recovery of those fragmented remains, multiple political acts and manifold temporalities. The intimation of a duration that is of tremendous importance—a photographic history of what was, what might have been, and what still could be.

After nearly seventy years, Higa's collaborators are still not safe from the actions of the state. The now that is indexed by this image of the dead irrupting into the everyday rapidly recedes into the historical past as well-intentioned volunteers gather the remains, processing them, disposing of them in the vast, undifferentiated collective of patriotic spirits that can only speak, mutely, on behalf of the state. Appearing as they did in the fields that would house the new city, the bones are just a temporally dislocated aberration, a disruption in the flow of the time of the nation. It is Higa's photography that helps them to remain materially present and visible: several weeks on the wall of a museum, a month in the color supplement to a popular journal, a potentially infinite cycle of digital storage, circulation, and exchange.[97]

What can be made of the moment—or rather the duration—that the image both captures and creates? In it unfolds a dialogue between subject and photographer. There is the Imperial Japanese soldier, one of the "war gods" whose collective sacrifice gave value to a sacrifier—the emperor—who discarded them once their offering had been made.[98] A soldier whose jewel-like body was shattered (*gyokusai*) so that the jeweled body of the emperor (*gyokutai*) could be preserved.[99] Whose brutality is remembered in countless Okinawan stories. Who failed in his obligation to preserve the lives of those Japanese citizens under his protection. Viewers see horror and abjection in the images—the shock that they showed when they saw the broken remains, left alone. There is also anger at the state that commanded this sacrifice. I heard this time and time again from friends who viewed the exhibition or read the *Sekai* collection. It is also possible to see—even in the images of soldiers who took their own lives by detonating a grenade in their laps—images of loyalty, patriotism, and courage. Many of their descendants and members of veterans groups that attended Higa's symposium spoke to these qualities.

And yet, the risk remains that this moment will be forced into the past as an excess of history overwhelms the act that Higa and the dead performed together. Too historical an interpretation misses a fundamental dimension of the relationship between Higa and his subjects that is represented in the images. Shawn Michelle Smith has written of the stunning response to photographs taken by US soldiers in Iraq: "Like shadowy nightmares, the Abu Ghraib photographs unleashed repressed cultural images, making them visible in new forms."[100] Viewing Higa's photographs as a record of wartime atrocities may offer an opportunity to critique the imperialist ideologies that made brutality possible. At the same time, it cedes the power to create the terrible aura that suffuses these images to that imperial ideology, acknowledging the persistence of the same ideological force that not only led to these events but to their memoration at places like Yasukuni. Is that enough? I want to go beyond that, following Smith's argument to ask about other shadowy dreams that Higa and the dead might have unleashed. The *sashindari* that he describes—the call to photograph—originates with the dead in what would be for them the present. It rises up from their hidden places, in the red Okinawan soil, and summons Higa to collaborate with them, bringing together a manifold of temporalities. It speaks to the Okinawans who see their images of other meanings, other duties, other rhythms, other possibilities that might have been overwhelmed by the demands of their daily lives.

Why have the dead returned, if not to offer testimony to their wartime experience? Nothing in Higa's exhibition suggests that they are seeking to atone for wrongs that they might have committed, to demand recognition for their courage, or to testify to their own victimhood. Those pasts are represented in the images, but it is also clear that the dead have changed.

The markers of their identities as soldiers have been shed. While they are represented in the first set of Higa's images at the exhibition, it is done in such a way that they are separated from the tokens of the lives that they have led. Inscribed pens, personal seals, other identifiable remains are shown on their own—away from the larger photographs of the material remains of the soldiers, of the bones themselves. When the bones are depicted, they are left in the final positions of their actions, but they have changed. Decades have weathered them, colored them, polished them, transformed them. There are those that appear in recognizable, near-human form, but there are others that may appear only as fragments, as traces indistinguishable from the pieces of coral that surround them.

It is here that Higa, unseen, comes into view. These images are his response to his summons. He is not, as Okamoto Tarō styled himself, a shaman with a camera. His opportunity to mediate the relationship between the living and the dead comes from the work of photography that he has practiced for decades, the collection of images of Okinawa that he has spent his life assembling, and the unexpected summons that he hears from the Japanese soldiers. It is the work of an Okinawan photographer who has found the strength and courage to reach out to the very soldiers whose failures, duplicity, cowardice, and violence shattered his world. His images capture the power and resolve of the dead soldiers that he stands alongside, but he rejects the brutal imperial ideology of ruin and fragmentation. He does not forget; perhaps he does not even forgive. Still, he offers the dead a gift—the opportunity to be visible again, to remain, to take place. In doing so, he calls on an aesthetic of unity, a cultural valorization of binding and of care, and a radical collective politics. Drawing on the same logic that once organized *senkotsu* (bone washing), he helps to make the remains of the dead beautiful and whole again. Older generations of Okinawans once used farming tools, bottles of local rice liquor, handcrafted ceramic urns, and the intercession of priestesses and shamans to reincorporate their dead into the community.[101] Higa uses digital cameras, laptop computers, inkjet printers, video monitors, digital storage systems, museum exhibitions, and popular publications to bring the solitary and forgotten dead to the point where they are able to become part of a new, reflexively constructed collective. Without his intervention, those who cannot otherwise take advantage of the mediation of *yuta* and priestesses, who find themselves in a milieu in which their presence is not expected, their stories are no longer told, or their particular memories forgotten, would find themselves consigned to melancholy places like Yasukuni Shrine or a meeting of a society of the bereaved. With Higa's help, they have the freedom to act and to speak.

What is the ground for this to take place? The call that Higa describes, the actions that he undertakes on their behalf, are not unusual in Okinawa. And yet, they are most often an index of already existing sets of relationships—with kin, with friends, with autochthonous entities. It may be that the living are not materially aware of these relationships, but the call reveals them. What kind of prior relationship exists that would allow these dead soldiers—these one-time colonizers, occupiers, men who may have caused the suffering and death of Okinawans—to call on Higa from their places of abjection? Why do they expect that he will answer their call? Beyond that, why does Higa take on the responsibilities for transforming these remains, even when it requires him to move beyond—as he did in the fieldwork of his *Nanamui* project—gendered dimensions of labor and power, social and legal proscriptions concerning death, and unresolved anger toward the Japanese Army and its actions? For Higa, there's no reason to think that this represents some belated acknowledgment of his patriotic duties as a citizen.

I think it is necessary to understand the ongoing effects of the new forms of kinship that were created between soldiers and citizens as the Battle of Okinawa approached, and that Gushiken Takamatsu described earlier. As false and grotesque as it may seem, as compelling as it may be to focus on military orders, executions, and the question of compulsory suicides, this murderous fusion of nation and family also contributed to the catastrophic wartime irruption of suffering, sacrifice, and death. Could ordinary people have simply worked through this intense, affective commitment in the years since the war ended, any more than they could have forgotten traumatic memories of pain and death? Or does something remain, an often unacknowledged force, stirring somewhere in those who once experienced it? As an elderly Okinawan businessman once told me, shifting to English to begin his admission with a curse, "Since the war, I've spent every day doing my best to rebuild Okinawa and make a good life here. I hate everything about the Japanese state and what it did in Okinawa. But, even now, I still believe. I still believe in the emperor." Perhaps Higa is recognizing these durable forms of *en*—the networks of obligation, reciprocity, and care that constitute social life. And, as the work of Shunsuke Nozawa, Kumaki Hiroko, and Ryo Moriomoto have shown, *en* can reveal itself in unexpected ways and in forgotten places.[102] What's more, these relationships are constructed and reproduced in action—the category of *yuimāru* or binding that is so central to Okinawan discussions about the labor of community life. What were the consequences of *yuimāru* when Okinawans bound themselves, as family, to Japanese soldiers and the state? We have seen the courage that Gushiken has described of soldiers who pushed back against those bonds and refused to kill. But what of those like Kinjō Shigeaki and his brothers who killed their families and themselves out of patriotism and love? Are these the capacities and the relationships that *sashindāri* allowed Higa to discover in himself, between himself and the soldiers who summoned him? Is this what led him to say that he must reconsider his own work and his own positions?

This is not to say that Higa has found beauty and comradeship in violence and corruption. He is uninterested in the efforts of veterans' and survivors' groups to equate the images to patriotic qualia of loyalty and commitment. Unlike Gushiken, Higa does not try to give refuge to those who have been unfairly bound up in oppressive forms of *en*. What he does is create a kind of temporal realignment. His images interrupt the expected flow of time, disclosing something that had been there all along. By rejoining these dead soldiers in the extended duration of their sacrifice, he can take into account their own transformation, buried in the soil of Okinawa. Okinawa has done the initial work of secondary burial—stripping away torn flesh, scouring the bones. Blood, most of the markers of their military status, have been removed. And so, when Gamafuyā, when the Promise Keepers, when community volunteers, when Higa find them and clean them, the final stages of preparation are completed, long after the initial death.

Higa creates a place for them to remain in spite of efforts, intentional and otherwise, to hide them away. The aesthetic transformation that Higa effects does not remove the traces of their violent deaths. Their remains are a token of their sacrifice, and a material trace of the power and commitment that they once showed. They have remained resolute, as have the Okinawans who answer their call. What of the Imperial institution and the Japanese state that abandoned them?

Here is where Higa draws on his own abilities as well as the relationships he has uncovered. He acknowledges them, even if their origin is in oppression, horror, and death. The artistic production here goes beyond Higa's personal representational practice, beyond stunning photographs of the dead. Higa brings together the kinds of networks that he has labored on for decades—establishing exhibitions in galleries and museums, carrying out fieldwork, publishing, organizing critical discussions and symposia. He is certainly attentive to the ways in which an auratic image is produced— the juxtaposition of past and present, battlefield and home, combat and the present—the representation of transmission over a distance in space and time. He pulls representations of the patriotic dead, with all of the respectful remoteness that implies, into the presence of the living. In doing so, he subverts conventional notions of distance and nearness that are immanent in fascist iconography. These soldiers are not removed to the distant places of the state and replaced by truly detemporalized traces—colorized portraits of young cadets or enlisted soldiers in freshly issued uniforms, smiling images of a group of soldiers going about their daily routines in garrison, poignant images of mourning families with carefully packaged remains. They have emerged from their waiting and they are present, here and now.

Their representations are integrated into the expanding constellation of Higa's work that Nakazato and Tōmatsu critiqued, alongside photographs of Okinawan war survivors, of shamanic rituals, of streets filled with demonstrators, of rural and urban Okinawan neighborhoods. By acknowledging their incorporation, their presence in these other networks (other *en—yuimāru*), they are recognized as placed in new fields of force. The power that was installed in and radiated from tombs and *butsudan* has been extended to galleries, journals, digital files in the cloud and in thumb drives. This is a repetition of the kinds of representational practice that Higa has engaged in for decades, but it is different too.

Other capacities have been mobilized and their values transformed. The power of sacrifice, the ambiguous violent and murderous commitment between Japanese soldiers and Okinawan citizens, the creative capacities of Okinawans to build collaboration and enduring relationships with the dead. The dead have changed everything—they are not what they were expected to be, they are not what they have been. Higa, too, is not who he thought himself to be, and the ability of the dead to call upon him indexes other Okinawan pasts that had not yet emerged in his work. Veterans' groups, government bureaucrats, their survivors or descendants, may come to claim them and install them in the places of the state or in their homes. They can also remain in their new place in Okinawa. In their hidden places, in their engagement with Higa, they have undergone a sea change.

Does this challenge viewers to see Higa's photographs in a different way? I think again about the path that Higa and his curators created through the images displayed at the exhibitions in Okinawa and Tokyo. The turn toward the massive photographs of the dead soldiers after watching the video of Gushiken and Higa's discovery of the soldier's brain takes on new weight. Rather than just expressing the bitter contradiction between responsibility and abandonment, could the image of the dead soldier stretched out alongside the ornate *jīshigāmi* be seen as a representation of two moments in the relationship between the living and the dead? One in which the Ryūkyūan dead were cared for by their families; the next where Higa joined the dead soldier in creating a new place in the world today. And the soldier who killed himself with a grenade? Higa's photograph captures him in the present as his murderous act has been gradually transformed and revalued in the Okinawan soil, in the moment where he is about to speak.

When the dead speak, what do they say? The question should be: What do they say to those who view them? Higa is quite explicit in what they have said to him. They have called him to photograph them. They have encouraged him to work with them and to reevaluate his life and his work. They speak of the Japan in which they no longer belong, and the Okinawa to which they have returned. What's more, he has written that their call is about what is happening in Okinawa *now*. Like the character Girū of *Uchinā shibai* or Takamine's *Untamagirū*, they committed their life to a social order, to an ideology, that demanded everything of them. And yet, they can no longer believe that their sacrifices, as Brad Weiss has written, violate a "moral order in order to affirm the truth of a wider moral universe."[103] Instead, their actions protected the elites that had called for their sacrifice, reinforced their exploitative ideology, and helped to establish a new, inequitable, and exclusionary postwar social order. They have begun to speak at a moment when Japan and the United States are expanding their military presence in Okinawa again, building a massive and controversial new Marine Corps air base to the north in Henoko, and constructing new Jieitai (Japanese Self-Defense Forces) installations across the islands. At a moment when their games of war in the seas and skies surrounding Okinawa have become increasingly confrontational and dangerous.

The image that they have created together gives them presence. It also creates a place from which their call can continue to be sent. What does this mean for the viewer who stands in the place of Higa, when he was responding to their call? To answer this question, one must be able to match the resolve of the photographer who created these images and the soldiers who summoned him. One must have the courage to stand with them and confront the excess of history that threatens any accounting with the past in Japan. One must do so without fear or pity, rejecting the injustice of closed narratives that valorize shared subordination to a state and a sovereign that demand everything but give so little in return. One must be attentive to the often inaudible murmurs, the subtle rhythms that reveal other abilities, other relationships, and other possibilities. Perhaps then, they can begin to speak about the new moment that they share, a new time to come.

Digging Together

I sat back against the wall in the ruined hotel, grateful for a break from the rain and the digging. The room was cool and the air thick with the musty smell of crumbling concrete.

Since early morning, we had been working in a grassy field between Nakagusuku Castle and the abandoned Nakagusuku Kōgen Hotel. To the east, a steep slope dropped off toward Awase and the Pacific Ocean beyond. It was August 18, 2010: my first day in the field with Gamafuyā. The Nakagusuku village government had invited them to look for bodies, and we had been joined by a dozen men from the Promise Keepers. A local researcher had heard that Japanese soldiers were buried somewhere around the hotel parking lot, and Okinawan civilians or conscripts might be in the group. We only had one day to dig, so we had to be efficient and lucky.

Before we began, an older man from the community made an offering of fruit, rice cakes, salt, sake, spirit money, and incense, intoning a prayer to the dead. He apologized for disturbing them and asked that they reveal their locations to us as we searched. After that, Gushiken quickly identified a possible burial site. Municipal workers cleared the ground, revealing a small depression, the soil damp and soft. Working in teams, we cut a trench two meters wide and two meters deep, inspecting the soil as we carried it out. It was dirty, exhausting work. By lunchtime, the trench snaked across the field for fifteen or twenty meters. We dug for the rest of the day, but we only discovered an old soccer ball and a couple of empty beer bottles, perhaps from the hotel or the small amusement park and zoo that had been built here after the war. Gushiken thought that a shaft filled with softer soil might continue diagonally toward the ocean, but we ran out of time.

We broke for lunch between the rains that lashed us in the morning, and the searing heat of the afternoon. Everyone gathered in a rubble-filled dining room in the old hotel, the walls covered with decades of graffiti. The team from Gamafuyā discussed what we had done that morning and compared it with previous excavations, describing what they had learned about reading the signs of war in the landscape. A pair of women from the Nakagusuku municipal office brought us a box of *bento* (box lunches) and bottles of ice tea. They were joined by an older man wearing pressed trousers, a plaid

4.6.   Gushiken Takamatsu and other volunteers searching for
        the remains of the dead.

shirt, and the Promise Keepers' red vest and ball cap. He knew the members of Gamafuyā by name, and they greeted one another with a laugh. At first, I thought that he might be Yamauchi Masayoshi, the Baptist minister that directed the NGO. He took charge of passing out the *bento* to everyone with a hurried enthusiasm.

After he finished, he came and sat down next to me. Introducing himself in conversational English as Yamada, he told me that he had been one of the Promise Keepers since the beginning. For many years, he had worked in the Yokohama area, everything from sales to construction. He kept drifting west until he ended up in Okinawa—a story I often heard from mainland Japanese men in the Promise Keepers. With nowhere else to go and no money left from his last construction job, he was living in a park in Naha when the call went out for volunteers for *ikotsu shūshū*. For months, he worked on the excavations, and he has been at the House of the Rising Sun ever since.

As we talked, the women from Nakagusuku came back and offered extra *bento* to everybody. He immediately grabbed two, with the urgency of a man who knows what it's like to go hungry. "I'm a *kuishinbo*," he joked, a chow hound. Taking one of the *bento* with both hands, he bowed slightly and offered it to me. "Take this for later," he said. "You never know."

In the House of the Rising Sun

The song met me in the street. The rest of the neighborhood was quiet: warehouses, offices, apartment buildings, funeral homes, wedding halls, scrap-metal salvage and machine shops, bait and tackle stores, inexpensive restaurants and business hotels, the harbor facilities that handled container shipping and local fishermen. The churning chords of the organ filled the concrete alleyway, Sunday morning echoes of George Murasaki and Jon Lord.[104] In the building ahead of me, the crashing drums, rhythmic clapping, and unison singing seemed to be reaching a crescendo. How could I be so late? I hurried inside and Gibo Kiyoshi, the building manager, led me to an open seat. The hymn was as powerful as an encore at a nightclub in Koza, but I quickly realized that what seemed like the end was only the beginning of the service. Lyrics flashed on large video monitors although everyone seemed to know them by heart. The tempo changed as the band transitioned to the next song, the piano rhythmically measuring out what sounded like the introduction to Nilsson's cover of "Without You." We sang for another fifteen or twenty minutes, the congregation smiling in recognition as one familiar hymn followed another.

At the front of the room, Reverend Yamauchi Masayoshi stood at a podium, wearing a short-sleeved white shirt with a standing collar and a crucifix pendant. His congregation at the Okinawa Bethany Church faced him. Older couples in conservative suits and dresses, original members who have remained with him since he founded the church in Urasoe a decade earlier. Others have made their way here from the streets and parks where they live, a stream that has continued since he opened his ministry to the unhoused and impoverished several years ago. Since then, many have found a home here at the House of the Rising Sun or at Eden House in Nishihara. Some men are dressed in an assemblage of fragments, perhaps from earlier moments in their lives. *Sagyōfuku* (work clothes), a dress shirt, a staff jacket from a municipal festival a decade earlier. One wearing a T-shirt from the First Battalion, Ninth Marine Regiment with "The Walking Dead" and a graphic design printed on the back. Several of the parishioners have large bandages, dressings new and clean. Other men wear pressed trousers and *kariyushi* shirts or white shirts and ties.[105] A few dressed in dark, double-breasted suits, worn with style and swagger.

The Asahi no Ataru Ie, House of the Rising Sun, stands on a quiet street in Akebono-Cho, a coastal neighborhood on the northwestern side of Naha.[106] The new urban spaces of Shintoshin where Gushiken Takamatsu and Higa Toyomitsu worked to recover the dead are less than three kilometers to the south; the heights of Shuri are about two kilometers beyond that. Akebono-Cho and the neighborhoods to its west were built on reclaimed land in the frenzy of construction that accompanied Reversion in the early 1970s. Light out of darkness, land from the sea. Here and there, the trace of the old coastline is visible, marked by aging wooden homes and low limestone outcroppings covered in dense trees and old tombs. The transformational relationship between land and sea is familiar to most Okinawans. Some can recount stories about the exchange of gifts between their respective deities that brought agriculture to the islands; many use the term *hannō hangyō* to describe a rural lifestyle divided between farming and fishing. The practice of urban land reclamation also has a long history in Okinawa, and the shape of contemporary Naha is a result of hundreds of years of design and labor.[107] Akebono-Cho is also the consequence of a new spatialized division of labor that resettled Okinawa in the changing American and Japanese empires, integrating the bases and the surrounding communities into new commodity chains, strategic operations, and conduits for the circulation of capital. A successful Okinawan businessman who had grown up in a fishing village once explained to me the dangers in relying on this exchange between sea and land. Every beachcomber knew, he told me, that the sea often left things on the shore that were not gifts to those who found them, and the traces of catastrophe that clung to them might carry over to their new owners.

Several miles to the north along Highway 58, these dangers emerged in a new context with the US Marine Air Station at Futenma. After World War II, the occupying Americans built this base atop farms and villages forcibly confiscated from the Okinawans who lived there, everything bulldozed, their communities dispersed, and as Wendy Matsumura has written, their social order violently transformed.[108] And now? Military flight operations dominate a densely populated urban area. Landowners are still denied the

4.7.   The House of the Rising Sun.

use of their land, roads are congested, auto accidents are a daily hazard, land
and water contaminated, the surrounding air filled with constant noise.
This oppressive routine is punctuated by the horrific as parts fall from air-
planes onto schoolyards, a helicopter crashes into a university, and soldiers
assigned to the base commit acts of violence. Support or opposition to the
bases is a constant source of conflict among residents. Japanese and American bureaucrats turned to the sea for a solution to these problems. In 1998,
they announced that they would build a replacement base to the north in
Henoko, filling a harbor to create a new airfield.[109] Now, decades later, the
project itself seems both environmentally destructive and technically un-
feasible, and it has provoked endless debate and conflict across Okinawa. A
supposed deterrent, it has helped to lay the groundwork for another generation of conflict in the region. This new base—as yet unbuilt—seems to be

as troubled as the houses built from material scavenged from the beaches that the businessman described to me.

And what of the Christianity of today's service? I suppose it also arrived from the sea, brought to the Ryūkyū Kingdom by a small number of foreign missionaries, their numbers increasing after Okinawa's incorporation into Japan. Other Okinawans encountered Christianity in the turbulent debates that surrounded it in late nineteenth- and early twentieth-century Japan. They found it in mainland and Okinawan schools, churches and factories; in books and newspaper articles; in public lectures as well as discussions in their homes and neighborhoods. After the Pacific War, new flows of ideas and materials were brought from sea and air by the US military and the civilians that supported their occupation. They built churches on and off base, established Christian schools and seminaries, created pathways for missionaries to move through the islands. At the same time, other routes of transmission and exchange that had been interrupted by the war were reopened and transformed, linking Okinawa with other Japanese and global networks. It may not seem significant that only about 1 percent of the population of Okinawa identifies as Christian, but there are several hundred active Christian churches of varying denominations scattered throughout the islands.[110] Yamauchi himself had been exposed to Christianity as a boy growing up in Urasoe, near the base that occupied Shintoshin. However, the self-denial and otherworldliness of Christianity had little appeal for him. He was more excited by the possibilities of post-Reversion Okinawa and the pleasurable, chaotic flow of everyday life. Eventually, he became the hard-living manager of a chain of karaoke boxes. He said that it was only after business failure and personal crises that he began to pay attention to the message of Christian salvation.

In its name, the House of the Rising Sun captures something of the ambiguity and complexity of these histories. It evokes the Vietnam era and American rule, versions of the song by the Animals, the Ventures, or Frijid Pink blasting from juke boxes or covered by local bands in GI bars. Reference to a life of dissipation and failure that led to a brothel or prison would be weirdly familiar in these gritty industrial backstreets.[111]

And yet, this House of the Rising Sun is a very different space, and that provocative difference figures in widely known narratives in Okinawa. During my fieldwork, reports frequently appeared in local and national newspapers, journals, and television broadcasts. My friends discussed it with interest, and Gushiken Takamatsu and Higa Toyomitsu told me of their relationship with its residents. The broad contours of the discussion were generally the same. A decade earlier, Yamauchi had expanded the ministry

4.8.   Yamauchi Masayoshi (*far left*) at a Bethany Church service.

of his church to the unhomed, the poor, and the suffering. "Christianity is the origin of welfare. That's what the church should do. The vulnerable cannot live without help. Looking away is to ignore the will of Jesus. The church has to help."[112] In 2009, Yamauchi cobbled together loans and contributions to transform the spaces that were available to him for those in need. They converted this aging business hotel into the House of the Rising Sun, a kind of avocational workers' cooperative. The Promise Keepers, the nonprofit that he organized to coordinate their activities, shared space with the Bethany Baptist Church, and the residence of about 250 former unhoused people. They were mostly men, two thirds Okinawan with the remainder divided between mainland Japanese, and a few Taiwanese and Filipino men. Another hundred or so lived in Eden House, a defunct senior citizens home that Yamauchi's organization had also acquired in rural Nishihara. During my fieldwork, there was a staff of twenty-two: fifteen members of the Promise Keepers and the remainder drawn from Yamauchi's family and congregation.

Several weeks earlier, in an office down the hall from the space where the service was being held, Gibo Kiyoshi, the manager of the residence, told me his own version of this history. He began, where most of these accounts begin, with the discovery of the remains of Japanese soldiers, buried but uninterred, in the traces of the battlefield beneath the land that would become Shintoshin. Although construction continued, the irruption of the dead into these excavations overcame the ability of the workers to manage them. Local and national veteran groups also voiced their concerns that the remains of *eirei*, the heroic spirits of soldiers who had never wavered in their sacrificial commitment to the nation, might not receive the respectful treatment that they deserved. Contractors were unprepared—and perhaps unwilling—to directly engage the potentially dangerous spirits of the dead, and an adequate program of volunteers could not be organized in time to preserve the schedule of development.

The collaboration between Yamauchi and Gushiken is grounded in this moment. Together, they petitioned the minister of internal affairs and commerce for support. Yamauchi had already been ministering to the poor and unhoused for several years, and this created an opportunity to expand his work.[113] Yamauchi would organize these men and women into a group known as the Promise Keepers. Through Gamafuyā, Gushiken would then direct them to recover the remains of the dead from the construction sites around Shintoshin. The state was anxious to avoid the image of wage labor for this patriotic task; instead, it established a set of reciprocal, benevolent, and asymmetrical exchanges—gifts to the community from a state grateful for their loyal efforts.[114]

The word went out to unhoused and unemployed laborers. Gibo himself responded to the call. Once the owner of a small construction company, he had lost his business and his family, and was living in a Naha park. Members of Gamafuyā took charge of their untested collaborators. The first week was tense as everyone wondered if they could work together. By the second week, Gibo said that they were functioning as a team.

Workers had to be at the construction site by 08:00. They were given a lunch and ¥1,000 for their evening meal.[115] For most of the unhoused men, it was an hour by bicycle from the parks where they lived to the excavation. The fifty or so who started work managed to adapt themselves to this schedule. They would arrive each morning, sober and ready to go. Gibo assumed the duties of the foreman, organizing the workday. He was so excited that he got to the worksite an hour early every day. After the workers checked in, they even began doing *rajio taisō* (radio calisthenics) together, just like workers at any other company. They worked hard, trying to stay healthy despite the fact that many of them were still living rough. They did their best to take care of one another. Everyone came to believe in the importance of what they were doing.

Gibo paused, changing the narrative. Like Higa's earlier account, he also began with the voices of the dead. With a summoning. He said that he hesitated to tell anyone about it before finally confiding in Gushiken. Children from a local elementary school would often come and watch them work from along the fence surrounding the excavation. One day, a little boy called one of the workers over and said that he wanted to see whoever was in charge. Gibo went to talk to him. The boy said that earlier that morning, he had seen two Japanese soldiers in old-fashioned uniforms looking at the place where the Promise Keepers were working. Gibo asked the boy where they had been. The boy pointed to an area that was beyond the perimeter of their excavations. Gibo went back to work, but he couldn't get the story out of his mind. On Sunday—their day off—he and several friends returned to the site. They crossed the boundary and began to dig. After excavating a fairly deep hole, they found two skeletons on exactly the spot that the boy indicated. Although the little boy had been so insistent in telling them about the soldiers, they never saw him again.

What to make of the summoning that Gibo described, and of his increasingly personal commitment to recover the remains of the dead? We have seen that it is not unusual to be called by the dead, to be drawn into relationships with them. Gushiken Takamatsu's work speaks eloquently about the commitment of the dead to save the living. Higa Toyomitsu has crafted projects that represent the transformations of the dead and their determination to prevent further exploitation and suffering. He explicitly described this as *sashindāri* (called by the spirits to photograph their remains) in writing of his participation in the project of *ikotsu shūshū* in Shintoshin. How did Gibo and his friends figure in this design?

It is impossible to know the hearts of the other workers as they met with Gibo each morning. Without homes or jobs, owning nothing, bereft of family and community support, with no intimation of future possibilities, their lives are at the extreme of the conditions described in the ethnographic work of Anne Allison, Tom Gill, Klaus Hammering, and Jieun Kim.[116] Their precarity is no longer a potentiality that might be realized. They describe their lives as having failed, fallen, been expended. If the sacrifice that they might once have made for the industrial transformation of contemporary Japan had already taken place in the valorization of capital on the shop-floor or a construction site, they are not simply the abject remnants of a lifelong process of labor. Because of their relationship to the state in this project, they cannot even sell their labor power. Stripped of the possibility of laboring in a formal sense, their actions in *ikotsu shūshū*—as the state certainly intended—could only be a gift.

But what kind of gift was this? Given the conditions of the workers, certainly not one that could make any claims on real reciprocity. And yet, could it be more than the relationship of patriotic obligation and indebtedness implicit in the state's offer? Perhaps the notion of excessive and non-recuperable expenditure that Bataille developed can help us make sense of it.[117] Not Mauss's grand potlatch, not even the examples of the Marshall Plan or massive human sacrifices by the Aztecs that fueled Bataille's imagination. Instead, I am inspired here by Okamoto Tarō's provocative engagement with Bataille's early thoughts on sacrifice in his notion of *girigiri no utsukushisa*—beauty on the edge. The gift of everything by those who have nothing—nothing but their own bodies in action in a duration that could end at any time.

And so, if we follow the state's lead and see the practice of *ikotsu shūshū* as something like sacrifice, we can see the Promise Keepers as both sacrificer and sacrifice (the one who makes the offering, and that which is offered, in Mauss's formulation). Those who are nearly nothing offering that which is everything to them. Not simply labor power, if such a thing could be simple, but the presence of their afflicted bodies, the determination and commitment that has gone unwanted and unoffered. The concern that has been withdrawn from family, friends, selves. What of the sacrifier, the recipient of the gift of sacrifice? Here, I think it is important to turn from the state to the dead, and the ways that the Promise Keepers recognize them.

In the times that I have worked alongside the Promise Keepers, they brought a seriousness and attentiveness to their work. It was clear that they believed that what they were doing was important. And yet, I never saw anyone treat the remains of the dead that they uncovered or speak of them with the reverence accorded to the "warrior gods" or "heroic spirits of the dead" valorized in nationalist discourses and in my interaction with members of veterans' groups who often came to observe the recovery efforts or participate in public forums about *ikotsu shūshū*. Instead, they uncovered them, cleaned them, carried them to the Gamafuyā field office with a combination of concern, affection, and pity. Yoshihiro, a member of the Promise Keepers since the first excavations, described it to me in stark terms. "Every time I think about them, those tiny bones, I wonder—what was it all for? Sacrifice, dying for your country. It's madness. There was no reason to die in that senseless, unimportant war."

Like Gibo and the other workers that they summoned, the abjection of the Japanese soldiers left in the battlefields beneath Shintoshin is significant. The remains disclosed by the workers' labor were broken and alone. Abandoned by their comrades, the emperor and the nation they served and protected, they lie discarded in hastily dug fighting positions, in abandoned tombs where others had been kept with care. The entire tableau hidden away by the American occupation until brought to light by laborers' hands. It is at this moment of encounter that Gushiken's and Higa's projects take shape. To Gushiken, the dead can testify to their refusal of sacrifice, and their critique reveals their commitment that life must be preserved. For Higa, the dead emerge from a duration of transformation, bringing all that they have accumulated in the past to bear on the political conflicts of the moment. The encounter between the dead and the Promise Keepers seems different.

There is a kind of symmetry to these two interlocutors, the members of the Promise Keepers and the sacrificed soldiers who call to them, both struggling against their parallel durations of abjection. Moreover, the ground against which their exchange is understood is always a complex manifold: the failed, genocidal totality of the Pacific War, and the indeterminate, capitalist modernity of contemporary Okinawa.

This is where they come together, uncertain subjects, constituted by the sharing of this moment, of these gifts. Placed in relationship to one another by this exchange, by their recognition of their mutual humanity. It is communication defined against the unfulfilled promise of communion and the claims of Japanese—and American—sovereignty. And yet, for even a brief duration, they can become those who offer something of value, and those who accept the kindness—and perhaps even the forgiveness—of another. In this moment, the battlefield becomes a space charged with the same kind of possibility and power that Okamoto Tarō could not see there, concerned more with their traces in the wooded shrines and rustic villages where nativist discourses had already located them.

I remembered something that Hiroshi, my companion in the farm work that I described earlier, had told me about his experience of *ikotsu shūshū*. One afternoon, the summer before, we were sitting in the sun on the veranda of the House of the Rising Sun, looking at Higa Toyomitsu's photographs of the dead that had been published in the journal *Sekai*. Gesturing to an image depicting the remains of a soldier who had killed himself by detonating a grenade on his lap, Hiroshi paused and said, "In saving them, we saved ourselves."

While state capital may not have been a wage for these men and women, it allowed them to gradually reconstruct themselves as laborers, once again capable of value-producing activity. It enabled Yamauchi's organization to develop the possibilities that remained in a derelict hotel and a defunct senior home, creating the House of the Rising Sun and Eden House to house them. It opened the possibility for them to rejoin social networks from which they had been excluded, or to organize new ones. And yet, what does it say for their dreams of the future that they can only imagine themselves to be free through toil? What does it mean for their return to the everyday to be mediated in the space-time of deep militarization, to labor in sites and temporal durations saturated with colonial discipline, wartime genocide, and postwar military domination? Are there costs to accepting the capital that enables their aspirations and their actions? Can their work transform the multiple temporalities that they uncover? What possibilities beyond the excavation of the dead can they seize?

Certainly, the expected narrative of decline so popular in the Japanese media is interrupted. The tropes of failure and loss that commonly organize narratives of precarity, an implicit and explicit counterpoint to lives of aspirational growth, are disrupted in practice and in representation.[118] And yet, they do not—they cannot—remain bound up in these new lives of sacrifice, supported by state capital. They must do other things. In fact, during the two years that I worked with both Gamafuyā and the Promise Keepers, the time spent searching for and recovering the remains of the dead only accounted for several weeks of activity. Instead, a more complex set of rhythms and practices emerged.

Every morning when I arrived at the House of the Rising Sun, the space hummed with activity. In the lobby and the interior space where religious services were held on weekends, all the familiar practices that anticipate labor were taking place. Men and women hurried in and out of the business office on the far side of the space. There, calls were made, appointments scheduled, errands organized, visitors welcomed. An ongoing search for opportunities, for support, for new relationships. And in the open space itself, those men who had once been laborers gathered, dressed again for work. Tall rubber boots, woven cotton gloves, heavy trousers and vests, towels knotted around their heads. A note, a moment in a familiar set of rhythms, yet one that is conjugated in entirely different ways.

Quick conversations between residents and staff organized the morning. Soon, teams of residents boarded cars and vans to travel to the farming projects that had been set up by the staff. The Promise Keepers had borrowed unused farmland from parishioners of the Bethany Church. While few residents had been farmers, many Okinawans in the community were familiar with farm labor. Growing up, they often helped older relatives to harvest the subsidized sugar cane that they grew on available land. Sometimes, they spent weekends helping their extended family to tend fields or greenhouses. Farmers received the extra labor that they needed, but families also returned home with gifts of produce. Several residents told me that they fondly remembered working together like this with their grandparents, their

4.9.   Members of the Promise Keepers working in the fields.

aunts and uncles, their cousins. In the projects that involved the Promise Keepers, parishioners of the Bethany Church, and other supporters, new forms of community were nurtured.

Some days, we cleared fields in Nishihara, working with hand tools or small tractors to cut back the dense brush. Other days, we worked in gardens set up to grow *nira*, or garlic chives. The supermarket chain Kanehide had offered to sell their *nira*, and everyone felt a sense of responsibility to make this project work. We took turns hauling bucket after bucket of water from a concrete cistern, carrying it to the raised *nira* beds while other workers weeded the frames. It was hot, tiring work, but there was still time to laugh and talk, drinking bottled water and tea while we waited to be picked up later in the afternoon. There were days when we went up to fields on the slopes of Shuri, where the Promise Keepers were experimenting with ways to grow traditional Okinawan vegetables like *goya* and *nābīrā*. A group of workers had come up with an idea for framed nets to protect plants from the summer typhoons. I remember how proud everyone was when we found that the crops had survived a typhoon undamaged. As Yamauchi later told me, there are many ways to relearn the pleasure of cultivating life.

The House of the Rising Sun was itself a center of action. Some residents rode their bicycles through the surrounding streets or met with local businesses to collect recyclables that could be redeemed. A group worked upstairs in the dining facility, preparing meals for their fellow residents. Whoever was available would join in to clean the common spaces, and the floors always gleamed with wax, the clear but pleasant smell of disinfectant in the air. Each person took care of their own rooms. Teams worked to prepare a place for new residents, cleaning and painting rooms, and repairing furniture so that they could have a place of their own. Others drew on skills that they had developed in the construction industry. In 2011, a powerful typhoon smashed windows and tore the worn, spalling concrete from one of the exterior walls. Several residents worked alongside volunteer contractors to repair the damage while others tended the drying carpets and furniture lined up in the parking lot. Work to maintain the building was continuous.

Some residents turned their attention to the future, taking advantage of job training programs sponsored by the prefecture. A former copywriter from mainland Japan told me that he was excited to be enrolled in a course that would certify him as a home health-care worker. He told me that he could never imagine going back to his old life, working on advertising campaigns for products that meant nothing to him. Now he was beginning to think that he wasn't going to just survive. A real future was possible again. Others took time to care for those who remained unhoused and impoverished, distributing food and drink in the parks around Naha. They also joined in the weekly events at Yogi Park, to entertain, to preach, and to feed anyone who might be gathered there.

And yet, it was not all activity. After the morning rush, the House of the Rising Sun became a place of quiet. Not everyone had to work. Many residents were able to qualify for government assistance, often after significant effort by the staff on their behalf. Some used this time to focus on healing: to enter drug and alcohol rehabilitation programs or get long-deferred medical care. Several members that I knew worked with Yamauchi to tentatively reach out to those who had suffered from their actions or their neglect, exploring the possibilities to make amends or create new kinds of relationships.

Even those who regularly worked on Promise Keepers projects were not driven by the rhythm of labor. The restored hotel was also a place for them to rest when they needed to rest, to create a space for themselves, to read, to think, to write, to talk with one another. The exhausted and infirm received special consideration. For them, the House of the Rising Sun might not be an intermediate space, a place that they would pass through. They could remain there, living their lives in the secure company of supportive friends.

There was also time for creativity. A group of residents learned *eisā*, the Okinawan dance for the dead.[119] They chose songs, learned to play the handheld drums, and practiced the energetic choreography of the dances. This was a challenging task. Residents came from all over Okinawa and mainland Japan, so they hadn't been dancing since childhood and had no particular style on which to base their performance. What's more, the dance is extremely popular in Okinawa, and they could count on experienced and discerning viewers to be in their audiences. They worked to assemble a coherent pattern for their *eisā*, and they considered what it meant to perform in a Christian church. They danced before services, in the park, at revivals. Other residents volunteered for the band that performed in the church or learned to play the *sanshin* with the *minyō* (folk song) group.

Some residents joined Yamauchi and his wife in Bible study. The pace was slow, and sessions focused on a page or two of text. Each member came with notes for the day's discussion, their Bible painstakingly highlighted and annotated. The sessions that I attended were conscientiously collaborative. Yamauchi or his wife might provide historical context for the selections that they had chosen, but they were careful not to impose their interpretations on others. Members, quiet at first, became more confident as they saw that their participation was appreciated. They drew on their own experiences and were eager to express their ideas. When the session ended, they made plans to meet again the following week for a new discussion.

It seemed that the experience of working to recover the remains of the dead encouraged many residents to consider other entities whose existence had become interlaced with their own. Wartime sacrifice and the spirits of the dead remained important topics of discussion, but that was not all. Some residents told me that their encounter with the dead in the old battlefields had reminded them—reawakened them—to beliefs that they had long ago abandoned. One resident explained that he wasn't the eldest son in his family, so he didn't have any direct responsibilities for the ancestral dead. However, since *ikotsu shuhsu*, he had become more attentive to the presence of the dead in the world around him and to their needs. A quiet, middle-aged member told me that he had been preoccupied with the un-happy and abandoned spirits of the dead that he encountered during their excavations. He wondered if Christianity might offer him some possibility to reach out to them. As he tried to practice Christian prayer, he had a rev-elation that the dead were now in heaven with God, no longer in the world around him. He said that he felt a sense of relief that they would not suf-fer because of his inability to fully care for them in the way that his grand-mother and mother had diligently attended to their ancestral spirits. Others followed similar paths: according to Shirahase Tatsuya, 20 to 30 percent of the residents had converted to Christianity.[120] Hide, another member since the early days, told me what brought him to Okinawa also shaped his con-version. He had grown up in an old Shintō family in mainland Japan. They had lost their position generations ago because of the Shrine Merger Act, and their regional practices were marginalized during the centralization of State Shintō.[121] For years, he felt contempt for all forms of organized religion. His only inspiration came from the Nietzsche that he studied as a college student. Years later, after his life had careened out of control, he said that it was the kindness of Yamauchi and his parishioners that saved his life; their examples and the daily work of *ikotsu shūshū* brought him to Christianity. However, he said that it was not a conventional conversion. While digging for the remains of the dead alongside the other Promise Keepers and mem-bers of Gamafuyā, the Christian god came to him "from the side," like the Okinawan deities that dwell among the people. Their relationship developed slowly, emerging almost unnoticed during weeks of work.

All of this suggests that practices that came together in the battlefield extended to the other actions of the Promise Keepers, creating new kinds of space and time, new experiences, and new understandings. For his part, Yamauchi encouraged his parishioners to think reflexively and critically about their situation, to draw inspiration from Christianity and consider how they might be able to continue to transform their lives. He turned to this theme at the service, speaking to his congregation about desire. He cautioned his listeners against the dangers of belonging to a competitive society, with its ceaseless struggle to improve their material conditions. What's more, he is less concerned with consumption than production, a sharp critique of the valorization of work.

A quotation from Matthew 20:20 appeared on the screen: "Then the wife of Zebedee came to Jesus with her two sons, bowed before him, and asked him for a favor." Yamauchi began to talk about respect for parents. He said that we are fortunate to have what we have. Now we must think about what we can do for ourselves. He introduced the story of Zebedee's wife, the mother of the disciples John and James, and her visit to Jesus on their behalf. He smiled and asked: As Okinawans, isn't this a familiar thing to do? What could be more understandable than the love of a mother for her children and her willingness to make any request on their behalf? What does Zebedee's wife ask? She wants her children to be happy and successful, but she also wants them to be seated on either side of Jesus in the world to come—to be exalted above all others.

Yamauchi repeats himself for emphasis: As parents, we love our children. We want them to succeed, to exceed what we have accomplished. But is that what they want? He pauses for effect. "We can love them so much that we hurt them." This is not the way that we must lead our lives, he says. Think of parents who push their children into successful careers out of what they think is love, only for them to spend their lives unhappy, dissatisfied, angry with one another.

This is the problem with the competitive foundations of Japanese society and *risshin shusse*, the determination for material improvement. Extending his arms as if to embrace the island around them, he sadly acknowledges that even Okinawa has become a twenty-four-hour society built around consumption. Convenience stores, vending machines, so many places are open day and night. Every corner of daily life is filled with the opportunity to work, buy, and profit. But all this draws power. Everything works all the time. There is no respite. Why do we need so many things? He reminds the congregation that a minister from Fukushima had visited the week before, his community still reeling from the disaster. Yamauchi argued that people have become prisoners of the working day, a duration that has expanded to fill every moment. This expansion of labor has put unreasonable pressures on their world—the ceaseless demand for power to be consumed in production is what led to the catastrophe at Fukushima two months ago, he said. Is profit and production more important than human life? He urged them to reduce the time that they spent in this struggle and use what is saved—saved time—to serve others. Only then would they know *kokoro no yutakasa*, the true richness of the heart. At the same time, they must not think that they have to sacrifice everything. God wants them to be happy. This is the balance that richness of the heart rather than material acquisition will allow them to achieve.

His words are a stark contrast to the argument that Kuramoto Sō's spectral soldiers voice when they walk the streets of Tokyo. They also urge the living Japanese to accept less, valorizing the instrumentality of denial. It is an end in and of itself. This is closely tied to their romanticization of pain, as the brutal sergeant beats his nephew to introduce him to the humility that only comes with violence and suffering. The subjectivity that Kuramoto's play advocates is one of anticipatory sacrifice. Through self-denial, the minimization of personal desire, the willingness—the eagerness—to accept pain without question, and even to implore the forces of authority to demand their sacrifice. All this despite the evidence that the consequences of that sacrifice may well be meaningless.

At the same time, we might ask why Yamauchi chose the story of Zebedee's wife. Her desire for her children was not based on material accomplishment and recognition, but on spiritual recognition and salvation. Isn't this an objective that would resonate with a clergyman such as Yamauchi? Here, he is acknowledging both a sense of the importance of everyday life and a respect for others that allows them to make their own decisions. Rather than demand the security of a future now, Yamauchi recognizes the importance of a duration in which to think and act. He points out that both capitalist modernity and spiritual certainty figure an accelerated emphasis on the future that threatens to evacuate this moment—the moment that they have only just recovered—of its possibilities.

What Yamauchi is advocating is not simply the counterpoint to this orientation, but one that is made possible through a historical critique of precisely this attunement. Writing of the Paris Commune, Kristin Ross has argued that the Communards were determined to overcome "the certainty that sharing could only mean the sharing of misery."[122] If there was no historical example of soldiers sacrificing themselves for the state, of Okinawan citizens willing to be sacrificed, of dutiful laborers producing and consuming in order to sustain the subject of capital that subsumes, degrades, and eliminates them, there would be no practical, reflexive basis to Yamauchi's argument. Instead, it is grounded in the shared experiences of the members of his congregation, and in the material conditions that give shape to the very building that surrounds them.

I think of Okamoto Tarō's commitment to uncovering buried possibilities, of Ifa Fuyū's Nietzschean injunction to have the courage to dig into the material foundations of your world. It is the Promise Keepers who have done this. They had been fired from their last job, forced from their homes, put on a final bus or flight away from familiar circumstances. Many of them, as Gibo told me, paused just before drinking themselves to death in a Naha park or killing themselves in a deserted battlefield. And yet, these are the men and women who have the courage to return to the spaces of their abjection, to the construction sites where they could no longer work as wage laborers, to the parks and fields where they lived, unhoused. They have returned to these spaces to act.

And the House of the Rising Sun, where they have made their new home? It is also a discarded remnant of an earlier spatialized division of labor, a hotel that once housed temporary laborers, travelers, people whose futures were uncertain but who held out some hope for the future. It was structurally exhausted—its business failed, fragments of concrete spalling here and there, its rooms emptied of life. And yet, as the residents' actions slowly restored its spaces, new possibilities emerged that have been shaped by what has been. This transformation extends to the other spaces where the Promise Keepers act. The buried battlefields, the abandoned farms, the streets filled with trash. Their actions uncover possibilities that have been passed over, pushed aside, thrown away.

As the work of the Promise Keepers becomes more widely known, in popular and academic media, in public and private discourses, their practices are revaluated. So too are the workers themselves. Gushiken Takamatsu and Higa Toyomitsu have been widely praised, from senior conservative politicians and the members of patriotic veterans' groups, to peace activists and the opponents of American military occupation. And, while the soldiers who they rescued from their burials may have refrained from killing or have reconsidered their acts, they are nonetheless accorded the status of the heroic war dead. In their collaboration, this prestige has been extended to the Promise Keepers. It was their work, their dedication that uncovered the dead, that allowed Guishiken and Higa to incorporate them into their projects, that returned them to their families and to the nation. They are the ones who instantiated Higa's injunctions: do not kill, do not tolerate killing, do not kill yourself. They have gone beyond this, acting constructively to restore relationships and to cultivate life. Of course, no revaluation of their status or reputation will be totalizing, and stigma surely lingers from their unhomed pasts, to be confronted in the future. And yet, it is this very history that figures in their reputation, the burdens that they bore and still acted. It is what shapes their potlatch of nothingness, of everything. And it gives form to the transformations that they struggle to continue.

Perhaps the grounds for these transformations are already present. In the possibility of a Japanese citizenship that constitutionally rejects war, in the *moai* and other forms of mutual care, in the demand for action and equality by generations of demonstrators, artists, voters. History that may be weighted with failure and yet remain charged with possibility. As workers, as practicing subjects, people like the Promise Keepers do more than uncover existing forms of *en* that can then be reawakened. Given the agentive notion of *yuimāru*, connections are retied, remade, reimagined. And, with the critical dimension integrated into this renewed practice, it has the possibility to be collaborative rather than exploitative, for the participants to anticipate a new and more just future rather than a return to the melancholy embrace of aestheticized violence and cruelty.

The service ends and most of the parishioners go upstairs for lunch. The dining hall staff serves plates filled with glossy scoops of steamed rice and thick, unctuous beef curry. People eat quietly, smiling and nodding as other parishioners and residents come and go. Almost everyone returns to the serving counter for seconds. As I finish, I say goodbye to the residents at my table. On the way out, I thank Yamauchi for the service and briefly speak with Gibo about activities in the coming week.

Outside in the streets, the sounds of the city awakening. Traffic on the main street a few blocks over is louder. I can hear an aircraft in the clouds overhead, but I can't tell if it is heading for the airport at Naha or departing from Kadena or Futenma to the north. Still, the shops and factories around me are closed. Tomorrow they will reopen. Workers with grinders and torches will cut up salvaged pieces of metal. Trucks will load and unload. Restaurants will open their doors and post their menus. Laborers on their way to the harbor or a construction site somewhere will stop and pick up *bento* for their lunches.

There will also be activity at the House of the Rising Sun. Teams of workers will board vans at the entrance. Guests might arrive: a minister from Itoman, from Osaka, from the Philippines. A driver from a local restaurant with a gift of frozen food. Two or three civil servants from the prefectural offices. Perhaps a new arrival will stand where I am standing now, anxiously holding printed directions in his hand. A resident might leave, returning to the streets or the parks where they lived before. I've met men like this in Yogi Park, I've seen the friendship and concern that continues between them and the residents who remained, I've heard the invitations for them to come back home. Another resident might finish their stay, put aside their fears about life beyond the walls of the House of the Rising Sun, and set out for whatever comes next.

For now, the streets are quiet. I look back at the House of the Rising Sun. Inside, the work continues.

Conclusion

Even the dead will not be safe.

Walter Benjamin, "Theses on the Philosophy of History"
([1940] 2007)

My friend placed the bottle on the table in front of me. It was clear glass—a small, screw-top *awamori* bottle like the ones they sell to tourists on Kokusai Dōri in Naha or in convenience stores. The label had been peeled off and the glass was scrubbed clean. There was a couple of inches of amber liquid in the bottom. *Majo no sake*, his wife explained—not exactly "witches' brew," but close enough.

She told me that they had organized a performance a few months earlier at a municipal hall on one of the smaller islands off the coast. A place with no theaters or clubs, far enough away that it was inconvenient to cross over to Okinawa just to go to a movie or to see a show. After their performance, an elderly woman was waiting to speak with them. She said she and her friends had really enjoyed themselves. Things hadn't been that lively in years. Out of gratitude, she offered them a bottle filled with this *awamori*, a locally distilled rice liquor. She told them that they discovered it when they were cleaning the abandoned tombs at the edge of the village. After the war, many families moved to the growing base towns or to mainland Japan. Local jobs were scarce and the difficulties of farming and fishing on a small island could be overwhelming. The tombs were left behind. Sometimes families would return and reclaim the remains of the dead, moving them to new tombs closer to their homes. The islanders who stayed would try to consolidate whatever was left unattended. When they were cleaning one old tomb, they found a ceramic urn filled with *awamori* buried up to its neck near the entrance. This was like the practice that still continues of setting aside a container of *awamori* when a son is born. It would be kept somewhere secure, like the entranceway to the house, until the boy became an adult. Then it would be served at the celebration. This tradition was a little different. When the child was born, they set aside this *awamori* for him. However, it was kept in the family tomb until his death. When they opened the tomb to put him inside, they would bring out the *awamori*. You would never personally enjoy the *awamori* that was set aside for you. But you would know that everyone who gathered to commemorate your death would be treated well. It was hard to say how old the *awamori* was. Year after year spent inside the tomb had changed it. As I held the bottle up to the light, it was far darker than any *awamori* I had ever seen. Thick, leaving a honeylike trace on the glass as I turned it.

My friend told me that they had shared it out, little by little, among the members of the performance troupe. They had given some to their neighbors and to their close friends. But they saved this for me. "After all," his wife said, "this is the kind of thing that an anthropologist should understand." She poured it out into a glass. "Drink it, then go right to bed. The dreams you have tonight will be important." I drank it while I sat and talked. When I finished, I said my goodbyes and walked back through the darkened streets to my hotel. Tired from traveling, I turned on the air conditioning and stretched out on the bed.

I woke up with the morning sun streaming through my window. It took me a moment to gather my thoughts. I remembered the *awamori* the night before, and what my friends told me. I had no memory of any dreams. It was as if I had closed my eyes and moments later opened them again. I struggled to remember while I showered and dressed, but I couldn't recall anything. I left for the day with a feeling of disappointment. When I was doing fieldwork for my dissertation, the interpretation of dreams was a pleasant activity among friends. Many mornings, we sat around the community center drinking coffee while someone recounted a dream from the night before. Everyone would offer suggestions about what it might mean, drawing on their sense of a shared symbolic vocabulary, their intimate knowledge of one another and their families, and the conviction that dreams can carry important messages. I suppose I hoped that a memory of dreams this morning would give me an opportunity to discuss it with my friends after my long absence from Okinawa. Instead, it was as if there was nothing in the place where something should have been.

On March 1, 2021, Gushiken Takamatsu began a hunger strike in front of the Okinawa Prefectural Offices. For more than a decade, he had done his best to bind together the recovery of the remains of the war dead, and his urgent warning to those living today against war and death: "Do not kill. Do not tolerate killing. Do not kill yourself." He had been praised by the members of Okinawan anti-base movements, and members of patriotic veterans' organizations and peace activists had traveled from the mainland to join him in the field. Schoolchildren from all over Japan visited the sites where he had organized *ikotsu shūshū* projects. Japanese governmental ministers listened to his stories and funded his work. He won awards and was celebrated in the media.[1]

At the same time, construction continued on the new American base in Henoko. Political fortunes changed. Construction was supported and condemned locally, encouraged and prohibited by the prefecture, and subject to the slow, grinding pressure of the Japanese state. The world changed. American wars began in Iraq and Afghanistan, surged, and began to recede. Japan and the United States turned their attention to China, militarism grew, new self-defense troops were stationed in Okinawa. Relationships changed. Theorists wrote about China attacking US forces in Okinawa with drones as a prelude to their invasion of Taiwan. The US military, particularly the Marine Corps, still bloodied by two decades of war, reorganized for a littoral campaign along the Pacific Rim.[2]

Reports that the ocean floor in Henoko was so unstable that it resembled meters of mayonnaise made it seem like construction might be abandoned.[3] Then trucks from southern Okinawa began to head north, dumping load after load of soil into Oura Bay in Henoko. As long as land remained in the old battlefields to the south, there would be fill to transform the ocean floor, to allow the new Marine Corps air station to rise from the sea. The bones of the dead were disinterred and put to work again.

Gushiken continued his hunger strikes across Japan—at the prefectural office, in the shadow of Yasukuni Shrine in Tokyo, at the Ministry of Defense. His opposition to base construction was simple: "throwing the bones, the flesh and blood, the spirit of the war dead into the ocean is not something that human beings do."[4] It is a message that he presented relentlessly. Sitting cross-legged on the ground, dressed in a poncho and ball cap during the rain, his message written in block letters on a banner displayed by his side. It is a message that he conveyed insistently, even confrontationally. In a hearing with Ministry of Defense officials, he demanded to know how they could do this simple thing: How could they appropriate the remains of the dead to build another space of war? His performances brought together the same disparate groups that had been drawn to him before. Members of veteran and survivor groups would say that they supported the construction of the new base, but they could not condone the actions of the state that would build it from the remains of relatives who had already been sacrificed once. Okinawan survivors would silently stand by his side, holding framed photographs of family members who were killed in the war. Gushiken did not prophesize, he did not speak the words of the dead. Yet he spoke for them, and for the living as well.

A decade ago, after a visit to Gushiken's temporary office, I stood alone, looking out past the elementary school to a broken ridgeline. To the abandoned tombs on its slopes, surrounded by the scattered fragments of the dead. To the new ring road that lay at the bottom of a cut that had disgorged the remains of the dead as the dirt and clay was removed to create its path. To the dead—shattered fragments or entire forms—that might lie beneath my feet. I thought of the legendary practice of *hitobashira*, the human pillar.

Modern scholarly interest in *hitobashira* surged in 1925, when construction at the Imperial Palace in Tokyo disclosed a number of human skeletons, buried in the foundations of the old castle. This discovery inspired a debate among native ethnologists, all committed to explain the practice.[5] My own exposure to the term is less scholarly. Years ago, living in an old house in Hayama, Japan, I read a copy of Lafcadio Hearn's *Glimpses of Unfamiliar Japan* that some previous tenant had left behind. I was struck by what Paul Manning has called "Hearn's writings and his wanderings in the weird cosmopolitan conjunctures between spaces produced by colonialism and modernity."[6] The Japan that Hearn described was a dangerous place, and the works of human beings were always subject to interference from other entities. Months of labor and the massive expenditures required to build a stone bridge, necessary for commerce and the movement of troops, could be destroyed in moments by the actions of a malicious water spirit. A castle, index and token of the power of the local warlord, could fall under the weakest of assaults if the deities did not strengthen the ramparts. And so, a practice emerged that incorporated a human being into the site. Hearn wrote that a wonderful young dancer, recognized for her performances during Obon, the festival of the dead, was immured in the walls at Matsue Castle. Her grace and posture would give the same to the building. A stranger (*ijin*), long a figure of danger and power, might be snatched up from the road and buried in the footings of a bridge. A mother carrying her infant daughter, a model of loyalty and self-sacrifice, might be buried in the banks of an aqueduct.[7]

One night over drinks, an Okinawan friend and avocational ethnologist told me that *hitobashira* was like making *mochi*. The sacrificial victim would be beaten to death, pounded with massive wooden mallets until their bones were broken and their body was like a gelatinous mass. Like the sweet, steamed rice pounded in an *usu* (mortar), each grain gave up its own integrity under the blows of the mallet, but they gained a collective strength as they were beaten into a rice cake. Buried in the foundation of a building, in the pier of a bridge, in the walls of a castle, the form of the sacrifice, reshaped by tools, would add strength and integrity to the new place.

I have never been able to find a written account of my friend's explanation. In fact, there is little reliable evidence to suggest that any of these practices have taken place for centuries.[8] What of Okinawa? There is no evidence at all for a practice like *hitobashira*; when early twentieth-century theatrical performances speak of it, they are adaptations of performances popular in mainland Japan at the time.[9] All of that changed with the Battle of Okinawa. There, the bodies of soldiers and civilians—Okinawans, Americans, mainland Japanese, Korean, Chinese, Pinoy, intact or in fragments, killed during battle, executed by the soldiers that were sworn to protect them, dead from disease or neglect—were incorporated into the landscape. Embedded in the soil, they became something new—an offering to bind the projects of the present over into the future. But the objects of magic often exceed the scope of the acts that brought them into being, and the lives and ambitions of those crucial to their enactment. The emperor, the generals, the local commanders who ordered them to their deaths are themselves dead or debilitated. And still, the dead maintain their watch, holding their position, keeping the world in place. Deaths that were once offered to ensure the survival of the Japanese Empire now hold together Japan and the United States in the massive project of American hegemony.

As I stood there in the darkness I thought of them, all around, beneath my feet.

The dream that was offered to me did not take shape. I have tried to hear the voices of the dead, but they did not speak to me. Or they did not speak to me directly. And yet, I have learned so much from listening. I have had the good fortune to spend time with those who have heard those voices. I have tried to be attentive to their claims of pasts, of memories that might otherwise be overwritten or effaced. I have seen the creativity with which they contested assertions of auratic authority. I have learned about their courage in challenging and transforming sacrifice. I have watched them struggle to build new relationships that might offer a path to a more just future. I hope that this book can be a point in our construction of a new constellation, one in which we can extend ourselves toward them. To take our share of responsibility for a burden that they have long borne on our behalf.

Introduction

1 Chris Marker, dir., *Level Five* (France, 1997), 106 min. Screening at the Brooklyn Art Museum, September 2014.

2 Rancière, *Film Fables*, 214.

3 I am quoting the English version of the film captions, except as noted.

4 Rancière, *Film Fables*.

5 Otto Preminger, dir., *Laura* (USA, 1944), 88 min.

6 For important contemporary conceptualizations of fiction and anthropology, see McLean and Pandian, *Crumpled Paper Boat*.

7 Kinjō passed away in 2022 at the age of ninety-three. Yoshichika Yamanaka, "Survivor of Mass Suicide." For more on Kinjō's life, see Bradley, "Banzai."

8 Onishi, "Okinawans Protest Japan's Plan."

9 Rabson, "Politics of Trauma."

10 See Nelson, *Dancing with the Dead*.

11 Field, *In the Realm*, 67.

12 TMM, "Sinking of the Tsushima-maru."

13 Higa Toyomitsu, *Hone no Ikusayu*; Medoruma, *Okinawa Sengo Zero-nen*.

14 Kinjō's argument about imputability resonates with Ricœur, *Memory, History, Forgetting*, 457–506; and Weinrich, *Lethe*, 166–67.

15   Ikeda, *Okinawan War Memory*; Jahana, *Shōgen Okinawa "Shūdan Jiketsu"*; Ohnuki-Tierney, *Kamikaze*; Yoshimi, *Grassroots Fascism*.

16   This also resonates with concerns with the aesthetic representation of even the most critical representation of war. See Benjamin, "Theories of German Fascism"; see also Swofford, *Jarhead*, who has described this experiential appropriation as "war porn."

17   Sono, *Aru Shinwa no Haikei*.

18   In 1972, the American occupation of Okinawa formally ended, and Okinawa "reverted" to Japanese sovereignty. In the remainder of the text I will simply refer to this event as Reversion. See Akamatsu, "Shūdan Jiketsu no Shima"; Hoshi, "Tokushū Shūdan Jiketsu."

19   The lawsuit was filed in 2005 and settled in 2008. Ōe, "Misreading."

20   While no direct material traces of an order for civilians to commit suicide have been found, and some anecdotal evidence has been offered that suggests that there were no formal orders issued, there are far more records of survivors who insist that there were. Despite this ambiguity, a Japanese court nonetheless ruled that there was enough evidence to believe that such an order had been given, disseminated, and enforced.

21   Nelson, "No Better Friend."

22   Sledge, *With the Old Breed*, 269.

23   Bataille, *Guilty*, 45.

Chapter 1. Opening a Rift in the Everyday

1   For the history of the American occupation of Okinawa, see Hein and Selden, *Islands of Discontent*; Inoue, *Okinawa and the US Military*; McCormack and Norimatsu, *Resistant Islands*; Nelson, *Dancing with the Dead*.

2   The word *naichi* literally means "interior lands"—the four main islands of Japan, generally excluding Okinawa. An important construct in nationalist discourses.

3   For a more complex discussion that builds on a similar conceptualization, see Jefferson, Turner, and Jensen, "On Stuckness."

4   The oil storage site in question is the Okinawan petroleum refinery, sold to Taiyo Oil Company in 2016.

5   Promise Keepers is a nonprofit formed by the Okinawa Bethany Church to support unhomed laborers. See Chapter 4 for a more complete discussion.

6   For important studies of the Okinawan diaspora, see Matsuda and Iacobelli, *Rethinking Postwar Okinawa*; Nakasone, *Okinawan Diaspora*; Rabson, *Okinawan Diaspora*; Suzuki, *Embodying Belonging*.

7 I am thinking here of Agamben's discussion of the temporal orientation of "truth tellers" in the history of philosophy, especially Agamben, *Time That Remains*, 60. For a discussion of anxiety concerning the attitude and actions of the dead toward the living, see Clastres, *Chronicle*, 117.

8 Mitchell, *Poisoning the Pacific*.

9 I do not think that participants are unaware of this contradictory experience of daily life. My thoughts on this have benefited from Fink, Saine, and Saine, "Oasis of Happiness."

10 The exhibition discussed here is *The Perpetual Moment: Visions from Okinawa and Korea*, MoMA PS1, New York, October 17–December 13, 2004. For further details, see the exhibition website: https://www.moma.org /calendar/exhibitions/4825.

11 For more on the work of Noh Suntag, see their website, http://suntag.net/ (accessed November 15, 2024).

12 On August 13, 2004, a US Marine Corps CH-54D helicopter crashed into the main administration building at Okinawa Kokusai Daigaku and exploded. Burning wreckage was scattered across a large area and several homes in the surrounding neighborhood were damaged. Armed US Marines blocked streets and denied local media and government officials access to the site.

13 The most thoughtful ethnographic engagement with the planned construction of an American military base in Henoko remains Inoue, *Okinawa and the US Military*.

14 For more on Teruya Rinsuke's work, see Nelson, *Dancing with the Dead*, 69–99. Rinsuke's performance in Takamine Gō's film *Untamagirū* is discussed in chapter 4.

15 The street takes its name from the tree known in English as the golden trumpet (*Handroanthus chrysanthus*). As the *ipê-amarelo*, it is the national flower of Brazil.

16 Medoruma, "Stories."

17 Medoruma, "Stories."

18 *Mabui* that appear in Takamine Gō's 1985 avant-garde film *Paradaisu byū* (Paradise view) and the popular children's action series *Ryūjin Mabuya* are depicted in this way.

19 Sato, "Gyokusai."

20 Inoue, *Okinawa and the US Military*, 1–30, 126–55; see also Nelson, "Occupation Without End."

21 This is similar to Lock's description of the fractal distribution of personhood in each organ of the body. Lock, *Twice Dead*, 315–44.

22 For a provocative counterpoint, see Anne Allison's discussion of the trans-formation of contemporary mainland practices in Allison, *Being Dead Otherwise*, 123–71.

23 Lebra, *Okinawan Religion*, 21–45, 54–57, 74–94.

24 Ifa, "Yuta No Rekishiteki Kenkyū."

25 In a less intrusive way, several people in Uruma City have told me that the spirits of the dead can slip into a body during Obon so that they can more fully enjoy the holiday. Their living hosts feel nothing more than a tingling sensation in their face and hands, and the spirits return to their places when the festival ends.

26 Representations of *mabui* play an important role in Okinawan popular culture. Medoruma Shun's "Mabuigumi" (1998) depicts the plight of a middle-aged fisherman whose *mabui* becomes separated from his body; the rhythm of Takamine Gō's film *Paradaisu byū* is punctuated with im-ages of a dog carrying a *mabui* in its teeth. Most prominently, the cult hit film/TV show *Ryūjin Mabuya* represents the exploits of an Ultraman-like superhero known as Mabuya, the Spirit of Ryūkyū.

27 The practice of *buta benjo* involves the quartering of pigs in the outdoor privies of rural homesteads. It was thought that any fraction of the *mabui* lost by a member of the household would be consumed by the pigs along with the family's waste. When the pig is, in turn, consumed during a family gathering, the household member would be able to recover that which had been lost. The term *senkotsu*, literally "the washing of the bones," is a ritual in which the remains of the dead are cleaned and restored to a form, contained in a funerary urn and the family tomb, that can once again act intersubjectively. It continued under the disinterested supervision of the American occupation but was prohibited after 1972 as mainland laws ap-plying to mortuary practices were applied to Okinawa.

28 Since the Okinawa "boom" in the 1980s, this negative valuation has subtly changed. Okinawanness is valorized as authentic and powerful, but still inescapably different from the unmarked lives of ordinary (i.e., mainland) Japanese.

29 Wacker, "Onarigami," 346–47.

30 Matsumura, *Limits of Okinawa*; Matsumura, *Waiting*, 17–36, 134–92.

31 Allison, *Precarious Japan*; Arai, *Strange Child*; Ishida and Slater, *Social Class*; McCormack and Norimatsu, *Resistant Islands*.

32 These material exchanges are vehicles by which the immaterial essence of the gift—its pleasing yet intangible content as well as the intentionality of the giver augmented by his or her particular qualities—are conveyed to the spirits of the living and the dead.

33 While *chimu* is generally glossed as heart, liver is also a possible translation.

34 For his magisterial treatment of resistance to collective pressures, see Amino, *Zōho muen, kugai, raku.*

35 While *yuimāru* is often seen as a sign of hopefulness and concern, it could also be understood as a moral economy that includes forms of exploitation and appropriation. See Turner, "Beautiful."

36 Ames, "Mired in History," 249–313.

37 The Fukuharas are one of the most historically important musical families in Okinawa. See Rabson, *Okinawan Diaspora.*

38 For detailed ethnographies, see Ames, "Mired in History"; Angst, "Rape of a Schoolgirl."

39 Higashi, "Child of Okinawa."

40 Suzuki, "Divination."

41 For a discussion of the broader Japanese context, see Carter, "Power Spots."

42 Ivy, *Discourses of the Vanishing,* 29–65.

43 Adorno, "Theses Against Occultism."

44 Bloch, *Heritage of Our Times,* 97–148.

45 Adorno, "Theses Against Occultism," 130.

46 Translations of different versions of this song are available on recordings by Bob Brozeman and Ryuichi Sakamoto.

47 Important anthropological work on the relationship between cosmologies and reflexive social critique can be found in Chu, *Cosmologies of Credit*; Klima, *Funeral Casino*; Kwon, *Ghosts of War*; Smith, *Ancestor Worship.*

48 Ifa, "Yuta No Rekishiteki Kenkyū." While Mrs. Adaniya is inspired by this history, it was also her predecessors who were targeted by Sai On's interventions.

49 Obon is the festival for the dead.

50 Yamanokuchi, *Yamanokuchi Baku Shibunshū,* 137–38.

51 Yamanokuchi, *Yamanokuchi Baku Shibunshū,* 137–38.

52 At the time, ¥100 was roughly equivalent to US$1. Allen, *Identity and Resistance,* 157.

53 *Manzai* is a popular form of Japanese stand-up comedy that centers on banter, often insulting, between two partners.

54 Unfortunately, the videos mentioned are no longer available.

55 Onga, "Okinawaken Ni Okeru Chīkishi Henshū Jigyō to 'Hisutorīto.'"

56 *Katakana* is a Japanese syllabary, often used to provide phonetic representation for foreign utterances.

57 For an extensive discussion of the social and spatial organization of the American occupation, see Molasky, *American Occupation*; Shimabuku, *Alegal*.

58 The most sophisticated study of the semiotic and spatial transformation of American occupied Okinawa is Figal, *Beachheads*.

59 *Kankara sanshin* are musical instruments constructed from empty tin cans, a length of wood, and strings made from parachute cord.

60 Deleuze, *Difference and Repetition*, 1–69; Lefebvre, *Rhythmanalysis*, 1–70; Roberson, "'Doin' Our Thing.'"

61 Weiss, "Northwestern Tanzania."

62 Lemon, "'Your Eyes Are Green.'"

63 Hart, "Heads or Tails?" See also Kwon, "Ghosts of War," for a provocative use of Hart's work in the context of Vietnam.

64 Onga, "Okinawaken Ni Okeru Chīkishi Henshū Jigyō to 'Hisutorīto.'"

65 Sadoyama Yutaka, "Duchuimuni," track 4 on *Sayonara Okinawa* (Kyanpasu, TRYS005, 1996).

66 Nelson, *Dancing with the Dead*, 171–214.

67 Okinawashi Jieigyōsha, "Beihei no Joshi."

68 About $100 at the time of my fieldwork.

69 Nelson, "Moai."

70 Embree, *Suye Mura*, 112–57.

71 Satomura, "Okinawa 'Moai' Monogatari."

72 Sakurai, *Kōshūdan Seiritsu Katei no Kenkyū*.

73 Yanagita, quoted in Najita, *Ordinary Economies*, 70.

74 Embree, *Suye Mura*, 112–57.

75 Najita, *Ordinary Economies*, 175–209.

76 Lazzarato, *Making*, 8–9.

77 Najita, *Ordinary Economies*, 211–14.

78 Adaniya, "Moai o Gyō to Suru Hitobito."

79 About $1.3 million at the time.

80 In the postwar era, *bashōfu* production has declined and this textile, once the everyday wear of Ryūkyūan peasants, has been valorized and commodified as a rare surviving expression of native artistry.

81 Inoue, *Okinawa and the US Military*.

82 If the text were to use the Japanese term *doshi*, and gloss the pronunciation as *dushi*, it would suggest that Okinawan utterances are a kind of derivation of Japanese.

83　The contents of the *moaichō* reflect a legal requirement for honest and accurate recordkeeping that was established in civil law in 1915. The prefectural government required anyone organizing a *moai* to present all of this material to their local police station for inspection and approval. Any changes in the conduct of the *moai* would also have to be reported and authorized. No such requirement exists today, but the *moaichō* (or some variation on it—for example, several of my friends have told me that they use apps to manage their *moai*) remains extremely popular.

84　The person responsible for the conduct of a *moai* is known variously as an *oya*, *zamoto*, or *temoto*; the person who keeps its records is known as a *hissha* or *chōhissha*.

85　Handwritten signatures carry very little legal or practical weight in Japan. In most cases where some positive form of identification is necessary, seals bearing the name of the person in *kanji* (Chinese characters) and registered with the local municipal government are used.

86　I would have the same experience later during my own participation in *moai*. Once, my friends knew that I had a talk in Tokyo planned that would coincide with our *moai* meeting. They gently reminded me well in advance to make sure that I paid before I left. Another time, my daughter was suddenly hospitalized. When friends dropped by the hospital to visit and bring a gift of fruit, they assured me that they had me covered for the upcoming *moai*, so I had nothing to worry about.

　　Default in a *moai* can be catastrophic. The family of a close friend of mine ended up in Koza because their grandfather had acted as a guarantor for his brother in a *moai*. When his brother defaulted and fled to mainland Japan, he was forced to sell his rural home and farmland to cover the debt. After that, taking a job in a base town was his only alternative.

87　It is interesting to compare the conduct of early *moai* with those of the colonial era. All of the members registered in the early records that I've seen were men. It was not the member himself whose seal was affixed, it was that of his guarantor. The member himself is not registered by name but by *yagō* (the name of his household) and his number in the birth order of his family. Less a record of depersonalization than the communal nature of participation.

88　About $25,000 at the time of my fieldwork.

89　Deleuze, *Difference and Repetition*, 21.

90　Lefebvre, *Critique of Everyday Life*.

Chapter 2. Iphigenia in the China Sea

1　See Sand, "Open Letter."

2　See Kase, "To the 187 Scholars."

3   Vidal-Naquet, *Assassins of Memory*, 98.

4   Dentsū is the largest advertising agency in Japan. Fujisankei Communications Group is a major communications conglomerate.

5   Breen, *Yasukuni*; Takenaka, *Yasukuni Shrine*.

6   Kase, "To the 187 Scholars."

7   See Sand, "Year of Memory Politics."

8   Kase, "Response to the Updated Version."

9   Kase, "To the 187 Scholars." It is only peripherally relevant to my argument that it is unlikely that any of the claims made by the revisionists are true. Signatories were carefully vetted and confirmed; they were given several opportunities to remove their name from the letter. No one did. Instead, several hundred more scholars signed after the initial publication.

10   De Certeau, "On the Oppositional Practices," 34.

11   Ohnuki-Tierney, *Kamikaze*; Ohnuki-Tierney, *Kamikaze Diaries*; Tansman, *Aesthetics of Japanese Fascism*; Tansman, *Culture of Japanese Fascism*.

12   Axell and Kase, *Kamikaze*.

13   The Japanese-language website of the SDHF can be found at https://hassin .org/.

14   There is a robust literature on this category. Of course, Nora and Kritzman's *Realms of Memory* remains a significant collection addressing the relationship between history and memory. I have also been influenced by Halbwachs, *The Collective Memory* and *On Collective Memory*; as well as Winter, *Sites of Memory*.

15   I received this message from Moteki on March 29, 2016; it was sent from Japan on March 30, 2016.

16   Kase, "The Greater East Asian War."

17   Kase, "The Greater East Asian War."

18   Ricœur, *Time and Narrative*, 20.

19   Harootunian, *Archaism and Actuality*, 6–10, 83–84; Harootunian, *Uneven Moments*, 326–61.

20   For the most complex historical treatment of the valorization of rural life in Japan, see Harootunian, *Things Seen and Unseen*. An early and influential ethnographic engagement is Robertson, *Native and Newcomer*.

21   Ivy, *Discourses of the Vanishing*, 66–97.

22   LaCapra, "Trauma, Absence, Loss."

23   Runia, *Moved by the Past*, 48.

24   Euripides, *Euripides V*, 161.

25   This substitution is suggested in *Iphigenia at Aulis*. However, the sacrifice takes place offstage and Artemis's intervention is only reported by a messenger. There is also some thought that this is a later addition to the diegesis, the work of someone other than Euripides. Even so, it is interesting to suggest that the deities recognize the appropriateness of substitution within the act of sacrifice, even when the human sacrificers and the human sacrifice do not. In any event, other representations, including Mircea Eliade's contemporary reinterpretation, end with Iphigenia's sacrifice of herself. Derrida, *The Gift of Death*; Eliade, *The Sacred and the Profane*; Evens, *Anthropology as Ethics*.

26   Evens, *Anthropology as Ethics*, 47–75.

27   Ricœur, *Time and Narrative*, 52–87.

28   Nakaima Hirokazu served as governor of Okinawa from December 10, 2006, to December 10, 2014. Supported by the Liberal Democratic Party (LDP) and Kōmeito in his candidacy, Nakaima supported the construction of a massive new Marine Corps air base in Henoko. He was defeated in his reelection bid by Onaga Takeshi, long-time mayor of Naha and himself a member of the LDP who, nonetheless, opposed base construction in northern Okinawa.

29   Slater, "3.11 Politics."

30   Ohnuki-Tierney, *Kamikaze*, 27–60, 102–24.

31   For a critical discussion of the category of *ibasho*, see Allison, *Precarious Japan*, 174–76.

32   Nelson, *Dancing with the Dead*, 3, 91, 184.

33   Figal, *Beachheads*, 34–35, 51–57.

34   Nora, "Between Memory and History," 23.

35   Yonetani, "Contested Memories."

36   Angst, "Gendered Nationalism."

37   I am inspired in my interpretation here by Prost, "Monuments to the Dead."

38   Despite their appearance, many were reconstructed after their destruction in the Battle of Okinawa. For a complex and sophisticated discussion of the transformation of the spaces of remembrance at Shuri Castle, see Loo, *Heritage Politics*, 55–118, esp. 96–97.

39   Nora, "Between Memory and History," 20.

40   For a discussion of colonial and other overseas shrines, see Nakajima, "Shinto Deities."

41   For a popular guide and description of the Naminoue Shrine, see http://naminouegu.jp/english.html.

42 For footage of the event, see "Abe Faces Angry Mourners at Okinawa Commemoration," YouTube, https://www.youtube.com/watch?v=k8v6HUJ5KZc.

43 See chapter 1 for my translation of Yamanokuchi's poem.

44 Tomiyama, "Okuni Wa?"

45 See Takada's memoir for a compelling account of his life and career. Takada, *Bābon, Sutorīto, Burūsu.*

46 *Tatami* is a mat made of woven grass, used as floor covering.

47 *Zabuton* is a cushion for seating.

48 Yamanokuchi, *Yamanokuchi Baku Shibunshū*, 36–37.

49 Runia, *Moved by the Past*, 1–16.

50 For me, the most compelling work on class, labor, and creativity remains Rancière, *Proletarian Nights*. For important critiques of proletarian literature in Japan, see Bowen-Struyk and Field, *For Dignity*; Perry, *Recasting Red Culture*.

51 Christy, "Making of Imperial Subjects."

52 Matsumura, *Limits of Okinawa*; Tomiyama, *Senjō no kioku.*

53 Gillan, *Songs*; Roberson, "'Doin' Our Thing."

54 This is the English translation of Article IX provided in Japanese government publications. See "The Constitution of Japan," https://japan.kantei.go.jp/constitution_and_government_of_japan/constitution_e.html.

55 At the same time, constitutional revision, especially relating to Article IX, has been a stated objective of the LDP leadership for many years.

56 Munn, "'Becoming-Past' of Places," 375.

57 For more on fields of action, see Munn, "Excluded Spaces."

58 The *shīsā*, a lion-like guardian entity, is conventionally used as a symbol of Okinawa.

59 Beginning in 1959, ANPO protests expressed opposition to United States-Japan mutual security arrangements.

60 Since the period of my fieldwork, the Naha Shimin Kaikan has been closed because of structural issues. Originally slated to be demolished, efforts are now underway to preserve it. For an extended reflection on both the aesthetic and pragmatic dimensions of his work, see Kinjō, *Okinawa genkūkan.*

61 Loo, *Heritage Politics*; Smits, *Maritime Ryūkyū.*

62 My account is based on my field notes and a recording that I made during the performance. I have also consulted a recording of a performance produced for television, and shown on affiliate channels of the Japanese

broadcaster TBS on August 14, 2010. See https://www.tbs.co.jp/tbs-ch/item/d1995.

63 The time reckoning here is marked. It either rejects or is unaware of post-war temporality in which the Showa era ended at year 64 (1989), with the death of the Showa emperor. These spirits of the dead know something of life beyond their death, but they are not aware that the emperor has been replaced and they have returned during the diminished reign of his son. Or, bound to an earlier set of social relations, they are unable to act on that knowledge.

64 The Okinawa shrine is one of a series of Shinto shrines across Japan to commemorate soldiers killed in war, as well as police, firemen, and others who die in the line of duty.

65 Derrida, *Gift of Death*, 69.

66 Turner, "Beautiful."

67 Ohnuki-Tierney, *Kamikaze*, 79–80.

68 Ohnuki-Tierney, *Kamikaze*, 1–25, 157–85.

69 Lambek, "Sacrifice."

70 Kockelman, *Chicken and the Quetzal*, 87–123.

71 Takenaka, *Yasukuni Shrine*, 90–93.

72 Takenaka, *Yasukuni Shrine*, 114.

73 In the televised performance of *Kikoku*, Ōmiya is played by Kitano Takeshi (Beat Takeshi), and the character seems like a variation on the gruff, violent, yet somehow sympathetic soldier that he portrayed in Nagisa Ōshima's film, *Merry Christmas, Mr. Lawrence* (Japan/New Zealand/UK, 1983).

74 Garon, "Luxury Is the Enemy." For a provocative discussion of the dissonance between the ideology of personal and household frugality and contemporary management debates, see Tsutsui, *Manufacturing Ideology*.

75 Caillois once suggested that, in sacrifice, human beings arrogate for themselves the position of creditor. By tactically initiating a circuit of exchange, they compel the deities, who insist on equilibrium in all things, to respond with a counter prestation of some kind. Caillois, *Man and the Sacred*, 28. Kuramoto's production takes precisely the opposite situation. In abstract terms, they argue that human beings are already indebted and must be prepared to effect a return at any time through sacrifice.

76 Harootunian, *Marx After Marx*, 153–96; Matsumura, "Expansion"; Walker, *Sublime Perversion of Capital*, 29–74, esp. 35–36.

77 For detailed arguments about precarity and contemporary capitalist crisis in Japan, see Allison, *Precarious Japan*; Gill, *Men of Uncertainty*.

78 Bakhtin, "Forms of Time"; Graeber, "It Is Value"; Munn, "Cultural Anthropology of Time." See also Ball and Harkness, "Kinship Chronotopes."

79 Casey, *Remembering*, esp. 154–258; Ricœur, *Memory, History, Forgetting*, esp. 3–35. Under Kuramoto's direction, performers attempt to represent the quotidian experience of soldiers as an unending present, uninterrupted by moments of contradiction and the critical reflection that they enable. It is an attempt to represent what for modern viewers is a memory, but to do so from within the form of the memory itself. A duration called back to immanence, disrupting the expected relationship between past and present.

80 Bataille, *Visions of Excess*; Bataille et al., *Sacred Conspiracy*.

81 Blanchot, *Unavowable Community*, 25.

82 Unlike the promise of memory work that Rancière has explored, the appropriation of the dead that takes place in performances such as this seems to be dignified in form alone. See Baronian and Rosello, "Jacques Rancière and Interdisciplinarity."

83 Later, I learned that this closing song was sung by Nagabuchi Tsuyoshi, the famous folk singer and actor, who played Akiyoshi in the televised performance of *Kikoku*.

Chapter 3. Unburying the Future

Epigraphs: Claude Lévi-Strauss's essay "Herodotus in the China Sea" appears in *The Other Face of the Moon*. Walter Benjamin's comments, made in relation to Roger Caillois's *L'aridité*, are quoted from Carlo Ginzburg, *Clues, Myths, and the Historical Method*.

1 For a provocative critique of Okamoto's fascination with Jōmon culture and his refiguration of the traditional, see Reynolds, *Allegories*, 54–85. See also Akasaka, *Okamoto Tarō to iu Shisō*, 109–90 passim; Chong et al., *Tokyo 1955–1970*; Morando, "Le mythe à l'épreuve"; Munroe, *Japanese Art After 1945*; Winther-Tamaki, "To Put On a Big Face."

2 For all citations, I refer to the 2009 edition of *Okinawa Bunkaron* unless otherwise noted. I have also consulted the original articles in *Shūkan Asahi* and the first edition of *Wasurerareta Nihon: Okinawa Bunkaron*, published in 1961.

3 Okamoto Tarō's father, Ippei, was a well-known journalist and illustrator. His mother, Kanoko, was a respected novelist.

4 Rancière, *Short Voyages*, 2.

5 Bourdieu, *Logic of Practice*, 145–46.

6 Okamoto, *Okinawa Bunkaron*, 219–20.

7   Although the statue itself bears the inscription in English, "Youth's time tower," on its base, it is often translated as "Young clock tower" in English sources.

8   "Ginza-Sukiyabashi Kōen'Wakai Tokeidai o Shūfuku-Okamoto Tarō Seitan 100 Shūnen de," *Ginza Keizai Shinbun*, June 27, 2011; Surya, *Bataille*, 192.

9   See Bakhtin, "Forms of Time"; Graeber, "It Is Value"; Munn, "Cultural Anthropology of Time." See also Ball and Harkness, "Kinship Chronotopes."

10   Okamoto, *Okinawa Bunkaron*, 220.

11   Okamoto, *Okinawa Bunkaron*, 226–28.

12   Okamoto, "Kamigami no Shima," 90–91.

13   In contemporary Japan, the characters would be read as Goshō, and, when used in Buddhist discourse, indicate a recently dead entity about to embark on the path of reincarnation.

14   The practice is known as *fūsō*, a form of primary burial once practiced throughout Okinawa. In the case of Kudaka, secondary burial takes place in the ornate ceramic urns (*zushigame* or, in Okinawan, *jīshigāmi*) that Okamoto and his companions saw on the beach. Okamoto, *Okinawa Bunkaron*, 238.

15   Okamoto, *Okinawa Bunkaron*, 238.

16   Okamoto, *Okinawa Bunkaron*, 239. Okamoto is contrasting mortuary practices in American-occupied Okinawa with legally required cremation in the main islands of Japan and, presumably, Western forms of burial.

17   Okamoto, "Kamigami no Shima," 91. The contested photograph was not included with others reproduced in Okamoto, *Okinawa Bunkaron*, 239–40.

18   OHBK, *Seitan 100nen Kinenten*.

19   Akasaka Norio noted that the photograph had been printed, but the curators decided not to display it.

20   Although neither man referred to it at the time, Takara and Akasaka have, in the past, debated ideological appropriations of Okinawa by Okamoto Tarō, Yoshimoto Takaaki, and others, and collaborated on the production of a collection of essays on the same topic. See Yoshimoto, *Ryūkyūko No Kankiryoku to Nantōron*.

21   Sahlins, *Culture and Practical Reason*, 174.

22   In fact, the color photographs of *jīshigāmi* (ceramic urns) published earlier in his essay received no criticism.

23   Increasingly, color photographs are also used in funeral services.

24   While it is possible that he based this initial description on his discussions with the *noro* and her family who hosted him during that visit, the

text closely follows what Orikuchi and Yanagita had written about Izaihō. Orikuchi, *Ryūkyū no Shūkyō*; Yanagita, *Kainan Shōki*.

25 Rancière, *Short Voyages*, 3–4 (bracketed word in original).

26 Augé, *Oblivion*, 56.

27 Leiris, *Phantom Africa*. See also Izzo, *Experiments with Empire*, 17–54.

28 Otto, *Idea of the Holy*; Eliade, *Sacred and the Profane*.

29 Iizawa, "Introduction."

30 TOMM, "Genshi," https://taro-okamoto.or.jp/exhibition/%e3%80%8e%e5 %8e%9f%e5%a7%8b%e3%80%8f.

31 Arutoki, totsujo, kare wa shaman ni naru. Okamoto Toshiko, "Introduction," *Shinpi*, 3.

32 On his return to Japan after the war, Okamoto would have found that the category of the shaman was being addressed with renewed interest. Francophone authors such as Lévi-Strauss wrote memorable studies on shamanism and the production of knowledge. That Okamoto had so heavily annotated his copy of Eliade's *Shamanism* is an indication of the seriousness of his interest. At the same time, there was much to attract Okamoto to contemporary Japanese social sciences and popular discourses. Renewed interest was paid to figures such as Yanagita Kunio and Orikuchi Shinobu, who appropriated the work of the Okinawan polymath Ifa Fuyū, and equated living Okinawan priestesses and necromancers with figures in the timeless Japanese past who were able to travel between the seen and unseen worlds, mediating the relationship between the living, the dead, and their deities. In the aftermath of war, scholars such as Hori Ichirō and Sakurai Tokutarō developed wide-ranging, systematic projects that explored the emergent category of spiritual intermediaries in the context of Japanese history, rural sociology, religious studies, and native ethnology. It is a subject that Okamoto returned to again and again in his work: in his essays about Tōhoku (*itako* in *Shinpi Nihon*) and Okinawa, and in a whole sequence of paintings and sculpture created in the postwar era.

33 Reynolds, *Allegories*, 67.

34 Reynolds, *Allegories*, 68.

35 Regardless of his dismissal of the category of shamanism, Taussig's work is crucial here: see Taussig, *Shamanism*. See also Bacigalupo, *Shamans of the Foye Tree*; Bacigalupo, *Thunder Shaman*; Taylor, "Healing Translations"; Viveiros de Castro, *Cannibal Metaphysics*; Viveiros de Castro, *From the Enemy's Point of View*; Viveiros de Castro, *Relative Native*.

36 Carneiro da Cunha, "Points of View."

37 Lewitsky was the deputy director of the Musée de l'Homme, and a scholar of Siberian shamanism. In 1942 he was executed as one of the leaders of a

French Resistance group organized by the staff of the museum. See Bataille et al., *Sacred Conspiracy*, 472; Weingrad, "College of Sociology," 153.

38 The indispensable guide to Okamoto's life in Paris is Akasaka, *Okamoto Tarō no mita Nihon*, 19–66. Okamoto mentions Breton in passing, but Surya contends that Breton neither spoke at nor attended any meetings. Bataille et al., *Sacred Conspiracy*; Okamoto, "Bataiyu to no deai"; Okamoto, "Waga tomo Joruju Bataiyu"; Surya, *Georges Bataille*.

39 Bataille et al., *Sacred Conspiracy*, 123–24.

40 Documentary evidence of Okamoto's participation is scant. There is good reason to believe that Okamoto was a valued and central member of the collective: unlike many other potential members, Bataille excused him from any initiation or probationary period, and he advanced him beyond the other initiates. Patrick Waldberg accounts for Okamoto's attendance at virtually all events, but there is no record of Okamoto having, for example, taught a session or published anything related to the Collège de Sociologie. He is not mentioned in Michel Surya's biography of Bataille, and there are no clear references to his work in any of Denis Hollier's collections of material related to the Collège de Sociologie. A list of names written by Bataille indicates that T. O. is to be "proposed by" Bataille at an upcoming session, and this most likely refers to "Tarō Okamoto," as he would have been known to his French colleagues. Bataille et al., *Sacred Conspiracy*, 268. See also Okamoto, "Bataiyu to no deai"; Okamoto, "Waga tomo Joruju Bataiyu"; Waldberg, *Tarō Okamoto*.

41 Okamoto, "Bataiyu to no Deai."

42 For a comprehensive collection of texts representing the work of the collective, see Bataille et al., *Sacred Conspiracy*; Hollier, *College of Sociology*. Details of Okamoto's participation are traced in Morando, "Le mythe à l'épreuve." On Benjamin's ambiguous participation, see Hollier, *College of Sociology*, xxi; Weingrad, "College of Sociology."

43 Caillois and Lanser, "Collège de Sociologie"; Surya, *Bataille*, 250.

44 Okamoto, "Bataiyu to No Deai"; Okamoto, "Waga tomo Joruju Bataiyu."

45 Bataille et al., *Sacred Conspiracy*, 175.

46 Okamoto, "Bataiyu to no deai," 268–69.

47 Mauss, quoted in Fournier, *Marcel Mauss*, 327–28.

48 See Benjamin, *Arcades Project*, 79, 97, 98, 110, 142, 199, 399, 415, 439, 469, 555, 615, 696, 774, 798.

49 Benjamin, "Theories of German Fascism."

50 See Weingrad, "College of Sociology."

51 Benjamin, quoted in Weingard, "College of Sociology," 147.

52 Okamoto, "Bataiyu to no deai," 269. It is worth noting that Okamoto omits any mention of this break in "Waga tomo Joruju Bataiyu," writing that he had to leave Paris when the Germans invaded. He recounts his farewell with Bataille and Bataille's hope that they would be able to continue their work together. Patrick Waldberg's memories of Okamoto's participation generally agree with the latter essay, making no mention of any disagreement with Bataille. Okamoto, "Waga tomo Joruju Bataiyu," 202–3; Waldberg, *Tarō Okamoto*.

53 In the postwar years, Okamoto's personal library included works, primarily in French, by Bataille, Eliade, Kojève, Lévi-Strauss, and Mauss. For a more detailed discussion of Okamoto's library and his reading of Eliade, see Sasaki, "Okamoto Tarō."

54 See esp. Yanagita, *Kainan shōki*; Yanagita, *Kaijō no michi*.

55 Christy, "Fantasy of Ancient Japan." While Lévi-Strauss himself traveled to Okinawa, this came after Okamoto's research visits, and I was unable to find any evidence that they directly communicated or otherwise cited the influence of their experiences. See Lévi-Strauss, *Other Face of the Moon*, 73–90.

56 Yanagita, *Kainan shōki*, 1–8.

57 Leiris, *Phantom Africa*.

58 Leiris, *Phantom Africa*, 6.

59 Okamoto, *Okinawa Bunkaron*, 35.

60 Watsuji, *Koji Junrei*, 1–15. For images of motion in representations of Japanese modernity, see Figal, *Civilization and Monsters*, 155–96; Marotti, *Money*, 245–83.

61 Okamoto, *Nihon no Dentō*, 44–72, esp. 50–55.

62 Hōryūji wa yakete kekkō . . . jibun ga Hōryūji ni nareba yoi no desu. Okamoto, *Nihon no Dentō*, 50–51.

63 Okamoto, *Okinawa Bunkaron*, 8.

64 Yanagita, *Yama no jinsei*.

65 Harootunian, *Overcome by Modernity*, 317–18.

66 Felman and Laub, *Testimony*; Hirsch, *Family Frames*; Hirsch, *Generation of Postmemory*; Koga, *Inheritance of Loss*.

67 Ivy, *Discourses of the Vanishing*, 67.

68 Akasaka, *Okamoto Tarō no Mita Nihon*, 217–21.

69 Miyamoto, *Nihon Zankoko Monogatari*.

70 Kojève, "Idea of Death."

71 Figal, *Civilization and Monsters*; Ivy, *Discourses of the Vanishing*.

72   Benjamin, *Charles Baudelaire.*

73   Okamoto, *Okinawa Bunkaron,* 9.

74   Okamoto, *Okinawa Bunkaron,* 71–72.

75   Kojève, "Idea of Death," 149.

76   Kojève, "Idea of Death."

77   Okamoto, "Ancient Blood," 110.

78   Okamoto, *Okinawa Bunkaron,* 30–31.

79   Okinawa Taimusushakan, *Tetsu no Bōfū.*

80   Figal, *Beachheads.*

81   Okamoto, *Tarō Tanjō,* 524.

82   Okamoto, *Tarō Tanjō,* 524–49.

83   Okamoto, *Okinawa Bunkaron,* 50–54.

84   Okamoto, *Okinawa Bunkaron,* 56–59.

85   Okamoto, *Okinawa Bunkaron,* 59–60.

86   Okamoto, *Okinawa Bunkaron,* 58.

87   Clastres, *Society Against the State.*

88   Okamoto, *Okinawa Bunkaron,* 64.

89   Okamoto, *Okinawa Bunkaron,* 64.

90   Matsumura, *Limits of Okinawa.*

91   Rabson, *Okinawan Diaspora.*

92   Arasaki and Kawamitsu, *Okinawa*; Koikari, *Pedagogy of Democracy*; Matsumura, *Limits of Okinawa*; Mori, *Okinawa Sengo Minshūshi*; Mori, Toriyama, and Kokuba, "*Shimagurumi tōsō*"; Shimabuku, *Alegal.*

93   Okamoto, *Okinawa Bunkaron,* 219–43.

94   Okamoto, *Okinawa Bunkaron,* 65.

95   Eliade, *Images and Symbols*; Otto, *Idea of the Holy*; Ricœur, *History, Memory, Forgetting.*

96   Okamoto, *Okinawa Bunkaron,* 40–41.

97   The woman was one of two *noro* on the island, each dwelling in their own village. *Noro* are the primary public ritual practitioners, the remaining member of the dual structure of priestesses and rulers that characterized the Ryūkyūan political system at every level of social organization.

98   Okamoto, *Okinawa Bunkaron,* 165–68.

99   Eliade, *Images and Symbols,* 27–56.

100   At this point, Okamoto also engages in a strange anti-Semitic digression, a joke of sorts. The passage is particularly repellent considering his reverence

for Mauss and the members of *Acéphale*'s disdain for anti-Semitism. See Okamoto, *Okinawa Bunkaron*, 181.

101   Okamoto, *Okinawa Bunkaron*, 75.

102   Okamoto, *Okinawa Bunkaron*, 75.

103   Okamoto, *Okinawa Bunkaron*, 77.

104   Weingrad, "College of Sociology."

105   Benjamin, *Arcades Project*; Cadava, *Words of Light*; Hansen, "Benjamin's Aura."

106   Benjamin, "On Some Motifs in Baudelaire," 338. See also Hansen, "Benjamin's Aura."

107   Okamoto, *Okinawa Bunkaron*, 184–85.

108   Okamoto, *Okinawa Bunkaron*, 187–91.

109   Okamoto, *Okinawa Bunkaron*, 173.

110   Horkheimer and Adorno, *Dialectic of Enlightenment*, 35–62.

111   Ivy, *Discourses of the Vanishing*.

112   Okamoto, *Okinawa Bunkaron*, 73.

113   Yanagita, *Kaijō no michi*.

114   Okamoto, *Okinawa Bunkaron*, 130–31.

115   Gell, *Art and Agency*, 68–72.

116   Benjamin, *Arcades Project*; Benjamin, *Work of Art*; Hansen, "Benjamin's Aura."

117   Harada, Maeshiro, and Miyahira, *Sasagerareru seimei*; Miyahira, *Ryūkyū Shotō no dōbutsu girei*. The anthropologist Maetakenishi Kazuma has argued that this incommensurability between mainland Japanese and Okinawan categories of sacrifice continues to be enacted in the exploitation of rural Okinawan communities for the storage of national strategic reserves of petroleum. See Maetakenishi, "Kichi-Dōbutsu kugi-Shakai undō."

118   Ifa, "Yuta no rekishiteki kenkyū."

119   Maetakenishi, "Kichi: Dōbutsu kugi: Shakai undō," 212–15.

120   Nelson, *Dancing with the Dead*, 48–53.

121   Harada, Maeshiro, and Miyahira, *Sasagerareru seimei*, 97–165.

122   Harada, Maeshiro, and Miyahira, *Sasagerareru seimei*; Miyahira, *Ryūkyū shotō no dōbutsu girei*.

123   Willerslev, Vitebsky, and Alekseyev, "Sacrifice as the Ideal Hunt."

124   Valeri, *Kingship and Sacrifice*, 46–50.

125   Winther-Tamaki, "To Put on a Big Face."

126   Figal, *Beachheads*.

127   Ōya Sōichi, "Shin Nihon Onna Keizu."

128 Rancière, *Philosopher and His Poor.*

129 Akasaka, *Okamoto Tarō no Mita Nihon*, 224–25; Okamoto, *Okinawa Bunkaron*, 20.

130 Okamoto, *Okinawa Bunkaron*, 245–51.

131 Mauss, *Gift*, 78; See also Bogoras, *Chukchee Mythology.*

132 Nietzsche, *On the Genealogy of Morals*, 61.

133 "Police Officer Dispatched from Osaka Insults Protestors in Okinawa," *Japan Times*, October 19, 2016.

134 Rancière, *Future of the Image*, 1–31. Rancière describes generosity as the characteristic of art that does not impose responses on viewers.

Chapter 4. From Among the Dead

The chapter title is inspired by Boileau-Narcejac, *D'entre les mortes.*

1 Kano, *Okinawa No Fuchi*, 1–33.

2 For a detailed, critical exploration of this moment, see Christy, "Making of Imperial Subjects"; Loo, *Heritage Politics*; Matsumura, *Limits of Okinawa.*

3 The quotation is taken from Nietzsche, *The Gay Science*. English translation by Walter Kaufmann in Nietzsche, *The Gay Science*, 41.

4 Aguni, "Ifa Fuyū."

5 Ifa, "Introduction," in Shimabukuro, *Okinawaken Kunigamigunshi*, 8.

6 Higa Shunchō (1883–1977) was an influential Okinawan historian. His copy of Ifa's book is held at the Okinawa Prefecture Library in Yogi Park, Naha.

7 Nietzsche, *Gay Science*, 41.

8 Kinmonth, *Self-Made Man*, 102–110.

9 Deleuze, *Nietzsche and Philosophy*, 1–37, esp. 34–35.

10 Tomiyama, "On Becoming 'a Japanese,'" https://apjjf.org/tomiyama-ichiro /2160/article.

11 For a broader sense of the ways in which the social experience of movement and acceleration goes beyond that of individuals in motion, see Ingold, "Back to the Future"; Keane, "Perspectives on Affordances"; Manning, "No Ruins."

12 The question of automobility is not limited to the Japanese experience of modern life. See Hansen and Nielsen, *Cars*; Lutz and Fernandez, *Carjacked*; Stuesse and Coleman, "Automobility."

13 McCormack and Norimatsu, *Resistant Islands*; Mori, *Okinawa Sengo Minshūshi.*

14 These ideas are inspired by an idiosyncratic reading of Martin Hägglund's work on Derrida. See Hägglund, *Radical Atheism*. Fisher sees this torn

and distorted experience as central to everyday life. Fisher, *Ghosts of My Life*, 18.

15 Lefebvre, *Rhythmanalysis*, 1–70.

16 Bakhtin, "Forms of Time."

17 Shīmī is a spring festival in which members of the community visit their family tombs, cleaning them and conversing with the spirits of the dead. Obon is a late summer festival in which the spirits of the dead return to their homes to spend time with their living families.

18 An image of both nostalgia and presence, the power spot has become a compelling category. See Carter, "Power Spots"; Rots, "This Is Not a Powerspot"; Rots and Teeuwen, *Sacred Heritage*.

19 For a graphic representation of the military imagination of this space, see Nash, *Battle of Okinawa*.

20 Kitamura, *Shishatachi no sengoshi*; Shima, "Bones."

21 Fisher, *Weird*, 8–13.

22 Yonaha, "From Traditional to Contemporary."

23 Smits, *Visions of Ryūkyū*, 50–99.

24 Rancière, "Aesthetic Dimension," 11.

25 For an exhaustive critique of everyday life during the Japanese colonial era, see Matsumura, *Limits of Okinawa*; Loo, *Heritage Politics*.

26 Takamine Gō, dir., *Untamagirū* (Japan, 1989), 120 min.

27 Nakazato Isao's readings of Takamine's work are sharp and perceptive. Nakazato, "Hanmo suru Guntō;" Nakazato, "Komamushitachi no Hanran." Although Takamine has received little critical attention in English, interviews and provocative criticism can be found in Gerow, "From the National Gaze"; Ko, *Japanese Cinema and Otherness*, 77–114; Nakazato, "Documentarists of Japan #20."

28 Adorno, "On the Fetish Character"; Yonaha, "From Traditional to Contemporary."

29 Nelson, *Dancing with the Dead*, 3, 91, 184.

30 Benjamin, *Arcades Project*, 107.

31 Benjamin, *Arcades Project*, 119.

32 Benjamin, *Arcades Project*, 104.

33 Fisher, *Weird*, 8–13.

34 My thoughts on duration are indebted to Halbwachs, *On Collective Memory*; Ricœur, *Memory, History, Forgetting*.

35 For a contrasting perspective on the remains of military bases, see Weiss, "Not Built to Last."

36   Anthropologists have found a productive space for criticism in the ambivalent experience of ruination. See Abu El-Haj, *Genealogical Science*; Dawdy, *Patina*; Finkelstein, *Archive of Loss*; Gordillo, *Rubble*; Middleton, "Becoming-After"; Navaro-Yashin, *Make-Believe Space*.

37   The foundational arguments within anthropology on qualia are Munn, *Fame of Gawa*, 10–13, 74–75. See also Fehérváry, *Politics in Color and Concrete*, 1–26.

38   Blaxell, "Preparing Okinawa."

39   Ōshiro, "Tennyo no Yūrei," 83.

40   For a provocative discussion of the nonhuman traces of the past shaping the present, see Kim, *Making Peace*.

41   These tropes are explored in Edwards, "Between Two Worlds"; Gillan, *Songs*.

42   Ōshiro, "Tennyō no Yūrei."

43   Noah Sneider has written that Gushiken seems to work with dental equipment, although Gushiken does not publicly discuss his private life in any detail. Sneider, "Second World War."

44   For critical interpretations of the category *genba*, see Onaga and Wu, "Articulating Genba."

45   Figal, *Beachheads*, 51–88; Kitamura, *Shishatachi no sengoshi*, esp. 277–345.

46   Gushiken, *Boku ga ikotsu o horu hito*.

47   Benjamin, "Theories of German Fascism."

48   For compelling anthropological engagements with the social world of the living and the dead, see Koga, *Inheritance of Loss*; Kwon, *Ghosts of War*; Renshaw, *Exhuming Loss*; Rubin, "Exhuming Dead Persons"; Sadruddin, "Death."

49   Gushiken's primary references are Hayashi, *Okinawa-Sen: Kyōseisareta "Shūdan Jiketsu"*; Hayashi, *Okinawa-Sen to Minshū*.

50   Gushiken, *Boku ga ikotsu o horu hito*, 16–17. See also the discussion of *gyokusai* in chapter 2.

51   Gushiken, *Boku ga ikotsu o horu hito*, 22.

52   Gushiken, *Boku ga ikotsu o horu hito*, 13–22, esp. 22.

53   Nancy, *Inoperative Community*, 1–42.

54   Valeri, "Wild Victims," 110.

55   Gushiken, *Boku ga ikotsu o horu hito*, 30.

56   Gushiken, *Boku ga ikotsu o horu hito*, 31.

57   Gushiken, *Boku ga ikotsu o horu hito*, 31–32.

58   In 2020, the Japanese Ministry of Health, Labor, and Welfare began a program to use more sophisticated forensic methods to identify remains. See

Kōseirōdōshō, *Senbotsusha Izoku nado e no Engo*, https://www.mhlw.go
.jp/stf/seisakunitsuite/bunya/0000172647_00005.html.

59   Gushiken, *Boku ga ikotsu o horu hito*, 33–34.

60   Hansen, "Benjamin's Aura," 352–54.

61   For a contemporary political history of other uses of the category of "voiceless voice," see Kapur, *Japan at the Crossroads*, 177–180.

62   Ricœur, *Memory, History, Forgetting*, 111–15, 314–42, 466–70.

63   Edwards, "Between Two Worlds," 143–44.

64   For compelling work on the contemporary implications of *en*, see Goldfarb,
"Coming to Look Alike"; Jensen, Ishii, and Swift, "Attuning"; Morimoto,
"Wild Boar Chase"; Nozawa, "Phatic Traces." The foundational discussion
remains Amino, *Zōho muen, kugai, raku*.

65   Okamoto, *Okinawa Bunkaron*, 73–75, 99–101.

66   "Jūku no Haru" has been regularly recorded as a duet between well-known
singers and was a local hit for Takada Wataru and Ōshiro Misako when
I was doing my dissertation research. The song itself is based on "Yoron
Kouta," a prewar working song in which a coal miner in Kyūshū longs for
his lover on Yoron, the small Ryūkyūan island where they grew up together.

67   Marc Augé makes the point in *Oblivion* that the notion of waiting and
hoping is often conceptually bound together—witness Dumas's phrase in
The Count of Monte Cristo: "toute la sagesse humaine sera dans ces deux
mots: 'Attendre et espérer'" (all human wisdom is summed up in these two
words: "Wait and hope!"). Augé, *Oblivion*, 10.

68   Govindrajan, *Animal Intimacies*, 31–61; Keane, "Killing Animals"; Singh
and Dave, "On the Killing and Killability of Animals."

69   Weiss, *Real Pigs*, 196.

70   See chapter 2 for a detailed analysis of *Kikoku*.

71   Gushiken, *Boku ga ikotsu o horu hito*, 50–64.

72   Gushiken, *Boku ga ikotsu o horu hito*, 62–64.

73   Morimoto, "Wild Boar Chase."

74   This is an intentional photographic style associated with Higa, especially
in the early years of his career.

75   The quotation comes from the introduction to a special issue of *Sekai*,
September 2010. Reproduced in Higa, "Hone ni yobarete," in *Hone no
Ikusayu*, 2.

76   A detailed history of postwar residential construction based on American
military models can be found in Ogura, "Gaijin Jūtaku."

77   The last was previously published as *Bideo Salon*.

78 Ryūdai Photo Club is based at Ryūkyū Daigaku, also known as the University of the Ryūkyūs.

79 For complex critiques of postwar American occupation, see Koikari, *Pedagogy of Democracy*; Shimabuku, *Alegal*.

80 Nakazato, *Fotoneshia*, 59–90.

81 Tōmatsu, *Hikaru Nanamui*, 126.

82 Rancière, "Notes on the Photographic Image," 15.

83 Nakazato, *Fotoneshia*, 14–58, 59–68.

84 Nakazato, *Fotoneshia*, 68–74.

85 Nakazato, *Fotoneshia*, 75.

86 Nakazato, *Fotoneshia*, 75–76.

87 The catastrophic consequences of the political exploitation of these images are discussed at length in Ohnuki-Tierney, *Kamikaze*, 1–25, 157–85.

88 For a productive discussion of *ibasho*, see Allison, *Precarious Japan*, 174–76.

89 Higa, "Hone ni yobarete," in *Hone no Ikusayu*, 2.

90 June 23 and August 15, respectively. The first date commemorates the cessation of hostilities during the Battle of Okinawa; the second, the Japanese surrender that ended the war in the Pacific.

91 The exhibition was scheduled for October 29 to November 5, 2010. Because of Typhoon Chaba, public events were canceled after the first day.

92 This is the same collection as that cited above: Higa, *Hone no Ikusayu*.

93 For a broader discussion of the return of the living survivors of war and their ideological representations, see Igarashi, *Homecomings*.

94 The history of the Battle of Okinawa is replete with accounts of Okinawan citizens trying to protect themselves from the battle by taking shelter in their household tombs. In many of these accounts, they were thrown out of the tombs or killed outright by the very soldiers who were charged with protecting them. See Rabson, *Okinawa*.

95 Rancière, *Aisthesis*.

96 See the discussion in chapter 2 that argues that a soldier's sacrifice of their own life in combat is also their extension of an attack to its limit. This is not to suggest that it would be a mistake to also consider it suicide. However, I think that one should not ignore the determination and commitment toward an external objective that it entailed. See also Ohnuki-Tierney, *Kamikaze*, 1–25, 157–85.

97 Osborne, "Infinite Exchange."

98 Here I follow Hubert and Mauss: in an act of sacrifice, the sacrifier is one to whom the benefits of the sacrifice accrue. Hubert and Mauss, *Sacrifice*, 1–49.

99   Ohnuki-Tierney, *Kamikaze*, 112–14.

100   Smith, *At the Edge of Sight*, 212.

101   Nelson, *Dancing with the Dead*, 141–54.

102   Kumaki, "Suspending Nuclearity"; Morimoto, "Wild Boar Chase"; Nozawa, "Phatic Traces."

103   Weiss, *Real Pigs*, 196.

104   George Murasaki is the leader and keyboard player of the eponymous Okinawan band, Murasaki. Jon Lord is primarily known as the keyboardist of Deep Purple.

105   Usually short sleeved, *kariyushi* shirts are made with textiles and patterns coded as traditionally Ryūkyūan. Perhaps inspired by Hawaiian shirts, they are worn in a wide variety of social settings.

106   The place name Akebono-Cho derives from *akebono* (dawn or daybreak), despite its location on the west side of the island associated with picturesque sunsets.

107   Figal, "Life with Tetrapods"; Hiroya, *Naha No Kūkan Kōzō*.

108   Matsumura, "Isahama Women Farmers."

109   Inoue, *Okinawa and the US Military*.

110   Alam, "Diverging Spirituality."

111   However, the House of the Rising Sun also has a complex history apart from the occupation. Japanese rockers took inspiration from the versions of the song mentioned, but the folksong movement reached back to older versions by Woody Guthrie, Leadbelly, Joan Baez, and Bob Dylan. In 1969, Takada Wataru interpreted it in his familiar style, and other versions by Asakawa Maki and Chiaki Naomi were very popular.

112   Shirahase, *Shūkyō no Shakaikōken*, 157.

113   Japanese government studies suggest that there were between 136 and 102 unhoused people in Okinawa prefecture at this time, the majority in the Naha area. As Shirahase suggests, the number declined from a high of 200 in 2009 due to increased availability of public funds. However, both Yamauchi and Gibo have told me that this number significantly undercounts the actual total of unhoused people, and they have been working with Okinawa prefecture to conduct more accurate surveys. Regardless, Yamauchi's ministry extends to the disabled, the elderly, the precarious, and the bereft. Shirahase, *Shūkyō no Shakaikōken*, 153–56.

114   A group of interested prefectural and local representatives, led by Itokazu Keiko (Sangiin/House of Councilors), worked to overcome bureaucratic hurdles and create an actual working budget. Shirahase, *Shūkyō no Shakaikōken*, 158–61.

115   About $11 in 2009.

116   See Allison, *Precarious Japan*; Gill, *Men of Uncertainty*; Hammering, "Gambling"; Kim, "Necrosociality."

117   Bataille, *Accursed Share*.

118   For a vital introduction to this critical and expanding field, see Allison, *Precarious Japan*; Gill, *Men of Uncertainty*; Hammering, "Gambling"; Kim, "Necrosociality."

119   See Nelson, *Dancing with the Dead*.

120   Shirahase, *Shūkyō no Shakaikōken*, 167–80.

121   For a more detailed orientation to the history of the routinization and formalization of spiritual practices (including Shintō) in the modern era, see Figal, *Civilization and Monsters*; Hardacre, *Shintō and the State*; Harootunian, *Overcome by Modernity*.

122   Ross, *Communal Luxury*, 65.

Conclusion

1   Sneider, "Second World War."

2   Hammes, "America Is Well Within Range"; USMC, "Marine Corps Vision and Strategy 2025."

3   Lummis, "On a Firm Foundation."

4   "Senbotsusha Ikotsu no Sengoshi (56) 'Ikotsu wa Donna ni Chīsakute mo Ningen,'" *Mainichi Shimbun*, September 9, 2021.

5   Koishikawa, *Ikeiniei to Hitobashira no Minzokugaku*.

6   Manning, "Goblin Spiders," 263.

7   Hearn, *Glimpses of Unfamiliar Japan*.

8   Andrea De Antoni has found evocative intimations of *hitobashira* in accounts of hauntings by dead Korean laborers in urban Kyoto. See De Antoni, "Down in a Hole."

9   Nakamura, "Okinawa Tomigusukuson No Densetsu."

Abu El-Haj, Nadia. *The Genealogical Science: The Search for Jewish Origins and the Politics of Epistemology*. Chicago: University of Chicago Press, 2012.

Adaniya Seiji. "Moai o gyō to suru hitobito." *Aoi Umi* 11, no. 5 (1981): 9–49.

Adorno, Theodor W. "On the Fetish Character in Music and the Regression of Listening." In *The Culture Industry: Selected Essays on Mass Culture*, 29–60. New York: Routledge, 1981.

Adorno, Theodor W. "Theses Against Occultism." *Telos* 19 (1974): 7–12.

Agamben, Giorgio. *The Time That Remains: A Commentary on the Letter to the Romans*. Stanford, CA: Stanford University Press, 2005.

Aguni Kyōko. "Ifa Fuyū to Suekichi Bakumontō (Ankyō) no kōryū." *Urasoe Shiritsu Toshōkan Kiyō* 8 (1997): 76–78.

Akamatsu Yoshitsugu. "Shūdan jiketsu no shima: Tokashikijima no heishi to muramin: 'Watashitachi o shinjite hoshii.'" *Aoi Umi* 6 (1971): 12–14.

Akasaka Norio. *Okamoto Tarō no mita Nihon*. Tokyo: Iwanami Shoten, 2007.

Akasaka Norio. *Okamoto Tarō to iu shiso*. Tokyo: Kodansha, 2014.

Alam, Bachtiar. "Diverging Spirituality: Religious Processes in a Northern Okinawan Village." PhD diss., Harvard University, 1995.

Allen, Matthew. *Identity and Resistance in Okinawa*. Lanham, MD: Rowman and Littlefield, 2002.

Allison, Anne. *Being Dead Otherwise*. Durham, NC: Duke University Press, 2023.

Allison, Anne. *Precarious Japan*. Durham, NC: Duke University Press, 2013.

Ames, Christopher A. "Mired in History: Victimhood, Memory, and Ambivalence in Okinawa Prefecture, Japan." PhD diss., University of Michigan, 2007.

Amino Yoshihiko. *Zōho muen, kugai, raku: Nihon chūsei no jiyū to heiwa*. Tokyo: Heibonsha, 1996.

Angst, Linda. "Gendered Nationalism: The Himeyuri Story and Okinawan Identity in Postwar Japan." *Political and Legal Anthropology Review* 20, no. 1 (1997): 100–113.

Arai, Andrea. *The Strange Child: Education and the Psychology of Patriotism in Recessionary Japan*. Stanford, CA: Stanford University Press, 2016.

Arasaki Moriteru and Kawamitsu Shin'ichi, eds. *Okinawa: tennōsei e no gyakkō*. Tokyo: Shakai Hyōronsha, 1988.

Augé, Marc. *Oblivion*. Minneapolis: University of Minnesota Press, 2004.

Axell, Albert, and Kase Hideaki. *Kamikaze: Japan's Suicide Gods*. Harlow, UK: Longman, 2002

Bacigalupo, Ana Mariella. *Shamans of the Foye Tree: Gender, Power, and Healing Among Chilean Mapuche*. Austin: University of Texas Press, 2007.

Bacigalupo, Ana Mariella. *Thunder Shaman: Making History with Mapuche Spirits in Chile and Patagonia*. Austin: University of Texas Press, 2016.

Bakhtin, M. M. "Forms of Time and Chronotope in the Novel." In *The Dialogic Imagination: Four Essays*, 84–258. Austin: University of Texas Press, 1981.

Ball, Christopher, and Nicholas Harkness, eds. 2015. "Kinship Chronotopes." Special issue, *Anthropological Quarterly* 88, no. 2 (2015).

Baronian, Marie-Aude, and Mireille Rosello. "Jacques Rancière and Interdisciplinarity." Translated by Gregory Elliott. *Art and Research* 2, no. 1 (2008). https://pure.uva.nl/ws/files/4285124/63487_298522.pdf.

Bataille, Georges. *The Accursed Share: An Essay on General Economy*, 3 vols. New York: Zone Books, 1988–1993.

Bataille, Georges. *Guilty*. Albany: State University of New York Press, 2011.

Bataille, Georges. *Visions of Excess: Selected Writings 1927–1939*. Minneapolis: University of Minnesota Press, 1985.

Bataille, Georges, Roger Caillois, Pierre Klossowski, Michel Leiris, and André Masson. *The Sacred Conspiracy: The Internal Papers of the Secret Society of Acéphale and Lectures to the College of Sociology*. London: Atlas Press, 2017.

Benjamin, Walter. *The Arcades Project*. Cambridge, MA: Belknap Press of Harvard University Press, 2002.

Benjamin, Walter. *Charles Baudelaire: A Lyric Poet in the Era of High Capitalism*. London: Verso, 2023.

Benjamin, Walter. "On Some Motifs in Baudelaire," *Walter Benjamin: Selected Writings, 4: 1938–1940*. Cambridge, MA: Belknap Press of Harvard University Press, 2006.

Benjamin, Walter. "[Review of] Roger Caillois, 'L'Aridité,'" et al., *Zeitschrift für Sozialforschung* VII (1938): 463. Quoted in Weingrad, Michael, "The College of Sociology and the Institute of Social Research." *New German Critique* 84 (2001): 129–61.

Benjamin, Walter. "Theories of German Fascism: On the Collection of Essays War and Warrior, Edited by Ernst Jünger." *New German Critique* 17 (1979): 120–28.

Benjamin, Walter. "Theses on the Philosophy of History." In *Illuminations*, 253–64. New York: Schocken Books, 2007.

Benjamin, Walter. *The Work of Art in the Age of Its Technological Reproducibility, and Other Writings on Media*. Cambridge, MA: Belknap Press of Harvard University Press, 2008.

Blanchot, Maurice. *The Unavowable Community*. Barrytown, NY: Station Hill Press, 2006.

Blaxell, Vivian. "Preparing Okinawa for Reversion to Japan: The Okinawa International Ocean Exposition of 1975, the US Military and the Construction State—1975." *The Asia-Pacific Journal: Japan Focus* 8, no. 2 (2010): 3386. https://apjjf.org/vivian-blaxell/3386/article.

Bloch, Ernst. *Heritage of Our Times*. Berkeley: University of California Press, 1991.

Bogoras, Waldemar. *Chukchee Mythology*. London: Forgotten Books, 2007.

Boileau-Narcejac. *Sueurs froides (D'entre les mortes)*. Paris: Gallimard, 2020.

Bourdieu, Pierre. *The Logic of Practice*. Stanford, CA: Stanford University Press, 1990.

Bowen-Struyk, Heather, and Norma Field, eds. *For Dignity, Justice, and Revolution: An Anthology of Japanese Proletarian Literature*. Chicago: University of Chicago Press, 2016.

Bradley, Michael. "'Banzai!' The Compulsory Mass Suicide of Kerama Islanders in the Battle of Okinawa." *Asia-Pacific Journal: Japan Focus* 11, no. 3 (2014): 4125. https://apjjf.org/2014/11/22/michael-bradley/4125/article.

Breen, John, ed. *Yasukuni, the War Dead, and the Struggle for Japan's Past*. New York: Columbia University Press, 2008.

Cadava, Eduardo. *Words of Light: Theses on the Photography of History*. Princeton, NJ: Princeton University Press, 2018.

Caillois, Roger. *Man and the Sacred*. Champaign: University of Illinois Press, 2001.

Caillois, Roger, and Susan Lanser. "The Collège de Sociologie: Paradox of an Active Sociology." *SubStance* 4, nos. 11/12 (1975): 61–64.

Carneiro da Cunha, Manuela. "Points of View on the Amazon Forest: Shamanism and Translation." Robert Hertz Lecture, Association pour la Recherche en Anthropologie Sociale, Paris, July 9, 1997.

Carter, Caleb. "Power Spots and the Charged Landscape of Shinto." *Japanese Journal of Religious Studies* 45, no. 1 (2018): 145–73.

Casey, Edward S. *Remembering: A Phenomenological Study*, 2nd ed. Bloomington: Indiana University Press, 2009.

Chong, Doryun, Hayashi Michio, Yoshitake Mika, Miryam Sas, Mitsuda Yuri, and Nancy Lim. *Tokyo 1955–1970: A New Avant-garde*. New York: Museum of Modern Art, 2012.

Christy, Alan S. "A Fantasy of Ancient Japan: The Assimilation of Okinawa in Yanagita Kunio's Kainan Shoki." Select Papers of the East Asia Center: Productions of Culture in Japan, no. 10. Chicago: East Asia Center, University of Chicago, 1995.

Christy, Alan S. "The Making of Imperial Subjects in Okinawa." *Positions* 1, no. 3 (1993): 607–39.

Chu, Julie Y. *Cosmologies of Credit: Transnational Mobility and the Politics of Destination in China.* Durham, NC: Duke University Press, 2010.

Clastres, Pierre. *Chronicle of the Guayaki Indians.* New York: Zone Books, 1998.

Clastres, Pierre. *Society Against the State: Essays in Political Anthropology.* New York: Zone Books, 1987.

De Antoni, Andrea. "Down in a Hole: Dark Tourism, Haunted Places as Affective Meshworks, and the Obliteration of Korean Laborers in Contemporary Kyoto." *Japan Review* 33 (2019): 271–97.

De Certeau, Michel. "On the Oppositional Practices of Everyday Life." *Social Text* 3 (1980): 3–43.

Deleuze, Gilles. *Difference and Repetition.* New York: Columbia University Press, 1994.

Deleuze, Gilles. *Nietzsche and Philosophy.* London: Athlone Press, 1983.

Derrida, Jacques. *The Gift of Death.* Chicago: University of Chicago Press, 1996.

Edwards, James Rhys. "Between Two Worlds: A Social History of Okinawan Musical Drama." PhD diss., University of California, Los Angeles, 2014.

Eliade, Mircea. *Images and Symbols: Studies in Religious Symbolism.* London: Harvill Press, 1961.

Eliade, Mircea. *The Sacred and the Profane: The Nature of Religion.* New York: Harcourt, Brace, 1959.

Embree, John F. *Suye Mura, a Japanese Village.* Chicago: University of Chicago Press, 1939.

Euripides. *Euripides V: Bacchae, Iphigenia in Aulis, The Cyclops, Rhesus.* Chicago: University of Chicago Press, 2013.

Evens, T. M. S. *Anthropology as Ethics: Nondualism and the Conduct of Sacrifice.* New York: Berghahn Books, 2008.

Fehérváry, Krisztina. *Politics in Color and Concrete: Socialist Materialities and the Middle Class in Hungary.* Bloomington: Indiana University Press, 2013.

Felman, Shoshana, and Dori Laub. *Testimony: Crises of Witnessing in Literature, Psychoanalysis, and History.* New York: Routledge, 1992.

Field, Norma. *In the Realm of a Dying Emperor.* New York: Pantheon Books, 1991.

Figal, Gerald. *Beachheads: War, Peace, and Tourism in Postwar Okinawa.* Lanham, MD: Rowman and Littlefield, 2012.

Figal, Gerald. *Civilization and Monsters: Spirits of Modernity in Meiji Japan.* Durham, NC: Duke University Press, 1999.

Figal, Gerald. "Life with Tetrapods: The Nature of Concrete in Okinawa." *Cross-Currents: East Asian History and Culture Review* 30 (2019): 150–70.

Fink, Eugen, Ute Saine, and Thomas Saine. "The Oasis of Happiness: Toward an Ontology of Play." *Yale French Studies* 41 (1968): 19–30.

Finkelstein, Maura. *The Archive of Loss: Lively Ruination in Mill Land Mumbai.* Durham, NC: Duke University Press, 2019.

Fisher, Mark. *Ghosts of My Life: Writings on Depression, Hauntology and Lost Futures*. Winchester, UK: Zero Books, 2014.

Fisher, Mark. *The Weird and the Eerie*. London: Repeater, 2017.

Fournier, Marcel. *Marcel Mauss: A Biography*. Princeton, NJ: Princeton University Press, 2015.

Garon, Sheldon. "Luxury Is the Enemy: Mobilizing Savings and Popularizing Thrift in Wartime Japan." *Journal of Japanese Studies* 26, no. 1 (2000): 41–78.

Gell, Alfred. *Art and Agency: An Anthropological Theory*. Oxford: Clarendon Press, 1998.

Gerow, Aaron. "From the National Gaze to Multiple Gazes: Representations of Okinawa in Recent Japanese Cinema." In *Islands of Discontent: Okinawan Responses to Japanese and American Power*, edited by Laura Hein and Mark Selden, 273–307. Lanham, MD: Rowman and Littlefield, 2003.

Gill, Tom. *Men of Uncertainty: The Social Organization of Day Laborers in Contemporary Japan*. Albany: State University of New York Press, 2001.

Gillan, Matt. *Songs from the Edge of Japan: Music-Making in Yaeyama and Okinawa*. Burlington, VT: Ashgate, 2012.

Ginzburg, Carlo. *Clues, Myths, and the Historical Method*. Baltimore: Johns Hopkins University Press, 1989.

Goldfarb, Kathryn E. "'Coming to Look Alike': Materializing Affinity in Japanese Foster and Adoptive Care." *Social Analysis* 60, no. 2 (2016): 47–64.

Gordillo, Gastón. *Rubble: The Afterlife of Destruction*. Durham, NC: Duke University Press, 2014.

Govindrajan, Radhika. *Animal Intimacies: Interspecies Relatedness in India's Central Himalayas*. Chicago: University of Chicago Press, 2018.

Graeber, David. "It Is Value That Brings Universes into Being." *HAU: Journal of Ethnographic Theory* 3, no. 2 (2013): 219–43.

Gushiken Takamatsu. *Boku ga ikotsu o horu hito 'Gamafuyā' ni natta wake*. Tokyo: Gōdō Shuppan, 2012.

Habu, Junko. *Ancient Jomon of Japan*. Cambridge: Cambridge University Press, 2004.

Hägglund, Martin. *Radical Atheism: Derrida and the Time of Life*. Stanford, CA: Stanford University Press, 2008.

Halbwachs, Maurice. *The Collective Memory*. New York: Harper and Row, 1980.

Halbwachs, Maurice. *On Collective Memory*. Chicago: University of Chicago Press, 1992.

Hammering, Klaus K. Y. "Gambling, Dignity, and the Narcotic of Time in Tokyo's Day-Laborer District, San'ya." *Cultural Anthropology* 37, no. 1 (2022): 150–75.

Hammes, Thomas X. "America Is Well Within Range of a Big Surprise, So Why Can't It See?" *War on the Rocks*, March 12, 2018. https://warontherocks.com /2018/03/america-is-well-within-range-of-a-big-surprise-so-why-cant-it-see/.

Hansen, Arve, and Kenneth Nielsen, eds. *Cars, Automobility and Development in Asia: Wheels of Change*. London: Routledge, 2019.

Hansen, Miriam. "Benjamin's Aura." *Critical Inquiry* 34, no. 2 (2008): 336–75.

Harada Nobuo, Maeshiro Naoko, Miyahira Moriaki. *Sasagerareru Seimei: Okinawa no dōbutsu kugi.* Tokyo: Ochanomizu Shobō, 2012.

Hardacre, Helen. *Shintô and the State.* Princeton, NJ: Princeton University Press, 1989.

Harootunian, Harry. *Archaism and Actuality: Japan and the Global Fascist Imaginary.* Durham, NC: Duke University Press, 2023.

Harootunian, Harry D. *Marx After Marx: History and Time in the Expansion of Capitalism.* New York: Columbia University Press, 2015.

Harootunian, Harry D. *Overcome by Modernity: History, Culture, and Community in Interwar Japan.* Princeton, NJ: Princeton University Press, 2000.

Harootunian, Harry D. *Things Seen and Unseen: Discourse and Ideology in Tokugawa Nativism.* Chicago: University of Chicago Press, 1988.

Harootunian, Harry D. *Uneven Moments: Reflections on Japan's Modern History.* New York: Columbia University Press, 2019.

Hart, Keith. "Heads or Tails? Two Sides of the Coin." *Man* 21, no. 4 (1986): 637–56.

Hayashi Hirofumi. *Okinawa-sen: Kyōseisareta "shūdan jiketsu."* Tokyo: Yoshikawa Kōbunkan, 2009.

Hayashi Hirofumi. *Okinawa-sen to minshū.* Tokyo: Ōtsuki Shoten, 2001.

Hearn, Lafcadio. *Glimpses of Unfamiliar Japan.* Rutland, VT: Tuttle Publishing, 2016.

Heidegger, Martin. *Being and Time.* London: SCM Press, 1962.

Hein, Laura Elizabeth, and Mark Selden. *Islands of Discontent: Okinawan Responses to Japanese and American Power.* Lanham, MD: Rowman and Littlefield, 2003.

Higashi Mineo. "Child of Okinawa." In *Okinawa: Two Postwar Novellas.* Translated and edited by Stephen Rabson, 79–118. Berkeley, CA: Center for Japanese Studies, 1989.

Higa Toyomitsu. *Hone no ikusayu: Foto-dokyumento: 65-nenme no Okinawasen.* Tokyo: Iwanami Shoten, 2010.

Hiroya Yoshikawa. *Naha no kūkan kōzō.* Naha: Okinawa Taimususha, 1989.

Hirsch, Marianne. *Family Frames: Photography, Narrative, and Postmemory.* Cambridge, MA: Harvard University Press, 1997.

Hirsch, Marianne. *The Generation of Postmemory: Writing and Visual Culture After the Holocaust.* New York: Columbia University Press, 2012.

Hollier, Denis, ed. 1988. *The College of Sociology (1937–39).* Minneapolis: University of Minnesota Press, 1987.

Horkheimer, Max, and Theodor W. Adorno. *Dialectic of Enlightenment.* New York: Herder and Herder, 1972.

Hoshi Masahiko. "Tokushū shūdan jiketsu: Shūdan jiketsu no hassō." *Urasoe Bungei* 14 (2009): 237–42.

Hubert, Henri, and Marcel Mauss. *Sacrifice: Its Nature and Function.* Chicago: University of Chicago Press, 1981.

Ifa Fuyū. "Introduction." Shimabukuro Gen'ichirō, ed. *Okinawaken Kunigamigunshi.* 6. Naha: Okinawaken Kunigamigun Kyōiku Bukai, 1919.

Ifa Fuyū. "Yuta no rekishiteki kenkyū." In *Ifa Fuyū Zenshyū, Vol. 9*, 342–66. Tokyo: Heibonsha, 1974.

Igarashi, Yoshikuni. *Homecomings: The Belated Return of Japan's Lost Soldiers*. New York: Columbia University Press, 2016.

Iizawa Kōtarō. "Introduction." In *Okamoto Tarō no Tōhoku*, 2–5. Tokyo: Mainichi Shinbunsha, 2002.

Ikeda, Kyle. *Okinawan War Memory: Transgenerational Trauma and the War Fiction of Medoruma Shun*. New York: Routledge, 2014.

Ingold, Tim. "Back to the Future with the Theory of Affordances." *HAU: Journal of Ethnographic Theory* 8, nos. 1/2 (2018): 27–38.

Inoue, Masamichi S. *Okinawa and the US Military: Identity Making in the Age of Globalization*. New York: Columbia University Press, 2007.

Ishida, Hiroshi, and David H. Slater. *Social Class in Contemporary Japan: Structures, Sorting and Strategies*. London: Routledge, 2009.

Ishihara Masaie and Aragaki Naoko, eds. *Sengo Koza ni okeru minshū seikatsu to ongaku bunka: Isihara Zemināru*. Ginowan: Yōjusha, 1994.

Ivy, Marilyn. *Discourses of the Vanishing: Modernity, Phantasm, Japan*. Chicago: University of Chicago Press, 1995.

Izzo, Justin. *Experiments with Empire: Anthropology and Fiction in the French Atlantic*. Durham, NC: Duke University Press, 2019.

Jahana Naomi. *Shōgen okinawa "shūdan jiketsu": Kerama Shotō de nani ga okita ka*. Tokyo: Iwanami Shoten, 2008.

Jefferson, Andrew, Simon Turner, and Steffen Jensen. "Introduction: On Stuckness and Sites of Confinement." *Ethnos* 84, no. 1 (2019): 1–13.

Jensen, Casper Bruun, Miho Ishii, and Philip Swift. "Attuning to the Webs of *En*: Ontography, Japanese Spirit Worlds, and the 'Tact' of Minakata Kumagusu." *HAU: Journal of Ethnographic Theory* 6, no. 2 (2016): 149–72.

Kano Masanao. *Okinawa no fuchi: Iha Fuyū to sono jidai*. Tokyo: Iwanami Shoten, 1993.

Kapur, Nick. *Japan at the Crossroads: Conflict and Compromise After Anpo*. Cambridge, MA: Harvard University Press, 2018.

Kase Hideaki. *The Greater East Asian War: How Japan Changed the World*. Tokyo: Society for the Dissemination of Historical Fact, 2017. Kindle.

Kase Hideaki. "The Greater East Asian War: How Japan Changed the World, Chapter 6—The Japanese Army's 'Spirit-First Policy.'" https://www.sdh-fact .com/book-article/661/.

Kase Hideaki. "Response to the Updated Version of the Open Letter in Support of Historians of Japan." Society for the Dissemination of Historical Fact, October 1, 2015. https://www.sdh-fact.com/essay-article/584/.

Kase Hideaki. "To the 187 Scholars and Their Followers Who Publicized Their Open Letter about the Comfort Women." Society for the Dissemination of Historical Fact, November 30, 2015. https://www.sdh-fact.com/essay-article /612/.

Keane, Webb. "Killing Animals: On the Violence of Sacrifice, the Hunt and the Butcher." *Anthropology of This Century* 22 (2018). http://aotcpress.com/articles/killing-animals-violence-sacrifice-hunt-butcher/.

Keane, Webb. "Perspectives on Affordances, or the Anthropologically Real." *HAU: Journal of Ethnographic Theory* 8, nos. 1/2 (2018): 27–38.

Kennai chūshō kigyō no moai jittai chōsa. Naha: Okinawaken sangyo shinko kosha chūshō kigyō jōhō senta, 1993.

Kim, Eleana J. *Making Peace with Nature: Ecological Encounters Along the Korean DMZ.* Durham, NC: Duke University Press, 2022.

Kim, Jieun. "Necrosociality: Isolated death and unclaimed cremains in Japan." *Journal of the Royal Anthropological Institute* 22, no. 4 (2016): 843–63.

Kinjō Nobuyoshi. *Okinawa genkūkan to no taiwa.* Naha: Jō Sekkei Kenkyūjo, 1983.

Kinmonth, Earl H. *The Self-Made Man in Meiji Japanese Thought: From Samurai to Salary Man.* Berkeley: University of California Press, 1981.

Kitamura Tsuyoshi. *Shishatachi no sengoshi: Okinawa senseki o meguru hitobito no kioku.* Tokyo: Ochanomizu Shobō, 2009.

Klima, Alan. *The Funeral Casino: Meditation, Massacre, and Exchange with the Dead in Thailand.* Princeton, NJ: Princeton University Press, 2002.

Ko, Mika. *Japanese Cinema and Otherness: Nationalism, Multiculturalism and the Problem of Japaneseness.* London: Taylor and Francis, 2013.

Kockelman, Paul. *The Chicken and the Quetzal: Incommensurate Ontologies and Portable Values in Guatemala's Cloud Forest.* Durham, NC: Duke University Press, 2016.

Koga, Yukiko. *Inheritance of Loss: China, Japan, and the Political Economy of Redemption After Empire.* Chicago: University of Chicago Press, 2016.

Koikari, Mire. *Pedagogy of Democracy: Feminism and the Cold War in the US Occupation of Japan.* Philadelphia, PA: Temple University Press, 2008.

Koishikawa Zenji. *Ikeniei to Hitobashira no Minzokugaku.* Tokyo: Hihyōsha, 1998.

Kojève, Alexandre. "The Idea of Death in the Philosophy of Hegel." *Interpretation: A Journal of Political Philosophy* 3, nos. 2/3 (1973): 114–56.

Kumaki, Hiroko. "Suspending Nuclearity: Ecologics of Planting Seeds after the Nuclear Fallout in Fukushima, Japan." *Cultural Anthropology* 37, no. 4 (2022): 707–37.

Kwon, Heonik. *Ghosts of War in Vietnam.* Cambridge: Cambridge University Press, 2008.

LaCapra, Dominick. "Trauma, Absence, Loss." *Critical Inquiry* 25, no. 4 (1999): 696–727.

Lambek, Michael. "Sacrifice and the Problem of Beginning: Meditations from Sakalava Mythopraxis." *Journal of the Royal Anthropological Institute* 13, no. 1 (2007): 19–38.

Lazzarato, Maurizio. *The Making of the Indebted Man: An Essay on the Neoliberal Condition.* Translated by Joshua David Jordan. Los Angeles: Semiotexte, 2012.

Lebra, William P. *Okinawan Religion: Belief, Ritual, and Social Structure*. Honolulu: University of Hawai'i Press, 2021.

Lefebvre, Henri. *Critique of Everyday Life*, vol 1. London: Verso, 2008.

Lefebvre, Henri. *Rhythmanalysis: Space, Time, and Everyday Life*. London: Continuum, 2004.

Leiris, Michel. *Phantom Africa*. Kolkata: Seagull Books, 2017.

Lemon, Alaina. "'Your Eyes Are Green Like Dollars': Counterfeit Cash, National Substance, and Currency Apartheid in 1990s Russia." *Cultural Anthropology* 13, no. 1 (1998): 22–55.

Lévinas, Emmanuel. *Totality and Infinity: An Essay on Exteriority*. Pittsburgh, PA: Duquesne University Press, 1969.

Lévi-Strauss, Claude. *The Other Face of the Moon*. Cambridge, MA: Belknap Press of Harvard University Press, 2013.

Lock, Margaret M. *Twice Dead: Organ Transplants and the Reinvention of Death*. Berkeley: University of California Press, 2002.

Loo, Tze May. *Heritage Politics: Shuri Castle and Okinawa's Incorporation into Modern Japan, 1879–2000*. Lanham, MD: Lexington Books, 2014.

Loo, Tze May. "Paradise in a War Zone: The US Military and Tourism in Okinawa, 1945–1972." *Japan Review* 33 (2019): 173–93.

Lummis, Douglas. "On a Firm Foundation of Mayonnaise: Human and Natural Threats to the Construction of a New US Base at Henoko, Okinawa." *Asia-Pacific Journal: Japan Focus* 16, no. 4 (2018): 5146. https://apjjf.org/2018/10/lummis.

Lutz, Catherine, and Anne Lutz Fernandez. *Carjacked: The Culture of the Automobile and Its Effect on Our Lives*. New York: Palgrave Macmillan, 2010.

Maetakenishi Kazuma. "Kichi: dōbutsu kugi: Shakai undō." *Ryūkyū bunkaken to wa nani ka [Bessetsu 6: Kan]* (June 3, 2003): 212–17.

Manning, Paul. "Goblin Spiders, Ghosts of Flowers and Butterfly Fantasies: Lafcadio Hearn's Transnational, Transmedia and Trans-Species Aesthetics of the Weird." *Japan Forum* 32, no. 2 (2020): 259–83.

Manning, Paul. "No Ruins. No Ghosts." *Preternature: Critical and Historical Studies on the Preternatural* 6, no. 1 (2017): 63–92.

Marotti, William A. *Money, Trains, and Guillotines: Art and Revolution in 1960s Japan*. Durham, NC: Duke University Press, 2013.

Matsuda, Hiroko, and Pedro Iacobelli, eds. *Rethinking Postwar Okinawa: Beyond American Occupation*. Lanham, MD: Lexington Books, 2017.

Matsumura, Wendy. "The Expansion of the Japanese Empire and the Rise of the Global Agrarian Question After the First World War." In *Cataclysm 1914: The First World War and the Making of Modern World Politics*, edited by Alexander Anievas, 144–73. Leiden: Brill, 2015.

Matsumura, Wendy. "Isahama Women Farmers Against Enclosure: A Rejection of the Property Relation in US-Occupied Okinawa." *Positions* 28, no. 3 (2020): 547–74.

Matsumura, Wendy. *The Limits of Okinawa: Japanese Capitalism, Living Labor, and Theorizations of Community*. Durham, NC: Duke University Press, 2015.

Matsumura, Wendy. "Okinawa: The Cold War Creation of a Model Jungle." *Funambulist* 9 (2017). https://thefunambulist.net/magazine/09-islands/okinawa-cold-war-creation-model-jungle-by-wendy-matsumura.

Matsumura, Wendy. *Waiting for the Cool Moon: Anti-Imperialist Struggles in the Heart of Japan's Empire*. Durham, NC: Duke University Press, 2024.

Mauss, Marcel. *The Gift*, expanded ed. Translated by Jane I. Guyer. Chicago: HAU Books, 2016.

McCormack, Gavan, and Satoko Oka Norimatsu. *Resistant Islands: Okinawa Confronts Japan and the United States*. Lanham, MD: Rowman and Littlefield, 2012.

McLean, Stuart, and Anand Pandian, eds. *Crumpled Paper Boat: Experiments in Ethnographic Writing*. Durham, NC: Duke University Press, 2017.

Medoruma Shun. "Mabuigumi." *Manoa* 23, no. 1 (2011): 112–34.

Medoruma Shun. *Okinawa sengo zero-nen*. Tokyo: Nihon hōsō shuppan kyōkai, 2005.

Medoruma Shun. "Stories from the Streets of Koza." *Words Without Borders*, July 1, 2012. https://wordswithoutborders.org/read/article/2012-07/july-2012-stories-from-the-streets-of-koza-shun-medoruma-sam-malissa/.

Middleton, Townsend. "Becoming-After: The Lives and Politics of Quinine's Remains." *Cultural Anthropology* 36, no. 2 (2021): 282–311.

Mitchell, Jon. *Poisoning the Pacific: The US Military's Secret Dumping of Plutonium, Chemical Weapons, and Agent Orange*. Lanham, MD: Rowman and Littlefield, 2020.

Miyahira Moriaki. *Ryūkyū shotō no dōbutsu girei*. Tokyo: Bensei shuppan, 2019.

Miyamoto Tsuneichi et al., eds. *Nihon zankoku mongatari*. Tokyo: Heibonsha, 1960.

Molasky, Michael S. *The American Occupation of Japan and Okinawa: Literature and Memory*. New York: Routledge, 1999.

Morando, Camille. "Le mythe à l'épreuve chez Taro Okamoto, peintre à la société secrète Acéphale et au Collège de sociologie (1936–1940)." In *Art et mythe*, edited by Fabrice Flahutez and Thierry Dufrêne, 59–71. Nanterre: Presses Universitaires de Paris Nanterre, 2011.

Morimoto, Ryo. "A Wild Boar Chase: Ecology of Harm and Half-Life Politics in Coastal Fukushima." *Cultural Anthropology* 37, no. 1 (2022): 69–98.

Mori Yoshio. *Okinawa sengo minshūshi: Gama kara Henoko made*. Tokyo: Iwanami Shoten, 2016.

Mori Yoshio, Toriyama Atsushi, and Kokuba Kōtarō. *"Shimagurumi tōsō" wa dō junbisareta ka: Okinawa ga mezasu "amayū" e no michi*. Tokyo: Fuji Shuppan, 2013.

Munn, Nancy D. "The 'Becoming-Past' of Places: Spacetime and Memory in Nineteenth-Century, Pre-Civil War New York." *HAU: Journal of Ethnographic Theory* 3, no. 2 (2013): 359–80.

Munn, Nancy D. "The Cultural Anthropology of Time: A Critical Essay." *Annual Review of Anthropology* 21 (1992): 93–123.

Munn, Nancy D. "Excluded Spaces: The Figure in the Australian Aboriginal Landscape." *Critical Inquiry* 22, no. 3 (1996): 446–65.

Munn, Nancy D. *The Fame of Gawa: A Symbolic Study of Value Transformation in a Massim (Papua New Guinea) Society.* Cambridge: Cambridge University Press, 1986.

Munroe, Alexandra. *Japanese Art After 1945: Scream Against the Sky.* New York: Harry N. Abrams, 1994.

Najita, Tetsuo. *Ordinary Economies in Japan: A Historical Perspective, 1750–1950.* Berkeley: University of California Press, 2009.

Nakajima, Michi. "Shinto Deities That Crossed the Sea: Japan's 'Overseas Shrines,' 1868 to 1945." *Japanese Journal of Religious Studies* 37, no. 1 (2010): 21–46.

Nakamura Fumi. "Okinawa Tomigusukuson no densetsu 'Madanbashi no hitobashira.'" *Otaru Shōka Daigaku Jinbun Kenkyū* 97 (1999): 298(1)–274(25).

Nakasone, Ronald Y., ed. *Okinawan Diaspora.* Honolulu: University of Hawai'i Press, 2002.

Nakazato Isao. "Documentarists of Japan #20: Takamine Go." Yamagata International Documentary Film Festival. Accessed January 24, 2024. https://www.yidff.jp/docbox/22/box22-1-1-e.html.

Nakazato Isao. *Fotoneshia: Me no kaikisen—Okinawa.* Tokyo: Miraisha, 2009.

Nakazato Isao. "Hanmo suru guntō." In *Okinawa, Imēji no ejji,* 213–31. Tokyo: Miraisha, 2007.

Nakazato Isao. "Komamushitachi no hanran." In *Okinawa, Imēji no ejji,* 239–58. Tokyo: Miraisha, 2007.

Nancy, Jean-Luc. *The Inoperative Community.* Minneapolis: University of Minnesota Press, 1991.

Nash, Douglas E., Sr. *Battle of Okinawa: III MEF Staff Ride Battle Book.* Quantico, VA: History Division, US Marine Corps, 2015.

Navaro-Yashin, Yael. *The Make-Believe Space: Affective Geography in a Postwar Polity.* Durham, NC: Duke University Press, 2012.

Nelson, Christopher T. "Against the Flow of Time: The Politics of Repetition in Postwar Japan." *Journal of Popular Music Studies* 27, no. 4 (2015): 424–36.

Nelson, Christopher T. *Dancing with the Dead: Memory, Performance, and Everyday Life in Postwar Okinawa.* Durham, NC: Duke University Press, 2008.

Nelson, Christopher T. "The Moai: Capitalism, Culture and Okinawan Rotating Credit Associations." *Journal of Pacific Asia* 7, no. 1 (2001): 15–26.

Nelson, Christopher T. "No Better Friend, No Worse Enemy." In *Anthropology and Global Counterinsurgency,* edited by John D. Kelly, Beatrice Jauregui, Sean T. Mitchell, and Jeremy Walton, 343–54. Chicago: University of Chicago Press, 2010.

Nelson, Christopher T. "Occupation Without End: Opposition to the US Military in Okinawa." *South Atlantic Quarterly* 111, no. 4 (2012): 827–38.

Nietzsche, Friedrich Wilhelm. *The Gay Science; with a Prelude in Rhymes and an Appendix of Songs*. New York: Vintage Books, 1974.

Nietzsche, Friedrich Wilhelm. *On the Genealogy of Morals*. New York: Vintage Books, 1989.

Nietzsche, Friedrich Wilhelm. *Unfashionable Observations*. Translated by Richard T. Gray. Stanford, CA: Stanford University Press, 1995.

Nora, Pierre. "Between Memory and History: Les Lieux de Mémoire." *Representations* 26 (1989): 7–24.

Nora, Pierre, and Lawrence D. Kritzman, eds. *Realms of Memory: The Construction of the French Past*, vol. 2: *Traditions*. New York: Columbia University Press, 1997.

Nozawa, Shunsuke. "Phatic Traces: Sociality in Contemporary Japan." *Anthropological Quarterly* 88, no. 2 (2015): 373–400.

Ōe Kenzaburō. "Misreading, Espionage and 'Beautiful Martyrdom': On Hearing the Okinawa 'Mass Suicides' Suit Court Verdict. UPDATE." *Asia-Pacific Journal: Japan Focus* 6, no. 10 (2008): 2915. https://apjjf.org/oe-kenzaburo/2915/article.

Ogura Nobuo. "Gaijin jūtaku no kensetu to sono naiyō." *Sengo Okinawa to Amerika: Ibunka Sesshoku No 50-Nen*. Naha: Okinawa Taimususha, 1995.

OHBK (Okinawakenritsu Hakubutsukan Bijutsukan Kikakuten). *Seitan 100nen Kinenten: Okamoto Tarō to Okinawa: Koko ga sekai no chūshin da*. Naha: Okinawa Bunka no Mori, 2011.

Ohnuki-Tierney, Emiko. *Kamikaze, Cherry Blossoms, and Nationalisms: The Militarization of Aesthetics in Japanese History*. Chicago: University of Chicago Press, 2002.

Ohnuki-Tierney, Emiko. *Kamikaze Diaries: Reflections of Japanese Student Soldiers*. Chicago: University of Chicago Press, 2006.

Oiji Akira. "Moai no rireki-Gendai Okinawa shakai ni okeru Uchinānchu no jinsei to moai no kinō ha'aku no kokoromi." *Kokuritsu Rekishi Minzoku Hakubutsukan Kenkyū Hōkoku* 91 (2001): 745–61.

Okamoto Tarō, "Ancient Blood, Contemporary Blood." *Review of Japanese Culture and Society* 23 (2011): 102–12.

Okamoto Tarō. "Bataiyu to no deai." In *Tarō Tanjō: Okamoto Tarō no uchū, vol. 2*, 264–69. Tokyo: Chikuma Gakugei Bunko, 2011.

Okamoto Tarō. "Kamigami no shima: Kudaka." *Shūkan Asahi*, January 20, 1961.

Okamoto Tarō. *Nihon no Dentō*. Tokyo: Kobunsha, 2010.

Okamoto Tarō. *Okamoto Tarō no Okinawa*. Tokyo: Shogakkan, 2016.

Okamoto Tarō. *Okinawa Bunkaron: Wasurerareta Nihon*. Tokyo: Chūkōbunko, 1996.

Okamoto Tarō. "Waga Tomo Joruju Bataiyu." In *Jujutsu Tanjō*, 200–204. Tokyo: Misuzu Shōbō, 2010.

Okamoto Tarō. *Wasurerareta Nihon: Okinawa Bunkaron*. Tokyo: Chūō Kōronsha, 1961.

Okamoto Toshiko. "Introduction." In *Shinpi*, 3–9. Tokyo: Nigensha, 2004.

Okinawashi Jieigyōsha. "Beihei no joshi Chūgakusei bōkō jiken megutte Koza bōdōji ni nite kita." *Jinmin no Hoshi* 5256 (2008). Accessed April 14, 2014. http://ww5.tiki.ne.jp/~peoplehs/data/5256-12.html.

Okinawa Taimusushakan. *Tetsu no bōfū: Okinawa senki*. Naha: Okinawa Taimu-susha, 1950.

Onaga, Lisa, and Harry Yi-Jui Wu. "Articulating Genba: Particularities of Expo-sure and Its Study in Asia." *Positions* 26, no. 2 (2018): 197–212.

Onga Takashi. "Okinawaken Ni Okeru Chīkishi Henshū Jigyō to 'Hisutorīto.'" *Dōjidaishi Kenkyū* 2 (2009): 65–76.

Onishi, Norimitsu. "Okinawans Protest Japan's Plan to Revise Bitter Chapter of World War II." *New York Times*, October 7, 2007.

Orikuchi Shinobu. *Ryūkyū no Shūkyō*. Tokyo: Aozora Bunko, 1923.

Osborne, Peter. "Infinite Exchange: The Social Ontology of the Photographic Image." *Philosophy of Photography* 1, no. 1 (2010): 59–68.

Ōshiro Tatsuhiro. "Tennyō no Yūrei." *Arashi* 8 (2006): 80–106.

Otto, Rudolph. *The Idea of the Holy*. Oxford: Oxford University Press, 1958.

Ōya Sōichi. "Shin Nihon Onna Keizu." *Fujin Kōron* (June 1959): 278–85.

Perry, Samuel. *Recasting Red Culture in Proletarian Japan: Childhood, Korea, and the Historical Avant-Garde*. Honolulu: University of Hawai'i Press, 2014.

Prost, Antoine. "Monuments to the Dead." In *Realms of Memory: The Construction of the French Past, Vol. 2—Traditions*, edited by Pierre Nora and Lawrence D. Kritzman, 307–32. New York: Columbia University Press, 1997.

Rabson, Steve. *Okinawa: Two Postwar Novellas*. Berkeley, CA: Center for Japanese Studies, 1989.

Rabson, Steve. *The Okinawan Diaspora in Japan: Crossing the Borders Within*. Honolulu: University of Hawai'i Press, 2012.

Rabson, Steve. "The Politics of Trauma: Compulsory Suicides During the Battle of Okinawa and Postwar Retrospectives." *Intersections: Gender and Sexuality in Asia and the Pacific* 24 (2010). http://intersections.anu.edu.au/issue24/rabson.htm#n23.

Rancière, Jacques. "The Aesthetic Dimension: Aesthetics, Politics, Knowledge." *Critical Inquiry* 36, no. 1 (2009): 1–19.

Rancière, Jacques. *Aisthesis: Scenes from the Aesthetic Regime of Art*. London: Verso, 2019.

Rancière, Jacques. *Film Fables*. Translated by Emiliano Battista. Oxford: Berg Publishers, 2006.

Rancière, Jacques. *The Future of the Image*. Translated by Gregory Elliott. London: Verso, 2019.

Rancière, Jacques. "Notes on the Photographic Image." *Radical Philosophy* 156 (2009): 8–15.

Rancière, Jacques. *The Philosopher and His Poor*. Durham, NC: Duke University Press, 2004.

Rancière, Jacques. *Proletarian Nights: The Workers' Dream in Nineteenth-Century France*. London: Verso, 2012.

Rancière, Jacques. *Short Voyages to the Land of the People*. Stanford, CA: Stanford University Press, 2003.

Renshaw, Layla. *Exhuming Loss: Memory, Materiality and Mass Graves of the Spanish Civil War*. Walnut Creek, CA: Left Coast Press, 2011.

Reynolds, Jonathan M. *Allegories of Time and Space: Japanese Identity in Photography and Architecture*. Honolulu: University of Hawai'i Press, 2015.

Ricœur, Paul. *Memory, History, Forgetting*. Chicago: University of Chicago Press, 2006.

Ricœur, Paul. *Time and Narrative*, vol. 1. Chicago: University of Chicago Press, 1984.

Roberson, James E. "'Doin' Our Thing': Identity and Colonial Modernity in Okinawan Rock Music." *Popular Music and Society* 34, no. 5 (2011): 593–620.

Robertson, Jennifer. *Native and Newcomer: Making and Remaking a Japanese City*. Berkeley: University of California Press, 1991.

Ross, Kristin. *Communal Luxury: The Political Imaginary of the Paris Commune*. London: Verso, 2015.

Rots, Aike P. "'This Is Not a Powerspot': Heritage Tourism, Sacred Space, and Conflicts of Authority at Sēfa Utaki." *Asian Ethnology* 78, no. 1 (2019): 155–80.

Rots, Aike P., and Mark Teeuwen, eds. *Sacred Heritage in Japan*. New York: Routledge, 2020.

Rubin, Jonah S. "Exhuming Dead Persons: Forensic Science and the Making of Post-Fascist Publics in Spain." *Cultural Anthropology* 35, no. 3 (2020): 345–73.

Runia, Eelco. *Moved by the Past: Discontinuity and Historical Mutation*. New York: Columbia University Press, 2014.

Sadruddin, Aalyia Feroz Ali. "Death in an Ordinary Time: Reflections from Rwanda." *Medical Anthropology Quarterly* 36, no. 2 (2022): 198–216.

Sahlins, Marshall. *Culture and Practical Reason*. Chicago: University of Chicago Press, 1976.

Sakurai Tokutaro. *Kōshūdan seiritsu katei no kenkyū*. Tokyo: Yoshikawa Kōbunkan, 1962.

Sand, Jordan. "Open Letter in Support of Historians in Japan." H-Net, May 15, 2015. https://networks.h-net.org/open-letter-support-historians-japan-japanese-language-version-0/.

Sand, Jordan. "A Year of Memory Politics in East Asia: Looking Back on the 'Open Letter in Support of Historians in Japan.'" *Asia-Pacific Journal: Japan Focus* 14, no. 9 (2016): 4886. https://apjjf.org/2016/09/sand.

Sasaki Hidenori. "Okamoto Tarō ni okeru Mirucha Eriāde no Eikyō." *Bigaku* 62, no. 2 (2011): 85–96.

Sato, Hiroaki. "Gyokusai or 'Shattering Like a Jewel': Reflection on the Pacific War." *Asia-Pacific Journal: Japan Focus* 6, no. 2 (2008): 2662. https://apjjf.org/hiroaki-sato/2662/article.

Satomura Minoru. "Okinawa 'moai' monogatari: Moai no oitachi." *Aoi Umi* 11, no. 5 (1981): 16–23.

Shimabuku, Annmaria M. *Alegal: Biopolitics and the Unintelligibility of Okinawan Life*. New York: Fordham University Press, 2018.

Shima Tsuyoshi. "Bones." In *Southern Exposure: Modern Japanese Literature from Okinawa*, edited by Michael Molasky and Steve Rabson, 156–71. Honolulu: University of Hawai'i Press, 2000.

Shirahase Tatsuya. *Shūkyō no shakaikōken o toinaosu*. Tokyo: Nakanishia Shuppan, 2015.

Singh, Bhrigupati, and Naisargi Dave. "On the Killing and Killability of Animals: Nonmoral Thoughts for the Anthropology of Ethics." *Comparative Studies of South Asia, Africa and the Middle East* 35, no. 2 (2015): 232–45.

Slater, David H. "3.11 Politics in Disaster Japan: Fear and Anger, Possibility and Hope." Society for Cultural Anthropology, July 26, 2011. https://culanth.org/fieldsights/series/3-11-politics-in-disaster-japan-fear-and-anger-possibility-and-hope.

Sledge, E. B. *With the Old Breed: At Peleliu and Okinawa*. New York: Presidio Press, 2007.

Smith, Robert J. *Ancestor Worship in Contemporary Japan*. Stanford, CA: Stanford University Press, 1974.

Smith, Shawn Michelle. *At the Edge of Sight: Photography and the Unseen*. Durham, NC: Duke University Press, 2013.

Smits, Gregory. *Maritime Ryukyu, 1050–1650*. Honolulu: University of Hawai'i Press, 2019.

Smits, Gregory. *Visions of Ryukyu: Identity and Ideology in Early-Modern Thought and Politics*. Honolulu: University of Hawai'i Press, 1999.

Sneider, Noah. "The Second World War Turned Okinawa into a Graveyard—Now It's in China's Sights." *1843 Magazine*, May 30, 2023. https://www.economist.com/1843/2023/05/30/the-second-world-war-turned-okinawa-into-a-graveyard-now-its-in-chinas-sights.

Sono, Ayako. *Aru shinwa no haikei: Okinawa-Keramato no shūdan jiketsu*. Tokyo: PHP Bunko, 1992.

Stuesse, Angela, and Mathew Coleman. "Automobility, Immobility, Altermobility: Surviving and Resisting the Intensification of Immigrant Policing." *City and Society* 26, no. 1 (2014): 51–72.

Sturdevant, Saundra Pollock, and Brenda Stoltzfus. *Let the Good Times Roll: Prostitution and the US Military in Asia*. New York: New Press, 1993.

Surya, Michel. *Georges Bataille: An Intellectual Biography*. London: Verso, 2002.

Suzuki, Kentarō. "Divination in Contemporary Japan: A General Overview and an Analysis of Survey Results." *Japanese Journal of Religious Studies* 22, nos. 3/4 (1995): 249–66.

Suzuki, Taku. *Embodying Belonging: Racializing Okinawan Diaspora in Bolivia and Japan*. Honolulu: University of Hawai'i Press, 2010.

Swofford, Anthony. *Jarhead: A Marine's Chronicle of the Gulf War and Other Battles*. New York: Scribner, 2003.

Takada Wataru. *Bābon Sutorīto burūsu.* Tokyo: Chikuma Shobō, 2001.

Takenaka, Akiko. *Yasukuni Shrine: History, Memory, and Japan's Unending Postwar.* Honolulu: University of Hawai'i Press, 2015.

Tansman, Alan. *The Aesthetics of Japanese Fascism.* Berkeley: University of California Press, 2009.

Tansman, Alan. *The Culture of Japanese Fascism.* Durham, NC: Duke University Press, 2009.

Taussig, Michael T. *Shamanism, Colonialism, and the Wild Man: A Study in Terror and Healing.* Chicago: University of Chicago Press, 1986.

Taylor, Anne-Christine. "Healing Translations: Moving Between Worlds in Achuar Shamanism." *HAU: Journal of Ethnographic Theory* 4, no. 2 (2014): 95–118.

TMM. (Tsushima-maru Memorial Museum). "The Sinking of the Tsushima-maru." Tsushima-maru Memorial Museum, August 22, 2004. https://www.tsushimamaru.or.jp/english.

Tōmatsu Shōmei. "Ketsujitsu shita hōjō no kiroku." In *Hikaru Nanamui no kamigami: Okinawa, Miyako, Nishihara (1997–2001),* by Higa Toyomitsu. Tokyo: Fūdosha, 2001.

Tomiyama Ichirō. "Okuni wa?" In *Oto no Tikara: Okinawa—Koza futtōhen,* 7–20. Tokyo: Inpakuto Shuppankai, 1998.

Tomiyama Ichirō. "On Becoming 'a Japanese': The Community of Oblivion and Memories of the Battlefield." *Asia-Pacific Journal: Japan Focus* 3, no. 10 (2005): 2160. https://apjjf.org/tomiyama-ichiro/2160/article.

Tomiyama Ichirō. *Senjō no kioku.* Tokyo: Nihon Keizai Hyōronsha, 2006.

TOMM (Taro Okamoto Memorial Museum). "Genshi." October 2, 2002. https://tarookamoto.or.jp/exhibition/%e3%80%8e%e5%8e%9f%e5%a7%8b%e3%80%8f/.

Tsuda, Noritake. "Human Sacrifices in Japan." *Open Court* 32, no. 12 (1918): 760–67.

Tsutsui, William M. *Manufacturing Ideology: Scientific Management in Twentieth-Century Japan.* Princeton, NJ: Princeton University Press, 1998.

Turner, Terence. "The Beautiful and the Common: Inequalities of Value and Revolving Hierarchy among the Kayapó." *Tipití: Journal of the Society for the Anthropology of Lowland South America* 1, no. 1 (2003): 11–26.

USMC (US Marine Corps). "Jungle Warfare Training Center." Accessed March 22, 2023. https://www.3rdmardiv.marines.mil/Units/Jungle-Warfare-Training-Center/.

USMC. "Marine Corps Vision and Strategy 2025." https://www.marforres.marines.mil/Portals/116/Docs/CmdDeck/usmc_vision_strategy_2025_0809.pdf.

Valeri, Valerio. *Kingship and Sacrifice: Ritual and Society in Ancient Hawaii.* Chicago: University of Chicago Press, 1985.

Valeri, Valerio. "Wild Victims: Hunting as Sacrifice and Sacrifice as Hunting in Huaulu." *History of Religions* 34, no. 2 (1994): 101–31.

Vidal-Naquet, Pierre. *Assassins of Memory: Essays on the Denial of the Holocaust.* New York: Columbia University Press, 1992.

Viveiros de Castro, Eduardo. *Cannibal Metaphysics*. Minneapolis: Univocal Publishing, 2014.

Viveiros de Castro, Eduardo. *From the Enemy's Point of View: Humanity and Divinity in an Amazonian Society*. Chicago: University of Chicago Press, 1992.

Viveiros de Castro, Eduardo. *The Relative Native: Essays on Indigenous Conceptual Worlds*. Chicago: HAU Books, 2015.

Wacker, Monika. "Onarigami: Holy Women in the Twentieth Century." *Japanese Journal of Religious Studies* 30, nos. 3/4 (2003): 339–59.

Waldberg, Patrick. *Taro Okamoto: Le baladin des antipodes*. Paris: Différence, 1992.

Walker, Gavin. *The Sublime Perversion of Capital: Marxist Theory and the Politics of History in Modern Japan*. Durham, NC: Duke University Press, 2016.

Watsuji Tetsurō. *Koji junrei*. Tokyo: Iwanami Shoten, 1979.

Weingrad, Michael. "The College of Sociology and the Institute of Social Research." *New German Critique* 84 (2001): 129–61.

Weinrich, Harald. *Lethe: The Art and Critique of Forgetting*. Ithaca, NY: Cornell University Press, 2004.

Weiss, Brad. "Northwestern Tanzania on a Single Shilling: Sociality, Embodiment, Valuation." *Cultural Anthropology* 12, no. 3 (1997): 335–61.

Weiss, Brad. *Real Pigs: Shifting Values in the Field of Local Pork*. Durham, NC: Duke University Press, 2016.

Weiss, Joseph. "Not Built to Last: Military Occupation and Ruination Under Settler Colonialism." *Cultural Anthropology* 36, no. 3 (2021): 484–508.

Willerslev, Rane, Piers Vitebsky, and Anatoly Alekseyev. "Sacrifice as the Ideal Hunt: A Cosmological Explanation for the Origin of Reindeer Domestication." *Journal of the Royal Anthropological Institute* 21, no. 1 (2015): 1–23.

Winter, Jay. *Sites of Memory, Sites of Mourning: The Great War in European Cultural History*. Cambridge: Cambridge University Press, 2014.

Winther-Tamaki, Bert. "To Put On a Big Face: The Globalist Stance of Okamoto Tarō's Tower of the Sun for the Japan World Exposition." *Review of Japanese Culture and Society* 23 (2011): 81–101.

Yamanokuchi Baku. *Yamanokuchi Baku shibunshū*. Tokyo: Kōdansha, 1999.

Yanagita Kunio. *Kaijō no michi*. Tokyo: Iwanami Shoten, 1978.

Yanagita Kunio. *Kainan shōki*. Tokyo: Kadokawa Gakugei Shuppan, 2013.

Yanagita Kunio. *Yama no jinsei*. Tokyo: Kyōdo Kenkyūsha, 1926.

Yeats, William Butler. *A Vision: The Revised 1937 Version*. Edited by Catherine E. Paul and Margaret Mills Harper. New York: Scribner, 2015.

Yonaha, Shoko. "From Traditional to Contemporary: Genealogy of Kumiodori in Modern Okinawan Theatre Called 'Okinawa Shibai.'" In *Modernization of Asian Theatres: Process and Tradition*, edited by Yasushi Nagata and Ravi Chaturvedi, 205–28. Singapore: Springer Singapore, 2019.

Yonetani, Julia. "Contested Memories: Struggles over War and Peace in Contemporary Okinawa." In *Structure and Subjectivity: Japan and Okinawa,* edited by Glenn D. Hook and Richard Siddle, 188–207. London: Routledge Curzon, 2003.

Yoshichika Yamanaka. "Survivor of Mass Suicide in Okinawa During WWII Dies at 93." *Asahi Shimbun*, June 25, 2022. https://www.asahi.com/ajw/articles /14678819.

Yoshimi, Yoshiaki. *Grassroots Fascism: The War Experience of the Japanese People.* New York: Columbia University Press, 1987.

Yoshimoto Takaaki, ed. *Ryūkyūko no kankiryoku to Nantōron: Shinpojiumu.* Tokyo: Kawade Shobō Shinsha, 1989.

INDEX

Note: Page numbers in italics refer to figures and captions.

mass media, 104
mass suicide, 5, 66
Masuzoe Yōichi, 191–92
material culture, 141, 198, 202, 240n32; in
    Hisutorīto museum, 35, 37, 38–39
Matsumura, Wendy, 72, 214
Mauss, Marcel, 105, 119, 122, 131, 154, 220,
    254n100, 259n98; Bataille and, 119–20;
    ethnology of, 106, 124; Okamoto and,
    118, 124, 252n53
McCarthyism, 9
"Medetai Bushi" (folksong), 43
mediators, 110, 113, 206
Medoruma Shun, 7, 19, 240n26
Meiji era, 22, 23, 33, 44, 166, 169; Meiji
    emperor and, 67–68
Meiji University (Tokyo), 201, 202
Mekarushi (courtly dance), 178
memorials, 9, 64, 67, 113, 190; Baku's,
    70–71; memorial rites and, 15, 21; to
    Okinawan victims, 6, 7; to Yamaokuchi,
    64, 65. See also monuments
memory, 1, 2, 6, 21, 24, 66, 70, 73, 87, 155;
    history and, 86, 100, 244n14; shared,
    16, 92; of World War II, 97, 171.
    See also remembrance
Merry Christmas, Mr. Lawrence (1983
    film), 247n73
militarism, 77, 132, 233
minotaur, 108
minyō, 64, 70, 101. See also folksongs
mise en abyme, 67
Mitchell, Jon, 15–16
Miura Baien, 43
Miyako, 133, 149, 155, 196
Miyamoto Tsuneichi, 129; Nihon Zankoku
    Monogatari, 128
moai (mutual aid organizations), 41–52,
    87, 229, 243n83, 243nn86–87
moai kiyaku (cooperative contract),
    47–48
moashibi (illicit outdoor parties), 173
mochi, 235
modernity and modernization, 22, 86,
    148, 159, 166, 172, 234; capitalism and,
    136, 137
MoMA PS1, 193
moment of action, 30, 34

monorail, 73, 175, 177
monuments, 64–67, 65, 100, 158, 181;
    peace, 73–74; World War II, 39, 58.
    See also memorials
Moteki Hiromichi, 57, 244n15
mujinkō (circles of endless reciprocity),
    43, 44
mundane, 198–99
Munn, Nancy, 74, 75
Murasaki (band), 37, 260n104
Murasaki, George, 213, 260n104
Musée de l'homme, 250–51n37
museums, 18, 35, 103, 104, 154, 193,
    239n10, 250–51n37. See also exhibits;
    and names of museums
music, musicians, 25, 37, 69–70, 85, 213,
    216, 241n37; songs, 32–33, 40, 69–70,
    169, 171, 187–88, 258n66. See also mu-
    sical instruments
musical instruments, 70, 242n59; sanshin
    (three-stringed instrument), 18, 23,
    43, 63, 66, 70
mutual assistance and mutual aid socie-
    ties, 23–24, 43, 44, 189
Mythe et l'homme, Le (Caillois), 122
myths, 146

Nagabuchi Tsuyoshi, 248n83
Nagasuku Castle, 211
Nagisa Oshima, 247n73
Nago, 8, 18, 150, 177
Naha, 6–8, 11, 62, 99, 145, 157, 160, 165,
    176, 182, 213, 224, 231, 260n113; air-
    port in, 134, 230; as capital of Oki-
    nawa Prefecture, 5, 176; downtown,
    77, 78; mayor of, 74, 137, 245n28;
    neighborhoods of, 174, 214; Oka-
    moto and, 107, 115, 132, 133; parks in,
    75–76, 218, 228; prefectural library in,
    61, 62; roads in, 166, 175; shrines in,
    67–68, 86
Naha Shimin Kaikan (Naha Civic Hall;
    Kinjō), 61, 79, 176–77, 246n60
Najita, Tetsuo, 43–44
Nakagusuku Kōgen Hotel, 211
Nakagusuku village, 211
Nakaima Hirokazu, 245n28
Nakanomachi, 41

www.ingramcontent.com/pod-product-compliance
Lightning Source LLC
Chambersburg PA
CBHW020829270326
41928CB00006B/465